Microsoft Power BI Visual Calculations: Simplifying DAX

Jeroen ter Heerdt
Madzy Stikkelorum
Marc Lelijveld

Microsoft Power BI Visual Calculations: Simplifying DAX

Published with the authorization of Microsoft Corporation by:

Pearson Education, Inc.

ISBN-13: 978-0-13-539692-6
ISBN-10: 0-13-539692-1

Library of Congress Control Number: 2025946899

1 2025

Trademarks

Warning and Disclaimer

EDITOR-IN-CHIEF
Julie Phifer

EXECUTIVE EDITOR
Loretta Yates

ACQUISITIONS EDITOR
Shourav Bose

DEVELOPMENT EDITOR
Kate Shoup

MANAGING EDITOR
Sandra Schroeder

SENIOR PROJECT EDITOR
Tracey Croom

COPY EDITOR
Charlotte Kughen

TECHNICAL EDITOR
Jeffrey Wang

INDEXER
Rachel Kuhn

PROOFREADER
Barbara Mack

COVER DESIGNER
Twist Creative, Seattle

COVER ILLUSTRATION
knssr/stock.adobe.com

COMPOSITOR
codeMantra

GRAPHICS
codeMantra

Dedication

For my wife, Ilse. You selflessly joined me on an adventure moving halfway across the globe, uprooting yourself from everything and everyone to allow me to fulfill my goals, which, among many other things, resulted in me working on visual calculations and writing this book. I am blessed with your unwavering support and love. We started on this adventure as a duo, and we embark on the next chapter as a trio with our daughter Chloë, and I couldn't be more excited.

—JEROEN

For my husband, Wouter, who has put up with me working on this book for so many evenings, weekends, and during nap times of our son without any complaints. You supported me through it all, taking our son for short outings so I could write, making sure I had the comfortable chair when my pregnant belly grew and moved my keyboard ever further away. Thank you for giving me the space to finish this book and even considering Dax as a name for our second son. I'm not saying that's going to be it, though!

—MADZY

For my wife, Kirsten, thank you for your patience, encouragement, and love during the late nights and long weekends spent writing this book. Your support carried me through the tougher moments, and I'm endlessly grateful for having you by my side. For my dad, Martin, your pride and unwavering belief in me have been a constant source of motivation since the start of my career.

—MARC

Contents at a Glance

Contents

Chapter 4 Organization and use of visual calculations 77

Chapter 5 The pillars: supportive functions 97

Chapter 6 The foundation: foundational functions 101

PART III   MASTERING VISUAL CALCULATIONS

Chapter 9   Breaking down visual calculations execution   195

Chapter 10 Applied visual calculations   225

Foreword

DAX is a critical piece of Power BI. It allows authors to build reusable semantic models to power exploration, reporting, and AI. DAX measures express business logic as dynamic, reusable calculations that work across a variety of dimensions and scenarios. However, DAX has a steep learning curve for new users.

Some of the concepts that make DAX so powerful—like filter context and the many features of semantic models—also make DAX challenging to learn. It demands clear thinking about row and filter context, which is hard for beginners, because it asks them to ignore the visual in front of them and reason in the abstract space of the semantic model.

Many common reporting and visualization tasks shouldn't require a complete understanding of these concepts. Tasks like showing the difference between two metrics or adding a running sum to a chart are easier to do using the data in a visualization. These ideas led us to add visual calculations to Power BI. Instead of pushing every calculation into measures that operate independently over base tables, you can work with the result set the visual already produced. That shift narrows the gap between how analysts think and how the engine executes.

Visual calculations are expressions defined as part of a visualization, and they work over the data in that visualization. This lets you write a calculation using specific numbers you can see rather than imagining how filter context might create those numbers from the semantic model. Visual calculations provide functions that already understand the structure of the visual to let you easily write running sums or moving averages. These are just two of the ways visual calculations make it easier to build powerful visualizations in Power BI.

There was a long path to visual calculations. Years before the team debated the investment, Amir Netz asked Jeffrey Wang to look at a performance escalation in a customer DirectQuery model. A measure was generating slow SQL. The customer was confused, and they were right to be. The visual already showed a small set of values from another measure—values that contained everything needed for the more complex result. Yet what looked simple on the canvas triggered a cascade of large, slow, and convoluted SQL. The gap between what is visibly simple and what the engine had to compute was a persistent source of friction. Incidents like this pushed us toward an approach that simplifies the mental model and speeds evaluation by operating at the level of the visual when it makes sense. It still took years and foundational work, including DAX window functions, before visual calculations officially took off.

Both newcomers and seasoned DAX users benefit from this approach. Newcomers can reason from what is on the screen and learn many DAX features without starting in the deep end. Experts can reduce model clutter by moving visual-specific calculations, such as formatting, into the visual and achieve more predictable cost in DirectQuery and composite models. *Microsoft Power BI Visual Calculations: Simplifying DAX* explains how visual calculations work, where they shine, how to keep performance stable as visuals grow more complex, and when classic measures remain the right tool. Visual calculations are still DAX expressions, and the power of DAX is still available when you need it. DAX measures are still a critical tool for building reusable semantic models that are the foundation of exploration, reporting, and AI in Power BI. However, visual calculations give you a way to more easily accomplish many common reporting and visualization tasks.

Use this book to shorten the path from a question to an answer, and to teach patterns your team can apply consistently. That is the value of visual calculations in Power BI. We hope this book helps you take advantage of visual calculations to accomplish your goals with Power BI.

Marius Dumitru, Partner Architect

John Vulner, Partner Architect

Jeffrey Wang, Partner Architect

Microsoft Power BI

Acknowledgments

We would like to express our sincere gratitude to all the people who have supported us while writing this book. Without their help and encouragement, this book would not have been possible. This includes the folks at Pearson/Microsoft Press: Loretta Yates and Shourav Bose for believing there was an audience for this and keeping us on track, and Kate Shoup, who turned our drafts into the book you are reading!

Visual calculations is a powerful and complex feature precisely because of its simplicity. It took years to get it to where it is now. We want to thank the entire Power BI visual calculations team at Microsoft for their efforts to make DAX easier for the rest of us. It all started with conversations at Microsoft between Jeroen and three architects: Jeffrey Wang, Marius Dumitru, and John Vulner. Without the guidance of Marius, Jeffrey, and John, visual calculations would not have existed.

We would like to thank Jeffrey for being our technical reviewer, keeping us honest and on track. Without him, this book would mostly be a collection of ambiguous information. Any mistakes still left in the book are solely because of the authors.

We'd also like to give a special thanks to Fowmy Abdulmuttalib, Injae Park, and Erik Svensen for showing the Power BI community what visual calculations can do and allowing us to use their examples in our book.

The Power BI community is the warmest and most welcoming community any of us have had the good fortune to be a part of. Its global reach, diversity, and passion are unparalleled. We are grateful that we're members of such an awesome collective. We learn so much from you all every day and look forward to sharing and learning for many years to come.

We want to thank you, the reader, for your interest in visual calculations. Our goal with this book is twofold. First, we want to help you be successful with Power BI by enabling you to do calculations using visual calculations; we hope that when you finish this book, you'll be ready to face any challenge with visual calculations. And second, we want to inspire you to explore new, innovative ways to use visual calculations while also looking beyond them toward the wide world of DAX and Power BI, where the possibilities are truly endless. We welcome your feedback and comments, and if you create a great visual calculation, tell us. We look forward to hearing from you!

Jeroen ter Heerdt

Duvall, Washington, United States of America

Madzy Stikkelorum

De Meern, Utrecht, The Netherlands

Marc Lelijveld

Haastrecht, Zuid-Holland, The Netherlands

About the Authors

Jeroen ter Heerdt Jeroen (Jay) ter Heerdt is a principal product manager on the Power BI team at Microsoft and one of the masterminds behind visual calculations. With a focus on advancing DAX and modeling in Power BI, Jeroen is passionate about delivering powerful features and improvements that empower users. Known as the "Dutch Data Dude," he is a seasoned speaker and advocate for data-driven insights, captivating audiences with his entertaining and thought-provoking presentations. Known for incorporating unique and delightfully "weird" elements into his keynotes, Jeroen leaves a memorable impression every time he takes the stage. You can find him sharing insights and connecting with the community on social media as @jaypowerbi, on Reddit as @dutchdatadude, on LinkedIn, and through his website, *https://www.dutchdatadude.com*. He frequently reminds himself to return to blogging more regularly. When not immersed in the world of data, Jeroen enjoys experimenting with artisanal food and drinks, home automation, and exploring the beauty of the Pacific Northwest.

Madzy Stikkelorum Madzy Stikkelorum has a master's degree in Mathematics, and analyzing data has always been one of her passions. She currently works as a data analytics consultant at Quanto, where she enjoys helping clients solve complex problems with Microsoft Power BI solutions. She shares her love for Power BI and DAX with the community by organizing the Power BI Summer School in the Netherlands, as a public speaker at international conferences, and in blog posts, which can be found at *https://quanto.eu/blog/*. Her very first video training about DAX, created with Michiel Rozema, launched in 2025 for Microsoft Press. Madzy is married to Wouter, and they already had one son together, but during the writing of this book, their second son was baking in the oven—inspiring Madzy to ensure she met the deadlines for her chapters! In her spare time, she loves to read, bake, and work on creative projects of all kinds. This is her first ever book as a co-author; she is extremely proud to have a book of her own making in her bookcase and is sure that more will follow.

Marc Lelijveld Marc Lelijveld is a Microsoft Data Platform Most Valuable Professional (MVP), solution architect, and technical evangelist with a passion for turning data into action. He focuses on Power BI and Microsoft Fabric, helping others make the most of these technologies through practical insights and real-world experience. Recognized as a Microsoft MVP since 2018, Marc is a regular speaker at international conferences, user groups, and community events. He's known for sharing his knowledge, best practices, and contagious enthusiasm—whether he's presenting deep technical content or inspiring others to level up their data journey. Marc blogs about Power BI and Microsoft Fabric at *https://data-marc.com* and can be found on most social platforms under his own name. When he's not working with data, you'll probably find him out exploring the world on one of his many bikes.

Introduction

"Data is the new oil!"

It wasn't too long ago that every consultancy and technology firm in the data space used that phrase, officially or unofficially. What they meant was that data is as important to the data revolution—driven by big data, massive data, and humongous data—as the use of oil was to the industrial revolution. In this exciting new era, all you needed was data, to buy their tools, and/or to hire their consultants, and your organization would magically be data driven!

If only that turned out to be true.

Data may indeed be the new oil. But just like crude oil, data needs refining. It must be transformed into information. This is why we clean, combine, model, and visualize data. The output of all this work—whether you do it on your own, get some help, or use a (semi-)automatic process—includes reports and dashboards that provide insights into various aspects of the organization's dealings, which decision-makers can then consume to make critical business decisions.

Ideally, your organization's data contains the answers needed to make informed decisions. But that data must be teased out—brought to the forefront. Adding calculations to the data is one way to achieve this. For example, providing a humble sum at the end of a list of sales transactions enables someone to understand how much was sold simply by looking at a single number rather than performing mental or computer-aided math to add up individual sales-transaction amounts.

Together with effective data cleansing, data modeling, and data visualization, calculations form the toolset to refine data into much needed information. However, this book focuses only on calculations—not on calculations in general, but rather on a specific way of performing calculations (visual calculations) in specific software (Power BI) that can help you transform your business into one that is data driven.

We assume you already know the basics of Power BI—or at the very least, even if you have a background in Excel and are a bit scared of using Power BI, you understand its role—so we do not include an exhaustive introduction to the software. We also assume you've heard a thing or two about DAX (spoiler alert: people say it's hard!) and perhaps decided it's not for you. However much you do or don't know about Power BI and DAX, it's OK. We're here to help. So, let's not delay any further and jump in.

What is DAX?

Data Analysis Expressions (DAX) is the native formula and query language for Microsoft PowerPivot, Power BI, and SQL Server Analysis Services Tabular models. This book focuses on the use of DAX with Power BI for reasons that will soon become apparent.

DAX is one of two languages you might use in Power BI to add calculations to your data. The other language is M. However, although you can do calculations with M, it's best suited for data transformations, such as data cleansing or grouping. If you must choose between M and DAX, follow this rule: Perform calculations in DAX—which is by far the superior option in terms of capabilities and speed—and transformations in M. Only deviate from this rule if you really must.

At first glance, DAX looks a lot like Excel formulas. It follows a similar structure in that you define an expression that applies functions to data and returns some result. In fact, many of the function names are the same. IF is IF, SUM is SUM, AVERAGE is AVERAGE, and so on. They do the same (or very similar) things. However, there are numerous functions that don't exist in Excel but do exist in DAX, and vice versa.

The fact that DAX looks a lot like Excel formulas is both a blessing and a curse. It's a blessing because new users, who most likely have some prior knowledge of Excel (because who doesn't?), feel empowered to add the calculations they need. But it's a curse because hidden beneath the seemingly simple, familiar expression syntax are concepts that are so alien to Excel that they might have come from a distant star. After dipping their toes into DAX waters, new users quickly discover that DAX supports functions they know nothing about, and that familiar functions they *do* know about from Excel are completely missing in DAX.

In some ways, it might be better if DAX did not seem so similar to Excel. Yes, it would have added hurdles in adoption, and users would have had to learn a new language. But beyond very basic usage, users still need to learn a new language because of the conceptual differences. The similarities in syntax provide a false sense of security, encouraging users to maintain an Excel mindset when using DAX and Power BI instead of preparing them to learn a fresh perspective on performing calculations.

What this book is about

This book is about visual calculations, a feature of Microsoft Power BI, aimed at making DAX easier to work with. Development of this feature started in June 2020, with visual calculations entering public preview in February 2024. At the time this book went to print, the visual calculations feature was still in preview; therefore, things might have changed by the time you read this. (We indicate features of visual calculations for which we anticipate changes in the book.)

Organization of this book

Here are the contents of this book at a glance:

Part I: Visual calculations fundamentals   This part covers the fundamentals of visual calculations and consists of the following chapters:

- **Chapter 1: Introduction to visual calculations**   This chapter introduces visual calculations and explains the problems with DAX that they are meant to solve.
- **Chapter 2: My first visual calculation**   This chapter provides a hands-on tutorial for building your first visual calculation.
- **Chapter 3: Visual calculations concepts**   In this chapter, you'll learn the core concepts behind visual calculations.
- **Chapter 4: Organization and use of visual calculations**   This chapter shows you how to work with visual calculations successfully and how to govern them.

Part II: Visual calculations functions   This part dives into the details of visual calculations exclusive functions and their foundations in DAX window functions. Because this is a hefty topic, it's divided into three chapters, so you can more easily find what you're looking for:

- **Chapter 5: The pillars: supportive functions**   This chapter introduces supportive functions, such as ORDERBY, that pave the way for the foundational functions.
- **Chapter 6: The foundation: foundational functions**   This chapter focuses on the foundational functions that form the basis of the functions that are exclusive to visual calculations.
- **Chapter 7: The floors and rooms: visual calculations exclusive functions**   This chapter discusses the exciting functions that are exclusive to visual calculations.

Part III: Mastering visual calculations   This part helps you master visual calculations. It consists of the following chapters:

- **Chapter 8: Comparing calculation options**   This chapter compares the various calculation options available to you in Power BI and discusses what to use when.

- **Chapter 9: Breaking down visual calculations execution**   This chapter explores the inner workings of visual calculations and their performance characteristics.

Part IV: The art of practical visual calculations   This final part focuses on practical applications of visual calculations and provides a detailed description of various use cases. It includes the following chapters:

- **Chapter 10: Applied visual calculations**   This chapter provides practical, real-world examples of how to use visual calculations to implement calculations that can be applied to many visuals.

- **Chapter 11: Charting with visual calculations**   Here, we explore how to create specific visuals that are missing from Power BI with the help of visual calculations.

Chapter 42: Beyond the page   Evaluates the goals we had for this book and provides guidance on what's next.

Appendices   Provides code snippets that support and expand on the main content.

Who should read this book?

This book is for anyone who wants to use the visual calculations feature of Power BI, as well as those who seek a deeper understanding of visual calculations, their foundation, and their inner workings. We present the DAX required to gain that understanding, but by no means is this book intended to cover everything there is to know about DAX. If learning DAX is your goal, there are way better materials available to you than this book.

We expect you, our reader, to have a basic knowledge of Power BI and some experience in the analysis of numbers. If you have already been exposed to DAX, this may be helpful because you might be able to skip some sections. However, previous experience with DAX is not required. Having used Excel formulas before will help.

Conventions and features in this book

This book uses the following conventions:

- We use US notation for numbers, such as a period (.) for decimal separators and a comma (,) for thousand separators.

- Power BI features (such as visual calculations, measures, and so on) are not capitalized.

- DAX functions are uppercase. For example: CALCULATE and RUNNINGSUM.

- Values supplied to parameters are uppercase. For example, HIGHESTPARENT and DEFAULT.

- Code is presented as follows:

  ```
  TheAnswerToTheUltimateQuestionOfLifeTheUniverseAndEverything = 42.
  ```

- Names of measures, visual calculations, and calculated columns are in italic: *Total Sales* measure, *VsPrevious* visual calculation.

- Parameter names are in italic: *axis*, *reset*.

- Whenever we reference a value you can find in the dataset, it's capitalized: Bikes, Yellow, Security products.

- Direct references to columns and tables are written with a capital: Product Category, Sales, Birth Date. Descriptive references are lowercase: the products listed.

- Of course, generic grammar still applies.

Here are some example snippets that show these conventions:

- This expression will return the total sales for products in the Computers category, within the current context. If it's executed in the same context as our *Total Sales* expression was in our last example, then *Total Computer Sales* represents the total amount for sales transactions of products in the Computers category for the year 2023 for stores in the United States.

- To calculate this, the column Category in the table Product Category is filtered based on the value Computers in the filter context to the DAX expression.

- To calculate the running sum of *Sales*, we are using the RUNNINGSUM function of DAX instead of CALCULATE, with the *axis* parameter set to the columns axis by specifying COLUMNS. This means the visual calculation will look like `MyVC = RUNNINGSUM ( [Sales], COLUMNS )`.

Signature, syntax, expression, and statement

The distinction between signature, syntax, expression, and statement sparked a debate among the authors of this book. We will not repeat the debate here, but it's important to know that throughout the book we use signature to refer to the unique identification of a function. You can think of it as the blueprint of a function, or what you would generally put in the header (.h) file if you were programming in languages such as C or C++. A function's signature includes its name and the parameters it accepts. A function's signature helps you to understand what a function does and how it should be used. The signature of a DAX function by itself is not executable. We will use the word signature throughout this book with this definition in mind.

In contrast, syntax refers to the rules and conventions that define the structure and format of valid statements in a programming language like DAX. It's like grammar in human languages. And just as improper grammar can make a sentence hard to understand, incorrect syntax can cause errors in code or make it difficult to read. In this book, we aim to avoid the word syntax and instead refer to pieces of executable DAX code in descriptive terms, such as "this visual calculation". If we need to, we will refer to pieces of executable DAX code as expressions or statements, such as "These three statements are equivalent because...."

These four terms also interact because statements can be syntactically correct but use functions with ambiguous or poorly designed signatures.

System requirements

We strongly urge you to follow along with the examples in this book and the tutorial provided in Chapter 2. To do so, we recommend you use the most recent Power BI Desktop version, but at minimum, you should be using the February 2024 version. In Power BI Desktop, be sure to turn on the visual calculations preview feature if it isn't turned on already. To do so, choose Options and Settings > Options > Preview features. Then select Visual calculations and click OK. Finally, restart Power BI Desktop to enable visual calculations.

If you're using Power BI in the web exclusively, you can also follow along, but keep in mind that the web version of Power BI Desktop doesn't have a ribbon at the time of this writing, so you will have to use the context menu of a visual (right-click), the three-dot menu of the visual to enter visual calculations edit mode, or the button in the bar at the top of the report.

When you have a supported visual selected while editing a report, there are multiple ways of entering visual calculations edit mode:

- Clicking the New visual calculation button in the ribbon, as shown in Figure 0-1 (Power BI Desktop only).

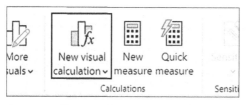

FIGURE 0-1 The New visual calculation button in the Calculations section of the Home ribbon.

- Right-clicking anywhere on the visual to open the context menu, choosing New visual calculation, and selecting the type of visual calculation you want to create (see Figure 0-2).

- Clicking the three-dot menu in the top-right corner of the visual, choosing New visual calculation, and selecting the type of visual calculation you want to create (see Figure 0-3).

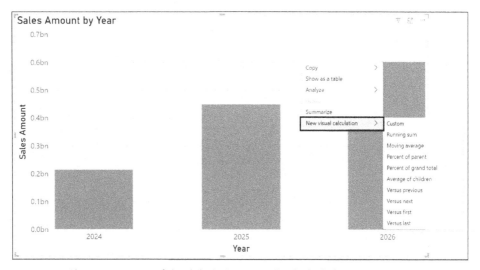

FIGURE 0-2 The context menu of visuals includes a New visual calculation entry.

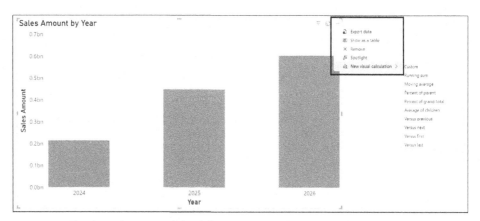

FIGURE 0-3 The three-dot menu of visuals includes a New visual calculation entry.

- Clicking the New visual calculation button in the bar at the top of the report, as shown in Figure 0-4 (browser only).

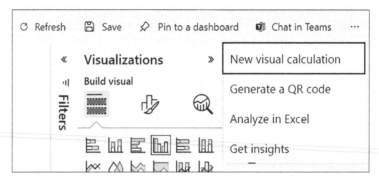

FIGURE 0-4 The bar at the top of the report while editing in the browser includes a New visual calculation button.

- Right-clicking an existing visual calculation and selecting Edit calculation (see Figure 0-5).

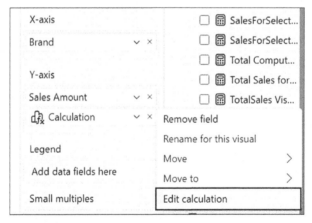

FIGURE 0-5 The context menu of a visual calculation is another way to enter visual calculations edit mode.

GitHub Repo

All examples and code snippets in the book are available on the book's website at *MicrosoftPressStore.com/powerbivis/downloads*.

The examples throughout the book use the same semantic model, available in the Contoso Sales.pbix file, which you can download from the aforementioned website.

The pbix file not only contains the semantic model but also includes multiple report pages showing the examples in the chapters in this book. The semantic model has some dimension tables like Customer, Date, Product, and Store and contains three fact tables with data about sales, orders, and order details.

The data in the model was generated using the free Contoso Data Generator published by SQLBI, which is available at *docs.sqlbi.com/contoso-data-generator/*.

Chapter 2, which walks you through creating your first visual calculation, will introduce the example model in more detail.

We also provide two more pbix files to download: Contoso Sales CH2 Start.pbix and Contoso Sales CH2 End.pbix. The Contoso Sales CH2 Start.pbix file is the starting point for following the tutorial in Chapter 2, and the Contoso Sales CH2 End.pbix is the result of the tutorial in that same chapter.

Errata, updates, and book support

We've made every effort to ensure the accuracy of this book and its companion content. You can access updates to this book—in the form of a list of submitted errata and their related corrections—at

MicrosoftPressStore.com/powerbivis/errata

If you discover an error that is not already listed, please submit it to us at the same page.

For additional book support and information, please visit *MicrosoftPressStore.com/ Support.*

Please note that product support for Microsoft software and hardware is not offered through the previous addresses. For help with Microsoft software or hardware, go to *support.microsoft.com.*

Visual calculations fundamentals

It's time to start your visual calculations journey! This first leg of the journey starts with an introduction (in Chapter 1, "Introduction to visual calculations") to visual calculations, in which we make the case for visual calculations and why you should take the time to learn about them. We then guide you through a step-by-step process of creating your first visual calculations (in Chapter 2, "My first visual calculation") before discussing important concepts that will solidify your understanding of visual calculations (in Chapter 3, "Visual calculations concepts"). The final chapter in this part, Chapter 4 ("Organization and use of visual calculations"), discusses the organization and use of visual calculations.

After completing this first leg of the journey, you will be able to create visual calculations successfully.

## CHAPTER 1

Introduction to visual calculations

The shortest description of a visual calculation goes like this: A visual calculation is a DAX calculation evaluated in the scope of a visual. This statement, however, assumes the reader possesses a lot of prior knowledge. As short as this statement is, it's not very simple, and it has far-reaching implications. There is a lot to unpack here. This chapter explores the challenges that many people face when using DAX and makes a case for how visual calculations help.

> **Note** This chapter is by no means a complete introduction to DAX, and it does not assume that you understand the problem with DAX. The goal of this chapter is to make you aware of the problem with DAX at a high level, not for you to become a DAX master. So, don't worry if the first part of the chapter, where we describe the problem with DAX before introducing our hero, visual calculations, is a bit too complex for you.

The problem with DAX

A lot of people say DAX is hard. We tend to agree—although it depends on what you do with it. Perhaps a better way of saying it is, "DAX is simple, but not easy." Another common expression used to describe the problem with DAX is, "DAX is easy until it isn't." Unfortunately, for many people, the moment DAX becomes difficult is very soon after they start using it. For these people, anything beyond a simple calculation, such as a SUM, DAX quickly becomes hard—often prohibitively so.

We think it's fair to say that everyone who attempts to use DAX struggles with it. Some users master it eventually. Some muddle through and find a way to coexist. Some ask for help from others. Some click the Export to Excel button to work with their data outside Power BI. Some just give up altogether. On the flip side, many users who master DAX, or at least get used to it, become frustrated every time a client asks how to export to Excel.

There are a couple reasons why DAX is perceived as difficult. One of them is that DAX expressions look so much like Excel formulas that you expect them to be as easy to work with, too. And they are, until they aren't.

What makes DAX hard has little to do with the functions themselves. The problem is also not its syntax—although DAX is a functional language, which means it uses an "inside-out" syntax instead of the more commonly used "top-to-bottom" syntax that is most used in programming. This requires some rethinking, particularly if you are coming from a procedural programming background or if, for example, you have written macros in Excel. To read and understand a DAX statement, you must find the innermost piece, parse it, then go to the next layer, which takes the innermost piece as a parameter, and work your way outward, as shown in Figure 1-1.

```
  a = DoThisFirst ()          FinallyDoThis (
  b = ThenDoThis (a)              ThenDoThis (
  c = FinallyDoThis (b)               DoThisFirst ()
                                  )
                              )
```

FIGURE 1-1 DAX is read from the inside out instead of from top to bottom.

Rather than the syntax, the real challenge with DAX lies in the evaluation context in which the statements are executed that determines its result. The existence of this evaluation context is a two-edged sword; it's what makes DAX so powerful and also what makes DAX so complex.

The evaluation context gives DAX users the ability to write a statement and have it return different results based on the context. On the one hand, it results in a high degree of flexibility. On the other, it means that DAX is never What You See Is What You Get (WYSIWYG). You can't simply look at a DAX statement and understand exactly what an evaluation of that statement will return because the result is subject to the evaluation context.

Let's look at a very basic example measure that involves just a SUM:

```
Sales Amount = SUM ( 'Order Detail'[Total Sales] )
```

You can't predict the results of this *Sales Amount* measure by just looking at its definition. Instead, the context in which it's evaluated dictates what it returns. Adding the *Sales Amount* measure to a visual that shows stores returns the sum of sales per store. Change the visual to show brand, and the same measure returns the sum of sales per brand.

Another issue is that it's extremely difficult in DAX to reliably and definitively refer to a value from an earlier (or later) row. These relative or absolute shifts from the current evaluation position are possible but surprisingly hard to do. After all, you're looking at a visual on your screen that shows data in a certain order, so it makes sense that you think that it should be easy to refer to an earlier (or later) row. However, if you try to do so, you'll soon discover DAX doesn't work that way. This is because DAX statements are evaluated in the model, which does not sort the data in the same way as the data is sorted in your visual. For all you know, that row that was at the top of your visual, is somewhere in the middle of the data when the DAX is evaluated, so the whole idea of referring to an earlier or later row is meaningless.

To make matters worse, let's say you refresh the data from the source and reload it into the model. However, the data did not change at all. The visual you're looking at still shows the same data in the same order as before. However, there's no guarantee that the order in the model is the same as before the refresh. Rows might have shifted positions, so what was the fiftieth row might now be the forty-second row in your table, rendering any thinking you had about the earlier rows meaningless.

Moreover, DAX offers an EARLIER function that seems to allow you to refer to earlier rows, but unfortunately it's only useful in calculated columns to access a different row context, precisely because of the evaluation context in which measures are evaluated. So, measures don't have the stable row context that EARLIER depends on.

Another reason why it's challenging to refer to a value in a previous row is that that row might contain the results of another measure. However, measures operate independently and are not aware of the existence of other measures, even when they're present in the same visual. Measures must work in any evaluation context and therefore cannot assume another measure is also in the context.

To summarize, DAX is perceived as hard, because

- Sorting isn't part of the evaluation context, so the sort order you see on the screen is not the sort order of the data when the DAX statement is evaluated.

- DAX measures are isolated from each other. Therefore, you cannot refer to another measure's result.

- You can't predict the results of DAX expressions by just looking at them because they're always executed in an opaque evaluation context that's unknown when the expression is authored.

There are two types of evaluation contexts: row context and filter context. Not only do these two types of contexts exist, but functions in DAX also often manipulate them, adding to or removing from the context and transforming one context into another. This last operation is called context transition. Together, evaluation context (consisting of row and filter context) and context transition are the key reasons why users are so often frustrated with DAX. There are, of course, more reasons why users are frustrated with DAX, but these are outside of the scope of this book.

By themselves, the concepts of row context, filter context, and context transition aren't hard to understand. In fact, we explain them in the next section. What's difficult to grasp is the fact that they work together in intricate ways to influence the results of your DAX statement and that they do so invisibly to the user. We discuss this later in the chapter, after we establish an understanding of the context.

Evaluating the context

As explained, evaluation context (which includes row context and filter context) and context transition make DAX hard. To master DAX means to master these concepts. Let's start with the easiest concept: row context.

Row context

Row context refers to the current row being processed. It's as simple as that. When DAX is operating on a row of data, the row that's currently being processed is called the row context. For example, consider the following table of data about customers. For each customer, apart from a unique key, we have columns for their Surname, City, and Age. (This is just a sample of the data we have available to us because we might have many more columns and customers.)

CustomerKey	Surname	City	Age
1200337	Holm	Los Angeles	38
1219923	Freeman	Los Angeles	37
145705	Horne	Los Angeles	61

After adding an age group calculation, our table would look like the following:

CustomerKey	Surname	City	Age	Age Group
1200337	Holm	Los Angeles	38	30-39
1219923	Freeman	Los Angeles	37	30-39
145705	Horne	Los Angeles	61	60-69

The definition of the *Age Group* calculation is as follows:

```
Age Group =
SWITCH (
    TRUE (),
    [Age] <= 19, "<20",
    [Age] >= 20 && [Age] <= 29, "20-29",
    [Age] >= 30 && [Age] <= 39, "30-39",
    [Age] >= 40 && [Age] <= 49, "40-49",
    [Age] >= 50 && [Age] <= 59, "50-59",
    [Age] >= 60 && [Age] <= 69, "60-69",
    "70+"
)
```

Notice that this calculated column divides all customers into age groups, with special groups for customers younger than 20 and everyone aged 70 or older.

In this calculated column, DAX evaluates the SWITCH function for each row of the table. The SWITCH statement takes an expression as its first parameter followed by a set of values and results. Then it includes a result to return in case none of the values match.

> **Note** We could have written this as an IF statement, but that would be less readable.

Because the expression parameter to SWITCH is TRUE(), the values that follow are evaluated top to bottom. The Age value of the row is then compared to each of the values. As soon as one of the values is true, the result is returned. If none of the values match, then the result "70+" is returned.

The row context ensures that the comparisons happen for the specific Age value in the current row being processed. The row context iterates over the table from top to bottom. You can think of this as a slide rule going down the table, making stops along the way at each data row, waiting until DAX finishes calculating for that row before moving to the next row.

> **Note** Even though we describe the order of execution as top to bottom, the actual execution of the DAX statement can be different. This is because, as discussed, the DAX evaluation context is unaware of the order of rows in the visual. However, in this example, this does not influence results.

Let's look at this process a little more closely. First, the cells for our *Age Group* column are all empty. The row context is set to the first data row:

CustomerKey	Surname	City	Age	Age Group
1200337	Holm	Los Angeles	38	
1219923	Freeman	Los Angeles	37	
145705	Horne	Los Angeles	61	

Now DAX evaluates the *Age Group* calculated column. Because the Age value is 38, the third value evaluates to true and "30-39" is returned.

```
Age Group =
SWITCH (
    TRUE (),
    [Age] <= 19, "<20",
    [Age] >= 20 && [Age] <= 29, "20-29",
    [Age] >= 30 && [Age] <= 39, "30-39",
    [Age] >= 40 && [Age] <= 49, "40-49",
    [Age] >= 50 && [Age] <= 59, "50-59",
    [Age] >= 60 && [Age] <= 69, "60-69",
    "70+"
)
```

The return value is inserted into the cell for *Age Group* in the current row and the context is moved to the next row:

CustomerKey	Surname	City	Age	Age Group
1200337	Holm	Los Angeles	38	30-39
1219923	Freeman	Los Angeles	37	
145705	Horne	Los Angeles	61	

Again, DAX evaluates the *Age Group* calculated column, which results in a value of 30-39. The context moves to the next row, and so on, until the *Age Group* calculation has been evaluated for all the rows, and the results are returned in their respective cells.

> **Note** While it might be tempting to think about row context as a special filter on your table, we recommend not doing that. The row context is not a type of filter; it simply indicates to DAX which row is currently responsible for providing the values to perform the calculation and where the result of the calculation should go. Whether a column in the table is used in a particular calculation is irrelevant; all columns of the table are part of the row context when a calculation is performed.

Filter context

Now that you understand row context, let's move on to filter context. Compared to row context, filter context is a harder concept to grasp because it's much less visual. Simply put, whereas row context is responsible for telling DAX in which row to evaluate any statement, filter context is responsible for telling DAX which subset of data to evaluate any statement against. That might mean filtering one table or many tables. Which subset of data is selected depends on the model and the selections the user made. That's why it's harder to visualize how calculations are affected by the filter context. Still, all on-demand calculations are affected by filter context. Notice that calculated columns and calculated tables in DAX aren't dynamically calculated and are therefore not subject to filter context. Similarly, custom columns in M aren't subject to any DAX context simply because they aren't part of the same evaluation engine. Instead, calculated columns, calculated tables, and custom columns (defined in M) are calculated as part of data refresh, as we discuss in more detail in Chapter 8, "Comparing calculation options."

Consider the following measure named *Unit Cost*, which calculates a sum of the UnitCost column of the Sales table:

```
Unit Cost = SUM ( 'Sales'[UnitCost] )
```

It's impossible to tell what the result of this measure represents, even if you have the data at hand. It could represent the sum of unit cost for all products ever sold in all stores in all countries in the world or, for example, it could represent the sum of unit cost of all green products sold in stores in the United States in December of 2023. These two results are vastly different, unless, of course, there were only green products sold, you only sell in the United States, and you only sold products in December 2023.

The filter context in which the measure is evaluated determines the result. Simply looking at the measure does not give you enough information to predict what the result represents.

You can set and manipulate filter context in many ways. One way is to use DAX. But most often, the filter context is set by selections made outside of the statement being evaluated—for example, when you use a slicer to set the current year to 2023 or because of another statement.

Exactly how the filter context was set outside of the statement is irrelevant, but it's important to know it most likely will be set. To determine the filter context, you must understand the filter context that was set outside of the statement before even looking at the statement in detail. Only with that understanding can you confidently create a mental picture of the filter context and stand a chance at explaining the results that a statement returns. Power BI does not help you here. There is no place in the software to see the filter context. However, by carefully inspecting the model and the report (don't forget the filter pane!), you can create this mental picture.

The order in which the filter context is determined is important. You start outside the statement before looking at the actual statement because the filter context set outside of the statement is provided to the statement. The statement can then manipulate that filter context but not the other way around. It's the filter context outside the statement that's set. The statement is evaluated in that context and can manipulate it for itself, but the statement cannot influence the context outside of its own evaluation.

If the filter context sets the year to 2024, then the result of our *Unit Cost* measure is the sum of all the unit costs for all products sold across the world in 2024; if the filter context additionally sets the store country to United States, then the result of our *Unit Cost* measure is the sum of all the unit costs for all products sold in stores in the United States in 2024; and so on. As you can see in the following table, the results of this one measure vary wildly depending on the filter context in which it's being evaluated.

Filter context	Result of evaluating *Unit Cost* measure
Year: 2024	28.07M
Country: US	85.63M
Year: 2024 Country: US	13.81M

 Note The filter context provided to DAX can come from many sources. It's the combination of all the filters from all those sources that forms the filter context in which DAX is evaluating the statement.

In addition to the filter context being set outside of the statement being evaluated, the statement can manipulate the filter context. It can, for example, add extra filters on top of the already existing filter context, or it can remove filters from the filter context. For example, the following measure adds an extra filter on top of whatever filter context is already set:

```
Total Computer Unit Cost =
CALCULATE ( SUM ( 'Sales'[UnitCost] ), 'Product'[CategoryName] = "Computers" )
```

This measure will return the total unit cost for products in the Computers category within the current context. If it's executed in the same context as our *Unit Cost* measure was in our last example, then *Total Computer Unit Cost* represents the total unit cost for sales transactions of products in the Computers category for the year 2024 for stores in the United States.

The preceding example added an extra filter, but you can also tell DAX to temporarily ignore filters set in the context—for example, by using the ALL function. To be precise, the ALL function overrides the filter context set to encompass everything that's in its parameter. For example, the following measure returns the unit cost for products in the Computers category for all stores in all countries, temporarily overriding any filter set on the CountryName column in the Store table from the filter context because the ALL parameter is set to Store[CountryName]:

```
Total Computer Sales All Countries =
CALCULATE (
    SUM ( 'Sales'[UnitCost] ),
    'Product'[CategoryName] = "Computers",
    ALL ( 'Store'[CountryName] )
)
```

Context transition

Row and filter context don't just stay row and filter context. Row context can transform into filter context through a mechanism called context transition. Context transition takes any active row context and transforms it into a filter in the filter context. Multiple functions do this automatically.

Learning how to use context transition to your advantage by knowing when it happens and knowing how and when to avoid it is key to your mastery of DAX. CALCULATE and CALCULATETABLE automatically execute this process. Therefore, any statement invoking either of these two functions performs a context transition. This happens regardless of whether you wrote these functions explicitly yourself by typing CALCULATE or CALCULATETABLE or if you are using a function that conveniently hides these functions from you but still invokes them, such as TOTALYTD. Of course, if you are calling a statement that is a black box to you—that is, you can't see its DAX—you would have a hard time telling when context transition happens. But it's safe to assume that it will happen. Power BI does not tell you context transition is happening or what part of the current filter context was transformed from a row context. Unless you are looking at DAX evaluation in detail you might miss it.

For context transition to happen, there must be something to transform. Thus, a row context must be present. This means that context transition happens in calculated columns, where a row context is present, and whenever you're using a function that iterates over multiple values, such as SUMX. This last group of functions are conveniently called iterators.

Let's look at an example. Suppose you're iterating a list of Store Descriptions, and the row context describes which Store Description is the current description. When that row context is subject to context transition, the current description from the row context is added to the existing filter context. If the filter context was previously empty, it would now contain a filter indicating the current Store Description. If it was not previously empty, it would now contain that filter and any filter that already existed, such as a filter to set the countries to Canada and the United States. (See Figure 1-2.)

Row context   Filter context

Store Description

Contoso Store Alaska

--context transition-▶

Store Description

Contoso Store Alaska

Store CountryName

Canada

United States

FIGURE 1-2 Context transition adds filters from the row context to the filter context.

Consider the table in Figure 1-3 that shows the *Sales* and *Maximum Product Sales* per store for stores located in Canada and the United States:

Description	Sales	Maximum Product Sales
Contoso Store Alaska	18,232,514.91	193,449.50
Contoso Store Arkansas	21,140,025.39	246,126.00
Contoso Store Connecticut	21,009,014.60	231,128.50
Contoso Store Hawaii	18,866,255.57	184,594.50
Contoso Store Idaho	18,768,667.04	268,897.50
Contoso Store Iowa	21,490,228.07	288,277.50
Contoso Store Kansas	22,082,097.40	331,299.50
Contoso Store Maine	18,422,638.69	245,832.50
Contoso Store Montana	18,032,263.12	203,005.50
Contoso Store Nebraska	20,067,174.96	290,404.00
Contoso Store Nevada	19,886,922.17	232,507.00
Contoso Store New Brunswick	20,871,020.59	265,506.00
Contoso Store New Hampshire	18,934,419.17	242,156.50
Contoso Store New Mexico	19,363,262.41	233,044.50
Contoso Store Newfoundland and Labrador	20,235,739.49	196,206.50
Contoso Store North Dakota	18,485,029.60	190,233.00
Contoso Store Northwest Territories	20,335,831.29	209,991.50
Contoso Store Nunavut	20,873,773.19	279,556.50
Contoso Store Oregon	21,567,692.30	332,367.00
Contoso Store Rhode Island	19,058,640.71	215,602.50
Contoso Store South Carolina	21,983,097.11	262,599.00
Contoso Store South Dakota	18,683,643.89	222,870.00
Contoso Store Washington DC	18,666,859.06	262,374.50
Contoso Store West Virginia	19,202,728.72	240,796.50
Contoso Store Wyoming	17,787,563.97	215,965.00
Total	**494,047,103.41**	**4,958,373.00**

FIGURE 1-3 The *Maximum Product Sales* measure calculates the sales amount for the most sold product per store based on the total sales.

The *Maximum Product Sales* measure looks like this:

```
Maximum Product Sales =
MAXX (
    Product,
    [Sales]
)
```

This measure uses the MAXX function to calculate the value for the *Sales* measure for the Product table. However, given context transition, you will soon see it doesn't calculate the *Sales* measure for all products. Rather, because of the context in which it's being used, *Maximum Product Sales* in our example returns the total sales amount for the most sold product for each store based on the *Sales*. To be more precise, for each store, it returns the total sales amount for the product that ranked the high-est by total sales for products that had at least one transaction in the Sales table for that store.

While doing that, it takes into account the current filter context, so you can further refine this statement. In this example, for each store located in either Canada or the United States, the *Maximum Product Sales* measure returns the total sales amount for the product that ranked the highest by total sales and that has at least one transaction in the Sales table for that store. Note that if a product is in stock but has never been sold in the current store, that product will not be considered. Indeed, if, for example, you added a filter to your filter context that set Year to 2024, then the return value of *Maximum Product Sales* changes even more.

The *Maximum Product Sales* for the Contoso Store Hawaii is 184,594.50 (for the Product Adventure Works Desktop PC2.33 XD233 White), and it's calculated by evaluating the preceding measure in a cer-tain context. Figure 1-4 shows the process of evaluating the *Maximum Product Sales* measure in detail. Let's walk through these steps in detail to understand how filter context, row context, and context transition work together. You will see context transition at work multiple times per store. To be exact, context transition happens 186,332 times.

1. At the start of the evaluation of *Maximum Product Sales*, the filter context has two filters:

   - The first filter selects Canada and United States for Store CountryName. This filter was set even before the context transition happened because the stores in the table were filtered to stores located in Canada or the United States.

   - The second filter selects Contoso Store Hawaii for Store Description. This filter is set because we are calculating *Maximum Product Sales* for each Store Description.

Note Depending on the model's value filter behavior setting, the filter context will have one or two filters. Because both the Description and CountryName columns belong to the Store table, they're combined into one filter if the value filter behavior is set to Coalesced and kept separately as two filters if the value filter behavior is set to Indepen-dent. At the time of this writing, the default value of this setting is Coalesced, so one filter is created. However, Microsoft has indicated plans to change this default to Independent in the future.

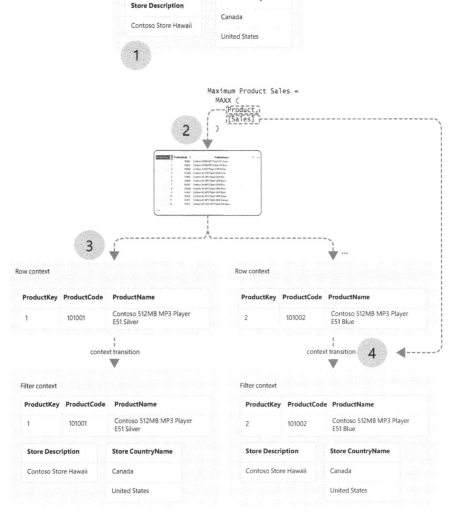

FIGURE 1-4 Context transition works to transform row context into filter context to retrieve expected results.

2. Within this filter context, the first parameter of MAXX is evaluated, which is a reference to the Product table. This returns all the rows (and all the columns) in the Product table because there are no filters in the current filter context that affect Product.

3. SUMX iterates (it's an iterator after all; see Chapter 8, "Comparing calculation options") over the results of the first parameter and evaluates the second parameter in a row context for each row of the first parameter. In this example, the *Sales* measure reference is evaluated in a row context for each row of Product, whereby the row context is always set to exactly one row of the Product table. To be exact, the row context is set to a one-row table containing all columns of the Product table. For example, when you're iterating over the first product, the row context is set as shown in Figure 1-5.

FIGURE 1-5 When evaluating the first product, the row context is set to all columns from the Product table for the first product. We added '...' for brevity.

4. The *Sales* measure reference in the second parameter applies context transition to the row context because there's an implicit CALCULATE surrounding any measure reference. This means that the following measure is equal to the one just after Figure 1-3:

```
Maximum Product Sales =
MAXX (
    Product,
    CALCULATE ( [Sales] )
)
```

Because a context transition occurs, the filter context in which *Sales* is evaluated equals the filter context set in the outer statement and adds the filter created by the context transition based on what was in the row context. The filter context now consists of the following three filters:

■ Store Country is Canada or United States.

■ Store Description is Contoso Store Hawaii.

■ Product ProductKey is 1, Product ProductCode is 101001, and so on.

Sales is then computed in the filter context. After that, the row context is updated to indicate the next Product. Then step 4 is performed again (including the context transition) until you have iterated over all Products.

After you have iterated over all products, MAXX computes the maximum of the results. Any blank values are ignored. Its results are then returned, and the evaluation for the Contoso Store Hawaii is complete. The filter on Store Description in the filter context is updated to reflect the next store and this process starts again to compute the *Maximum Product Sales* for the next store in the table visual.

After *Maximum Product Sales* is calculated for all stores, the total number of context transitions performed is (number of stores) * (number of products +1) = 74 * (2517+1) = 186,332 times! As you can see, context transition is a very common operation. The issue is that it's equally opaque, confusing many users about the inner workings of DAX, leaving them unable to reason about the results, and causing them to utter a frustrated, "DAX is hard!"

CALCULATE, the scary clown among the DAX functions

Many of us get tingles down our spine when we work with CALCULATE. Using CALCULATE can feel like riding a wild bull. You ride it, but you never feel fully in control.

While this is not true, it's understandable why it can feel that way. One of the reasons is what you saw earlier in this chapter: you end up using CALCULATE more often than you think, even if you didn't type it yourself. This implicit CALCULATE that surrounds any measure reference is surprising to many beginners. Because the implicit CALCULATE performs a context transition, the measure referenced is calculated within a filter context created by context transition. However, you didn't ask for that, did you? All you did was write a measure reference, expecting that measure to be evaluated within the context of the rest of the DAX you are writing. But no. Because of the implicit CALCULATE, that pesky context transition kicked in.

Often you explicitly use CALCULATE, and that's where you actively invoke context transition to help you out. While it can be tempting to solve any issues in DAX by adding CALCULATE around whatever you wrote, you shouldn't do this precisely because of the context transition. It can lead to situations in which the calculation works but you've lost all control over why.

What are visual calculations?

Now that we have identified the core issues with DAX that lead to the widespread opinion that DAX is hard, it's time to discuss visual calculation. Visual calculations are a way of performing DAX calculations in Power BI. These do away with this complexity and, as a result, make DAX easier to use.

DAX offers multiple options for performing calculations. This chapter offers a high-level comparison of the most relevant options. For a detailed review of all these calculation options, see Chapter 8.

A new tool in your toolbox

In DAX, you can perform calculations using the following:

- **Calculated columns** A calculated column is a column added to a table. The contents of the cells in the column are the output of a DAX statement. Calculated columns are most often used to perform row-by-row calculations within a table—for example, to obtain the difference between two columns for each row. Calculated columns are static, meaning they're calculated when the table is first loaded or refreshed, and their results cannot be changed until the table is refreshed again. Calculated columns are relatively easy to understand because you can inspect the DAX statement and predict the results.

- **Calculated tables** A calculated table is like a calculated column except, as its name implies, it calculates a table instead of a column. After the table is loaded or refreshed, the results for calculated tables and calculated columns are locked in and cannot be changed until the table is refreshed. The results are precomputed and aren't dynamically determined. Most often, calculated tables are relatively easy to understand, precisely because you can inspect the DAX statement and predict the results. The same statement always returns the same result for the same parameters until the table is refreshed.

- **Measures** Unlike calculated columns and calculated tables, measures aren't precalculated or static. Their output is dynamically calculated as needed and is determined not only by their definition but also by the filter context in which they're executed. The same definition can have a different meaning based on the filter context. Measures are evaluated within that filter context and often summarize multiple rows.

- **Visual calculation** Visual calculations are DAX calculations executed in the scope of a visual. They are by default executed on a row-by-row basis, much like a calculated column, but are calculated on the fly, like a measure. In contrast to both calculated columns and measures, visual calculations aren't part of the semantic model in Power BI but instead are part of a visual, such as a chart. This means visual calculations don't have to worry about filter context as much as measures need to do. In fact, the filter context is seen as external to the visual calculation on a visual. This doesn't mean the visual calculation isn't affected by or would ignore the filter context but rather that it's applied on a different level. The filter context dictates what the measures and fields on the visual return, and the visual calculation takes those values as input for its evaluation. In other words, a visual calculation is only indirectly affected by filter context, not directly, the way a measure or field reference is.

Visual calculations share behaviors with calculated columns and measures but also have important differences, particularly in how they can be used, where they are stored, and when they are computed. See Chapter 8 for more details.

Visual context

A visual calculation cannot refer to anything that is not on the visual. The only data the visual calculation is aware of is what is on the visual. The visual calculation is oblivious to any other data. How that data got there, or how it was determined that the visual should show this set of data through filter context, is irrelevant.

The universe for a visual calculation is extremely simple. Indeed, visual calculations do not know that a semantic model exists. Therefore, visual calculations are much easier to understand, and their results are easier to predict, check, and validate. Because there is no abstract filter context that directly affects the results of a visual calculation, you can visually inspect what's happening and confirm that the calculation does what you need it to do. Even a filter set in the filter pane to filter the data in the visual does not directly affect a visual calculation but does so indirectly. In other words, a visual calculation is aware of the visual context. Because the visual context can only contain the fields in the visual and nothing else, it's much easier to understand than the context in which measures (and calculated columns) are evaluated. Anything you see while working with visual calculations is part of the visual context, and anything you don't see isn't. It's that simple.

Why visual calculations?

You might be wondering, why use visual calculation? Why did Microsoft even bother to incorporate this capability in the first place? Well, let's face the truth: Power BI was never built for DAX masters. It was built for end users, for the masses—which is to say, easy to use with minimal education required. However, the reality is that DAX does require education and training for anything more than a simple sum. This problem becomes more pronounced if you don't have a proper semantic model.

The masses often don't care about building a good semantic model, best practices, or tweaking systems to obtain the best performance. They care about two things: getting their job done and doing it fast. That doesn't mean that they don't need to be able to trust the data. Of course they do. But they don't really care about all the intricate details of the DAX language or your semantic model. As long as what they have gets the job done in the time required, they're good. Doing something quick and easy is more important than developing a perfectly polished solution. DAX, for them, is not easy. This is one reason Excel is still so prevalent everywhere and that the Export to Excel button is the most popular button in any BI tool in the market—Power BI included. This doesn't mean that the masses disregard quality or best practices in the long term. In fact, the opposite is true. Many of them want to strike a balance between getting the job done efficiently while ensuring accuracy and reliability. However, when ensuring accuracy, reliability, and quality and following best practices get in the way of getting the job done, getting the job done always wins.

While Power BI was built for end users and not DAX masters, DAX masters of course have a role to play, in which they build the semantic model and provide the central, core solutions as part of it using measures. End users can then use visual calculations to bolt on these quick and easy solutions they need for a limited scenario. They think something that is simple in Excel should be simple in Power BI. But the reality is that it isn't. Visual calculations bring these worlds much closer together.

Ask yourself this: would you prefer your business users to do their calculations in Power BI or in Excel? If you enable them to do their calculations in Power BI, the data on which they base their calculation, and therefore decision, is the data that's centrally provided. If they export to Excel to add their calculations, you have zero visibility into what happened between the moment the data was exported to Excel and the moment the decision was made. You lose all control and insight into the quality of the data; as a result, the output cannot be trusted.

Visual calculations are Microsoft's latest effort to make DAX easier to use. They don't replace the powerful yet complicated DAX that already exists. Rather, they're another tool in your toolbox that you can use if you prefer. There are many reasons to use visual calculations, apart from the actual functional benefit it provides. These might include the following:

- Your knowledge level in DAX or that of the users for whom you're making reports and models might lead you to use visual calculations.

- You might be doing some prototyping before implementing the solution in the semantic model using a measure.

- You might be under a lot of time pressure.

- You might just need the solution for one visual or report and don't want to bother with expanding your semantic model.

Whatever your reason, visual calculations are a tool that come with their own benefits and downsides, and it's up to you to make an educated choice when to use them.

Benefits of visual calculations

Visual calculations come with some extra benefits that measures and calculated columns simply do not provide.

Simpler than measures, more trustworthy than Excel

Visual calculations make DAX easier. They're a great way to find solutions in a business context, in which getting an answer quickly and easily is more important than building a reusable, long-lived solution. In these situations, you or your end user need a one-off, quick, easy solution, and you don't care about updating the semantic model using a complicated DAX measure. In such cases, it's unacceptable to ask the Power BI developer to update the model, even if that would only take a day (which is very wishful thinking). Rather, the calculation must be performed quickly, the answer should be given right away, and the decision should be made right after. Business does not wait. Bogging business down with lengthy processes will only result in business intelligence efforts receiving less and less funding or the continued clicking of that dreaded Export to Excel button.

Note We strongly believe that enabling end users to perform their business calculations in Power BI on top of trusted data is the way to go every single time.

Let's take a look at a very simple visual, shown in Figure 1-6.

Description	Sales
Contoso Store Alaska	18,232,514.91
Contoso Store Arkansas	21,140,025.39
Contoso Store Connecticut	21,009,014.60
Contoso Store Hawaii	18,866,255.57
Contoso Store Idaho	18,768,667.04
Contoso Store Iowa	21,490,228.07
Contoso Store Kansas	22,082,097.40
Contoso Store Maine	18,422,638.69
Contoso Store Montana	18,032,263.12
Contoso Store Nebraska	20,067,174.96
Contoso Store Nevada	19,886,922.17
Contoso Store New Brunswick	20,871,020.59
Contoso Store New Hampshire	18,934,419.17
Contoso Store New Mexico	19,363,262.41
Contoso Store Newfoundland and Labrador	20,235,739.49
Contoso Store North Dakota	18,485,029.60
Contoso Store Northwest Territories	20,335,831.29
Contoso Store Nunavut	20,873,773.19
Contoso Store Oregon	21,567,692.30
Contoso Store Rhode Island	19,058,640.71
Contoso Store South Carolina	21,983,097.11
Contoso Store South Dakota	18,683,643.89
Contoso Store Washington DC	18,666,859.06
Contoso Store West Virginia	19,202,728.72
Contoso Store Wyoming	17,787,563.97
Total	**494,047,103.41**

FIGURE 1-6 This example is a list of stores and the Sales per store.

Let's say you want to grab the value of the Description column. You might be tempted to write
`Store Description = [Description]` in a measure because, well, the value is right there on the screen, and it's clearly named Description, is it not? Well, too bad. DAX doesn't allow you to grab it so easily. Instead, in a measure, you have to write something like this:

```
Store Description = SELECTEDVALUE ( Store[Description] )
```

This works because the Store Description measure is evaluated within a context that contains one Store. Therefore, you grab the aggregated value of the one Store's Description, which results in the one Description in context being returned. The results of doing this are shown in Figure 1-7.

Description	Sales	Store Description
Contoso Store Alaska	18,232,514.91	Contoso Store Alaska
Contoso Store Arkansas	21,140,025.39	Contoso Store Arkansas
Contoso Store Connecticut	21,009,014.60	Contoso Store Connecticut
Contoso Store Delaware		Contoso Store Delaware
Contoso Store Hawaii	18,866,255.57	Contoso Store Hawaii
Contoso Store Idaho	18,768,667.04	Contoso Store Idaho
Contoso Store Iowa	21,490,228.07	Contoso Store Iowa
Contoso Store Kansas	22,082,097.40	Contoso Store Kansas
Contoso Store Maine	18,422,638.69	Contoso Store Maine
Contoso Store Mississippi		Contoso Store Mississippi
Contoso Store Montana	18,032,263.12	Contoso Store Montana
Contoso Store Nebraska	20,067,174.96	Contoso Store Nebraska
Contoso Store Nevada	19,886,922.17	Contoso Store Nevada
Contoso Store New Brunswick	20,871,020.59	Contoso Store New Brunswick
Contoso Store New Hampshire	18,934,419.17	Contoso Store New Hampshire
Contoso Store New Mexico	19,363,262.41	Contoso Store New Mexico
Contoso Store Newfoundland and Labrador	20,235,739.49	Contoso Store Newfoundland and Labrador
Contoso Store North Dakota	18,485,029.60	Contoso Store North Dakota
Contoso Store Northwest Territories	20,335,831.29	Contoso Store Northwest Territories
Contoso Store Nunavut	20,873,773.19	Contoso Store Nunavut
Contoso Store Oregon	21,567,692.30	Contoso Store Oregon
Contoso Store Rhode Island	19,058,640.71	Contoso Store Rhode Island
Contoso Store South Carolina	21,983,097.11	Contoso Store South Carolina
Contoso Store South Dakota	18,683,643.89	Contoso Store South Dakota
Contoso Store Utah		Contoso Store Utah
Contoso Store Washington DC	18,666,859.06	Contoso Store Washington DC
Contoso Store West Virginia	19,202,728.72	Contoso Store West Virginia
Contoso Store Wyoming	17,787,563.97	Contoso Store Wyoming
Contoso Store Yukon		Contoso Store Yukon
Total	**494,047,103.41**	

FIGURE 1-7 The report author added a store description to the list of stores and the Sales per store.

At first glance, the Store Description measure did indeed do its job. However, after a closer look, it becomes clear that some things are different between Figure 1-7 and Figure 1-6. Figure 1-7 suddenly shows more stores! To be precise, the stores that had no Sales are now also shown in the table. This is because Power BI automatically removed these, as all calculations in the visual did return empty values. In Figure 1-6, the *Sales* measure was the only calculation, and it resulted in an empty value for those stores. However, because the *Store Description* measure always returns a value, there are no rows for which all the calculations in the visual returns empty values; hence, Power BI doesn't remove any rows.

> **Note** If you ever want to force Power BI to show all the items, even if all calculations in the visual return empty values, you can right-click the item (Stores in our example) and select Show items with no data. Keep in mind that this option is not compatible with visual calculations at this time.

Also, notice that on the total row, the Store Description returns no value. This is because in the context of the total, there is no single Store selected; therefore, SELECTEDVALUE doesn't return a value (unless you specified the *alternateResult* parameter).

Now, reflect on your first inclination of writing Store Description = [Description] to grab the Description. While this is invalid in a measure, this is perfectly valid in a visual calculation, assuming of course that the Description is on the visual on which the visual calculation is being evaluated. In regular DAX, you can't refer to a value by its name even though you're looking at it. In visual calculations, you can. This is just an example of how a visual calculation is easier; we will see many more throughout this book.

Referring to visual structure

Because visual calculations are executed as part of a visual, they have extra tricks up their sleeves. The visual context in which they operate not only describes what data is on the visual (which is then iterated over in a row context) but also the structure of the visual. This means a visual calculation can refer to the axes of a visual, such as the x-axis or the y-axis instead of the actual field. This enables visual calculations to be highly flexible; a visual calculation can continue to work even if the field that is on the x-axis changes by simply referring to the axis instead of the actual field. Much like with a calculation group or field parameter, this provides a high level of flexibility. We will dive much deeper into the concept of axes a little later in this book.

Just DAX, but simpler

If you already know DAX, you might be worried about applying your knowledge in visual calculations. While it's true that they operate a little differently, if you already know DAX, you will soon see that visual calculations are easier to work with than measures, and also, they're still DAX.

Most DAX will work in visual calculations. However, because a visual calculation operates in the visual context, it's blissfully unaware of the semantic model, so DAX functions that perform actions on that model don't work. Examples of these are DAX functions that manipulate or evaluate relationships, such as RELATED or USERELATIONSHIP. When used in visual calculations, these and other functions that need access to the semantic model return an error.

If you ever wonder whether you can use a function in visual calculations, simply look at the DAX documentation available at *https://learn.microsoft.com/dax*. Each function page has a header that indicates whether you can use that function in visual calculations. More details on which functions are available, blocked, or discouraged can be found in Chapter 3.

Because there is only visual context to work with, the DAX required for visual calculations is much simpler to write, edit, and understand compared to the DAX required for measures. CALCULATE is often not even required, although under the covers, as you will soon see, many visual calculation functions use it. The difference is that you don't have to worry about it, and you don't have to use it. It's there when you need it, but it's conveniently hidden away if you prefer. And let's be honest; who doesn't prefer it this way?

Exclusive functions

Although the language used in visual calculations is DAX, not all DAX can be used. The inverse is true as well: certain functions provided are available only in visual calculations and nowhere else. To understand which functions are exclusive to visual calculations, check the same documentation mentioned in the preceding section at *https://learn.microsoft.com/dax*.

Functions that are used exclusively by visual calculations are easier to use and often solve typical business problems such as adding a moving average, a difference versus previous, or a running sum. The reason most of these functions are exclusive to visual calculations is that they have an *axis* parameter, which is mostly optional. This parameter determines the direction in which the visual calculation moves across the data in the visual. It's much like a row context in a calculated column because it's set to select one row at a time from top to bottom by default, but it can be changed to selecting one column at a time from left to right or even operate over the data in the visual in a snaking pattern, making a Z or N pattern.

> **Note**   Chapters 3, "Visual calculations concepts" and 7, "The floors and rooms: visual calculations exclusive functions", discuss these functions in much more detail.

Highly visual

Visual calculations is a very clever name for this feature because they aren't just calculations on a visual; they're also highly visual. As we discuss in more detail later in this book, compared to the rest of DAX, they are WYSIWYG. The visual you're working on is shown to you all the time. On top of that, you're always shown the data the calculation works on, and tools are provided to easily validate the results. Additionally, you don't have to do all the typing. And unlike with measure, templates are provided, and even less typing is required. All of this provides an easier-to-use, more Excel-like way of working that is a breath of fresh air compared to measures.

Performance

It's impossible to compare the performance of visual calculations with calculated columns because calculated columns are precalculated and visual calculations are not. Therefore, this section compares the performance of visual calculations with measures.

Unless you have a trivial amount of data in your visual, visual calculations should perform better than measures because they're executed as part of the DAX query to fetch the results instead of independently. This eliminates the need to send multiple queries to the source, even though the DAX engine tries to optimize performance and fuses queries together. With visual calculations, a single query is sent to the source, whereas no such guarantee exists for analysis that relies on measures. How pronounced the effects are depends on the size of your data and the complexity of the DAX used.

 Note See Chapter 9, "Breaking down visual calculations execution," for more details on performance characteristics of visual calculations.

Downsides of visual calculations

Visual calculations aren't in the semantic model. Therefore, if you attempt to manage them using tools that focus only on your semantic model, you won't succeed. Instead of being in the semantic model, visual calculations are stored as part of the visual and are therefore part of the report file.

This also means they can't be reused across multiple reports as easily. Many organizations like to create central definitions of common calculations and provide them as measures or calculated columns in their semantic models so users can rely on them in their reports, increasing the chances that people will use common, agreed-upon definitions—for example, of what constitutes sales, risk, and exposure profiles. But visual calculations aren't in the model, so they aren't reusable across reports, nor are they as discoverable for tenant admins or central teams as measures are. This doesn't mean you have to open every single report a user makes to see if they used a visual calculation. There are tools to discover and monitor visual calculations in your organization as well as in reports.

 Note To learn more about how to manage and reuse visual calculations and where and how visual calculations are stored in the report file, see Chapter 4, "Organization and use of visual calculations."

In summary

Power BI visual calculations represent a new tool in your calculation toolbox, combining the best aspects of calculated columns and measures into one. They're executed in the visual context, not in the model, which makes them easier to understand. On top of that, they can do things measures can't, such as referring to the visual structure, and they're much faster.

Don't worry, visual calculations don't require you to learn a new language. They still use DAX, but the DAX you write is simpler. This is partly because of specialized functions that are exclusive to visual calculations but also because the visual context is easier to understand than filter context. On top of that, the visual context and data on the visual is shown to you, so it's easier to validate the results of the calculation.

Visual calculations make it easier to understand what makes DAX complicated for most users: filter context. It is still there but only affects the visual calculations in an indirect manner, so you don't have to worry about it as much. On top of that, the context in which visual calculations are evaluated only contains what you're working with on the visual. The model and its complex filter context, like CALCULATE, are hidden from sight, giving you peace of mind to focus on what really matters: writing the calculation you need to provide the insight you and your users require.

As with all things, there are some tradeoffs. The biggest one is that because visual calculations are not stored in the semantic model, but rather in the report, they're not as reusable as measures.

Visual calculations and measures are not mutually exclusive. If you're new to Power BI, we recommend you start with visual calculations and use measures only for the most basic of calculations, such as simple sums. Then, once you're ready, you can use more measures where it makes sense. If you're already used to working with measures, we encourage you to consider visual calculations because of the simplicity of the DAX required, their performance, and their visual aspect, which allows you to check your work more easily than with measures, while at the same time keeping in mind the downsides of using visual calculations. This recommendation applies to any calculation scenario, not just the scenarios in which visual calculations enable you to create calculations that are almost prohibitively complicated in measures as well, such as a running sum, as you will soon see.

## CHAPTER 2

My first visual calculation

Now that you have learned about visual calculations, how easy it is to use them, why they matter, and what problem they solve, you must be eager to try them out for yourself. To that end, this chapter switches from the theoretical approach presented in the previous chapter to real-world examples in which you could use visual calculations. This chapter starts by introducing the semantic model we will be using throughout the book. After that, it guides you through the process of creating visual calculations. You will be introduced to the process of creating visual calculations. Meanwhile, we will touch upon a few new concepts, which will be further explained in the next chapters of this book. The first examples are also building blocks for practical, real-world examples, which will be described in Part IV, "The art of practical visual calculations."

Introduction to the example semantic model

To help you create your first visual calculations, we have created an example of a semantic model that you can use, which you can find on this book's companion website (see Introduction). The pbix file Contoso Sales CH2 Start provides a starting point from which you can follow along to do all the steps described in this chapter. The pbix file not only contains the semantic model but also includes a report page called Chapter 2, which serves as the starting point on which we'll build in this chapter. On the website, you can also find the Contoso Sales CH2 End pbix file, which will match the final version that you will have created if you follow along with all the steps in this chapter. You can check that model to determine whether you did it correctly.

> **Note** It's also possible to create visual calculations directly in the service, but for the purpose of these first examples, we'll use the desktop version. In the service, the steps are similar.

To begin, open the example semantic model in Power BI Desktop. As shown in Figure 2-1, the example model contains data about sales transactions. It's a simple model that has some dimension tables like Customer, Date, Product, and Store, and contains three fact tables with data about Sales, Orders, and Order Detail. To enable you to start straight away with the visual calculations, we've already prepared the necessary relationships and some simple measures, which can be found in a table where all measures are stored. This table is named _Measures.

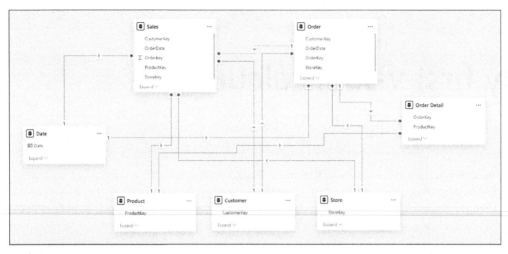

FIGURE 2-1 The model view of the example semantic model.

On the Chapter 2 report page, the clustered bar chart on the left shows the *Costs* and *Sales* per product category, and the clustered column chart on the right gives the *Sales* per Month. There is also a slicer to enable you to select different years.

Questions that could arise from this example model include the following:

- What is the profit per product category?

- What are the total year-to-date sales?

- How is the total profit divided over the different countries?

Of course, it's possible to create measures in Power BI that answer these questions and show them on the report page. However, we'll employ visual calculations instead because they're so easy to use.

Create your first visual calculation

A visual calculation is created inside a visual. For your first visual calculation, you'll enhance the sample visual that contains *Sales* and *Costs* per product category with the total profit per product category. Do so by first selecting the clustered bar chart on the left of the report page. When the visual is selected, there are multiple ways to add a visual calculation to this bar chart:

- Click the New visual calculation button in the Calculations section of the Home ribbon, as shown in Figure 2-2.

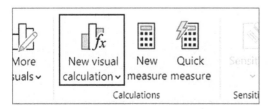

FIGURE 2-2 The New visual calculation button in the Calculations section of the Home ribbon.

- Click the More options button (it features three dots) in the top-right corner of the visual, and select the New visual calculation > Custom option, as shown in Figure 2-3.

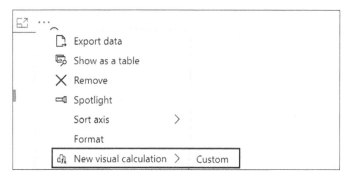

FIGURE 2-3 Click the New visual calculation option, then the Custom option in the More options button.

- Right-click the visual and select the New visual calculation option in the context menu that opens, as shown in Figure 2-4.

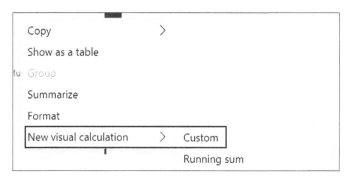

FIGURE 2-4 Right-clicking the visual opens a context menu with a New visual calculation > Custom option.

Performing one of these actions displays the visual calculations edit mode window, which shows your visual as it appeared on the report page at the top and a matrix with data beneath it. The matrix is a representation of the data in the visual and is conveniently called the visual matrix. In this case, the visual matrix contains values for the sales and costs per product category as well as the total sales and costs for all product categories combined. An empty Calculation column appears to the right of these values, as is shown in Figure 2-5. This is where you will create your first visual calculation.

The first question we want to answer is, what is the total profit per product category? The formula for this involves subtracting the costs from the sales. This is exactly what you'll do to create your first visual calculation.

As explained in Chapter 1, "Introduction to visual calculations," visual calculations are written in the DAX language. They have a similar syntax as regular measures and should thus begin with a name. We'll call our first visual calculation *Profit*.

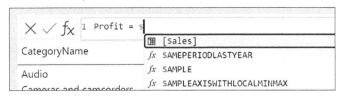

CategoryName	Sales	Costs	Calculation
Audio	13,765,422.62	5,829,616.19	
Cameras and camcorders	47,767,301.24	18,911,017.28	
Cell phones	68,195,741.37	29,601,158.73	
Computers	225,519,726.55	93,950,645.45	
Games and Toys	4,452,061.96	2,013,339.74	
Home Appliances	39,613,959.72	16,473,529.78	
Music, Movies and Audio Books	20,022,708.59	7,796,987.04	
TV and Video	29,526,412.37	11,933,364.18	
Total	**448,863,334.43**	**186,509,658.40**	

FIGURE 2-5 Add a visual calculation to an existing visual in the visual matrix.

To create this visual calculation, place your cursor in the formula bar and use ordinary DAX to write the formula. Notice that the IntelliSense feature provides suggestions as you type. In this example, after you type the name for your visual calculation and begin typing the formula, as you press the S key, you will see a list of suggestions that includes [Sales], as shown in Figure 2-6.

FIGURE 2-6 Defining *Profit* as a visual calculation.

 Note The suggestion, [Sales], has square brackets, like a column or measure. The icon that precedes this indicates a table column. However, we have used a measure in the visual. Furthermore, it does not have a table name in front of the square brackets, as would be typical when you are referring to a table column. This is because this [Sales] object actually refers to the column of Sales that is present in the visual matrix, which is visible in the visual calculations edit mode window. This concept will be further explained in the next section.

When you type a square bracket in the formula bar, you will see all the available columns for use in this visual matrix. In this example, there are three: CategoryName, Sales, and Costs. CategoryName is a column of the Product table. The Sales and Costs columns are the results of the DAX measures *Sales* and *Costs* that are defined in the _Measures table. These measures were added to the visual and return values for the context that is evaluated for the visual in which we are creating a visual calculation.

Back to our example. We wanted to create output for the profit, which is defined as the difference between sales and costs. In the formula bar, you can simply type the following DAX formula:

```
Profit = [Sales] - [Costs]
```

Press Enter or click the green check mark to finish. This will create a new column in the visual matrix with the name Profit, and in each row, the corresponding value of sales minus costs is evaluated, as shown in Figure 2-7. Congratulations, you have successfully created your first visual calculation!

CategoryName	Sales	Costs	Profit
Audio	13,765,422.62	5,829,616.19	7,935,806.43
Cameras and camcorders	47,767,301.24	18,911,017.28	28,856,283.96
Cell phones	68,195,741.37	29,601,158.73	38,594,582.64
Computers	225,519,726.55	93,950,645.45	131,569,081.09
Games and Toys	4,452,061.96	2,013,339.74	2,438,722.22
Home Appliances	39,613,959.72	16,473,529.78	23,140,429.95
Music, Movies and Audio Books	20,022,708.59	7,796,987.04	12,225,721.55
TV and Video	29,526,412.37	11,933,364.18	17,593,048.19
Total	**448,863,334.43**	**186,509,658.40**	**262,353,676.03**

FIGURE 2-7 *Profit* as a visual calculation in the visual matrix.

This new calculation is also added to your visual. As shown in Figure 2-8, the visual should now contain three values: *Sales* and *Costs* (which are measures) and *Profit* (which is your very first visual calculation).

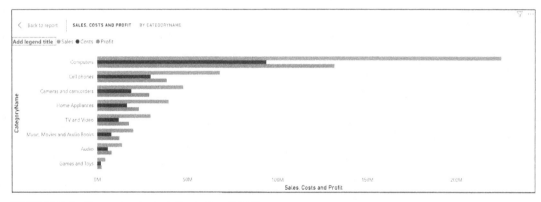

FIGURE 2-8 *Profit* as a visual calculation in the visual preview.

You can add a new visual calculation by writing another DAX statement in the formula bar. You can even use your newly created visual calculation in another visual calculation. For example, you can create a visual calculation to calculate the profit including a 10 percent tax amount by typing the following DAX formula in the formula bar and pressing Enter:

```
Profit incl tax = 1.1 * [Profit]
```

This will create a second visual calculation, and thus a new column in your visual matrix and a new bar in the visual preview.

It's also possible to go back to your report by clicking the Back to report button in the top-left corner of the window, as shown in Figure 2-9.

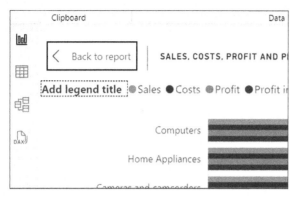

FIGURE 2-9 You can use the Back to report button to go back to the report.

In the Visualizations pane of the visual that you just edited, there are two new values on the X-axis, called *Profit* and *Profit incl tax* (assuming you created both visual calculations described so far), as shown in Figure 2-10. To help you differentiate between measures, columns and visual calculations, the visual calculations are identified by a small icon that shows a column chart with fx in front of it.

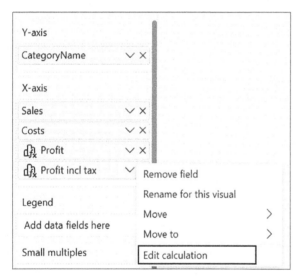

FIGURE 2-10 The X-axis of the visual contains four fields.

There are also different options in the dropdown on the right side of the data fields. For regular measures and columns, there are options for Show value as and New quick measure. But for visual calculations, there is an Edit calculation option instead. Clicking this option returns you to the visual calculations edit mode window, with the visual preview on top and the visual matrix, where you can edit your visual calculation, below it.

Create a year-to-date sales calculation

The report page contains a visual that shows the sales per month, but it's very common to look at sales on a year-to-date basis, instead—hence, our second question earlier in this chapter: what are the total year-to-date sales? Let's see if we can create another visual calculation for year-to-date sales. In this example, you will add a new year-to-date sales calculation to the clustered column chart that contains the sales per month, shown in Figure 2-11.

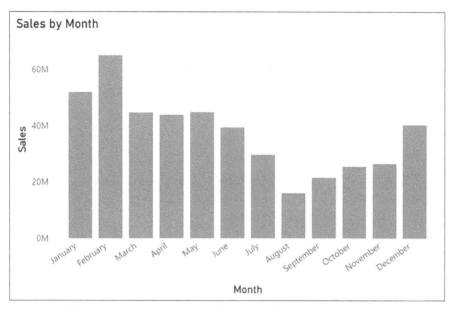

FIGURE 2-11 This clustered column chart visual shows the *Sales* per Month.

As before, begin by selecting the visual you want to work on—in this case, the column chart. Then add a visual calculation to open the visual calculations edit mode window, with the column chart on top and the visual matrix below it. This time, the visual matrix has one column for the month, which lists all the month names, and one column called Sales, where the values for the data in the column chart are listed. At the bottom, there's a total row that shows the total sales over all the months.

To calculate year-to-date sales, you add up the sales for all previous months, plus the sales for the current month. So, for January, the year-to-date sales would be the same as the regular sales because it's the first month of the year. But for February, the year-to-date sales would be the sum of the January sales and the February sales. And for March, it would be the sum of January, February, and March.

Note If you're familiar with DAX, you could use time intelligence functions to obtain the year-to-date value. However, because visual calculations are meant to be simple, and are available to any user who is not ready to use time intelligence functions, we will use visual calculations here.

Because users frequently need to obtain running sums, like year-to-date sales, visual calculations offer an expression template for this operation. An expression template is a predefined template to compute certain calculations in visual calculations. To view and insert available expression templates (of which there are several), click the fx button for the visual calculation to the left of the formula bar (see Figure 2-12). These expression templates can be selected in the visual calculations edit mode, as well as in the ribbon (refer to Figure 2-2), the More options button (refer to Figure 2-3), and the context menu (refer to Figure 2-4).

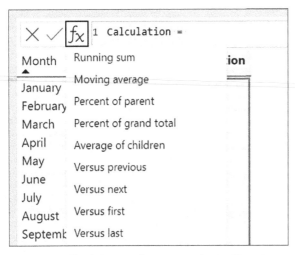

FIGURE 2-12 The fx button allows you to view and insert expression templates.

For this example, select the first expression template in the list, Running sum. As shown in Figure 2-13, expression templates provide easy-to-use parameter pickers that enable you to quickly select parameter values without having to type them. In addition, this expression template automatically names your visual calculation *Running sum* and adds the RUNNINGSUM DAX function. For this example, let's change the name of the visual calculation to *YTD Sales* instead of *Running sum* because that is a better description of what you want to calculate.

Month	Sales	Running sum
January	51,886,482.12	

`1 Running sum = RUNNINGSUM( ⊙ [Field])`

FIGURE 2-13 Using the Running Sum expression template is made easy thanks to the parameter picker.

The RUNNINGSUM function

The RUNNINGSUM DAX function is not available for measures, calculated columns, and calculated tables. Rather, it's a brand-new function created specifically for visual calculations. It calculates the sum of values by adding the current value to the preceding values—exactly what you need to calculate the year-to-date sales. However, the RUNNINGSUM function has much broader uses, and can be applied to all values on the axis. For example, suppose you have a process, and each step in that process takes a certain number of seconds to complete, and you've created a visual with all the steps on the axis. Using the RUNNINGSUM function, you can calculate exactly how much time has passed after each step. And if you add the starting timestamp for the first step, you even get the exact timestamp of when each process step completes. That's with just one DAX function! Truly, the possibilities are endless. We will discuss axis and related concepts in Chapter 3 and dive much deeper into the available functions, including RUNNINGSUM, in Part II, "Visual calculations functions", of this book.

As shown in Figure 2-13, the DAX function RUNNINGSUM asks for at least one parameter, as indicated by the [Field] parameter picker. However, our data does not contain a Field column, as indicated by the red squiggle. You need to replace this field with the column for which you want to calculate the running sum. To do that, either click the parameter picker and pick [Sales] as shown in Figure 2-14 or delete the [Field] placeholder in the formula bar and type a square opening bracket to see a list of all the available options for the current visual (in this case, Month and Sales).

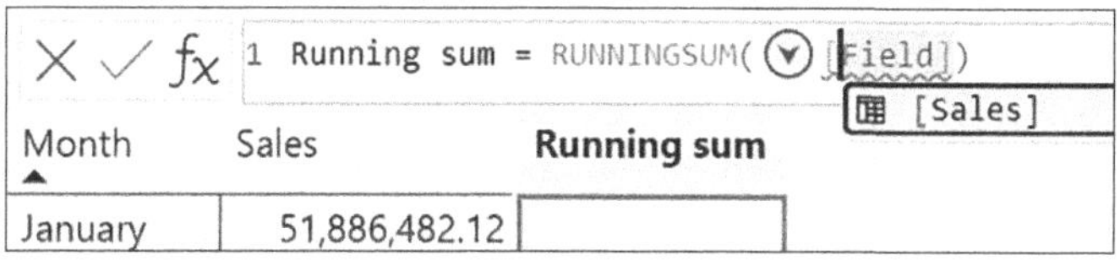

FIGURE 2-14 Use the parameter picker to select a column.

To calculate the running sum of the sales data, select [Sales] to generate the following DAX statement:

```
YTD Sales = RUNNINGSUM ( [Sales] )
```

Then press Enter or click the green check mark to the left of the formula bar to create the new visual calculation in your visual. The resulting visual calculation should appear in the visual preview in the top half of the screen (see Figure 2-15).

The values are exactly as you would expect, which is best seen in the visual matrix at the bottom of the screen (see Figure 2-16).

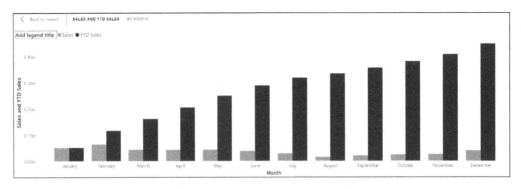

FIGURE 2-15 The *YTD Sales* visual calculation correctly calculates the running sum of *Sales*.

Month	Sales	YTD Sales
January	51,886,482.12	51,886,482.12
February	64,923,153.55	116,809,635.66
March	44,610,254.48	161,419,890.14
April	43,794,064.91	205,213,955.06
May	44,782,137.77	249,996,092.82
June	39,376,967.87	289,373,060.69
July	29,708,944.66	319,082,005.34
August	16,054,829.64	335,136,834.98
September	21,523,910.57	356,660,745.55
October	25,471,590.22	382,132,335.77
November	26,442,100.96	408,574,436.73
December	40,288,897.70	448,863,334.43
Total	**448,863,334.43**	**448,863,334.43**

fx   Create a new calculation or select one

FIGURE 2-16 The visual matrix of the visual shows *Sales* per Month and *YTD Sales*.

As expected, the two values for January are the same, because the YTD sales in January consist only of sales during that single month. The other values are also as expected, with YTD sales in February equaling the sum of the January and February sales, and YTD sales in March equaling the sum of the YTD sales in February and the March sales. And, as expected, at the end of the year, the YTD sales in December equal the grand total of all the individual sales per month, resulting in a total of approximately 449 million—which is also the total for the YTD Sales column.

> **Note** We are well aware that the TOTALYTD function restarts the sum at Year change, when the semantic model has a dimension marked as Date table. For this example, with visual calculations, we assume you only work with one year of data, and therefore, RUN-NINGSUM will suffice as well. At year change, the RUNNINGSUM function will continue summing up. This behavior can be influenced by using the *reset* parameter as described in Chapter 3, "Visual calculations concepts." We will also add this *reset* parameter later in this chapter to a visual calculation.

Suppose you want to view the YTD sales per month, but not the sales for each individual month. You cannot simply remove the *Sales* measure from the visual because you need that data to calculate the YTD sales. You can, however, hide that data. To do so, make sure you're in the visual calculations edit mode, locate the *Sales* measure in the Visualizations pane, and click the eye icon. (This is the same icon you use to hide or show columns or tables in the table view of a Power BI semantic model.) A diagonal line will appear through the icon, indicating that it's now hidden (see Figure 2-17).

FIGURE 2-17 The eye icon next to measures and visual calculations makes it possible to hide measures or visual calculations from the visual.

Notice that the visual matrix at the bottom of the visual calculations edit mode window is not affected by hiding the *Sales* measure. It still contains two columns, Sales and YTD Sales, and rows for each Month. However, the visual preview in the top part of the screen contains only the *YTD Sales* for each Month, as does the visual on the report page.

Notice, too, that the Y-axis setting in the Visualizations pane for the visual on the report page lacks an entry for the *Sales* measure. However, if you hover your mouse pointer over the information icon above the Y-axis setting (see Figure 2-18), Power BI informs you that there are more fields in the visual, but they are hidden. You can still access and use them when you open the visual calculations edit mode window.

FIGURE 2-18 The information icon indicates that this visual has hidden fields.

> **Note** You can create very complex visual calculations in steps and hide any irrelevant intermediate results. We'll look at an example of a more complex calculation that requires some intermediate steps later in this chapter. Chapter 3 includes more information about the concept of hiding elements in visuals.

Set a format

When you create a measure, you often need to format it, so it looks how you want it to in your report. But how does this work for visual calculations? To find out, let's use the example you just created for year-to-date sales.

The *YTD Sales* visual calculation doesn't have any format set; neither does the *Sales* measure from which it is calculated. So, let's start with that. If you change the *Sales* measure to a currency format with a dollar sign in front of it, you won't see any changes in the visual. This makes sense because even though the *Sales* measure is in that visual, it's hidden from view. If you switch to the visual calculations edit mode, though, you do see the change in the visual matrix, with all the values in the Sales column preceded by a dollar sign (see Figure 2-19). However, the YTD Sales column has not changed. This is because visual calculations do not take on the format of any measures used to create them—although it does try to guess, based on the function you used and your input data types. In this case, the result is not what we want. We want to format it with a dollar sign in front, just like the *Sales* measure.

Month	Sales	YTD Sales
January	$51,886,482.12	51,886,482.12
February	$64,923,153.55	116,809,635.66
March	$44,610,254.48	161,419,890.14
April	$43,794,064.91	205,213,955.06
May	$44,782,137.77	249,996,092.82
June	$39,376,967.87	289,373,060.69
July	$29,708,944.66	319,082,005.34
August	$16,054,829.64	335,136,834.98
September	$21,523,910.57	356,660,745.55
October	$25,471,590.22	382,132,335.77
November	$26,442,100.96	408,574,436.73
December	$40,288,897.70	448,863,334.43
Total	**$448,863,334.43**	**448,863,334.43**

fx Create a new calculation or select one to edit it h

FIGURE 2-19 The visual matrix shows the Sales with a currency format, but the YTD Sales are not formatted in the same way.

Fortunately, it's possible to set a format for a visual calculation. You do this in the visual's Visualizations pane. Simply click the General tab, open Data format, and choose YTD Sales from the Apply settings to menu. Then open the Format menu under Format options and choose Currency. Make sure that the Currency format menu is set to $ English (United States) as shown in Figure 2-20.

FIGURE 2-20 You can set data formats for visual calculations in the General section of the Visualizations pane, under the Data Format header.

> **Note** You can create custom formats for visual calculations. This gives you the freedom to display your visual calculations however you like. Advanced formatting options for visual calculations are described in Chapter 4, "Organization and use of visual calculations."

This change is also visible in the visual matrix, with entries in the YTD Sales column formatted as a currency with the dollar sign in front. Furthermore, because the visual matrix is just a matrix representation of the data in the visual, the change is also visible in the visual preview, with the axis now containing a dollar sign. The values in the tooltip are formatted as currencies as well.

Calculate the profit per country

The third question posed at the beginning of this chapter was, how is the total profit divided over the different countries?

Earlier you created a visual calculation to calculate the profit, but that visual calculation is not available in the Data pane of our model for use in a new visual. However, it's available in a visual that you have already created—the one that shows *Sales, Costs, Profit*, and *Profit incl tax* by CategoryName. So, you can copy that visual to a new report page and change it as needed to answer our question.

To start, copy the aforementioned visual and paste it on a new report page. Then remove the *Profit incl tax* entry from the Visualizations pane because you don't need that data. Finally, change the Y-axis data field from CategoryName to the CountryName from the Store table. The result will be a clustered bar chart that shows *Sales, Costs*, and *Profit* by CountryName, as shown in Figure 2-21.

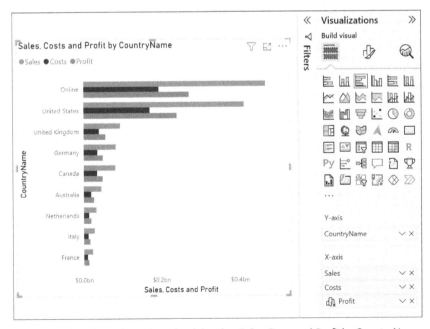

FIGURE 2-21 A clustered bar chart visual showing *Sales, Costs*, and *Profit* by CountryName, next to the Visualizations pane for the visual.

This visual currently contains *Sales* and *Costs* measures, which you don't need to show there. However, you do need these measures to calculate the profit. So, rather than removing the *Sales* and *Costs* measures from the visual, you need to hide them. To do so, open the visual calculations edit mode window and click the eye icon next to the Sales and Costs entries (see Figure 2-22).

FIGURE 2-22 The Visualizations pane of the visual where the *Sales* and *Costs* measures are hidden, and only the *Profit* visual calculation is visible.

You now have a visual that shows the profit for each country. But the visual does not show the percentage of the total profit for each country, which is what you're really after. One way to obtain this is to simply change the visual from a clustered bar chart to a pie chart. This will display the profit per country as part of the total profit, and it displays the percentages as well. However, because there is a known aversion to pie charts among the Power BI community (including some of the authors of this book), we will take a different approach: creating a visual calculation that shows these percentages in a bar chart.

To calculate the profit of each country as a percentage of the total profit, you need to divide the profit for each country by the total profit (which is already visible in the Total row of the Profit column). To achieve this, you can create a column that displays the total profit for all countries on each country row, and then divide each country's profit by this total profit to obtain a percentage.

If you were to do this using DAX measures, you would need to change the context to remove the filter that is set to a specific country for each row. So, you could use CALCULATE and a function like REMOVEFILTERS or ALL to obtain the total profit on the rows for each country. But in the spirit of making DAX easier, we'll use a pair of functions created specifically for visual calculations: COLLAPSE and COLLAPSEALL. These two functions make it possible to pick a field in the visual matrix and collapse the lattice, returning the collapsed value of the column. We will discuss how this works in Chapter 3 and discuss the functions in detail in Part II.

Note In this case, you only have one field on the rows (CountryName), so you can only collapse to one higher level—meaning COLLAPSE and COLLAPSEALL will generate the same result. However, if you have multiple levels on your axis—for example, the year, quarter, and month—you can use COLLAPSEALL to display the total value for all rows (including the subtotals).

Note You can use the COLLAPSE function to return different kinds of results, such as the total value for all rows (same as COLLAPSEALL), the quarter total for each month, the yearly total for each quarter (so, one level collapsed), and more. We'll dive deeper into this in Part II.

To start, create a visual calculation with the following DAX statement:

```
Total Profit = COLLAPSEALL ( [Profit], ROWS )
```

This creates another column in the visual matrix with the total profit displayed on each individual row, as well as the Total row (see Figure 2-23).

Create a new calculation or select one to edit it here

CountryName	Sales	Costs	Profit	Total Profit
Australia	$45,089,152.58	18,690,555.54	26,398,597.04	740,693,124.92
Canada	$82,316,364.56	34,119,408.06	48,196,956.50	740,693,124.92
France	$22,745,351.50	9,471,036.05	13,274,315.44	740,693,124.92
Germany	$83,272,724.41	34,548,906.68	48,723,817.72	740,693,124.92
Italy	$27,467,104.93	11,357,110.69	16,109,994.25	740,693,124.92
Netherlands	$32,290,656.77	13,396,522.28	18,894,134.48	740,693,124.92
Online	$465,981,615.52	193,372,577.81	272,609,037.70	740,693,124.92
United Kingdom	$94,934,581.28	39,254,650.66	55,679,930.62	740,693,124.92
United States	$411,730,738.85	170,924,397.70	240,806,341.15	740,693,124.92
Total	**$1,265,828,290.39**	**525,135,165.47**	**740,693,124.92**	**740,693,124.92**

FIGURE 2-23 The *Total Profit* visual calculation displays the total profit for each individual row in the visual matrix.

Note The second parameter, ROWS, indicates to the function that you want to collapse the rows. This implies that you can also collapse over different axes, which is something that we will explore later in this chapter.

The next step is to create yet another visual calculation to calculate the percentage of the profit per country as a part of the total profit. You can use the following DAX to obtain a new column that contains these values:

```
% Profit = DIVIDE ( [Profit], [Total Profit] )
```

Then use the General Format settings in the Visualizations pane to select the Percentage format for the visual calculation (see Figure 2-24). Figure 2-25 shows the resulting visual matrix.

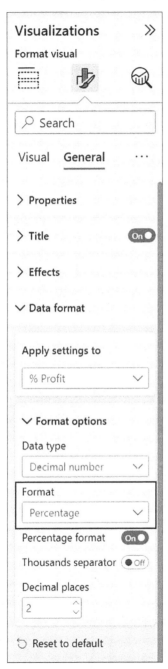

FIGURE 2-24 Use the General Format settings in the Visualizations pane to set the data format of the *% Profit* visual calculation to a Percentage.

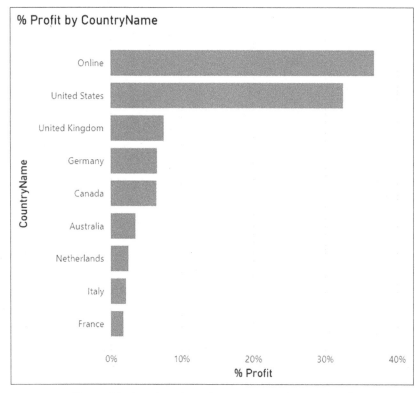

CountryName	Sales	Costs	Profit	Total Profit	% Profit
Australia	$45,089,152.58	18,690,555.54	26,398,597.04	740,693,124.92	3.56%
Canada	$82,316,364.56	34,119,408.06	48,196,956.50	740,693,124.92	6.51%
France	$22,745,351.50	9,471,036.05	13,274,315.44	740,693,124.92	1.79%
Germany	$83,272,724.41	34,548,906.68	48,723,817.72	740,693,124.92	6.58%
Italy	$27,467,104.93	11,357,110.69	16,109,994.25	740,693,124.92	2.17%
Netherlands	$32,290,656.77	13,396,522.28	18,894,134.48	740,693,124.92	2.55%
Online	$465,981,615.52	193,372,577.81	272,609,037.70	740,693,124.92	36.80%
United Kingdom	$94,934,581.28	39,254,650.66	55,679,930.62	740,693,124.92	7.52%
United States	$411,730,738.85	170,924,397.70	240,806,341.15	740,693,124.92	32.51%
Total	**$1,265,828,290.39**	**525,135,165.47**	**740,693,124.92**	**740,693,124.92**	**100.00%**

At the top of the visual matrix: *Create a new calculation or select one to edit it here*

FIGURE 2-25 The visual matrix showing *Sales, Costs, Profit, Total Profit*, and *% Profit* by country.

You can now hide both the *Profit* and the *Total Profit* visual calculations to obtain a bar chart with just the percentages of the profit per country, as was our goal (see Figure 2-26).

FIGURE 2-26 The resulting bar chart shows the percentage of the total profit per country.

Now, this approach works just fine. But you can obtain the percentage of the total profit per country more easily by using an expression template—specifically the Percent of grand total expression template. This expression template creates a visual calculation that does exactly what we did here, but all in one step. It uses the following syntax:

```
Percent of grand total = DIVIDE ( [Field], COLLAPSEALL ( [Field], Axis ) )
```

Simply replace the [Field] parameter picker with [Profit] (because you want to divide the profit by the total profit) and the Axis parameter picker with the keyword ROWS (to indicate that you want to collapse the rows to obtain the total profit) and press Enter. Change the format to a percentage, and you'll get the result as shown in Figure 2-27. To indicate that this calculation uses the Profit column, the header of the Profit column is lined with a dotted line. This uses the highlight functionality of visual calculations, as described in more detail in Chapter 4. Notice that the values of the *Percent of grand total* visual calculation are identical to those of the *% Profit* visual calculation.

CountryName	Sales	Costs	Profit	Total Profit	% Profit	Percent of grand total
Australia	$45,089,152.58	18,690,555.54	26,398,597.04	740,693,124.92	3.56%	3.56%
Canada	$82,316,364.56	34,119,408.06	48,196,956.50	740,693,124.92	6.51%	6.51%
France	$22,745,351.50	9,471,036.05	13,274,315.44	740,693,124.92	1.79%	1.79%
Germany	$83,272,724.41	34,548,906.68	48,723,817.72	740,693,124.92	6.58%	6.58%
Italy	$27,467,104.93	11,357,110.69	16,109,994.25	740,693,124.92	2.17%	2.17%
Netherlands	$32,290,656.77	13,396,522.28	18,894,134.48	740,693,124.92	2.55%	2.55%
Online	$465,981,615.52	193,372,577.81	272,609,037.70	740,693,124.92	36.80%	36.80%
United Kingdom	$94,934,581.28	39,254,650.66	55,679,930.62	740,693,124.92	7.52%	7.52%
United States	$411,730,738.85	170,924,397.70	240,806,341.15	740,693,124.92	32.51%	32.51%
Total	**$1,265,828,290.39**	**525,135,165.47**	**740,693,124.92**	**740,693,124.92**	**100.00%**	**100.00%**

FIGURE 2-27 The two visual calculations—*% Profit* and *Percent of grand total*—return the same results.

Reset your calculation

Now that you have seen some simple examples, it's time to explore additional functionality within visual calculations. If you recall the calculation you created for year-to-date sales per month, you might remember that there's a slicer on the report page to select only one year of data. This is on purpose; a year-to-date calculation that sums up values over different years might not give as much insight to a business user. So, you'll probably want to start a new calculation each year. In other words, you want to reset the calculation for each year. Fortunately, resetting a calculation is quite simple and involves a function you've already used: RUNNINGSUM.

When employing RUNNINGSUM to calculate the year-to-date sales, you used the following visual calculation:

```
YTD Sales = RUNNINGSUM ( [Sales] )
```

This statement has only one parameter, which is the field you want to sum over. However, the function RUNNINGSUM supports the use of additional parameters to enable you to create more complex calculations—specifically the *axis*, *orderby*, *blanks*, and *reset* parameters—as shown in the following function signature:

```
RUNNINGSUM ( Expression, [Axis], [OrderBy], [Blanks], [Reset] )
```

Only one of these parameters—the first one—is mandatory. The other four are optional. In this example, you want to apply the fifth parameter (*reset*) to reset your calculation. When you apply this parameter, the function resets the running sum whenever the parameter's value changes.

In this example, you want to reset the running sum each year. The effect of the *reset* parameter is best seen if you create a new matrix in the report with the Year and Month columns from the Date table on the rows and the *Sales* measure as the expression, or value. The expression for this is as follows:

```
YTD Sales = RUNNINGSUM ( [Sales], [Year] )
```

This expression is very similar to the one you used earlier, but in this case, you have added a *reset* parameter ([Year]) to indicate that you want to reset the calculation when the Year value changes on January 1 of the next year.

Note In all the previous examples, we have omitted the *reset* parameter—meaning it's set to NONE by default. So, the calculation is not reset in any of these examples.

Figure 2-28 shows the resulting visual matrix. Notice that the values for the first year are the same as in the example where we did not use the *reset* parameter. That is, for each month, the previous months are summed up to calculate the year-to-date sales, and the totals for 2024 are the same for both the sales and the year-to-date sales. The values are identical again for January 2025 because the calculation for the year-to-date sales has been reset for the new year. Finally, the value of the year-to-date sales for February 2025 is the sum of January 2025 and February 2025, and so on. Now the calculation does exactly what you want it to do, even if you show multiple years in your visual.

		fx	Create a new calculation or select one to edit it here
Year	Month	Sales	YTD Sales
2024	January	$14,091,130.12	14,091,130.12
	February	$18,652,745.19	32,743,875.31
	March	$13,707,027.63	46,450,902.94
	April	$13,617,953.40	60,068,856.34
	May	$16,025,489.67	76,094,346.00
	June	$15,987,048.83	92,081,394.84
	July	$15,846,857.82	107,928,252.65
	August	$9,561,371.47	117,489,624.12
	September	$16,331,213.97	133,820,838.08
	October	$20,374,371.26	154,195,209.35
	November	$23,371,076.56	177,566,285.91
	December	$36,497,380.10	214,063,666.00
	Total	**$214,063,666.00**	**214,063,666.00**
2025	January	$51,886,482.12	51,886,482.12
	February	$64,923,153.55	116,809,635.66

FIGURE 2-28 The visual matrix with a visual calculation for year-to-date sales that resets each year.

Note Chapter 3 dives more deeply into the possibilities associated with resetting your calculations.

Create calculations that navigate over the columns

So far, all of our examples have involved calculating over rows within columns in the visual matrix—summing up different values within one column in the running sum or collapsing all the values in a column to a total value. But what if you want to calculate over columns instead of rows?

Enter the *axis* parameter. You've already seen this parameter twice in this chapter. It was a mandatory parameter for the COLLAPSEALL function and an optional one for the RUNNINGSUM function. To see how this parameter works, you first need to create a visual with a field dimension on the columns in the visual matrix. In the example semantic model, you can create a report page with a matrix that contains CategoryName from the Product table on the rows, YearQuarter from the Date table on the columns, and the familiar *Sales* measure. Figure 2-29 shows the resulting matrix visual and part of the Visualizations pane.

CategoryName	Q1-2024	Q2-2024	Q3-2024	Q4-2024	Q1-2025	Q2-2025	Q3-20
Audio	$1,038,926.50	$1,352,971.01	$1,344,796.73	$3,079,619.26	$5,777,350.70	$3,872,147.54	$2,
Cameras and camcorders	$13,103,481.38	$8,068,930.08	$4,601,514.46	$7,170,858.79	$17,297,594.21	$15,264,808.87	$7,
Cell phones	$3,457,961.86	$4,192,581.24	$4,415,694.79	$9,837,632.88	$21,766,278.14	$18,930,868.88	$11,
Computers	$12,486,032.00	$17,535,223.77	$20,574,798.78	$39,850,193.68	$84,033,897.88	$68,453,202.94	$31,
Games and Toys	$309,864.12	$217,915.36	$153,667.18	$516,630.05	$1,476,095.23	$1,387,121.17	$
Home Appliances	$7,959,507.47	$7,835,943.35	$6,484,927.45	$11,627,617.65	$16,542,900.10	$8,850,746.44	$5,
Music, Movies and Audio Books	$1,530,029.18	$1,220,315.86	$937,936.91	$2,750,497.52	$5,613,217.98	$4,505,880.43	$4,
TV and Video	$6,565,100.43	$5,206,611.23	$3,226,106.96	$5,409,778.09	$8,912,555.89	$6,688,394.27	$5,
Total	**$46,450,902.94**	**$45,630,491.90**	**$41,739,443.25**	**$80,242,827.92**	**$161,419,890.14**	**$127,953,170.55**	**$67,2**

Rows

CategoryName   ∨ ×

Columns

YearQuarter   ∨ ×

Values

Sales   ∨ ×

Drill through

Cross-report   ● Off

FIGURE 2-29 The matrix visual shows the sales per category and per quarter.

If you add a visual calculation to this visual, you'll notice that the visual matrix now has a different format than in all the previous examples. You'll still see the CategoryName on the rows, but because the YearQuarter is on the columns, you'll get a new column for each value of YearQuarter. If you first create a new visual calculation, you'll see two columns for each YearQuarter: Sales (with the value of the *Sales* measure) and Calculation (which is empty), as shown in Figure 2-30. This is where you'll create your new visual calculation.

For the sake of example, let's create a calculation that returns the moving average for multiple quarters by applying the MOVINGAVERAGE function and specifying an axis. The signature of this function is as follows:

```
MOVINGAVERAGE ( <Column>, <WindowSize>[, <IncludeCurrent>][, <Axis>][, <OrderBy>]
[, <Blanks>][, Reset] )
```

| YearQuarter | Q1-2024 | | Q2-2024 | | Q3-2024 | | Q4-2024 |
CategoryName	Sales	Calculation	Sales	Calculation	Sales	Calculation	Sales
Audio	$1,038,926.50		$1,352,971.01		$1,344,796.73		$3,079,61
Cameras and camcorders	$13,103,481.38		$8,068,930.08		$4,601,514.46		$7,170,85
Cell phones	$3,457,961.86		$4,192,581.24		$4,415,694.79		$9,837,63
Computers	$12,486,032.00		$17,535,223.77		$20,574,798.78		$39,850,19
Games and Toys	$309,864.12		$217,915.36		$153,667.18		$516,63
Home Appliances	$7,959,507.47		$7,835,943.35		$6,484,927.45		$11,627,61
Music, Movies and Audio Books	$1,530,029.18		$1,220,315.86		$937,936.91		$2,750,49
TV and Video	$6,565,100.43		$5,206,611.23		$3,226,106.96		$5,409,77
Total	**$46,450,902.94**		**$45,630,491.90**		**$41,739,443.25**		**$80,242,82**

FIGURE 2-30 A new calculation was added for each YearQuarter on the columns.

Note The MOVINGAVERAGE function is also available as an expression template. However, we have chosen not to use that expression template here, so you'll better grasp how the function works.

The first two parameters are mandatory. However, all the others are optional, as indicated by the square brackets. In this example, it makes sense to calculate a moving average over the last four values so that for each quarter you calculate the average for a whole year (all four previous quarters). This will help business users look at their data without a seasonality pattern. For example, if you sell ice cream, it's expected that you'll sell much more during the months when the temperature is higher. To see if your sales have increased since the previous year, you can compare this year's monthly value with the same month of the previous year, but that only gives you insight about that one month. If you calculate the average sales over the last 12 months, however, you can see per month whether your sales have increased on a yearly basis.

Note The default behavior of the *axis* parameter is to calculate over the first axis in the visual shape. In most cases, this corresponds to the ROWS value that you saw in the COLLAPSEALL function, for example. If the *axis* parameter is optional in the function you are using and you omit it, it falls back to the default setting—so the first axis in the visual shape. Chapter 3 discusses the other possible values.

In our example, to calculate the moving average over the last four quarters, you can use the following visual calculation:

```
MA = MOVINGAVERAGE ( [Sales], 4, TRUE, COLUMNS )
```

The *windowSize* parameter is set to 4, indicating that you would like to average over the last four values. The *includeCurrent* parameter is set to TRUE because you want to include the current value when you calculate the moving average for the four values that you are averaging. (You could skip this, because it's an optional parameter and its default value is TRUE, but we've included it here for clarity.) Finally, the *axis* parameter is set to COLUMNS, indicating that you want to calculate this moving average over the columns. Figure 2-31 shows the result.

YearQuarter CategoryName	Q1-2024 Sales	MA	Q2-2024 Sales	MA	Q3-2024 Sales	MA	Q4-2024 Sales	MA	Q1-2025 Sales	MA
Audio	$1,038,926.50	1,038,926.50	$1,352,971.01	1,195,948.75	$1,344,796.73	1,245,564.74	$3,079,619.26	1,704,078.37	$5,777,350.70	2,888,684.42
Cameras and camcorders	$13,103,481.38	13,103,481.38	$8,068,930.08	10,586,205.73	$4,601,514.46	8,591,308.64	$7,170,858.79	8,236,196.18	$17,297,594.21	9,284,724.39
Cell phones	$3,457,961.86	3,457,961.86	$4,192,581.24	3,825,271.55	$4,415,694.79	4,022,079.29	$9,837,632.88	5,475,967.69	$21,766,278.14	10,053,046.76
Computers	$12,486,032.00	12,486,032.00	$17,535,223.77	15,010,627.89	$20,574,798.78	16,865,351.52	$39,850,193.68	22,611,562.06	$84,033,897.88	40,498,528.53
Games and Toys	$309,864.12	309,864.12	$217,915.36	263,889.74	$153,667.18	227,148.88	$516,630.05	299,519.18	$1,476,095.23	591,076.95
Home Appliances	$7,959,507.47	7,959,507.47	$7,835,943.35	7,897,725.41	$6,484,927.45	7,426,792.76	$11,627,617.65	8,476,998.98	$16,542,900.10	10,622,847.14
Music, Movies and Audio Books	$1,530,029.18	1,530,029.18	$1,220,315.86	1,375,172.52	$937,936.91	1,229,427.32	$2,750,497.52	1,609,694.87	$5,613,217.98	2,630,492.07
TV and Video	$6,565,100.43	6,565,100.43	$5,206,611.23	5,885,855.83	$3,226,106.96	4,999,272.87	$5,409,778.09	5,101,899.18	$8,912,555.89	5,688,763.04
Total	$46,450,902.94	46,450,902.94	$45,630,491.90	46,040,697.42	$41,739,443.25	44,606,946.03	$80,242,827.92	53,515,916.50	$161,419,890.14	82,258,163.30

FIGURE 2-31 The visual calculation successfully calculates a moving average.

To confirm that the values are as you would expect, look at the row for the Audio category. You'll see that the moving average value of Q1-2024 is the same as the sales value. This is because there are not yet any additional values to include in the moving average. The moving average for Q2-2024, however, is different from the sales value, because it now averages two values (Q1-2024 sales and Q2-2024 sales). The same is true of the moving average for Q3-2024 (which averages sales values of the first three quarters of the year) and Q4-2024 (which averages sales values of the first four quarters). The first quarter of 2025 is the interesting one. Here, you would expect the moving average to average sales values of Q2-2024 ($1.35 million), Q3-2024 ($1.34 million), Q4-2024 ($3.08 million), and Q1-2025 ($5.78 million). The average of these numbers is approximately $2.89 million, which equals the value returned by the moving average calculation for Q1-2025. So, it works exactly as anticipated.

Note This example shows how a more complex calculation can be performed using just one simple line of DAX. This is exactly what visual calculations are meant to do: make DAX easier.

How does this work?

Now that you've seen a few examples of visual calculations and how easy it is to create them, and you've caught a glimpse of the possibilities associated with visual calculations, it's time for us to explain how they work.

Figure 2-32 shows the visual calculations edit mode window for a visual calculation, with all relevant elements highlighted. These include the following:

- **Visual preview** The visual preview shows you what the visual will look like when you leave the visual calculations edit mode and return to your report. You can see what impact newly added visual calculations have on your visual, and what your visual will look like if you hide certain measures or visual calculations.

- **Visual matrix** The visual matrix is the data representation of your visual. As mentioned, it shows you the outcomes of all newly added calculations.

- **Formula bar** You use the formula bar to write and edit visual calculations.

- **Panes** The visual calculations edit mode window includes the same panes as the report, such as the Visualizations pane (shown here). You use these panes to select other visual calculations that you might want to edit or to format them.

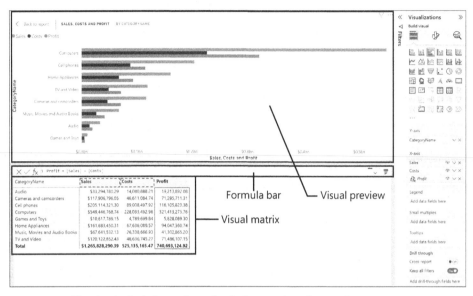

FIGURE 2-32 The visual calculations edit mode window consists of many elements.

The most important concept you need to grasp is that every visual—whether it's a clustered bar chart, a table, or even a simple card visual—can be viewed as a visual matrix, with the different dimensions of the visual on the visual matrix's rows and columns, and the calculated values for each combination of dimensions within the visual matrix. Viewing a visual as a visual matrix enables you to add more calculations, which can be seen as new columns in the visual matrix.

It's important to note that you can only use the values that are already inside a visual matrix for any new calculations you want to add. You cannot create new calculations based on measures or dimensions that are not present in the visual matrix. You can, however, add the necessary measures in the visual and then hide those measures so that they don't appear in the visual, but they do exist in the visual matrix and can therefore be used in new calculations. It's even possible to create a visual that displays only visual calculations, as you saw in the year-to-date sales example. In this approach, you can hide intermediate steps in your calculations and show only the final result.

As you have seen, you can perform a calculation in two different ways: by writing a DAX expression that uses measures or visual calculations that are already present in the visual, or by applying expression templates, which provide you with the structure of the calculation, leaving you to fill in the specifics by typing or using the provided parameter pickers.

Power BI includes several new functions created specifically for visual calculations. These include the RUNNINGSUM, COLLAPSEALL, and MOVINGAVERAGE functions discussed in this chapter, but (spoiler alert) there are many more! Part II describes these functions in greater detail.

These new functions include some new parameters, like the *axis* and *reset* parameters, which you saw earlier in this chapter. Both of these parameters are discussed in greater detail in Chapter 3. The *reset* parameter enables you to reset your visual calculation so it starts again from a specific data point. This is very useful if, for example, you are calculating year-to-date values for multiple years in the same visual. As for the *axis* parameter, it enables you to navigate within the visual matrix in various ways, such as by rows, by columns, or other patterns (discussed further in Chapter 3).

In summary

Chapter 1 explained why visual calculations were created: to enable every end user to get more out of Power BI *without* having to master DAX. The purpose of this chapter was to demonstrate this using a few basic examples.

This chapter showed you how easy it is to create visual calculations for existing visuals in a Power BI report, without the need to write complex DAX measures. If you are familiar with Excel formulas, adding visual calculations to your Power BI model should be easy. Alternatively, you can use one of several expression templates to create quite complex calculations with just a few clicks.

The learning curve for visual calculations is short, enabling every business user to create quick insights based on the existing reports and enhanced with visual calculations. Moreover, because the outcome of the new visual calculation appears in the visual calculation edit mode window's visual preview and in the visual itself, you're not left to sift through a big table of data to glean these insights. Rather, you can visualize them directly in your report. You can even create complex calculations with multiple steps and hide intermediate results. In this way you can more easily follow exactly what is being calculated in the visual calculation edit mode window but display only the final result on the report page.

Visual calculations also offer a performance improvement compared to measures because visual calculations work only on the data available in the visual matrix (which is usually a small set). Chapter 9, "Breaking down visual calculations execution," explains this in more detail.

We hope you have grasped some of the possibilities that arise with visual calculations. The rest of this book dives deeper into these possibilities, as well as important concepts that pertain to visual calculations (Chapter 3), functions used for visual calculations (Part II), and how visual calculations compare to other calculation options within Power BI (Chapter 8, "Comparing calculation options").

Visual calculations concepts

Visual calculations involve several new concepts that do not exist in regular DAX. This chapter focuses on these concepts, which include the following:

- **Visual matrix** The visual matrix is central to visual calculations. It offers a way to structure data dynamically based on rows and columns in a What You See Is What You Get (WYSIWYG) fashion.

- **The *axis* parameter** An *axis* parameter brings flexibility to calculations by defining directions, much like the axes of a chart.

- **The *reset* parameter** A *reset* parameter restarts a calculation at a certain point on the axis, returning it to its default state.

- **Hidden field** A hidden field enables you to break complex calculations into smaller pieces to ease debugging and increase understandability.

Through explanations and examples, this chapter will help you understand these concepts and how they increase the possibilities of visual calculations.

Visual matrix

The visual matrix is the key component of visual calculations. You can think of the visual matrix as the simplest representation of the data used to create the visual. The visual matrix displays the data in the visual as well as the result of the visual calculation as you add it. It does not, however, display any formatting that may be applied to the visual itself.

> **Note** Every Power BI report visual can be represented in a visual matrix, regardless of whether it's a column chart, scatter plot, or any other type of visual.

Ultimately, generating a visual in a report involves a DAX expression that queries the semantic model. The resulting table forms the visual matrix. If you want to know more about this process and the queries involved, see Chapter 9, "Breaking down visual calculations execution," for more details.

Power BI automatically generates the visual matrix when you add or edit a visual calculation, with the visual calculation itself displayed as a column in the visual matrix. The visual calculation is also added as a new column to the virtual table that's used to generate the visual.

Hierarchies in the visual matrix

A Power BI visual may contain a hierarchy of model items, which you use to navigate across—for example, CategoryName, SubCategoryName, and ProductName. Using a hierarchy enables you to drill up and down to analyze a metric on different levels. In this scenario, the visual matrix always displays the data on the lowest hierarchy level as a flat table, while the visual itself shows the collapsed values on the highest hierarchy level.

Figure 3-1 shows a simple visual that includes a visual calculation to calculate the profit. In this case, the expression is a simple *Sales* minus *Costs*. This calculation references two columns, which are already part of the visual matrix. Anything that is not in the visual matrix cannot be referenced by a visual calculation.

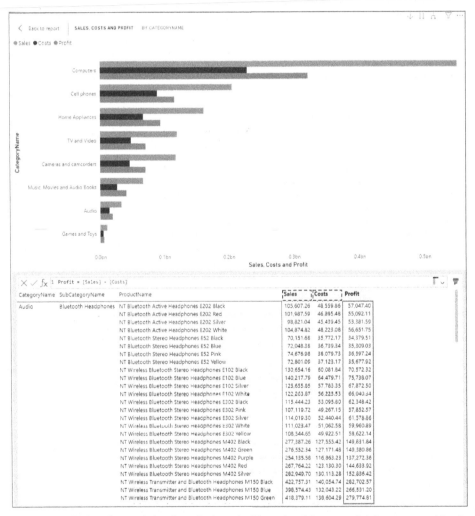

FIGURE 3-1 The bar chart and visual matrix show the hierarchy of Category, SubCategory, and Product.

In the example shown in Figure 3-1, a simple visual calculation was added to calculate the profit by using the following expression:

```
Profit = [Sales] - [Costs]
```

Calculation occurs at every level in the visual matrix, and subtotals and totals are calculated separately. Jumping from one level to another is described in more detail later in this chapter in the section "Navigating the lattice." Using the *axis* and *reset* parameters, as well as visual calculation functions like COLLAPSE, EXPAND, COLLAPSEALL, and EXPANDALL, enables you to navigate the lattice and calculate the visual calculation on different levels.

Understanding the *axis* parameter

A common parameter in visual calculations is the *axis* parameter. The *axis* parameter is not available in measures, calculated columns, or calculated tables. The easiest way to explore the use of the *axis* parameter is by looking at the RUNNINGSUM function. With RUNNINGSUM, the *axis* parameter defines the direction in which the running sum should be calculated: over rows, columns, or a combination. The possible values for the *axis* parameter are ROWS, COLUMNS, ROWS COLUMNS, and COLUMNS ROWS.

The axis can be seen as the axis of a chart, which has an x-axis and a y-axis. But because we're referring to the visual matrix in visual calculations, the names of the axes could be more intuitive. Therefore, in visual calculations, the x-axis is represented by columns and the y-axis by rows (see Figure 3-2).

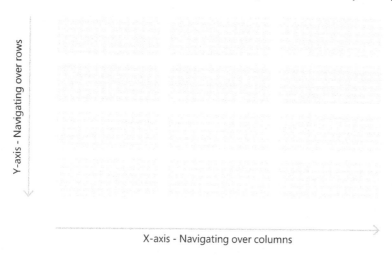

FIGURE 3-2 Understanding the axis properties in the visual matrix.

Business functions in visual calculations are RUNNINGSUM and MOVINGAVERAGE, explained in more detail in Chapter 7, "The floors and rooms: visual calculations exclusive functions." Both these high-level functions have an optional *axis* parameter. However, they are not the only functions in visual calculations that use the *axis* parameter. In any case, if the parameter is not filled, the default behavior is to move across the first axis in the visual shape. The alternative values for the *axis* parameter are COLUMNS, ROWS COLUMNS, and COLUMNS ROWS, which are described in more detail later in this chapter in the section "Practical uses for the axis parameter."

Some functions have a signature that includes a mandatory *axis* parameter. These include the following:

- COLLAPSE
- COLLAPSEALL
- EXPAND
- EXPANDALL

Each of these functions and their signature is described in detail in Chapter 7.

Navigating the lattice

The lattice is formed by all the fields on all the axes. Visual calculations calculate results on various levels on the lattice. For example, you calculate a total or a subtotal for a visual calculation by moving around on the lattice to remove that field from the context. (This is illustrated by the tables in Figure 3-3.) Using lattice navigation functions (COLLAPSE, COLLAPSEALL, EXPAND, and EXPANDALL), you can explicitly move around in the lattice. The *axis* parameter lets you define how you want to navigate the lattice and in which direction. In other words, you can move over different levels of aggregation of the visual matrix. In the following example, we use the *Sales* measure, with Year and Quarter on columns and CategoryName and SubCategoryName on rows.

Figure 3-3 shows all possible combinations of aggregation levels. The most granular data is in the bottom table. The visual matrix shown in visual calculations edit mode is the most granular level of data with all hierarchies expanded.

You navigate the lattice using the EXPAND, EXPANDALL, COLLAPSE, and COLLAPSEALL functions. As an example, suppose you use the COLLAPSE function to collapse the Quarter column from the most granular data in the bottom table of Figure 3-3. You will then be working with sales data aggregated on the year level, meaning the sales value will reflect the total sales for each year. From there, you could collapse the Year column to aggregate sales for all years.

If you keep going, eventually there will be no more fields to collapse. At this point, you will arrive at the highest level of granularity, with just one value for sales: the total sales for all quarters, years, subcategories, and categories. If you want to jump directly to this aggregated total, you can use the COLLAPSEALL function. Alternatively, if you want to jump directly down to the lowest level, you can use EXPANDALL.

Let's zoom in to a smaller set of data and explore the exact functions to navigate the lattice. Figure 3-4 shows only the top section of Figure 3-3.

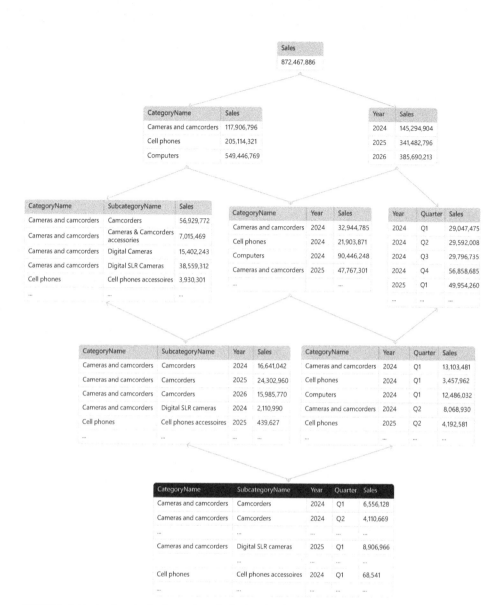

FIGURE 3-3 Navigating the lattice and results in the visual matrix.

To grasp what you see in Figure 3-4, compare it to building a regular visual in a Power BI report. Suppose you build a measure to calculate sales. If you put only that measure on the report canvas, you will see only the aggregated total. Well, this is exactly what you see as result at the top of Figure 3-4. As soon as you add the Year column to that, however, you follow the lattice down and to the right and you expand the visual matrix. As a result, you will now have Year and sales data in your visual matrix. Similarly, if you navigate from the top down to the left, the visual matrix will be expanded with the CategoryName column. Because a visual matrix can have rows and columns, these can also be combined, with CategoryName, Year, and Sales in the visual matrix, as shown in the center-bottom portion of Figure 3-4. Similarly, you could navigate further down from Year by adding Quarter and expand the visual matrix to include Year, Quarter, and Sales, as shown in the bottom-right section.

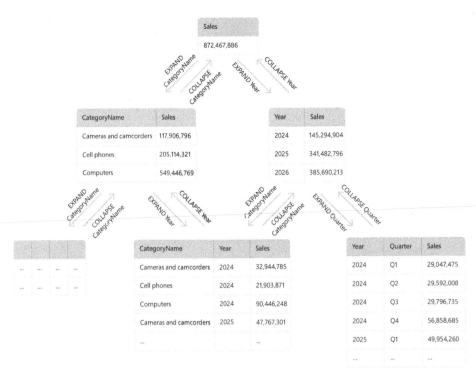

FIGURE 3-4 A zoomed-in view of the lattice.

Why is it important to understand this behavior and how to navigate the lattice? Well, in a business scenario, you might want to calculate the percentage of something compared to the total. For example, suppose you want to calculate the percentage of sales in each quarter compared to the grand total sales. Of course, percentage of total is a templated calculation in visual calculations. But using the COLLAPSEALL function, you can jump directly to the top of the lattice and compare the individual row in which Year and Quarter are in the context versus the total of all years and quarters. The visual calculation to achieve this would be as follows:

```
Percent of grand total = DIVIDE ( [Sales], COLLAPSEALL ( [Sales], ROWS ) )
```

This visual calculation compares an individual row in the context of Year and Quarter to the total of all years together—that is, the grand total. If you want to compare to the total within a year and compare the year's individual total against the grand total, this is where the COLLAPSE function comes in, and it's why you must understand navigating across the lattice. This is called percentage of parent, and is calculated in this visual calculation:

```
Percent of parent = DIVIDE ( [Sales], COLLAPSE ( [Sales], ROWS ) )
```

> **Note** See Chapter 7 for more information on the COLLAPSE and EXPAND functions.

Practical uses for the *axis* parameter

Taking the RUNNINGSUM function as an example and specifying the *axis* parameter, the input values are similar to what has been discussed for *axis*. You can either calculate a running sum over rows (moving vertically from top to bottom over the visual matrix) or over columns (moving horizontally from left to right over the visual matrix). For the RUNNINGSUM function, the *axis* parameter is optional. If you omit the *axis* parameter, it will often navigate over the rows in the visual matrix. However, you can change this behavior to calculate a running sum over the columns in the visual matrix.

In total, there are four different values that can be used for the *axis* parameter:

- ROWS
- COLUMNS
- ROWS COLUMNS
- COLUMNS ROWS

The first two are fairly straightforward. The second two are more complex, following a snake pattern across the visual matrix. The following table describes each of these options.

Icon	Axis name	Description
↓↓	ROWS	Calculates vertically across rows from top to bottom.
→→	COLUMNS	Calculates horizontally across columns from left to right.
↓↓	ROWS COLUMNS	Calculates vertically across rows from top to bottom, continuing column by column from left to right.
→→	COLUMNS ROWS	Calculates horizontally across columns from left to right, continuing row by row from top to bottom.

The following sections detail the behavior of each parameter value using the sample data shown in Figure 3-5. This is based on a visual matrix that displays sales amounts, with years in rows and quarters in columns. In some examples, monthly data is added to explain certain patterns.

Year	Q1	Q2	Q3	Q4	Total
2024	46,450,902.94	45,630,491.90	41,739,443.25	80,242,827.92	**214,063,666.00**
2025	161,419,890.14	127,953,170.55	67,287,684.86	92,202,588.87	**448,863,334.43**
2026	217,110,293.97	160,281,816.38	96,367,837.21	129,141,342.40	**602,901,289.96**
Total	**424,981,087.05**	**333,865,478.82**	**205,394,965.32**	**301,586,759.19**	**1,265,828,290.39**

FIGURE 3-5 Sample data to explain the *axis* parameter.

ROWS

If the *axis* parameter is not specified, the default value is the first axis in the visual shape. In our example, that is ROWS. For example, if you were to add the following RUNNINGSUM to the visual matrix in Figure 3-5, it would by default sum over rows from top to bottom:

```
RunningSum = RUNNINGSUM ( [Sales Amount] )
```

Notice in the preceding expression that the *axis* parameter—which is optional—is not specified. In contrast, the following expression explicitly defines the *axis* parameter, yielding the exact same result:

```
RunningSum = RUNNINGSUM ( [Sales Amount], ROWS )
```

Both statements return the visual matrix shown in Figure 3-6.

Quarter	Q1		Q2		Q3		Q4		Total	
Year	Sales Amount	Running sum	Sales Amount	Running sum	Sales Amount	Running sum	Sales Amount	Running sum	Sales Amount	Running sum
2024	46,450,902.94	46,450,902.94	45,630,491.90	45,630,491.90	41,739,443.25	41,739,443.25	80,242,827.92	80,242,827.92	214,063,666.00	214,063,666.00
2025	161,419,890.14	207,870,793.08	127,953,170.55	173,583,662.45	67,287,684.86	109,027,128.11	92,202,588.87	172,445,416.79	448,863,334.43	662,927,000.43
2026	217,110,293.97	424,981,087.05	160,281,816.38	333,865,478.82	96,367,837.21	205,394,965.32	129,141,342.40	301,586,759.19	602,901,289.96	1,265,828,290.39
Total	424,981,087.05	424,981,087.05	333,865,478.82	333,865,478.82	205,394,965.32	205,394,965.32	301,586,759.19	301,586,759.19	1,265,828,290.39	1,265,828,290.39

FIGURE 3-6 RUNNINGSUM over rows in a visual matrix.

One could argue whether the result presented in Figure 3-6 is useful. It places the sum of all first quarters of every year in one column, the sum of all second quarters in the next, and so on. But it would be more useful to take the running sum over all quarters of a given year. To achieve this, you could either change the visual to place years on columns and quarters on rows or change the behavior of the axis for the RUNNINGSUM expression.

COLUMNS

If you specify COLUMNS as the *axis* parameter, the expression runs from left to right over the y-axis of the visual matrix. In a running sum, having years on rows and quarters on columns, as in the previous example, you can specify the *axis* parameter as follows:

```
RunningSum = RUNNINGSUM ( [Sales Amount], COLUMNS )
```

The result will look like the visual matrix in Figure 3-7, taking the sum over years. Although the preceding expression did not explicitly specify a reset parameter, the running sum will automatically reset to zero for every row, so in this case, for every year. The sum starts from zero because the *axis* parameter is set to COLUMNS. This results in the visual calculation taking the sum over all columns for that row in the visual matrix. The running sum ends at the end of the visual matrix for each row.

✕ ✓ fx	1	Running sum = RUNNINGSUM(|Sales Amount|, COLUMNS)								
Quarter	Q1		Q2		Q3		Q4		**Total**	
Year	Sales Amount	Running sum	Sales Amount	Running sum	Sales Amount	Running sum	Sales Amount	Running sum	Sales Amount	Running sum
2024	46,450,902.94	46,450,902.94	45,630,491.90	92,081,394.84	41,739,443.25	133,820,838.08	80,242,827.92	214,063,666.00	**214,063,666.00**	214,063,666.00
2025	161,419,890.14	161,419,890.14	127,953,170.55	289,373,060.69	67,287,684.86	356,660,745.55	92,202,588.87	448,863,334.43	**448,863,334.43**	448,863,334.43
2026	217,110,293.97	217,110,293.97	160,281,816.38	377,392,110.35	96,367,837.21	473,759,947.56	129,141,342.40	602,901,289.96	**602,901,289.96**	602,901,289.96
Total	424,981,087.05	424,981,087.05	333,865,478.82	758,846,565.88	205,394,965.32	964,241,531.20	301,586,759.19	1,265,828,290.39	**1,265,828,290.39**	1,265,828,290.39

FIGURE 3-7 Running sum over columns moving over the y-axis.

ROWS COLUMNS

As you have seen, with rows, the running sum automatically resets when it arrives at a new column. Similarly, if you set the *axis* parameter to COLUMNS, the running sum will start from zero at the end of each row. However, if you add more complexity by combining rows and columns, a snake pattern emerges. For example, if you set *axis* to ROWS COLUMNS, a running sum will calculate vertically across rows from top to bottom, continuing column by column from left to right as shown in Figure 3-8.

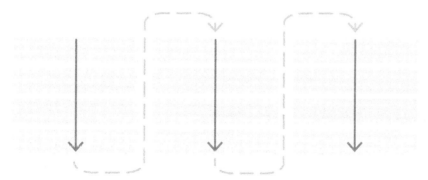

FIGURE 3-8 Conceptual explanation of ROWS COLUMNS behavior.

By slightly changing the preceding example, you put the quarters on rows and years on columns. If you now calculate a running sum and specify ROWS COLUMNS for the *axis* parameter, you will snake through the visual matrix, combining all quarters and all years together (see Figure 3-9).

`fx` `1 RunningSum = RUNNINGSUM([Sales Amount], ROWS COLUMNS|`

Year Quarter	2024 Sales Amount	RunningSum	2025 Sales Amount	RunningSum	2026 Sales Amount	RunningSum	Total Sales Amount	RunningSum
Q1	46,450,902.94	46,450,902.94	161,419,890.14	375,483,556.14	217,110,293.8?	880,037,294.40	424,981,087.05	424,981,087.05
Q2	45,630,491.90	92,081,394.84	127,95?,170.55	503,436,726.69	160,28?,816.38	1,040,319,110.78	333,865,478.82	758,846,565.88
Q3	41,739,443.25	133,820,838.08	67,28?,684.86	570,724,411.56	96,36?,837.21	1,136,686,947.99	205,394,965.32	964,241,531.20
Q4	80,242,827.92	214,063,666.00	9?,?02,588.87	662,927,000.43	1??,?41,342.40	1,265,828,290.39	301,586,759.19	1,265,828,290.39
Total	214,063,666.00	214,063,666.00	448,863,334.43	662,927,000.43	602,901,289.96	1,265,828,290.39	1,265,828,290.39	1,265,828,290.39

FIGURE 3-9 Practical example of snake behavior of ROWS COLUMNS.

COLUMNS ROWS

COLUMNS ROWS follows a snake pattern, just like ROWS COLUMS. But with COLUMNS ROWS, the calculation moves horizontally across all columns and continues on the next row (see Figure 3-10).

Use cases for this pattern are limited, although an example could be when adding a dimension on columns like Brand while still having Year and Quarter on rows. In this example, you still want to calculate the running sum over years; applying a RUNNINGSUM function with COLUMNS ROWS as the *axis* parameter will do the job (see Figure 3-11).

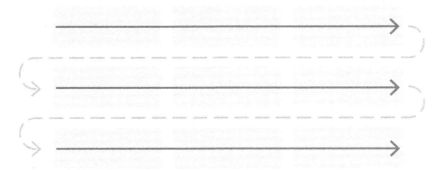

FIGURE 3-10 Conceptual behavior of COLUMNS ROWS behavior.

`fx` `1 RunningSum = RUNNINGSUM([Sales Amount], COLUMNS ROWS )`

Year	Quarter	Brand A. Datum Sales Amount	RunningSum	Adventure Works Sales Amount	RunningSum	Contoso Sales Amount	RunningSum	Total Sales Amount	RunningSum
2024	Q1	3,141,619.52	3,141,619.52	9,981,114.09	13,122,733.61	8,664,030.99	21,786,764.61	21,786,764.61	21,786,764.61
	Q2	1,862,432.16	23,649,196.77	11,081,808.21	34,731,004.98	8,005,975.51	42,736,980.49	20,950,215.88	42,736,980.49
	Q3	1,051,657.60	43,788,638.09	9,872,864.58	53,661,502.67	6,652,121.81	60,313,624.48	17,576,643.99	60,313,624.48
	Q4	1,681,084.21	61,994,708.69	19,144,878.97	81,139,587.66	12,852,493.34	93,992,081.00	33,678,456.52	93,992,081.00
	Total	7,736,793.49	7,736,793.49	50,080,665.87	57,817,459.36	36,174,621.65	93,992,081.00	93,992,081.00	93,992,081.00
2025	Q1	4,033,845.27	98,025,926.27	37,802,841.26	135,828,767.53	23,867,997.55	159,696,765.07	65,704,684.07	159,696,765.07
	Q2	3,478,494.24	163,175,259.31	30,632,172.17	193,807,431.48	17,372,877.48	211,180,308.96	51,483,543.89	211,180,308.96
	Q3	1,786,341.19	212,966,650.15	15,137,888.18	228,104,538.34	10,148,364.22	238,252,902.56	27,072,593.59	238,252,902.56
	Q4	1,714,706.29	239,967,608.85	21,190,185.44	261,157,794.29	14,784,874.80	275,942,669.09	37,689,766.53	275,942,669.09
	Total	11,013,386.99	105,005,467.99	104,763,087.05	209,768,555.04	66,174,114.05	275,942,669.09	181,950,588.09	275,942,669.09
2026	Q1	2,898,022.49	278,840,691.58	49,980,811.46	328,821,503.04	37,363,995.44	366,185,498.48	90,242,829.40	366,185,498.48
	Q2	2,069,212.92	368,254,711.40	35,439,733.43	403,694,444.83	31,334,816.92	435,029,261.75	68,843,763.26	435,029,261.75
	Q3	1,488,739.80	436,518,001.55	18,434,928.50	454,952,930.05	19,580,100.35	474,533,030.40	39,503,768.65	474,533,030.40

FIGURE 3-11 Practical example of snake behavior of COLUMNS ROWS.

Understanding reset

The section "Understanding the *axis* parameter" earlier in this chapter explained the patterns that can be achieved with, for example, a running sum. You have seen that specifying ROWS or COLUMNS as the *axis* parameter will automatically reset at the end of a column or row—for example, at the start of a new year. However, using ROWS COLUMNS or COLUMNS ROWS continues the running sum over multiple rows or columns.

Most organizations will more likely need a running sum that starts over from zero for each new year. You can achieve this using the *reset* parameter. With the *reset* parameter, you can easily calculate the total sales amount over all months and quarters but start over from zero for every new year. Although the running sum continues, you can define on which change in data the running sum should start over (see Figure 3-12).

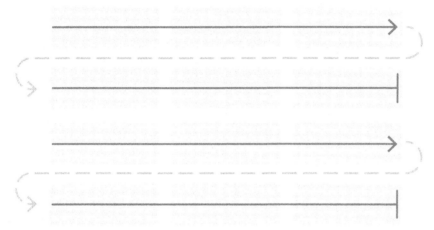

FIGURE 3-12 Conceptual behavior of COLUMNS ROWS behavior with *reset* parameter.

In Figure 3-12, the running sum continues over two rows and stops at the end of each second row. This might be useful if, for example, you have two rows for each year, and you would like to split your analysis in the first half and second half of the year. If in this scenario you want to take a running sum of *Sales* but start over for each new Year, the *reset* parameter should be used. Just using RUNNINGSUM with the *axis* parameter set to COLUMNS will not be enough to incorporate the second row. This is where the *reset* parameter comes in to explicitly define when the running sum must be reset. To make the *reset* parameter work, the visual matrix must contain some level or hierarchy. In this example, we have a hierarchy of Year and field that splits the year into two halves. This hierarchy is used and referenced to by the *reset* parameter.

> **Note** The preceding example uses a split of years in two equal parts. This field is not available in the sample semantic model and is solely used as an example to describe the behavior of the *reset* parameter with COLUMNS ROWS specified for the *axis* parameter.

The *reset* parameter is available on visual calculations exclusive functions but is easiest to comprehend for business functions like RUNNINGSUM and MOVINGAVERAGE. (More details can be found in Chapter 6, "The foundation: foundational functions.") Some functions in visual calculations also have a *partitionBy* parameter, which is not available for these business functions. In fact, one could argue that the *reset* parameter is mapped to *partitionBy*, in which the data is sliced in sections on which the calculations are applied in isolation. Thinking of the *reset* parameter as being mapped to *partitionBy* will not only help you to understand the reset functionality, but also to convert visual calculations into DAX measures if desired. Typically, the defined partitions form the hierarchy that you can use as the target for the *reset* parameter.

Reset modes

Reset can work in two different modes: absolute and relative. Also, the *reset* parameter accepts five different input values. They are broken down per category as follows:

- **Absolute mode**   In this mode, the accepted parameter values are NONE, positive integer values, HIGHESTPARENT, and field references.

- **Relative mode**   In this mode, the accepted parameter values are LOWESTPARENT and negative integer values.

To better understand how each mode affects your visual calculations, imagine a hierarchy consisting of Year, Quarter, Month, and Day. The way a running sum or similar calculation resets—whether at a fixed level like Quarter or more dynamically, depends entirely on the mode you choose. Absolute mode uses fixed positions within the hierarchy to determine where the calculation should reset, while relative mode applies a more flexible approach based on the current level in hierarchy. In this section, we'll discuss both modes in detail and use clear examples to show how they impact your results across different hierarchy levels.

Absolute mode

Absolute mode indicates the calculation is partitioned by the target column on which the reset is defined and all columns above in the hierarchy. For example, you define a reset on Quarter; in that case, the partitioning is happening on the combination of Year and Quarter only, but Month and Day are left out of scope. This means that Quarter is the target column, and if the target column is out of scope, the reset will not happen. So, when you build a visual calculation taking a running sum and resetting on Quarter level, you will not see the running sum performed on Year level or Quarter level as the specified reset comes in. Instead, it just returns the Sales of that respective Year or Quarter. But, as soon as you drill down to Month level, you'll see the visual calculation is performed and nicely reset for each Quarter.

When a positive numeric value is specified for the *reset* parameter, the reset is operating in absolute mode. The positive integer value identifies the target column starting from the top (the top column is 1, the next is 2, and so on). It goes up to N (the number of columns in the hierarchy), and any higher values are trimmed down. Alternatively, one can also specify the column directly. Following the example hierarchy we described before, the following table defines which columns will define the partitioning depending on the level of reset.

Level / value	Reset = 1 or [Year]	Reset = 2 or [Quarter]	Reset = 3 or [Month]	Reset = 4 or [Day]
Day level	Year	Quarter and Year	Month, Quarter and Year	Day, Month, Quarter and Year
Month level	Year	Quarter and Year	Month, Quarter and Year	Month, Quarter and Year
Quarter level	Year	Quarter and Year	Quarter and Year	Quarter and Year
Year level	Year	Year	Year	Year
Grand total level	None	None	None	None

Relative mode

When a negative numeric value is specified for the *reset* parameter, the reset is performed in relative mode. Valid values for this mode are between –1 and –N+1 (where N is the number of columns in the hierarchy), and any lower values are trimmed up. Consider the visual calculation described earlier, having a hierarchy with Year, Quarter, Month, and Day, and using *Sales Amount*, the behavior will be slightly different from what you've seen with absolute mode. The following table shows how the calculation will be partitioned at each level depending on the value of reset.

Level / value	Reset = -1	Reset = -2	Reset = -3
Day level	Month, Quarter and Year	Quarter and Year	Year
Month level	Quarter and Year	Year	None
Quarter level	Year	None	None
Year level	None	None	None
Grand total level	None	None	None

Reset parameter values

In the previous section, we explored how the *reset* parameter operates in absolute and relative modes, controlling how calculations are partitioned within a hierarchy. Now, we turn our attention to the different values you can assign to the *reset* parameter itself—each offering varying degrees of control and flexibility. Whether you choose to leave it unset (NONE), reference a specific field, or rely on hierarchy-based options like HIGHESTPARENT or LOWESTPARENT, each option results in a different setup when a calculation restarts. You can also use numeric values to dynamically target positions in the hierarchy, which becomes particularly powerful in reports using field parameters.

This section breaks down these options, building from the most straightforward to more advanced and adaptive scenarios in order:

- NONE
- Field reference
- HIGHESTPARENT
- LOWESTPARENT
- Numerical value

NONE

The default value of the *reset* parameter is NONE. With this value, the *reset* parameter is not specified, and the calculation will not reset to zero for any value change in rows or in columns.

Field reference

When you specify a field reference for the *reset* parameter, the visual calculation will reset at that field. For example, if you set *reset* to the field reference for years, the visual calculation will start over every time a new year appears on the specified *axis*. But as long as the year is the same, the visual calculation will continue.

As an example, consider the visual matrix in Figure 3-11, which shows years and quarters on rows and brands on columns. If you want to calculate the running sum for all brands and quarters within one year, you can set the *axis* parameter to COLUMNS ROWS. However, suppose you instead want to take all years into account, and you want to reset the running sum to zero for the start of every new year. In this case, you can specify a field reference for Year as the *reset* parameter, as in the following expression:

```
RunningSum = RUNNINGSUM ( [Sales Amount], COLUMNS ROWS, [Year] )
```

Figure 3-13 shows the result, with the running sum reset to zero for the start of each new year.

FIGURE 3-13 Practical example of applying the *reset* parameter on Year in a running sum.

HIGHESTPARENT

Setting the *reset* parameter to HIGHESTPARENT resets the calculation when the value of the highest parent on the axis changes. For example, suppose you have a COLUMNS ROWS *axis* in which brands are defined on columns and years and quarters are defined on rows. In this case, if you set the *reset* parameter to HIGHESTPARENT, the visual calculation resets based on a value change in the Year column, because Year is higher in the hierarchy of Year and Quarter. It will not perform a reset based on the ROWS value, however, because COLUMNS come first in the *axis* parameter.

The following expression uses HIGHESTPARENT as the *reset* parameter. (Figure 3-14 shows the resulting visual matrix.)

```
RunningSum = RUNNINGSUM ( [Sales Amount], COLUMNS ROWS, HIGHESTPARENT )
```

FIGURE 3-14 Reset on HIGHESTPARENT.

LOWESTPARENT

As its name implies, LOWESTPARENT is the opposite of HIGHESTPARENT, resetting the calculation based on the lowest value in the hierarchy. For example, the following expression uses LOWESTPARENT as the *reset* parameter, causing the visual calculation to reset based on a value change in the Quarter column. (Figure 3-15 shows the resulting visual matrix.)

```
RunningSum = RUNNINGSUM ( [Sales Amount], COLUMNS ROWS, LOWESTPARENT )
```

✕ ✓ *fx* 1 RunningSum = RUNNINGSUM([Sales Amount], COLUMNS ROWS , LOWESTPARENT)

Year	Brand Quarter	A. Datum Sales Amount	RunningSum	Adventure Works Sales Amount	RunningSum	Contoso Sales Amount	RunningSum	Total Sales Amount	RunningSum
2024	Q1	3,141,619.52	3,141,619.52	9,981,114.09	13,122,733.61	8,664,030.99	21,786,764.61	21,786,764.61	21,786,764.61
	Q2	1,862,432.16	1,862,432.16	11,081,808.21	12,944,240.37	8,005,975.51	20,950,215.88	20,950,215.88	42,736,980.49
	Q3	1,051,657.60	1,051,657.60	9,872,864.58	10,924,522.18	6,652,121.81	17,576,643.99	17,576,643.99	60,313,624.48
	Q4	1,681,084.21	1,681,084.21	19,144,878.97	20,825,963.18	12,852,493.34	33,678,456.52	33,678,456.52	93,992,081.00
	Total	**7,736,793.49**	**7,736,793.49**	**50,080,665.87**	**57,817,459.36**	**36,174,621.65**	**93,992,081.00**	**93,992,081.00**	**93,992,081.00**
2025	Q1	4,033,845.27	4,033,845.27	37,802,841.26	41,836,686.53	23,867,997.55	65,704,684.07	65,704,684.07	65,704,684.07
	Q2	3,478,494.24	3,478,494.24	30,632,172.17	34,110,666.41	17,372,877.48	51,483,543.89	51,483,543.89	117,188,227.96
	Q3	1,786,341.19	1,786,341.19	15,137,888.18	16,924,229.37	10,148,364.22	27,072,593.59	27,072,593.59	144,260,821.56
	Q4	1,714,706.29	1,714,706.29	21,190,185.44	22,904,891.73	14,784,874.80	37,689,766.53	37,689,766.53	181,950,588.09
	Total	**11,013,386.99**	**11,013,386.99**	**104,763,087.05**	**115,776,474.04**	**66,174,114.05**	**181,950,588.09**	**181,950,588.09**	**275,942,669.09**
2026	Q1	2,898,022.49	2,898,022.49	49,980,811.46	52,878,833.95	37,363,995.44	90,242,829.40	90,242,829.40	90,242,829.40
	Q2	2,069,212.92	2,069,212.92	35,439,733.43	37,508,946.35	31,334,816.92	68,843,763.26	68,843,763.26	159,086,592.66
	Q3	1,488,739.80	1,488,739.80	18,434,928.50	19,923,668.30	19,580,100.35	39,503,768.65	39,503,768.65	198,590,361.31

FIGURE 3-15 Reset on LOWESTPARENT.

LOWESTPARENT comes with an additional complexity. In this case, because the visual calculation is reset based on the quarter, this indirectly affects the calculation for the running sum on the year. Because the calculation was already reset on the quarter level, it implicitly means the calculation will also reset on the year level or any other level above that. So, to understand the behavior of LOWESTPARENT, you must know the order in which columns are placed in the hierarchy. On a time axis, like that used in Figure 3-15, this is fairly easy to understand. But for other contexts, which might include columns like CategoryName or Brand that inherently have nothing to do with each other, the order of items in the hierarchy determines the reset behavior.

> **Note** Field references behave like LOWESTPARENT, in that the order of items in the hierarchy will dictate their behavior.

Numerical value

In addition to specifying a textual field reference for the *reset* parameter, you can enter a numerical value. These values are stand-ins for other values we have already discussed.

Using numerical values will in principle not add additional functionality to what has been discussed before based on field references, HIGHESTPARENT or LOWESTPARENT. However, it can be useful to use numerical values.

- **0**   This is equivalent to specifying NONE. With 0 specified, the visual calculation does not reset.

- **Positive value**   This identifies the field starting from the highest field on the axis, independent of grain. A value of 1 is equivalent to HIGHESTPARENT. A positive value indicates a reset in absolute mode as described in the previous section.

- **Negative value**   This identifies the field starting from the lowest field on the axis, relative to the current grain. A value of –1 is equivalent to LOWESTPARENT. A negative value indicates a reset in relative mode as described in the previous section.

Example: choosing a *reset* parameter value

When you aren't sure which columns will be part of the visual matrix, it will be very challenging to understand the HIGHESTPARENT or LOWESTPARENT options for the *reset* parameter. Moreover, working with field references will be impossible, because the field referenced must be part of the visual matrix; if it isn't, an error will occur. This is a problem, because if field parameters are used in a Power BI report, then the resulting visual matrix will contain dynamically changing fields, enabling users to dynamically change the measures or dimensions being analyzed in the report. If you're not familiar, field parameters help users explore and customize data and analyses by dynamically selecting other dimensions they're interested in.

Suppose you create a field parameter in a Power BI report that enables users to employ a slicer to dynamically select fields in the rows of the visual matrix, with potential values of Year, Quarter, Month, and Day of Week. Depending on the functionality of the field parameter, the user might select one or multiple columns—meaning there's no way to know exactly which columns will be part of the visual matrix. Therefore, you cannot use a field reference for the *reset* parameter.

If you always want to reset on the highest or lowest level in the hierarchy, the easiest approach would be to use HIGHESTPARENT or LOWESTPARENT. But what if you want to reset on an intermediate level in the hierarchy? Consider an example in which Year, Quarter, and Month are selected in the slicer, which together form the hierarchy presented on the rows of the visual matrix. You could set up your visual calculation to reset on the second level in the hierarchy by using the following expression:

```
RunningSum = RUNNINGSUM ( [Sales Amount], COLUMNS ROWS, 2 )
```

This expression results in the matrix shown in Figure 3-16, which resets the running sum back to zero whenever a new quarter starts, because Quarter is the second level in the hierarchy.

FieldParam		Axis = COLUMNS ROWS with RESET on Numerical values					
■ Year	Brand	Adventure Works		Contoso		**Total**	
■ Quarter	Year	Sales Amount	RunningSum	Sales Amount	RunningSum	**Sales Amount**	**RunningSum**
■ Month	⊟ 2024	**50,080,665.87**	**50,080,665.87**	**36,174,621.65**	**86,255,287.51**	**86,255,287.51**	**86,255,287.51**
Day of Week	⊞ Q1	9,981,114.09	9,981,114.09	8,664,030.99	18,645,145.09	**18,645,145.09**	**18,645,145.09**
	⊞ Q2	11,081,808.21	11,081,808.21	8,005,975.51	19,087,783.72	**19,087,783.72**	**19,087,783.72**
	⊞ Q3	9,872,864.58	9,872,864.58	6,652,121.81	16,524,986.39	**16,524,986.39**	**16,524,986.39**
	⊟ Q4	19,144,878.97	19,144,878.97	12,852,493.34	31,997,372.31	**31,997,372.31**	**31,997,372.31**
	⊟ 2025	**104,763,087.05**	**104,763,087.05**	**66,174,114.05**	**170,937,201.10**	**170,937,201.10**	**170,937,201.10**
	⊟ Q1	37,802,841.26	37,802,841.26	23,867,997.55	61,670,838.80	**61,670,838.80**	**61,670,838.80**
	⊞ Q2	30,632,172.17	30,632,172.17	17,372,877.48	48,005,049.65	**48,005,049.65**	**48,005,049.65**
	⊟ Q3	15,137,888.18	15,137,888.18	10,148,364.22	25,286,252.40	**25,286,252.40**	**25,286,252.40**
	⊟ Q4	21,190,185.44	21,190,185.44	14,784,874.80	35,975,060.24	**35,975,060.24**	**35,975,060.24**
	⊞ 2026	**123,326,997.71**	**123,326,997.71**	**115,835,779.06**	**239,162,776.77**	**239,162,776.77**	**239,162,776.77**
	Total	**278,170,750.62**	**278,170,750.62**	**218,184,514.75**	**496,355,265.38**	**496,355,265.38**	**496,355,265.38**

FIGURE 3-16 Reset based on second level in the hierarchy, which is Quarter in this example.

So far, the numeric value specified in the *reset* parameter has enabled you to do the same thing as a field reference. But suppose the user changes the column in the matrix visual based on the field parameter. After the change, the rows contain Quarter, Month, and Day of Week. So, you can no longer use the same field reference when you want to reset on the second level, because the second level as specified in this visual calculation has become Month. Unless you change the expression for the visual calculation, Month will be used for the *reset* parameter (see Figure 3-17).

Axis = COLUMNS ROWS with RESET on Numerical values							
Brand	Adventure Works		Contoso		Total		
Quarter	Sales Amount	RunningSum	Sales Amount	RunningSum	Sales Amount	RunningSum	
⊟ Q1	97,764,766.81	97,764,766.81	69,896,023.98	167,660,790.80	167,660,790.80	167,660,790.80	
⊟ January	29,825,442.26	29,825,442.26	21,207,968.89	51,033,411.15	51,033,411.15	51,033,411.15	
Sunday	2,284,827.22	2,284,827.22	1,864,586.93	4,149,414.15	4,149,414.15	4,149,414.15	
Monday	2,750,489.14	6,899,903.29	2,056,784.26	8,956,687.55	4,807,273.40	8,956,687.55	
Tuesday	3,701,757.15	12,658,444.70	2,438,651.39	15,097,096.09	6,140,408.54	15,097,096.09	
Wednesday	5,174,155.29	20,271,251.38	3,707,552.72	23,978,804.10	8,881,708.01	23,978,804.10	
Thursday	5,286,436.83	29,265,240.93	3,634,227.21	32,899,468.13	8,920,664.03	32,899,468.13	
Friday	4,182,674.00	37,082,142.13	3,021,447.87	40,103,590.00	7,204,121.87	40,103,590.00	
Saturday	6,445,102.63	46,548,692.64	4,484,718.51	51,033,411.15	10,929,821.14	51,033,411.15	
⊞ February	39,225,221.49	39,225,221.49	27,842,824.32	67,068,045.81	67,068,045.81	67,068,045.81	
⊞ March	28,714,103.06	28,714,103.06	20,845,230.77	49,559,333.84	49,559,333.84	49,559,333.84	
Total	278,170,750.62	278,170,750.62	218,184,514.75	496,355,265.38	496,355,265.38	496,355,265.38	

FieldParam — Year, Quarter ■, Month ■, Day of Week ■

FIGURE 3-17 Reset based on second level in the hierarchy, which has become Month after changing the field parameter.

Field parameters generate a dynamic range of items that are part of the hierarchy. If only one column is selected in the slicer, there is no second level on which the *reset* parameter can operate. In this scenario, visual calculations will automatically detect this. Positive numbers that are out of range are mapped to the lowest level (not parent) in the hierarchy. Negative numbers that are out of range are mapped to the highest level in the hierarchy.

Understanding hidden fields

As the name implies, hidden fields enable you to hide elements from the visual in your Power BI report. Hiding items is not entirely new; you can hide model objects in the semantic model and hide entire visuals from a report. However, visual calculations introduce the ability for the user to hide individual fields from a visual. By doing so, users can break down complex calculations into smaller steps. This applies to any value that is part of the visual matrix, whether it's a measure from the model or an existing visual calculation.

> **Note** Fields used on the axes cannot be hidden. The ability to hide fields is limited to values in the visual matrix.

You can hide items from the resulting visual by clicking the small eye icon in the Build pane under Values (see Figure 3-18). Toggling this button shows or hides the value from the resulting visual. When you edit a visual calculation, all values are always visible in the visual matrix.

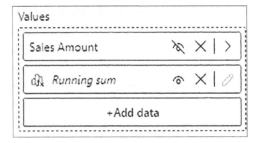

FIGURE 3-18 Values defining a visual in the Build pane, showing the option to hide elements from the visual.

There are two main scenarios in which hiding elements can be useful:

- To show only the resulting visual calculation, in which the original measure from the model is hidden.

- To break down complex calculations in small steps for understandability and debugging.

Only showing visual calculations

Every value in a visual calculation must exist in the visual matrix. By default, this means that both the original value residing in the model and the visual calculation will be shown in the resulting visual. However, there might be times when you want to show only the result of a visual calculation—for example, to show only the running sum, leaving out the original values. Hiding the original values will remove them from the visual presentation but leave them intact in the visual matrix.

Figure 3-19 provides an example. Notice how the columns in the chart show only one value (the result of the visual calculation), while the visual matrix still shows the original *Sales Amount* measure that resides in the semantic model. Because the original value is hidden, the resulting visual shows only relevant information.

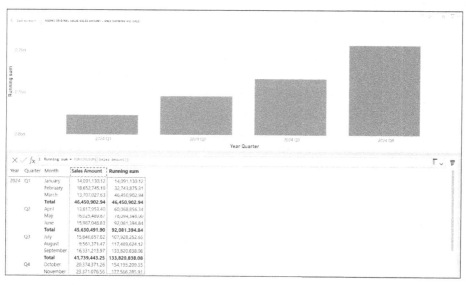

FIGURE 3-19 The resulting column chart shows only one data bar, although the visual matrix shows the original value as well as the visual calculation.

Breaking down complex calculations

You can use visual calculations to create complex calculations, especially when employing concepts like the *axis* and *reset* parameters (covered earlier in this chapter). Sometimes, though, visual calculations can become so complex, it's difficult to fully grasp how they work. Breaking complex calculations into multiple steps can help users better understand the resulting numbers. You can then hide intermediate steps to show only the desired calculation in the report visual. Similarly, if you want to debug a complex calculation, breaking it down in small steps can help to find where the issue is.

An example could be calculating the percentage sales of a certain product subcategory, as part of the category. Visual calculations contain an expression template to get you started, but validating the outcome might be challenging. The expression template that can be used is as follows:

```
Percent of parent = DIVIDE ( [Field], COLLAPSE ( [Field], Axis ) )
```

If the COLLAPSE function were new to you, you might want to get a better idea of what this function is doing. You could break the calculation into a few steps by calculating the denominator separately in its own visual calculation like so:

```
Total of Category = COLLAPSE ( [Sales Amount], ROWS )
```

This expression calculates the total sales for the product category to which the subcategory belongs. Looking at the visual matrix, you can validate whether the outcome matches the one you expected. As a next step, you can add the following expression to divide the current row sales by the total of the category:

```
Percentage of product category = DIVIDE ( [Sales Amount], [Total of Category] )
```

The result will be exactly the same as the original calculation. However, you can then hide the intermediate step to show only the result of the calculation that returns the percentage of product category (see Figure 3-20).

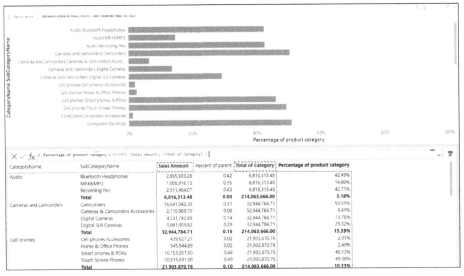

FIGURE 3-20 You can break down complex calculations in multiple steps and showing only the end result.

Available functions, and their relation to regular DAX

As discussed, visual calculations simply use regular DAX just as in measures, calculated columns, and calculated tables. They do not introduce any new DAX language elements.

The majority of DAX functions also work in visual calculations. However, there are a few important differences. These are shown in Figure 3-21.

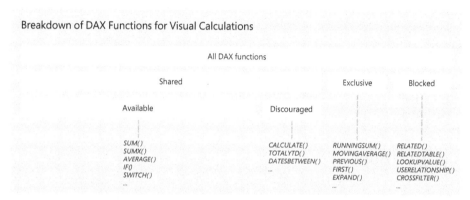

FIGURE 3-21 Breakdown of available DAX functions for visual calculations.

If you ever wonder whether you can use a DAX function in visual calculations, simply look at the DAX documentation available at *https://learn.microsoft.com/dax*. Each function page has a header that indicates whether it can be used in visual calculations. Figure 3-22 shows an example of such a header.

FIGURE 3-22 An example header that shows where a function can be used.

Shared functions

You can break DAX down into model-related elements, like measures, calculated columns, and calculated tables. Each of these can refer to objects that are part of the semantic model.

Shared functions are DAX functions which are shared across all experiences. These functions work in measures, calculated columns, calculated tables as well as visual calculations. Typically, these are generic functions like SUM, MIN, MAX but also functions that help to check conditions like IF and SWITCH.

Available

Available functions are typically functions that can be used in all different contexts. These could be aggregation functions like SUM, AVERAGE, MIN, and MAX, as well as the iterator versions SUMX, AVERAGEX, MINX, and MAXX. The majority of DAX functions can basically be used anywhere. Functions like IF and SWITCH that validate a condition are also available everywhere.

Discouraged

Although these functions will not return an error if used in a visual calculation, you should use them with caution because their results will likely not be what you expected. These functions expect to work in a filter context in a semantic model. Although they do not refer to the model structure directly, the way USERELATIONSHIP does, they do expect that model all the same. Therefore, when used in the visual context as part of a visual calculation, their expectations are violated, and they are not likely to return sensible results.

Exclusive functions

Several functions have been introduced in DAX solely for visual calculations. These functions are exclusive to visual calculations. These functions work only within the visual matrix and cannot reach back out to the semantic model.

Categories of visual calculations exclusive functions are as follows:

- **Business functions**   These include RUNNINGSUM and MOVINGAVERAGE.

- **Medium-level functions**   These include absolute movement functions (FIRST and LAST), relative movement functions (PREVIOUS and NEXT), lattice navigation functions (EXPAND, EXPANDALL, COLLAPSE, and COLLAPSEALL), and other functions (ISATLEVEL, RANGE, LOOKUP, and LOOKUPWITHTOTALS).

- **Foundational functions**   These include OFFSET, INDEX, WINDOW, RANK, and ROWNUMBER.

- **Supportive functions**   These include ORDERBY, PARTITIONBY, and MATCHBY.

Visual calculations exclusive functions only have signatures that support the *axis* parameter. Many visual calculations exclusive functions can be mapped to window functions for use in regular DAX. Chapters 6 and 7 describe exclusive functions and their relation to regular DAX in more detail.

Blocked functions

Blocked functions are the functions that reach out to the model. Visual calculations can work only with values that are part of the visual matrix. If a calculation requires another value, this value must be brought into the visual matrix. If you don't want to show this value in the visual, you can hide it from the output.

Note Although the formula bar in visual calculations enables you to write any of the semantic model–related functions, using these functions will result in errors.

Types of functions that reach out to the model and are therefore not supported in visual calculations include the following:

- **Functions that cross a relationship to look up data** These include RELATED and RELATEDTABLE.

- **Relationship behavior functions** Examples of these are USERELATIONSHIP and CROSSFILTER.

Limitations

Although visual calculations work in the majority of scenarios in Power BI reports, there are situations in which visual calculations have limitations. The next sections describe the current limitations at the time of this writing. As we expect Microsoft to further evolve on visual calculations, we recommend that you check the most recent limitations in the documentation at *https://learn.microsoft.com/power-bi/ transform-model/desktop-visual-calculations-overview#considerations-and-limitations*.

Signatures of functions

Because visual calculations are in public preview at the time of this writing, various features—but especially signatures of functions—are subject to change. New parameters will likely be introduced, and new features will be added as the visual calculations feature is made generally available.

Reuse of visual calculations

Other calculation types like measures and calculated columns save their definition to the semantic model and can easily be reused across different visuals and reports. Because visual calculations are defined on the visual itself and use the visual matrix, the calculations cannot easily be reused across different visuals. The topic of reuse and adoption of visual calculations is described in more detail in Chapter 4, "Organization and use of visual calculations."

Visual types

Visual calculations are not available for all types of visuals. Although the majority of standardized visuals like column and bar charts are supported, more exclusive visual types are not, such as the following:

- Visuals with external computations, like R and Python visuals.

- AI-influenced visuals, like key influencers, decomposition trees, Q&A visuals, and smart narratives.

- Visuals with external integrations, like paginated reports, metrics, Power Apps, and Power Automate.

Visual interactions

If a visual calculation is added to a visual, user interactions are limited in the following ways:

- Unlike model objects, which can be used as filters on a visual, page, or report, visual calculations do not show up in the Filter pane.

- Visuals with a visual calculation cannot be drilled through to navigate from one page to another.

- The Personalize visual feature that enables a report's consumer to change the visual types or fields used in a visual is not available for any visuals that have visual calculations.

Formatting

There are some limitations with regard to formatting a visual calculation. For example:

- You cannot visually change the sort order of a visual calculation. If you want to change the sort order, you must do so with DAX. The limited formatting options available are discussed in Chapter 4.

- Although data categories (like measures and columns) can be applied to model objects in Power BI to define how a field appears in a visualization (for example, with thousand separators and decimal places), this is not supported for visual calculations because they are not part of the model. Visual calculations must be formatted in the visual through the Properties section of the Format pane (see Chapter 4).

- Dynamic format strings, which enable users to determine how measures appear in visuals by conditionally applying a format string with a separate DAX expression, are not supported for visual calculations.

External effects of visual calculations

If you want to use the output of a visual calculation externally, there are various limitations:

- The results from visual calculations are not included when underlying data for a visual is exported because this exported information comes from the source model in which the visual calculations are not present. The key is that you're exporting the underlying data from the model in this example, whereas the visual calculations are created at visual level.

- Reports cannot be published to the web if visual calculations are used in the report.

- Reports using visual calculations cannot be used in Power BI Embedded.

If you create a visual calculation that contains an error or calls a function that's not available for visual calculations, it will return an error. In most cases, this error will tell you what is going on. To resolve the error, you first have to open the visual calculations edit mode. From there, you can start debugging. One of your options will be to break any complex calculation down into steps, as discussed earlier in this chapter.

In summary

With the introduction of visual calculations, important new concepts were introduced to Power BI. This chapter discussed the following concepts:

- **Visual matrix** The visual matrix is the simplest representation of the data used to create the visual. The visual matrix displays the data in the visual as well as the result of any visual calculations added to the visual.

- **The *axis* parameter** This parameter determines how the visual calculation traverses the visual matrix.

- **The *reset* parameter** This parameter defines whether a visual calculation resets while traversing the visual matrix.

- **Hidden fields** Hidden fields enable you to hide fields from the visual in your Power BI report.

Visual calculations also introduced a number of new DAX functions that are exclusive to visual calculations. However, you can use many DAX functions in visual calculations, but not all. Because it is important to know which functions are available for use, the DAX documentation shows the availability on each individual function's page.

Finally, as great as visual calculations are, they have their limitations, which are also important to remember when working with them. The most important limitations have to do with the support visual types and other features in Power BI.

## CHAPTER 4

Organization and use of visual calculations

This chapter explores where to find visual calculations in Power BI and how to use them effectively. You'll learn about their formatting options, how they interact with different data types, and how the user interface is designed to support a seamless experience. It also covers strategies for managing and discovering visual calculations using concepts like Power BI enhanced report format and API-based discovery of visual calculations, and it dives into how these calculations can integrate with external features such as the explore functionality in the Power BI Service.

Where to find visual calculations in Power BI

Visual calculations are integrated throughout Power BI Desktop. This section explores where in the application you can find visual calculations and how you can apply them directly. Because visual calculations are part of a visual, our starting point will be a semantic model in which data has been imported and a first visual has been built. In this scenario, we have a simple report page on which the measure for *Sales* is shown in a column chart combined with a Year field.

Chapter 2, "My first visual calculation," explained how to add a visual calculation. At the time of this writing, there are three places where visual calculations can be added to a visual. Here is an overview of the different ways to create new visual calculations:

- **Ribbon**   When a visual on the screen is selected, and the visual type supports visual calculations, a button appears on the ribbon in two tabs—Home and Modeling—to create a new visual calculation in the selected visual. Click this button in either tab to open the visual calculations edit mode. You can choose several standard options or create a custom calculation.

- **Right-click**   Right-clicking a visual that supports visual calculations opens a context menu with a New visual calculation option. From here, you can choose from several standard options or create a custom calculation.

- **Context menu**   Each visual has a context menu, which you can access by clicking the ellipsis menu (...) located at the top-right corner of the visual. This context menu offers the same options for visual calculations as with the menu that opens when you right-click the visual.

Figure 4-1 shows the three choices in Power BI Desktop, and where you can find them. No matter which one you choose, the available options will all be the same.

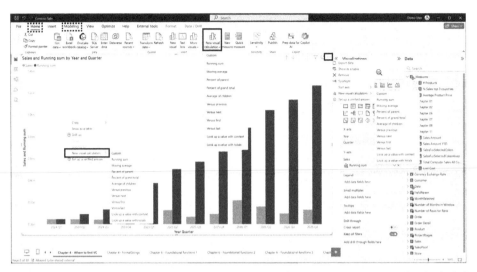

FIGURE 4-1 There are three places in the Power BI Desktop where you can create new visual calculations.

Visual-level formatting and data type support

To visualize the outcome of calculations in the most optimal way, formatting is required. Format strings enable you to customize how items appear in Power BI.

Format strings should not be confused with data types. Data types define whether a number is, for example, a whole number, decimal number, or postal code. In contrast, format strings allow for a more fine-grained level of formatting—for example, defining how many decimal places a decimal number should show or the formatting of date fields in order from year, month, and day.

You can use format strings to format three different levels of objects in Power BI:

- **Model**   You can apply format strings to any model object, like columns and measures. Changing the format string in the model influences the default appearance for that object. As soon as you drag and drop that object on the report canvas, it will use these default formatting settings.

- **Visual**   On the visual level, you can apply additional formatting by overwriting the model format strings. You can format any column, measure, or visual calculation for that visual only. The default formatting set at the model level will not change when you update visual-level formatting. Visual-level format strings for fields are persisted for fields but not for visual calculations. If you set a visual-level format string on a field and then remove and re-add that field to the same visual, the visual-level format string will be reinstated. In contrast, for a visual calculation, the format string will not be reinstated when you have removed a visual calculation and recreate it later. When you just hide a visual calculation and show it later again, the visual-level format string will be reinstated.

- **Element** Formatting on the element level overwrites any previously set formatting on the model and/or visual level. Element-level formatting can apply to specific parts of a visual, for example tooltips or data labels.

Format strings on these three levels are hierarchical, and one level can overwrite another. Also, because visual calculations are not stored in the model, only visual- and element-level formatting can be used to format them.

Level	Impact	Available for
Model	All visuals, all pages, all reports on the same semantic model	Columns and measures
Visual	Selected visual	Columns, measures, and visual calculations
Element	Selected element of the selected visual	Columns, measures, and visual calculations

Let's look at an example. Suppose you have a chart with a *Sales* measure. As shown in Figure 4-2, the measure is initially formatted as a decimal number (but not as currency), with two decimal places configured.

FIGURE 4-2 The model-level format strings define the default formatting of a model object.

Now suppose you use the General tab in the Format pane to apply visual-level formatting, configuring *Sales* as a Currency, which displays the dollar sign in front of the numbers. Also, you've added thousands separators to improve readability of the values (see Figure 4-3). This overrules the model-level formatting.

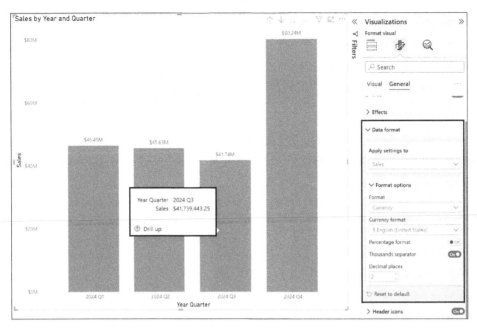

FIGURE 4-3 You can assign visual-level formatting using the Format pane in Power BI Desktop.

Figure 4-4 shows formatting on the element level, with a visual calculation built on top of the *Sales* measure. The visual calculation calculates the running sum over all Quarters of a Year and resets each time a new Year starts. The following expression is used:

```
Running sum = RUNNINGSUM ( [Sales], ROWS, [Year] )
```

By default, visual calculations use the decimal value for formatting. Here, we added the visual calculation as a secondary bar in this column chart, and we wanted to format its data labels to show millions rather than thousands because the quarterly numbers can become quite high. At the same time, we wanted to keep the *Sales* measure formatted as thousands. The formatting is on the element level and applies only to the data labels. If this visual calculation were to be used as input for any other visual calculation, the original formatting (in thousands) would apply. Also, because it's only formatting and doesn't change how values are computed, we don't lose accuracy.

> **Note** At the time of this writing, by default, the data type of a visual calculation is decimal number. If a visual calculation returns a text string, this may result in unexpected errors. Explicitly changing the data type on either the visual or element level will solve this. Microsoft is aware of this issue, and we expect this to be addressed in the future.

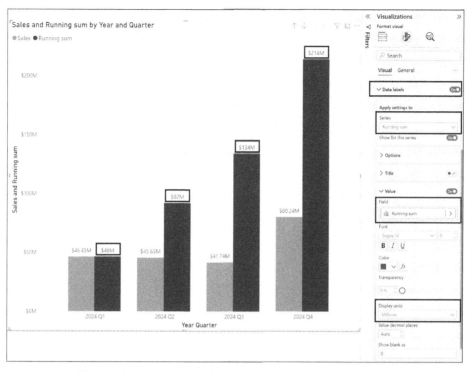

FIGURE 4-4 In this example, we set element-level formatting to change the display units for the running sum visual calculation to show in millions, whereas the original value is shown in thousands.

Development of visual calculations through the user interface

While traditional code developers are known for barely touching their mouse—preferring to navigate, code, and execute everything through keyboard shortcuts—Power BI caters to a different kind of audience (although Power BI does support keyboard shortcuts). Most Power BI users are more visually driven, often working through intuitive interfaces rather than complex text-based environments. This distinction becomes especially clear when developing visual calculations. The user experience for creating visual calculations is designed with accessibility and ease of use in mind. Rather than having to memorize syntax and type every function, users are guided through a more structured, template-based approach. Two main features drive this accessible interface: parameter pickers and matrix highlights.

Parameter picker for required parameters

When building a new visual calculation, templates offer a solid starting point, helping users to quickly frame their logic without needing to worry about every technical detail. They can use parameter pickers to easily select parameters and fields with just a few clicks, significantly lowering the barrier to entry for building dynamic, context-aware calculations directly within a visual.

This guided development experience not only speeds up the process but also helps ensure consistency and reduces errors, especially for users who are newer to DAX or visual calculations. It's available in visual calculations for required parameters. By simply clicking the dropdown, users can select one of the fields that is part of the visual matrix, as shown in Figure 4-5.

FIGURE 4-5 The formula bar of the visual calculations includes the parameter picker for required parameters.

 Note You can also use the Ctrl+spacebar keyboard shortcut to parameter pickers.

Matrix highlights

When creating a visual calculation, it can be challenging to understand the exact fields that are used to compute the value. To better understand which fields are used, visual calculations include matrix highlights. You can find this option in the visual calculations edit mode. These highlights can be compared to cell highlights in Microsoft Excel, although they are not entirely the same because matrix highlights in visual calculations are limited to columns, whereas Excel can also highlight individual cells.

Figure 4-6 shows the *Sales* and *Costs* measures. We will add a new visual calculation to subtract the costs from the sales to calculate profit. Once we add a new visual calculation, matrix highlights can help us to directly build our new metric. The highlight icon appears in the top-right of the editor; it's available only when you are editing a visual calculation. Once clicked, the colors in the formula bar correspond with the highlights in the visual matrix.

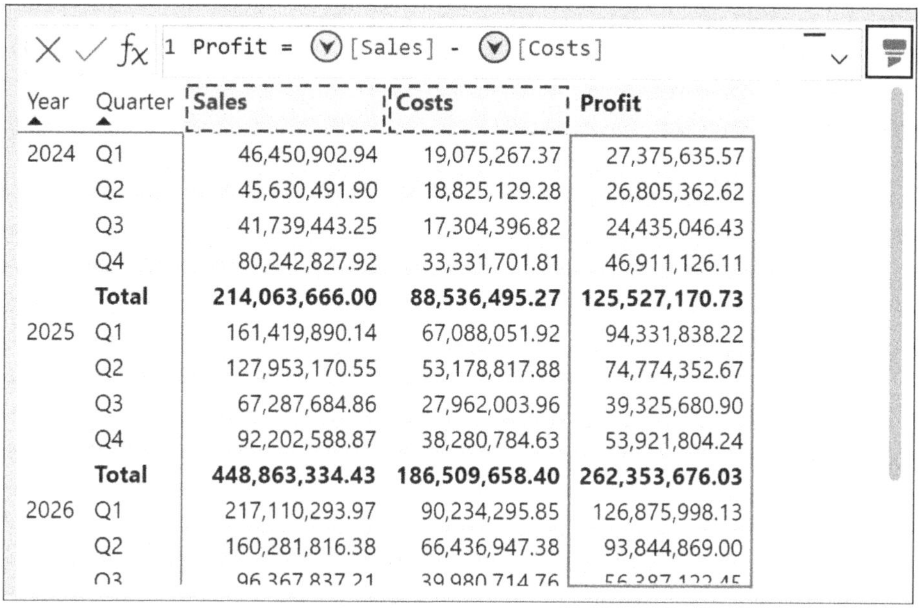

Year	Quarter	Sales	Costs	Profit
2024	Q1	46,450,902.94	19,075,267.37	27,375,635.57
	Q2	45,630,491.90	18,825,129.28	26,805,362.62
	Q3	41,739,443.25	17,304,396.82	24,435,046.43
	Q4	80,242,827.92	33,331,701.81	46,911,126.11
	Total	**214,063,666.00**	**88,536,495.27**	**125,527,170.73**
2025	Q1	161,419,890.14	67,088,051.92	94,331,838.22
	Q2	127,953,170.55	53,178,817.88	74,774,352.67
	Q3	67,287,684.86	27,962,003.96	39,325,680.90
	Q4	92,202,588.87	38,280,784.63	53,921,804.24
	Total	**448,863,334.43**	**186,509,658.40**	**262,353,676.03**
2026	Q1	217,110,293.97	90,234,295.85	126,875,998.13
	Q2	160,281,816.38	66,436,947.38	93,844,869.00
	Q3	96,367,837.21	39,980,714.76	56,387,122.45

Formula bar: `1  Profit = [Sales] - [Costs]`

FIGURE 4-6 Matrix highlights and colors in the formula bar match the selected columns in the visual matrix.

Note The parameter picker, discussed in the previous section, works seamlessly with visual matrix highlights, which makes the interface even more intuitive—especially since the colors of the parameter picker match the highlights in the visual matrix.

Visual calculations in pbip format

By default, Power BI solutions are saved in a binary file, the pbix file. Power BI Desktop also supports saving the solution as a Power BI Project, which breaks down the solution in folders and separates the semantic model from the report metadata. Because visual calculations are part of the report metadata, the definitions of visual calculations are also saved inside the report definition.

Note At the time of this writing, saving a solution as a Power BI Project is a preview feature, and you must explicitly enable it in the Power BI Desktop settings.

The breakdown of a Power BI solution into multiple files allows for programmatic approaches to generate and edit items, as well as source control and deployment through continuous integration and continuous delivery. With the source control capabilities, you can store semantic model and report item definitions in a source control system, like Git. With Git, you can track version history, compare revisions (diff), and revert to previous versions.

Saving reports in pbip format breaks down even the report elements in text-editable files. Visual calculations can be found in the report definition files, where the report folder contains subfolders for each report page, among many other files. The definition folder contains components of the report, in the following subfolders and files:

- **bookmarks/**   This stores bookmark definitions, each in its own file.

- **pages/**   This contains one folder per report page (named by GUID), each with a page.json and a visuals/ folder. Inside the visuals/ folder, each visual has a visual.json file defining visual settings.

- **report.json**   This contains report-wide metadata.

- **version.json**   This manages pbip schema versioning.

- **StaticResources/**   This holds assets like images.

- **definition.pbir**   This acts as the entry point for Power BI Desktop to load the report.

For each visual on the screen, the page subfolder contains another folder. A file called visual.json is located in the folder for the visual, which contains the visual configuration. This includes the type of visual, columns used in the visual, and visual calculation definitions. The visual calculation is saved in the NativeVisualCalculation container that describes the language, name, and expression of the visual calculation:

```
{
  "field": {
    "NativeVisualCalculation": {
      "Language": "dax",
      "Expression": "[Sales] - [Costs]",
      "Name": "Profit"
    }
  },
  "queryRef": "select",
  "nativeQueryRef": "Profit"
}
```

The preceding code snippet shows a part of the visual.json file, in which the visual calculation for *Profit* is defined. This contains only part of the visual.json; many other elements like visual sort order and any other visual settings are defined in this json file.

Although the reuse of visual calculations is limited (described in the "Reuse of visual calculations" section later in this chapter), having a code-based interface and file per visual, it's easier to copy-paste an entire visual from page to page or elements of a visual like a visual calculation from one visual to another visual. Also, in scenarios in which bulk changes are required, like changing the name of an item, the enhanced report format will help to bulk search-and-replace field references in multiple visual calculations at a time.

Management and discoverability

From an administrative, governance, and compliance perspective, understanding and monitoring the use of visual calculations across your organization is essential. Visual calculations provide a flexible way for users to create tailored metrics directly within visualizations, offering dynamic and context-specific insights. However, this flexibility can also introduce challenges when it comes to maintaining a single source of truth within the organization's data ecosystem.

Striving for a single source of truth is key to effective data governance, ensuring consistency, accuracy, and transparency in reporting and analysis. When users create visual calculations independently, bypassing centralized measures defined within the semantic model, inconsistencies may arise. These inconsistencies can lead to errors in key metrics, conflicting interpretations between reports, and diminished trust in organizational data over time.

Visual calculations are intended to make DAX easier and excel at tasks such as customizing titles, subtitles, and conditional formatting. However, because they're not reusable, they lack the standardized reliability of centralized measures. This limitation can cause fragmentation and deviation from a single definition across reports because similar calculations may be created differently across teams.

To address these risks, organizations must think about the discovery and management of visual calculations. Power BI Administrators should establish clear guidelines on when to use visual calculations versus centralized measures. Visual calculations should be employed primarily for tasks specific to visualization design, such as formatting or highlighting, while critical metrics used in business decisions should remain standardized within the semantic model. However, if users do not have direct access to the semantic model, visual calculations can be added in reports for custom calculations, next to report-level measures. Also, if a user does not have the appropriate level of knowledge, visual calculations can provide an easier way to get started. Finally, visual calculations are useful when specific visual calculations functions such as RUNNINGSUM and MOVINGAVERAGE provide an easier way out than setting up the equivalent in measures. Training programs can help users understand these distinctions and encourage responsible usage. By fostering collaboration and maintaining proper governance, organizations can effectively balance the agility of visual calculations with the need for data integrity.

Traceability

Traceability is essential for Power BI Administrators to maintain data governance and consistency across reports and dashboards. It enables the monitoring of visual calculations' origins, changes, and usage, helping to detect discrepancies and maintain trust in organizational data.

APIs, such as Power BI Scanner APIs, allow administrators to track key metadata like creation, modification, and dependencies. This helps resolve issues when they occur and ensures calculations align with organizational standards. However, at the time of this writing, visual calculations are not traceable through the Scanner API, nor through any of the other APIs.

Traceability also prevents redundancy and conflicting definitions by identifying inconsistent calculations. Using audit trails and versioning systems further enhances accountability and enables swift corrections when needed. Power BI provides audit logs that contain information about all actions performed by users in the Power BI Service (cloud). Because this is limited to the web environment, nothing that occurs in Power BI Desktop is traced. The creation of visual calculations is also not traced as activity in audit logs but is covered in a generic activity named Update Report Content.

> **Note** The full list of operations as they appear in the audit logs can be found at *https://learn.microsoft.com/fabric/admin/operation-list*.

Telemetry

Telemetry refers to the collection and analysis of data to monitor, measure, and optimize system performance. In the context of data governance and reporting, telemetry can provide valuable insights into the usage patterns, dependencies, and performance of visual calculations. By leveraging telemetry, administrators can identify discrepancies and ensure that visual calculations align with organizational standards.

Fabric workspace monitoring collects all kinds of operations that happen within Microsoft Fabric and also for Power BI as one of the platform workloads. Microsoft Fabric is an end-to-end data and analytics platform designed to empower organizations with a unified solution for data integration, engineering, storage, and business intelligence. Built on the foundations of Power BI, it has a single architecture with enterprise-grade security, governance, and compliance. It streamlines decision-making by enabling teams to collaborate on a shared data foundation.

Workspace monitoring is a Fabric database that collects and organizes logs and metrics from a range of Fabric items in your workspace. Workspace monitoring lets workspace users access and analyze logs and metrics related to Fabric items in the workspace. The data is saved in an Eventhouse containing all sorts of diagnostic logs and metrics from all items in the workspace. The data is aggregated and stored in the monitoring database, where it can be queried using Kusto Query Language (KQL) or SQL. The database supports both historical log analysis and real-time data streaming.

> **Note** Fabric workspace monitoring is the latest and newest addition to Microsoft Fabric to collect telemetry. If workspace monitoring is not available in your tenant, Azure Log Analytics integration on the workspace level provides similar functionality. Read more on Log Analytics integration in the documentation at *https://learn.microsoft.com/power-bi/transform-model/log-analytics/desktop-log-analytics-configure*.

Semantic model operation logs are part of the workspace monitoring logs and are registered in the Eventhouse KQL database. A wide range of logs is collected, containing information such as the used application, workspace, and capacity, as well as performance-related information.

> **Note** All details of telemetry captured in workspace monitoring for semantic models can be found in the documentation at *https://learn.microsoft.com/power-bi/enterprise/semantic-model-operations*.

Workspace monitoring is part of the Power BI/Fabric Service. Power BI Desktop cannot be monitored directly; therefore, the semantic model must first be published to the service. After publishing, every time an event happens with the semantic model or the report, the telemetry is collected by workspace monitoring.

As an example, we will continue with the rather simple calculation to calculate profit that we set up in Figure 4-6. We used the following visual calculation to calculate the profit:

```
Profit = [Sales] - [Costs]
```

When we open the report, the first data should be picked up by workspace monitoring. When opening the monitoring KQL Database, we will find all operations that occurred in the workspace. Among the semantic model operation logs, QueryStart and QueryEnd events indicate the beginning and end of a query sent to the semantic model. These events help trace the execution lifecycle of each query, including those triggered by visuals. While visual calculations are executed on the visual matrix and not pushed directly down to the model engine, it's still possible to capture their logic through the semantic model logs. This is evident in the EventText field of the QueryEnd log, which contains the full DAX query—enhanced with the DSVisualCalcs syntax—that describes the visual calculation applied on the visual. Figure 4-7 shows an example of this.

> **Note**   The query in the monitoring database looks slightly different from the query we have defined in the visual calculation. This is due to the underlying structure of visual calculations, which is described in more detail in Chapter 9, "Breaking down visual calculations execution."

FIGURE 4-7 Workspace monitoring in Microsoft Fabric shows a QueryEnd event from the SemanticModelLogs table. It reveals the executed DAX query of a visual calculation, including the use of DSVisualCalcs, useful for tracing and auditing calculation logic.

The fact that we find the visual calculation query here may seem counterintuitive, but it enables monitoring and auditing of calculations that are technically scoped to the visual layer. However, workspace monitoring is a solution that is not intended for larger-scale monitoring because it will allow users within a workspace to trace all traffic going through the semantic model engine, including the visual calculations, potentially exposing them to more detail than they should be seeing.

> **Note** Workspace monitoring is a Fabric feature and requires a Power BI Premium or Fabric capacity. Creation of Fabric items next to workspace monitoring must be explicitly enabled in the tenant settings.

API discoverability

As a solution owner or Power BI Administrator, you might want to find out where visual calculations are used to spot the ones that may derive from organization set standards and definitions. One way to do this is to use an API call to scan across all Power BI Workspaces at one time. This is where the Scanner API comes in. It's an API designed for metadata scanning. However, the level of detail required to return individual visual objects and their specifics, like visual calculations, is not available in the Scanner API at the time of this writing.

> **Note** You can find the most up-to-date details about the Scanner API in the documentation at *https://learn.microsoft.com/fabric/governance/metadata-scanning-overview*.

Semantic link labs to get visual calculations definitions

There are other ways to discover visual calculations in the Power BI Service. For example, Microsoft Fabric notebooks allow for a code-based integration with any objects that are available in the Power BI Service. Semantic link, a python package in Fabric notebooks, bridges the gap between the code-first world of notebooks and the low-code experience of Power BI by enabling interaction with semantic models as well as functionalities to read report metadata. With semantic link, users can query, analyze, and manipulate semantic models and reports directly from notebooks (see Figure 4-8).

Semantic link labs is an experimental additional package, designed to explore new features and capabilities built on top of semantic link. It allows users to test early-stage ideas and prototypes that enhance semantic link functions, helping shape the future of data-driven development in Microsoft Fabric. Often, functions in semantic link (labs) are wrappers for already-existing APIs. Both semantic link and the experimental labs package are available only for notebooks in Microsoft Fabric and are not available for any platform.

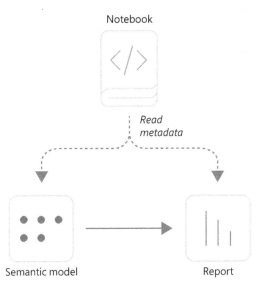

Notebook

Read
metadata

Semantic model

Report

FIGURE 4-8 We've diagrammed a notebook reading metadata from a semantic model and a report, with a data flow from the semantic model to the report.

Note You can find the most up-to-date information about semantic link and its capabilities in the documentation at *https://learn.microsoft.com/fabric/data-science/semantic-link-overview.*

Before you start exploring options to find visual calculations using semantic link labs in a notebook, you must know that visual calculations expressions are identified as Native Visual Calculations in the report metadata, as discussed earlier in the "Visual calculations in pbip" section. The notebook starts by specifying the report and workspace you want to work with. The ReportWrapper is used to load the report definition, which includes various artifacts like layout, visual configurations, and internal settings. These are returned in a Base64-encoded format, so the notebook decodes them to get the raw JSON structure of the report.

Visual calculations aren't surfaced through the standard semantic model metadata (like measures or calculated columns are) because they are saved in the report definition. Therefore, you can't just query visual calculations directly. Instead, the full report JSON definition must be parsed to look for any traces of NativeVisualCalculation objects. These can be hidden deep within nested structures or even embedded inside escaped JSON strings within the config sections of visuals.

After all occurrences of the NativeVisualCalculation object are collected, the notebook extracts just the useful parts, such as the name of the visual calculation, the language used (DAX), and the expression itself. These results are put together in a dataframe, which is effectively a table definition.

The output can help with documentation, governance, or simply getting a better overview of how visual calculations are used across a report—something that's otherwise quite hidden from view. Figure 4-9 shows a sample output.

	Name	Language		Expression
0	Highlight	dax		VAR _h = COLLAPSE (EXPAND (MAX ([Sales Amount]), ROWS), ROWS) RETURN IF (MONTH ([Date]) = [MonthSelected Value], _h * 1.2, BLANK ())
1	Versus next	dax		[Average Product Price] - NEXT([Average Product Price])
2	Versus previous	dax		[Costs] - PREVIOUS ([Costs], 2)
3	Versus previous OFFSET	dax		[Costs] - CALCULATE ([Costs], OFFSET (-2))
4	Vs prev cols rows	dax		[Costs] - PREVIOUS([Costs], COLUMNS ROWS)
5	Vs prev cols	dax		[Costs] - PREVIOUS([Costs], COLUMNS)
6	Versus next	dax		[Average of Price] - NEXT ([Average of Price])
7	Versus next in Category	dax		[Average of Price] - NEXT ([Average of Price], HIGHESTPARENT)
8	Versus next in Category OFFSET	dax		[Average of Price] - CALCULATE ([Average of Price], OFFSET (1, ROWS, HIGHESTPARENT))

FIGURE 4-9 This dataframe in a Fabric notebook shows extracted DAX visual calculations from a Power BI report, with columns for name, language, and expression.

Note   You can find sample code that can be used in a notebook using semantic link labs to find visual calculations in Appendix F.

Other places where you can find visual calculations

Looking at other places where visual calculations can be found, we aim for anything outside of Power BI Desktop and reports in the Service. At the time of this writing, visual calculations are available in only one other place: the *Explore functionality in the Power BI Service.*

Explore enables you to explore your data in a focused way. It allows users to quickly create one visual for ad hoc analysis. For building this visual, objects like tables, columns, and measures from the semantic model are available. On top of that, new visual calculations can be created.

As an example, we've used the explore functionality to analyze the profit by adding a visual calculation by simply clicking the New visual calculation button in the ribbon of the visual. We use the following expression (Figure 4-10 shows the result):

```
Profit = [Sales] - [Costs]
```

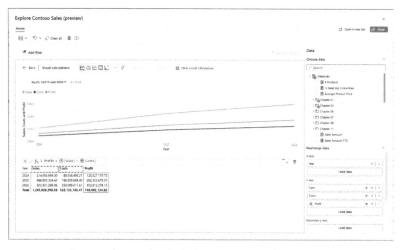

FIGURE 4-10 You can also use visual calculations in the explore functionality.

One of the options to open the explore functionality is from the semantic model directly, as well as from the ellipsis menu of an existing visual on a report page. Results can be saved in the workspace of the Power BI Service, where the explore item appears as a new object.

Reuse of visual calculations

Visual calculations in themselves are not reusable. They're saved in the metadata of the report, inside the visual definition. Considering that visual calculations work based on the visual matrix and all objects that are part of that visual matrix (discussed in more detail in Chapter 3, "Visual calculations concepts"), it's also difficult to simply copy-paste a visual calculation from one visual to another; if one of the objects in the visual matrix isn't present (a column, measure, or other visual calculation), the added visual calculation will cause the visual to return an error.

The limited reusability of visual calculations means that visual calculations can only be used inside one report and that definitions cannot be shared across multiple reports that share the same semantic model. Therefore, it's recommended that you create measures for any key calculations that should be reused across multiple reports.

Despite this limitation, visual calculations can add significant value—especially for ad hoc analysis but also for anything visual specific, like dynamic formatting of visuals. Many visual formatting options allow for dynamic settings through an expression, which could be saved in a measure, but this easily bloats the model with measures that are only used for a single visual. Visual calculations also make complex calculations much easier. Typical scenarios are RUNNINGSUM or MOVINGAVERAGE, which are highly complex and require many steps in a measure. We will show some examples of these uses in Part IV, "The art of practical visual calculations."

In summary

Visual calculations can be found in multiple places in Power BI Desktop, like the ribbon, visual context menu, and in the right-click menu. However, Desktop is not the only place where you can find visual calculations. They're also in Power BI Service, mostly in the same places, and in the explore functionality for ad hoc analysis.

To ease development of visual calculations, options like the parameter picker and matrix highlights are available. Both options make editing visual calculations more accessible and make it easier to see which columns are used in the calculations.

Creation of visual calculations is a first step, after which formatting for correct display comes in. Three levels of formatting are available: model, visual, and element. Because visual calculations are not saved to the model, visual calculations can only be edited on the visual and element level.

Discoverability of visual calculations is important. For administrators, it can be useful to detect where visual calculations are used by extracting the report definitions with APIs or tools like semantic link in notebooks. Also, telemetry can be collected using workspace monitoring or log analytics integration to detect execution of visual calculations on the workspace level.

## PART II

Visual calculations functions

As discussed in Chapter 3, "Visual calculations concepts," visual calculations just use DAX. However, not all DAX functions are available in visual calculations, whereas some functions are available in visual calculations but not elsewhere.

This part focuses on the functions that are exclusively available for visual calculations and a selection of functions that you can employ in other places DAX is used. To be precise, this part discusses the shared functions that form the foundation of visual calculations functions—namely, the window functions. Indeed, most visual calculations are easier-to-use versions of these window functions. First, this part discusses how these functions interact. Then it dives into their inner workings.

Don't worry if the details on the supportive and foundational functions are lost on you. You don't need them to be successful starting out with visual calculations. In fact, you might never need them. However, we think it's good to know they exist, just in case you ever do need to explore the foundations of visual calculations.

Chapter 3 divided DAX functions into three categories: shared functions, exclusive functions, and blocked functions. Each of these categories contains various groups of functions. This part focuses on two of these categories: shared (this includes functions that are available anywhere DAX is used) and exclusive (these are functions that are available only in visual calculations). The following table contains a list of the functions discussed in this part.

Figure II-1 shows the functions that are exclusively available in visual calculations, as well as the shared foundational and supportive functions that support them. Except for these foundational and supportive functions, all functions shown in Figure II-1 are available exclusively in visual calculations.

Notice how Figure II-1 looks a bit like a house. We like to think of the various functions as elements of a house—specifically, a house in Amsterdam. Why Amsterdam? Because in Amsterdam, houses are built on pillars, because the soil conditions are bad. There is even a famous Dutch children's rhyme about this by Johannes van Vloten, which includes the line "Amsterdam, die grote stad, is gebouwd op palen." This translates to "Amsterdam, that big city, is built on pillars." Just as the pillars underneath a house in Amsterdam support the foundation of that house (and the foundation in turn supports the rest of the house), the supportive functions in visual calculations support the foundational functions, which in turn support the rest of the visual calculations functions, which form the floors and the rooms of the house.

Category	Group	Included functions
Exclusive	Business functions	MOVINGAVERAGE RUNNINGSUM
	Absolute movement functions	FIRST LAST LOOKUP LOOKUPWITHTOTALS
	Relative movement functions	PREVIOUS NEXT
	Lattice navigation functions	COLLAPSE COLLAPSEALL EXPAND EXPANDALL
	Other functions	ISATLEVEL RANGE
Shared	Foundational functions	INDEX OFFSET RANK ROWNUMBER WINDOW
	Supportive functions (can only be used as part of other functions)	MATCHBY ORDERBY PARTITIONBY

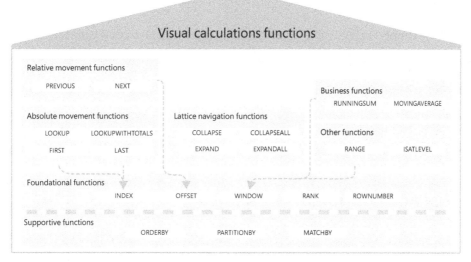

FIGURE II-1 This house represents the available visual calculations functions.

Visual calculations exclusive functions

Fortunately, the names of the functions that are exclusive to visual calculations are very descriptive. You can pretty much just read them to understand what they do. But just in case you're confused, here is a high-level description of each visual calculations exclusive function:

- **Business functions** These perform a running sum or running total calculation (RUNNING-SUM) or a moving average (MOVINGAVERAGE). Both functions are easier-to-use versions of the WINDOW foundational function.

- **Absolute movement functions** These enable you to jump to a fixed position on the axis. FIRST retrieves a value from the first element on the axis, while LAST retrieves a value from the last element on the axis. These functions are an easier-to-use version of the INDEX foundational function. The other functions in this group, LOOKUP and LOOKUPWITHTOTALS, allow you to retrieve values in the visual matrix by specifying filters, mimicking a very similar behavior of XLOOKUP in Excel.

- **Relative movement functions** These enable you to perform movements from the current position on the axis. PREVIOUS retrieves a value from a previous element on the axis, while NEXT retrieves a value from a next element on the axis. For both these functions, you can determine how many steps to take along the axis. These functions are a shortcut for the OFFSET foundational function.

- **Lattice navigation functions** These enable you to navigate upward (COLLAPSE) or downward (EXPAND) within the hierarchy levels on the axes. Whereas COLLAPSE and EXPAND enable you to determine how many levels to move up or down on the axis, the special variants

COLLAPSEALL and EXPANDALL enable you to jump to the highest and lowest level on the axis, respectively.

- **Other functions**   These enable you to check whether a column is at the current level (ISATLEVEL) so you can return a different result for the subtotal and total. The RANGE function returns an interval of rows on the axis. RANGE is an easier-to-use version of the WINDOW foundational function.

Many of the visual calculations exclusive functions are easier-to-use versions of foundational or other functions that are available anywhere DAX can be used. When we discuss each function, we indicate which shortcut it provides.

Foundational and supportive functions

The foundational and supportive functions are not exclusively for use with visual calculations. They don't provide the *axis* or *reset* parameters. Instead, they share a common set of parameters, which include parameters that require the ORDERBY, PARTITIONBY, and MATCHBY functions. These special functions cannot be used on their own; rather, they support other functions.

How the remainder of this part is organized

The following chapters discuss supportive functions, foundational functions and visual calculations exclusive functions. For each function, we cite parameters and provide examples. We also include the equivalent measure (or calculated column) of sample visual calculations.

When building a house, you start at the bottom, placing pillars if needed before laying the foundation. Only then can you start building the floors. We follow the exact same approach—starting with the pillars formed by the supportive functions (discussed in Chapter 5) before continuing on to the foundation (Chapter 6), before finally making our way up to the floors and rooms of the house, where we discuss the visual calculations exclusive functions (discussed in Chapter 7).

If you aren't interested in learning about the supportive and foundational functions, you can simply skip those chapters. However, we do recommend that you at least peruse them so you have a grasp of what they do in case you need them down the line—for example, if you find yourself dealing with an advanced scenario in which the visual calculations exclusive functions do not provide enough flexibility. Having some understanding of these functions will also enable you to better appreciate the power and elegance of the visual calculations exclusive functions.

## CHAPTER 5

The pillars: supportive functions

Let's start at the pillars of our construction: the supportive functions. Like the foundational functions we discuss in Chapter 6, these functions are not exclusive to visual calculations and can be used anywhere you can use DAX. However, the functions in this group can't be used on their own. They must be used within other functions.

The available supportive functions are as follows:

- ORDERBY

- PARTITIONBY

- MATCHBY

These functions are used as inputs to specific foundational function parameters with the same name. That is, ORDERBY is used in the *orderBy* parameter, PARTITIONBY in the *partitionBy* parameter, and, you guessed it, MATCHBY in the *matchBy* parameter.

On their own, these functions provide no value. It's when you use them as parameters for other functions that they add value. Therefore, we do not provide a lot of examples in this chapter. Instead, to see examples of these functions in action, refer to the examples in Chapters 6 and 7.

ORDERBY

This function enables you to define the sorting order within each partition (defined with PARTITIONBY) of the relation or axis on which the function operates. For example, you might use it to order categories alphabetically or years in a descending order.

ORDERBY takes one or more expressions and optional accompanying ordering indicators. The expressions are scalar expressions and define what is used to sort, while the optional ordering indicators indicate how the expression is sorted.

The ordering indicator is specified per expression and can be set to either ASC (short for ascending) or DESC (short for descending). If you do not specify an ordering indicator, it's set to ascending. You can also specify 1 (or TRUE) or 0 (or FALSE) to set an ascending or descending order, respectively. In addition to ascending or descending order, you can use the ordering indicator to specify how to sort blank values. This is optional and accepts the following options:

- **BLANKS DEFAULT**   This is the default value. With this value, blank numerical values are ordered between zero and negative values, while blank string values are ordered before all strings, including empty strings.

- **BLANKS FIRST**   This ensures that blanks are always sorted at the top, regardless of the ascending or descending sort order specified in the ordering indicator.

- **BLANKS LAST**   This ensures that blanks are always sorted at the bottom, regardless of the ascending or descending sort order specified in the ordering indicator.

Because ORDERBY accepts multiple expressions, the following four equivalent statements sort the data in the partitions first by Year ascending, putting the blanks first, followed by Country descending, and leaving any blank values for Country to be sorted in the default manner:

```
ORDERBY ( [Year], BLANKS FIRST, [Country], DESC )
ORDERBY ( [Year], ASC BLANKS FIRST, [Country], DESC )
ORDERBY ( [Year], ASC BLANKS FIRST, [Country], DESC BLANKS DEFAULT )
ORDERBY ( [Year], BLANKS FIRST, [Country], DESC BLANKS DEFAULT )
```

Providing an ORDERBY value when calling a function is optional. If you do not specify anything, every column in the relation or on the axis that is not specified in PARTITIONBY or *reset* will be used to sort.

PARTITIONBY

PARTITIONBY indicates if and how you want to slice up the data in the relation or axis on which the foundational function operates. Because you do not have to define any slices, you do not have to specify PARTITIONBY in the foundational functions. If you do use PARTITIONBY, the data within each slice is sorted by the sort order defined in ORDERBY.

This function takes one or more column names to be used to divide the data into partitions. The columns need to be present in the relation or on the axis. You may also use the RELATED function to return a column name in a table related to the relation, but you cannot do so when using PARTITIONBY as part of a visual calculation. This is because, as noted in Chapter 3, "Visual calculations concepts," RELATED is a blocked function in visual calculations.

For example, the following statement divides the data in the relation or on the axis by CategoryName and SubCategoryName:

```
PARTITIONBY ( 'Product'[CategoryName], 'Product'[SubCategoryName] )
```

As a result, slices are created for every subcategory within each product category. Even if the same SubCategoryName is present in two product categories, they will be in different slices. If instead we had written PARTITIONBY ('Product'[SubCategoryName]), then any subcategories with the same name would have been in the same slice, even if they were part of different product categories.

If you specify a column in PARTITIONBY that is not present in the relation or on the axis, the foundational function will return an error. If you do not define any slices, then all data in the relation or on the axis is treated as one slice.

MATCHBY

The final supportive function, MATCHBY, enables you to instruct DAX on how to determine the current row. You can specify one or more column names. The same rules as for PARTITIONBY apply:

- The columns need to be present in the relation or on the axis on which the foundational function operates.

- You may use RELATED to refer to a column in a table related to the relation, but you can't do so when using MATCHBY as part of a visual calculation. This is because, as noted in Chapter 3, RELATED is a blocked function in visual calculations.

You use this function to help DAX determine the current row, which is most useful if you have data in the relation that does not include a key that can be used to uniquely identify each row. If multiple columns must be used to uniquely identify each row, then DAX might not be able to handle this. Even if the data that's in the relation can be uniquely identified using a value in the relation, there is no guarantee that it will stay the same after the context changes or data gets updated, in which case DAX might still require you to specify a value for MATCHBY. Therefore, we recommend that you specify MATCHBY whenever the data the foundational function operates over does not include a unique identifier for each row, even if DAX is not explicitly asking for your help by showing you an error message such as the following: "OFFSET's relation parameter may have duplicate rows, which isn't allowed."

If you specify MATCHBY, then the columns you provide, together with any columns you provide to PARTITIONBY, are used to identify each row. If you do not specify MATCHBY, and the columns in ORDERBY and PARTITIONBY cannot uniquely identify every row in the relation or axis, the foundational function will try to find the least number of additional columns required to uniquely identify the rows and append these to the ORDERBY value (even if you did not specify ORDERBY). If no such columns can be found, the preceding error message is returned, requiring you to specify MATCHBY

In summary

This chapter discussed the ORDERBY, PARTITIONBY, and MATCHBY supportive functions. These functions can only be used as part of other functions (which we will discuss in Chapters 6 and 7).

ORDERBY defines sorting within partitions created by PARTITIONBY. It accepts scalar expressions and optional ordering indicators such as ASC, DESC, BLANKS FIRST, and BLANKS LAST to customize sorting behavior. Specifying ORDERBY is optional, but if omitted, all unspecified columns are sorted automatically.

The PARTITIONBY function creates slices for each unique combination of specified column values. If a column is specified that is not in the relation or axis, an error is returned. When no slices are defined, all data is treated as one slice.

MATCHBY helps DAX identify the current row, especially when data lacks a unique identifier. This function is crucial when multiple columns are required to uniquely identify rows or when context changes or data updates make unique identification unreliable. If no unique identifier exists, DAX may append additional columns to ORDERBY to uniquely identify rows, or an error message will demand the use of MATCHBY. MATCHBY can work in conjunction with PARTITIONBY to ensure accurate identification.

These functions collectively provide robust tools for managing data relations within DAX, ensuring accurate slicing, row identification, and ordering for complex datasets.

In Chapter 6, we move up to the next level of functions: the foundational functions.

The foundation: foundational functions

Now that we have discussed the supportive functions, let's talk about the foundational ones. Even though these functions are available outside of visual calculations, we discuss them here because they were introduced as part of the work on the visual calculations feature and because visual calculations exclusive functions provide shortcuts to most of them. Available foundational functions are as follows:

- INDEX

- OFFSET

- WINDOW

- RANK

- ROWNUMBER

When not used in visual calculations, these foundational functions provide ways of achieving certain results that are difficult—sometimes prohibitively so—without them.

Foundational functions are not exclusive to visual calculations. You can use them wherever DAX is used, including calculated columns, measures, and, of course, visual calculations. They're used in visual calculations when you need a bit more flexibility than the visual calculations exclusive functions provide.

Signature and parameters

All foundational functions provide an easy-to-recognize signature:

```
X (
    …
    [, <relation> or <axis>]
    [, <orderBy>]
    [, <blanks>]
    [, <partitionBy>]
    [, <matchBy>]
    [, <reset>]
)
```

As you can see from this signature, apart from function-specific parameters, indicated by ..., all foundational functions provide the parameters shown in the following table.

Parameter	Definition	Required	Skippable
relation	A table expression that defines from which output a value is returned. When used in a visual calculation, also accepts an axis.	No	Yes
orderBy	Specifies how each partition on the relation or axis is sorted; accepts the ORDERBY function.	No	Yes
blanks	Defines how blank values are handled.	No	Yes
partitionBy	Specifies how the relation or axis is partitioned; accepts the PARTITIONBY function.	No	Yes
matchBy	Defines how to match data to identify unique rows; accepts the MATCHBY function.	No	Yes
reset	Dictates whether the calculation resets, and if so, how.	No	Yes

The *relation* parameter accepts an axis value as well as a table expression. If you specify *reset* (even if it's the default value of NONE), you can specify an axis value for *relation*, but you cannot specify anything else for *relation*, nor can you specify a value for *orderBy* or *partitionBy*. If you do not specify *reset*, then the values for *orderBy* and *partitionBy* are used.

Because of this, when using foundational functions in visual calculations, we recommend you specify an axis value for the *relation* parameter and use *reset* as needed to achieve your goals. If you use foundational functions anywhere else but in visual calculations, *axis* and *reset* are not available, so you must use *relation*, *orderBy*, *partitionBy*, and *matchBy*.

The *blanks* and *orderBy* parameters are the exceptions to these rules. You can always use them, regardless of whether you are using the foundational function in a visual calculation. In fact, they are also available on visual calculations exclusive functions.

Whether a parameter is required, the values each parameter accepts, and each parameter's default value are quite intricate, so let's look at these parameters in more detail.

The *relation* parameter

The *relation* parameter defines what will return the output. A table expression is expected here. This can be as simple as just the name of a table, such as Store, or a DAX statement that returns a table, such as ADDCOLUMNS or SUMMARIZECOLUMNS. Any columns specified in the *partitionBy* parameter must come from the *relation* parameter or from a related table.

If you're using a foundational function in a visual calculation, you should most often specify an axis reference for *relation* to determine the axis along which the calculation will traverse the visual matrix. For a detailed discussion on the *axis* parameter, refer to Chapter 3, "Visual calculations concepts." You can think of the axis reference as being mapped to the *relation* parameter. In addition to helping you understand how the foundational functions work, this can also be helpful if you need to convert from a visual calculations exclusive function to other DAX functions.

If you're using a foundational function in anything that is not a visual calculation, such as a measure, and you do not specify a *relation* parameter, then you must provide a value to the *orderBy* parameter. In addition, anything you provide to the *orderBy* and *partitionBy* parameters must be fully qualified. This means you must include the table name as well as the column name, such as `Store[Description]`. Also, any columns you specify for the two parameters must come from a single table.

If you do not specify the *relation* parameter, then it takes on a value that is dependent on what you provide in the *orderBy* and *partitionBy* parameters. To be exact, *relation* will be set to the result of the ALLSELECTED function applied to all columns in those parameters.

The *orderBy* parameter

This parameter specifies how you want each partition in the *relation* or *axis* parameter to be sorted. It only accepts the ORDERBY function. Partitions are defined by using either *partitionBy* or *reset*. If you do not specify *orderBy*, then you must specify *relation* if you're using the foundational function in anything but a visual calculation. In visual calculations, the *axis* parameter is used automatically.

The *orderBy* parameter defaults to ordering by every column that is in the *relation* or on the *axis* that is not specified in *partitionBy* or *reset*. See Chapter 5, "The pillars: supportive functions," for a more in-depth discussion of ORDERBY.

The *blanks* parameter

Use this parameter to specify how blank values on the axis should be ordered while the calculation traverses the axis (in a visual calculation) or the relation. This parameter is optional and takes the following values:

- **DEFAULT**   This is the default value. It indicates that blank numerical values are ordered between zero and negative values. For blank textual values, the blank values are ordered before all text values, including empty text values.

- **FIRST**   Blank values are always ordered at the beginning, regardless of ascending or descending sorting order.

- **LAST**   Blank values are always ordered at the end, regardless of ascending or descending sorting order.

This parameter does not sort anything in the values of the visual matrix, such as visual calculations or measures. Instead, it sorts the values of the fields on the axis used. If those values contain a blank value, then that blank value (and its corresponding row) will be sorted according to the setting in this parameter. As a result, a visual calculation that is sort-order dependent, such as a running sum calculation, will return a different value depending on where the blank value on the axis is sorted.

The *partitionBy* parameter

Use this parameter to divide the data on the relation or axis into slices. This parameter accepts only the PARTITIONBY function. For more details on this function, see Chapter 5. Each slice is sorted according to the *orderBy* setting, and then the calculation is performed within the slice. If you don't specify any value for *partitionBy* (or *reset*), then *relation* (or *axis*) is treated as a single slice.

We do not recommend using *partitionBy* in visual calculations. Instead, use *reset* because it's the easiest way of achieving the same result. After all, who doesn't like easy?

The *matchBy* parameter

This parameter specifies how to match data to identify the current row. It accepts only the MATCHBY function. For more on this function, see the "MATCHBY" section in Chapter 5. You use this parameter if you do not have anything that can uniquely identify the rows in your relation—for example, if you have a composite key.

Assuming you stick to using *axis* in visual calculations, you should not need to use *matchBy* in visual calculations because the *axis* always has unique identifiers.

If you do not specify *matchBy*, and the columns in *orderBy* and *partitionBy* cannot uniquely identify every row in the relation, the foundational function will try to find the least number of additional columns required to uniquely identify the rows and append these to the *orderBy* value (even if you did not specify *orderBy*). If no such columns can be found, an error is returned, requiring you to specify a value for *matchBy*.

The *reset* parameter

This parameter is available only for visual calculations. It dictates whether a calculation resets while it traverses the visual matrix. Refer to the section "Understanding reset" in Chapter 3 for more details.

The calculation is reset by dividing the data on the axis into slices, the same way *partitionBy* does. You cannot specify both *reset* and *partitionBy*. In fact, you can think of the *reset* parameter as being mapped to the *partitionBy* parameter. Keep in mind, however, that *reset* automatically includes parent levels and *partitionBy* does not. In addition to helping you understand how the foundational functions work, this can also be helpful if you need to convert from a visual calculations exclusive function to other DAX functions.

Now that you know all about the parameters of the foundational functions, let's look at each function in a bit more detail. Because this book is about visual calculations, we will be brief here.

INDEX

INDEX returns a row in an absolute position.

Visual calculations shortcut functions

FIRST, LAST

Signature

```
INDEX(
        <position>
        [, <relation> or <axis>]
        [, <orderBy>]
        [, <blanks>]
        [, <partitionBy>]
        [, <matchBy>]
        [, <reset>]
)
```

Parameters

In addition to the parameters shared with the other foundational functions, INDEX supports the use of a *position* parameter, which is its first parameter. The *position* parameter defines the absolute position on the relation or axis from which to obtain the data.

You can pass both negative and positive values to *position*. The first row is 1, the second row is 2, the last row is -1, the second-last row is -2, etc. As you might have noticed, FIRST is a shortcut to INDEX (1, …), and LAST is a shortcut to INDEX (-1, …).

If you specify a position that doesn't exist on the partition, or if you specify 0 or BLANK(), then INDEX will return an empty table.

> **Note** You don't need to provide an actual number. Any DAX expression that returns a scalar value is valid.

Examples

Let's write a measure that uses INDEX to retrieve the sales for each year's final month:

```
Last Month in Year Sales =

CALCULATE (
    [Sales],
    INDEX ( -1,
        ALLSELECTED ( 'Date'[Year], 'Date'[MonthNumber] ),
```

```
        ORDERBY ( 'Date'[Year], ASC, 'Date'[MonthNumber], ASC ),
        PARTITIONBY ( 'Date'[Year] )
    )
)
```

The *Last Month in Year Sales* measure specifies Year and MonthNumber as the *relation* and divides it into slices by year (using PARTITIONBY). Then each slice is ordered by Year and MonthNumber in ascending order (using ORDERBY). Finally, the last row (notice the -1 value for the *position* parameter) within each ordered slice is retrieved, and the value of *Sales* for that row is calculated and returned. Figure 6-1 shows the slices and ordering. It also illustrates that the *Last Month in Year Sales* measure returns the expected results.

Year	MonthNumber	Sales	Last Month in Year Sales
2024	1	14,091,130.12	36,497,380.10
2024	2	18,652,745.19	36,497,380.10
2024	3	13,707,027.63	36,497,380.10
2024	4	13,617,953.40	36,497,380.10
2024	5	16,025,489.67	36,497,380.10
2024	6	15,987,048.83	36,497,380.10
2024	7	15,846,857.82	36,497,380.10
2024	8	9,561,371.47	36,497,380.10
2024	9	16,331,213.97	36,497,380.10
2024	10	20,374,371.26	36,497,380.10
2024	11	23,371,076.56	36,497,380.10
2024	12	36,497,380.10	36,497,380.10
2025	1	51,886,482.12	40,288,897.70
2025	2	64,923,153.55	40,288,897.70
2025	3	44,610,254.48	40,288,897.70
2025	4	43,794,064.91	40,288,897.70
2025	5	44,782,137.77	40,288,897.70
2025	6	39,376,967.87	40,288,897.70
2025	7	29,708,944.66	40,288,897.70
2025	8	16,054,829.64	40,288,897.70
2025	9	21,523,910.57	40,288,897.70
2025	10	25,471,590.22	40,288,897.70
2025	11	26,442,100.96	40,288,897.70
2025	12	40,288,897.70	40,288,897.70

FIGURE 6-1 *Last Month in Year Sales* returns the *Sales* for each Year's last month.

To return the first year in the Date table using a calculated column, you can write either of these equivalent statements using INDEX:

```
First Year =
INDEX ( 1, ALL ( 'Date'[Year] ) )

First Year2 =
INDEX ( 1, ORDERBY ( 'Date'[Year] ) )
```

Notice that the *First Year2* calculated column does not specify a relation. Instead, it relies on the fact that if not specified, the *relation* parameter will be set to the result of applying the ALLSELECTED function to all columns specified in the *orderBy* and *partitionBy* parameters.

 Note Although this example demonstrated this behavior in a calculated column, the behavior is the same in measures.

OFFSET

OFFSET returns a row in a relative position.

Visual calculations shortcut functions

PREVIOUS, NEXT

Signature

```
OFFSET (
        <delta>
        [, <relation> or <axis>]
        [, <orderBy>]
        [, <blanks>]
        [, <partitionBy>]
        [, <matchBy>]
        [, <reset>]
)
```

Parameters

In addition to the parameters shared with the other foundational functions, OFFSET supports the use of a *delta* parameter, which is its first parameter. This parameter specifies the relative position on the relation or axis from which to obtain the data. You can pass both negative and positive values to *delta*. The previous row is -1, the next row is 1, and so on. As you might have noticed, PREVIOUS is a shortcut to OFFSET (-1, …), and NEXT is a shortcut to OFFSET (1, …).

If you specify a delta that causes a relative movement that does not exist on the partition, or if you specify 0 or BLANK(), then OFFSET will not perform a relative movement, and the context is set to the current row.

> **Note** You don't need to provide an actual number. Any DAX expression that returns a scalar value is valid.

Examples

The Order Detail table contains information about orders and the lines on each order. Each order can have multiple lines because a customer might buy more than one product per order. Each product is captured on its own order line within the same order.

The following calculated column extends the Order Detail table and returns the previous sales for the same product, in descending order of sales. So, if the product was sold for a larger or equal amount in another order, then the column will return the value of the order in which that product was sold that is ranked just above the current order. In other words, it finds the amount for a previous order of the same product that was an equal or slightly greater amount.

This calculated column requires the use of MATCHBY. Without it, the columns used in it are not enough to uniquely identify the rows, and the following error is returned: "OFFSET's relation parameter may have duplicate rows. This is not allowed."

This is because the Order Detail table doesn't have a single key column because each order can have multiple order lines. To uniquely identify each row, you need to use both the unique identifier of the order (OrderKey) and the order line number (LineNumber). Power BI, however, does not support such composite keys. Even so, you can use MATCHBY as follows to tell DAX how to uniquely identify each row:

```
Previous Sales Amount Of Same Product =
CALCULATE (
    [Sales],
    OFFSET (
        -1,
        'Order Detail',
        ORDERBY ( 'Order Detail'[Total Sales], DESC ),
        PARTITIONBY ( 'Order Detail'[ProductKey] ),
        MATCHBY ( 'Order Detail'[OrderKey], 'Order Detail'[LineNumber] )
    )
)
```

Adding MATCHBY to this calculated column enables it to return the correct results, as shown in Figure 6-2.

ProductKey	OrderKey	Total Sales	Previous Sales Amount Of Same Product
552	20017	62,475.00	
552	4060042	44,982.00	62,475.00
552	4360209	39,984.00	44,982.00
552	7660815	37,485.00	39,984.00
552	7680046	37,485.00	37,485.00
552	7790836	37,485.00	37,485.00
552	8130491	37,485.00	37,485.00
552	3960788	34,986.00	37,485.00
552	4770040	34,986.00	34,986.00
552	4870047	34,986.00	34,986.00
552	5280325	34,986.00	34,986.00
552	1140035	31,237.50	34,986.00
552	2090177	31,237.50	31,237.50
552	2770060	29,988.00	31,237.50
552	4090265	29,988.00	29,988.00
552	4120080	29,988.00	29,988.00
552	5350348	29,988.00	29,988.00
552	5480366	29,988.00	29,988.00
552	6460063	29,988.00	29,988.00
552	7650100	29,988.00	29,988.00
552	7360097	26,239.50	29,988.00
552	7450250	26,239.50	26,239.50

FIGURE 6-2 *Previous Sales Amount of Same Product* returns the sales amount for the same product ordered by Total Sales descending.

Note The table in Figure 6-2 is filtered to show just one product to make it easier to see the results of the calculated column.

WINDOW

The WINDOW function returns multiple rows, which are positioned at a selectable absolute or relative interval.

Visual calculations shortcut functions

RUNNINGSUM, MOVINGAVERAGE, RANGE

Signature

```
WINDOW (
        from
        [, from_type]
        , to
        [, to_type]
        [, <relation> or <axis>]
        [, <orderBy>]
        [, <blanks>]
        [, <partitionBy>]
        [, <matchBy>]
        [, <reset>]
)
```

Parameters

In addition to the parameters shared with the other foundational functions, WINDOW accepts the parameters shown in the following table.

Parameter	Definition	Required	Skippable
from	Indicates where the window starts.	Yes	No
from_type	Specifies whether the window starts at a relative (REL) or absolute position (ABS); the default value is REL.	No	Yes
to	Specifies where the window ends; the last row is included in the window.	Yes	No
to_type	Specifies whether the window ends at a relative (REL) or absolute position (ABS); the default value is REL.	No	Yes

The *from* and *to* parameters indicate where the window starts and ends, respectively. If the corresponding _type parameter is REL, then a negative value provided for this parameter specifies the number of rows to go back from the current position to get the first (or last) row in the window. A positive value indicates the number of rows to move forward from the current row.

If the corresponding _type parameter is set to ABS, then the *from* and *to* parameters indicate the 1-based absolute position in the current partition of the start and end of the window, respectively. For example, 1 means the window starts (or ends) at the beginning of the partition. However, if from or to are negative, then these parameters indicate the position of the start (or end) of the window from the end of the partition, where -1 means the last row in the partition.

The following table summarizes the interaction of the *from*, *from_type*, *to*, and *to_type* parameters and the values provided:

| Parameter | Parameter value is | Matching_*type* parameter value | |
		ABS	REL (default)
from	Negative	Specifies the position of the start of the window from the end of the partition.	Specifies the number of rows to go back from the current position to find the start of the window.
	0	Specifies that the position of the start of the window is the first row in the partition (same as 1).	Specifies that the start of the window is the current row.
	Positive	Specifies the position of the start of the window from the start of the partition.	Specifies the number of rows to go forward from the current position to find the start of the window.
to	Negative	Specifies the position of the end of the window from the end of the partition.	Specifies the number of rows to go back from the current position to find the end of the window.
	0	Specifies that the position of the end of the window is the first row in the partition (same as 1).	Specifies that the end of the window is the current row.
	Negative	Specifies the position of the end of the window from the start of the partition.	Specifies the number of rows to go forward from the current position to find the end of window.

To understand how these parameters work, let's look at some basic examples:

- `WINDOW ( 1, ABS, 4, ABS, … )` This creates a window that starts at the beginning of the partition and stops after the fourth position on the partition. The window is four elements long.

- `WINDOW ( -1, REL, 0, REL, … )` This creates a window that starts at the previous position on the partition and stops after the current position on the partition. The window is a maximum of two elements long.

If you specify values where the end of the window falls before the start of the window, such as `WINDOW ( 0, REL, -1 REL, … )` or `WINDOW ( 4, ARS, 1, ABS, … )`, WINDOW will return an empty table.

Note You don't need to provide an actual number. Any DAX expression that returns a scalar value is valid.

Examples

The following measure defines a moving average starting a configurable number of months back and ending on the current month:

```
Moving average of Sales Measure WINDOW Configurable =
IF (
    ISBLANK ( [Sales] ),
    BLANK (),
    AVERAGEX (
        WINDOW (
            0 - [Number of Months in Window Value],
            REL,
            0,
            REL,
            ALLSELECTED ( 'Date'[Year], 'Date'[MonthNumber] )
        ),
        [Sales]
    )
)
```

As you can see, the WINDOW function's *from* parameter is calculated based on another value—in this case, *Number of Months in Window Value*. This could be anything, such as another measure or other logic you want to use. In this case, however, it's a numerical parameter. A slicer is provided on the page to configure this parameter, which in turn changes the results of the *Moving average of Sales Measure WINDOW Configurable* measure. We have also included an IF statement to check for blank values of *Sales* to avoid showing the moving average line for periods with no sales.

Figure 6-3 shows the result if the parameter is set to its default value of 3. Figure 6-4 shows the result if the parameter is set to 42. Notice how the smoothness of the line changes with the new parameter settings made through the slicer.

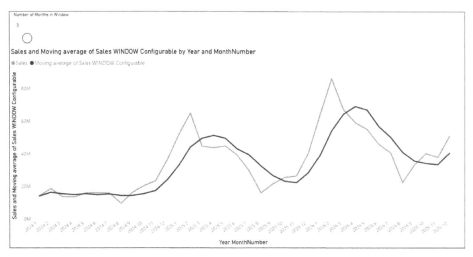

FIGURE 6-3 Using a low value for the parameter makes the moving average line follow the actuals more closely.

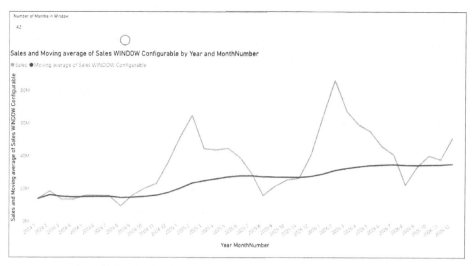

FIGURE 6-4 Using a high value for the parameter smooths out the moving average line.

RANK

Use this function to obtain a ranking of each row within a partition, sorted by the specified sort order. RANK returns a blank value for total rows when used in measures but returns a value on those rows when used in visual calculations.

Although its name is similar, RANK is not the column-based version of RANKX, like SUM is to SUMX. Rather, RANK is considered a window function instead because of relation-based calculations and partitioning. In contrast, RANKX is a function that expects a table and applies an expression to rank the rows in the table.

Visual calculations shortcut functions

None

Signature

```
RANK (
        [<ties>]
        [, <relation> or <axis>]
        [, <orderBy>]
        [, <blanks>]
        [, <partitionBy>]
        [, <matchBy>]
        [, <reset>]
)
```

Parameters

In addition to the parameters shared with the other foundational functions, RANK supports the use of an optional *ties* parameter. This parameter defaults to SKIP, which means that if two rows end up with the same rank, they will both be assigned the same rank and the next rank number will be skipped. Alternatively, you can specify DENSE, which means the next rank number will not be skipped.

Examples

For an example of RANK, see the section "Comparing RANK and ROWNUMBER" later in this chapter.

ROWNUMBER

Use this function to obtain a unique ranking of each row within a partition, sorted by the specified sort order. ROWNUMBER returns an error if it cannot uniquely identify each row.

Visual calculations shortcut functions

None

Signature

```
ROWNUMBER (
          [<relation> or <axis>]
          [, <orderBy>]
          [, <blanks>]
          [, <partitionBy>]
          [, <matchBy>]
          [, <reset>]
   )
```

Parameters

ROWNUMBER does not have special parameters other than the parameters shared with the other foundational functions.

Examples

For an example of ROWNUMBER, see the next section, "Comparing RANK and ROWNUMBER".

Comparing RANK and ROWNUMBER

RANK and ROWNUMBER are very similar because both are window functions. The difference lies in the fact that with ROWNUMBER, you can guarantee that the same number will never be assigned twice, and if it is, the function will return an error. RANK offers no such guarantee and will, like RANKX, assign the same number twice as necessary.

Let's look at a detailed example of these functions. For this, we define the following measures:

```
Rank by Birthday skip = RANK ( SKIP, ALLSELECTED ( 'Customer' ), ORDERBY
( 'Customer'[Birthday] ) )

Rank by Birthday dense = RANK ( DENSE, ALLSELECTED ( 'Customer' ), ORDERBY
( 'Customer'[Birthday] ) )

Rownumber by Birthday = ROWNUMBER ( ALLSELECTED ( 'Customer' ), ORDERBY
( 'Customer'[Birthday] ) )
```

Adding these measures to a table visual of unique identifiers for each customer (CustomerKey) and customer birthday (Birthday) returns the results shown in Figure 6-5.

As you can see in Figure 6-5, *Rownumber by Birthday* returns a unique number for each row, if each row can uniquely be identified. In this case, the relation allows that to happen because it contains CustomerKey, which is unique for each customer. The *matchBy* parameter for ROWNUMBER can be used to influence how rows are uniquely identified. In contrast, both *Rank by Birthday skip* and *Rank by Birthday dense* show repeating, although different, results.

CustomerKey	Birthday	Rank by Birthday skip	Rank by Birthday dense	Rownumber by Birthday
1204686	Sunday, February 03, 1935	1	1	1
1299282	Sunday, February 03, 1935	1	1	2
184766	Monday, February 04, 1935	3	2	3
1088286	Monday, February 04, 1935	3	2	4
1168084	Monday, February 04, 1935	3	2	5
1360870	Monday, February 04, 1935	3	2	6
1433548	Monday, February 04, 1935	3	2	7
1454207	Monday, February 04, 1935	3	2	8
1519673	Monday, February 04, 1935	3	2	9
1696179	Monday, February 04, 1935	3	2	10
279428	Tuesday, February 05, 1935	11	3	11
438712	Tuesday, February 05, 1935	11	3	12
835184	Tuesday, February 05, 1935	11	3	13
863912	Tuesday, February 05, 1935	11	3	14
1161057	Tuesday, February 05, 1935	11	3	15
1170676	Tuesday, February 05, 1935	11	3	16
1391337	Tuesday, February 05, 1935	11	3	17
1399102	Tuesday, February 05, 1935	11	3	18
1494926	Tuesday, February 05, 1935	11	3	19
1526766	Tuesday, February 05, 1935	11	3	20
241911	Wednesday, February 06, 1935	21	4	21

FIGURE 6-5 ROWNUMBER guarantees unique values, whereas RANK does not.

In summary

This chapter discussed the foundational functions, which serve as essential tools for achieving complex outcomes that might otherwise be highly challenging or even impossible. The foundational functions rely in no small part on the supportive functions discussed in Chapter 5. In addition to parameters matching the supportive functions, the foundational functions have a shared set of parameters that include *relation*, *blanks*, and *reset*. Together, these parameters offer a high degree of flexibility:

- The *relation* parameter provides the context in which calculations are performed.

- The *blanks* parameter determines how blank values are treated during calculations, which can significantly impact results in scenarios with missing data.

- The *reset* parameter defines how calculations are restarted, allowing for greater control over how values are segmented or grouped during computation.

The foundational functions are INDEX, OFFSET, WINDOW, RANK, and ROWNUMBER. Each of these functions offers unique capabilities:

- INDEX facilitates the retrieval of specific rows based on their absolute position within a table.

- OFFSET allows navigation across rows by specifying an offset relative to a given reference.

- WINDOW enables the aggregation of data within a defined range or window, supporting dynamic calculations.

- RANK provides a mechanism to rank rows based on specific criteria, making it easier to evaluate relative positions.

- ROWNUMBER assigns unique row numbers within a dataset, aiding in indexing and organization.

Although introduced as part of the visual calculations feature, these functions are versatile and not exclusive to visual calculations. They have broadened the scope of what DAX can achieve and can be utilized across a wide range of DAX contexts, including calculated columns, measures, and visual calculations. Within visual calculations, they are particularly useful when a higher degree of flexibility is required compared to the shortcuts offered by visual calculations exclusive functions, which we will discuss in Chapter 7, "The floors and rooms: visual calculations exclusive functions."

The floors and rooms: visual calculations exclusive functions

Congratulations! You've made it past the pillars and the foundation. Now let's start exploring the floors and rooms of the house: the visual calculations exclusive functions. These functions have been created specifically for visual calculations and rely on the *axis* parameter. For more information about the *axis* parameter, refer to Chapter 3, "Visual calculations concepts."

> **Note** The functions discussed in this chapter are exclusive to visual calculations and cannot be used elsewhere.

This chapter discusses the visual calculations exclusive functions and provides examples of each. It also shows equivalent measures. Because our goal is not to write a DAX book, we did not ensure that the measure equivalents provided work on all levels. They are equivalent on the detail level of data, but adapting them so they also return the correct results on subtotal and total levels is beyond the scope of this book, and the measures would be even more complicated than they appear in this chapter. Our goal in including the measure equivalents is to show you that visual calculations require less complicated DAX, and even the measures required to achieve the same results just on the detail level are complicated enough to achieve this goal. We've left it as an exercise for the so-inclined reader to expand these measures further so they return the correct values on the subtotal and total levels.

After discussing shared signatures and parameters, as well as skippable parameters, this chapter discusses each function in detail. For each function, we describe what the function does, what shortcut it provides to more complex DAX, and what a typical use case is. We also show what each function returns and what parameters it takes. Finally, we provide examples and the equivalent measures.

Signature and parameters

You can recognize visual calculations exclusive functions by their signature, which consists of the following, in addition to any function-specific parameters:

```
X ( <column> [, <axis>] [, <blanks>] [, <reset>] )
```

Many visual calculations exclusive functions also provide an *orderBy* parameter, but not all.

The *axis* parameter

Except for lattice-navigation functions, which require you to specify the *axis* parameter, this parameter is optional. It requires an axis reference and determines the axis along which the calculation will traverse the visual matrix, as discussed in the section "Understanding the *axis* parameter" in Chapter 3. You can think of the *axis* parameter as being mapped to the *relation* parameter on foundational functions. Keep this in mind if you ever need to convert from a visual calculations exclusive function to other DAX functions.

The *orderBy* parameter

This parameter specifies how you want each partition in the *axis* parameter to be sorted. It only accepts the ORDERBY function. Partitions are defined using *reset*. The *orderBy* parameter defaults to ordering by every column that is on the *axis*. See Chapter 5, "The pillars: supportive functions" for a more in-depth discussion of ORDERBY. Not all visual calculations exclusive functions provide this parameter; the parameter is available on the business functions (RUNNINGSUM, MOVINGAVERAGE), some of the absolute movement functions (FIRST, LAST), the relative movement functions (PREVIOUS, NEXT), and the RANGE function.

The *blanks* parameter

You use the *blanks* parameter to specify the order of blank values on the axis while the calculation traverses the axis. This parameter is optional and takes the following values:

- **DEFAULT**   This is the default value. It indicates that blank numerical values are ordered between zero and negative values. For blank textual values, the blank values are ordered before all text values, including empty text values.

- **FIRST**   With this value, blank values always appear at the beginning, regardless of ascending or descending sorting order.

- **LAST**   With this value, blank values are always ordered at the end, regardless of ascending or descending sorting order.

This parameter does not sort the values of the visual matrix, such as visual calculations or measures. Instead, it sorts the values of the fields on the axis used. If these include a blank value, that blank value (and its corresponding row) will be sorted as specified by this parameter. As a result, a visual calculation that is sort-order dependent, such as a running sum calculation, will return a different value depending on where the blank value on the axis is sorted.

The *reset* parameter

This optional parameter indicates whether a calculation resets as it traverses the visual matrix. Refer to Chapter 3 for more details. You can think of the *reset* parameter as being similar to the *partitionBy* parameter of foundational functions, the difference being that *reset* automatically includes parent levels, whereas *partitionBy* does not. Keep this in mind if you ever need to convert from a visual calculations exclusive function to other DAX functions.

Although these functions are easier to use, they are less flexible than their foundational counterparts. If you need more flexibility than these visual calculations exclusive functions provide, you can rewrite your visual calculation using DAX that, instead of using visual calculations exclusive functions, relies on other functions such as SUM, SUMX, or foundational functions such as INDEX, OFFSET, or WINDOW.

You will often need to use CALCULATE in combination with these other functions, which comes with an extra layer of complexity. Effectively, you're trading ease of use for flexibility. That is, visual calculations exclusive functions are easier to use but less flexible, while other functions are more flexible but can quickly become very complex. We recommend starting with the easier-to-use visual calculations exclusive functions and resorting to other functions only when needed.

Skippable parameters

With visual calculations exclusive functions, you don't need to specify optional parameters, even if you want to specify a value for a later parameter. In other words, these optional parameters are skippable.

This new DAX concept of skippable parameters was introduced with visual calculations. Skippable parameters allow for cleaner code because you can simply omit any unnecessary optional parameters. And unlike with DAX functions that do not support skippable parameters, you do not need to include empty commas (, , etc.). We hope that all DAX functions will support skippable parameters in the future because none of us like these empty commas.

For example, if you want to specify a value for *blanks*, which is the third optional parameter in the signature of most visual calculation functions, you could just write this:

```
X ( [Column], DEFAULT )
```

This does not specify any value for *axis* (which is the first optional parameter) or *orderBy* (the second optional parameter) and only specifies a value for the *blanks* parameter. This is equivalent to the following two visual calculations:

```
X ( [Column], , , DEFAULT )
X ( [Column], ROWS, ORDERBY(…), DEFAULT )
```

Business functions

The functions in this category are arguably the most exciting new functions that visual calculations provide. They offer an easy way to add common business calculations that are otherwise surprisingly hard to do in measures (as the measure equivalents for many of these functions will show).

RUNNINGSUM

As its name suggests, this function performs a running sum, also known as a running total calculation. Calculating a running sum simply means adding together all the values up to and including the current value. In addition to simply generating a running sum, RUNNINGSUM is often used for Pareto analysis.

For more information on Pareto and other uses of RUNNINGSUM, see Chapter 11, "Charting with visual calculations." Figure 7-1 provides a conceptual illustration of this function.

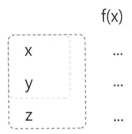

FIGURE 7-1 This is a conceptual illustration of RUNNINGSUM.

RUNNINGSUM provides an easier-to-use shortcut to the WINDOW function. Specifically, it's a shortcut to WINDOW (1, ABS, 0, REL, …). For more details on WINDOW see Chapter 6, "The foundation: foundational functions."

RUNNINGSUM returns the sum of all values in a column on the axis since the last time the calculation was reset, up to and including the current value. If no reset is defined, RUNNINGSUM starts at the top of the visual matrix and continues to the end, following the sort order.

Parameters

RUNNINGSUM takes the following parameters:

Parameter	Definition	Required	Skippable
column	Indicates the column to sum, which provides the value of each element.	Yes	No
axis	Specifies an axis, which determines how the calculation traverses the visual matrix.	No	Yes
orderBy	Specifies how each partition on the axis is sorted; accepts the ORDERBY function.	No	Yes
blanks	Defines how blank values are handled.	No	Yes
reset	Dictates whether the calculation resets, and if so, how.	No	Yes

Examples

Typically, users want to perform a running sum calculation over time, such as years and quarters. As an example, Figure 7-2 shows *Sales* for each Quarter in 2024.

You can add a running sum for *Sales* by Quarter by creating the following visual calculation for this chart:

```
Running sum of Sales = RUNNINGSUM ( [Sales] )
```

As shown in Figure 7-3, *Running sum of Sales* does precisely what you expect: it sums up the values for each quarter and keeps going until the end. Notice that the line never decreases; rather, it always increases with exactly the value of that quarter's sales.

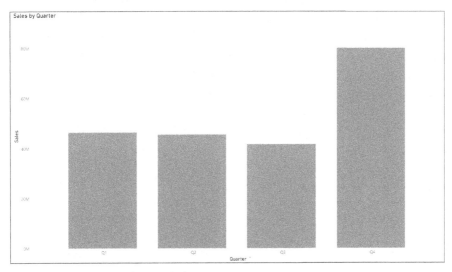

FIGURE 7-2 This example shows *Sales* by Quarter.

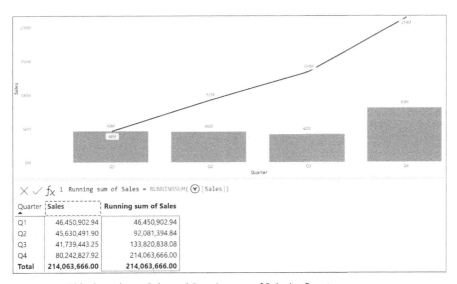

FIGURE 7-3 This chart shows *Sales* and *Running sum of Sales* by Quarter.

Notice the *Running sum of Sales* visual calculation does not refer explicitly to Quarter. This is because Quarter is on the rows axis of the visual matrix; because ROWS is the default value for the *axis* parameter for our example (because it's the first parameter in the visual shape), you don't need to specify it. In fact, this visual calculation is equivalent to

```
Running sum of Sales = RUNNINGSUM ( [Sales], ROWS )
```

This works great, but as soon as we add data for multiple years to the visual, *Running sum of Sales* keeps summing values across the years (see Figure 7-4).

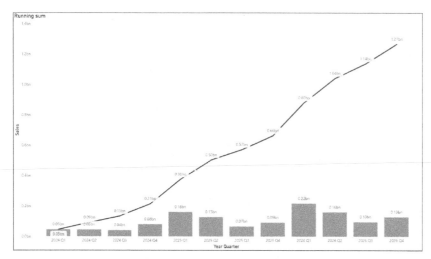

FIGURE 7-4 This chart shows *Sales* and *Running sum of Sales* by Year and Quarter.

If you show this to users, you most likely will see quite a few raised eyebrows. This is because people instinctively think about a running sum over time as occurring within one year and expect the running sum to restart for each year. In visual calculations, we call this behavior a reset, explained in detail in Chapter 3 in the section "Understanding *reset.*" By adjusting the *Running sum of Sales* visual calculation to leverage the *reset* parameter, you can obtain the desired result, as shown in the following expression. Figure 7-5 shows the result.

```
Running sum of Sales with Reset on Year = RUNNINGSUM ( [Sales], [Year] )
```

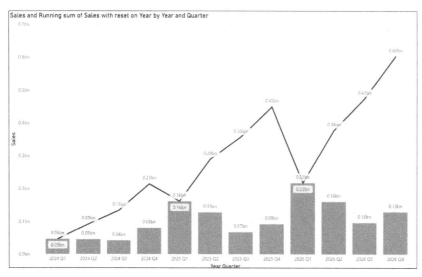

FIGURE 7-5 The chart shows *Sales* and *Running sum of Sales with Reset on Year* by Year and Quarter.

Interestingly, the *Running sum of Sales with Reset on Year* visual calculation is equivalent to this expression:

```
Running sum of Sales with Reset on HighestParent = RUNNINGSUM( [Sales],
HIGHESTPARENT )
```

It is also equivalent to the following:

```
Running sum of Sales with Reset on 1 = RUNNINGSUM( [Sales], 1 )
```

The reason these three statements are equivalent is because of the structure of the visual matrix. Year is the highest level on the rows axis of the visual matrix. Therefore, resetting on Year is the same as using HIGHESTPARENT (or its equivalent numerical value of 1) to reset on the highest parent field on the rows axis (see Figure 7-6). If Year were no longer the highest parent field on the rows axis, however, the preceding three DAX statements would no longer be equivalent.

Year	Quarter	Sales	Running sum of Sales	Running sum of Sales with Reset on Year	Running sum of Sales with Reset on 1	Running sum of Sales with Reset on Highestparent
2024	Q1	46,450,902.94	46,450,902.94	46,450,902.94	46,450,902.94	46,450,902.94
	Q2	45,630,491.90	92,081,394.84	92,081,394.84	92,081,394.84	92,081,394.84
	Q3	41,739,443.25	133,820,838.08	133,820,838.08	133,820,838.08	133,820,838.08
	Q4	80,242,827.92	214,063,666.00	214,063,666.00	214,063,666.00	214,063,666.00
	Total	214,063,666.00	214,063,666.00	214,063,666.00	214,063,666.00	214,063,666.00
2025	Q1	161,419,890.14	375,483,556.14	161,419,890.14	161,419,890.14	161,419,890.14
	Q2	127,953,170.55	503,436,726.69	289,373,060.69	289,373,060.69	289,373,060.69
	Q3	67,287,684.86	570,724,411.56	356,660,745.55	356,660,745.55	356,660,745.55
	Q4	92,202,588.87	662,927,000.43	448,863,334.43	448,863,334.43	448,863,334.43
	Total	448,863,334.43	662,927,000.43	448,863,334.43	448,863,334.43	448,863,334.43
2026	Q1	217,110,293.97	880,037,294.40	217,110,293.97	217,110,293.97	217,110,293.97
	Q2	160,281,816.38	1,040,319,110.78	377,392,110.35	377,392,110.35	377,392,110.35
	Q3	96,367,837.21	1,136,686,947.99	473,759,947.56	473,759,947.56	473,759,947.56
	Q4	129,141,342.40	1,265,828,290.39	602,901,289.96	602,901,289.96	602,901,289.96
	Total	602,901,289.96	1,265,828,290.39	602,901,289.96	602,901,289.96	602,901,289.96
Total		1,265,828,290.39	1,265,828,290.39	1,265,828,290.39	1,265,828,290.39	1,265,828,290.39

FIGURE 7-6 This is the visual matrix for the various running sum visual calculations.

Note Refer to Chapter 3 for more details on the visual matrix structure and how resetting visual calculations works.

You can also implement a running sum in a visual calculation using the WINDOW foundational function or other shared functions. For example, the following visual calculation is equivalent to the earlier *Running sum of Sales with Reset on Year* visual calculation:

```
Running sum of Sales Visual Calculation restart on Year WINDOW =
SUMX ( WINDOW ( 1, ABS, 0, REL, ROWS, HIGHESTPARENT ), [Sales] )
```

This visual calculation works as follows:

- The *axis* parameter for WINDOW is set to ROWS; therefore, we are operating over the rows in the visual matrix.

- The *from* and *from_type* parameters for WINDOW are set to 1 and ABS (short for absolute), respectively, which fixes the start of the window to the first element of the axis. Because *axis* is set to ROWS, this is the first row, and because *from_type* is set to ABS, this is a fixed position and will not move as the calculation traverses the axis.

- The *to* and *to_type* parameters for WINDOW are set to 0 and REL (short for relative), respectively. This ensures that the end of the window is always at the current element on the axis. Because *axis* is set to ROWS, the end of the window is always at the current row, including that row. If the calculation is calculated on the third row, the window spans from the first row up to and including the third row, and so on.

- The *reset* parameter is set to HIGHESTPARENT. This partitions the window into multiple slices— one for each distinct value of the column that is the HIGHESTPARENT on the ROWS axis, which is the Year column. Note that we could also have written [Year] or 1 here.

- WINDOW is passed as the table parameter to SUMX, which then evaluates the *Sales* measure for every row in the window and returns the sum of the results.

Measure equivalent

Of course, it's possible to write a running sum in a measure. In fact, there are multiple ways to achieve this. The first way shown here does not leverage foundational functions. The *Running sum of Sales Measure* measure that follows is equivalent to the previous *Running sum of Sales* visual calculation:

```
Running sum of Sales Measure =
CALCULATE (
    [Sales],
    FILTER (
        ALL ( 'Date' ),
        'Date'[Year] < MAX ( 'Date'[Year] )
            || (
                'Date'[Year] = MAX ( 'Date'[Year] )
                    && 'Date'[Quarter] <= MAX ( 'Date'[Quarter] )
            )
    )
)
```

To restart the *Running sum of Sales Measure* each year, you use the following:

```
Running sum of Sales Measure restart on Year =
CALCULATE (
    [Sales],
    FILTER (
        ALL ( 'Date' ),
        'Date'[Year] = MAX ( 'Date'[Year] )
            && 'Date'[Quarter] <= MAX ( 'Date'[Quarter] )
    )
)
```

Another way to achieve the same result is to use foundational window functions, which leverage WINDOW, as follows:

```
Running sum of Sales Measure restart on Year WINDOW =
SUMX (
    WINDOW (
        1,
```

```
        ABS,
        0,
        REL,
        ALLSELECTED ( 'Date'[Year], 'Date'[Quarter] ),
        PARTITIONBY ( 'Date'[Year] )
    ),
    [Sales]
)
```

In this measure, the *relation* parameter is set to all selected years and quarters. This relation is then divided into multiple slices, one for each distinct value of Year (as indicated using PARTITIONBY). The other parameters are the same as the ones you saw in the *Running sum of Sales Visual Calculation Restart on Year WINDOW* visual calculation example.

Looking back at that example, note that the *axis* parameter has been replaced by the corresponding relation; because Year and Quarter are on the rows axis, the equivalent relation is the selected years and quarters. The same goes for the value of the *reset* parameter in the *Running sum of Sales Visual Calculation restart on Year WINDOW* visual calculation; it's translated into the equivalent values for the *partitionBy* parameter. This is because a measure is unaware of the axes of the visual matrix it's operating on; thus you cannot use the *axis* and *reset* parameters in a measure. Instead, you use the *relation*, *orderBy*, and *partitionBy* parameters to achieve the same result—although in this case, we didn't need to use *orderBy*.

> **Note** The measure equivalents include explicit references to columns on which the calculation works. So, if the user changes the columns on the visual, the measure will return unexpected results and will have to be updated to reflect the changes.

MOVINGAVERAGE

As its name suggests, this function performs a moving average calculation. Calculating a moving average involves selecting a slice of the values on an axis and returning the average over that slice. MOVINGAVERAGE is most often used to calculate averages across periods. Figure 7-7 provides a conceptual illustration of this function.

$$f(x)$$

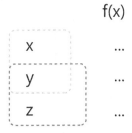

FIGURE 7-7 This is a conceptual illustration of MOVINGAVERAGE.

MOVINGAVERAGE provides an easier-to-use shortcut to the WINDOW function. Specifically, it's a shortcut to `WINDOW ( N, REL, M, REL, … )`, with N and M being the relative position where the window starts and ends, respectively. For more details on WINDOW see Chapter 6.

MOVINGAVERAGE returns the average of a configurable slice of values of the column on the axis since the last time the calculation was reset.

Parameters

MOVINGAVERAGE takes the following parameters:

Parameter	Definition	Required	Skippable
column	Indicates the column to average, which provides the value of each element.	Yes	No
windowSize	Specifies the number of values on the axis to average.	Yes	No
includeCurrent	A true/false parameter that specifies whether to include the current row in the values to average.	No	Yes
axis	Specifies an axis, which determines how the calculation traverses the visual matrix.	No	Yes
orderBy	Specifies how each partition on the axis is sorted; accepts the ORDERBY function.	No	Yes
blanks	Defines how blank values are handled.	No	Yes
reset	Dictates whether the calculation resets, and if so, how.	No	Yes

Examples

A common use for MOVINGAVERAGE is to calculate a moving average over a number of time periods. For example, in a visual that shows *Sales* by Year and Quarter, you can add a moving average over the last three quarters, including the current, in a visual calculation like this:

```
Moving average of Sales = MOVINGAVERAGE ( [Sales], 3 )
```

Figure 7-8 shows the resulting visual and its visual matrix.

As in the examples provided for RUNNINGSUM, you can reset the moving average. For example, you could use the *reset* parameter to calculate a moving average for only three quarters within a year instead of across years like so:

```
Moving average of Sales with reset by Year = MOVINGAVERAGE ( [Sales], 3, [Year] )
```

Figure 7-9 shows the result of this expression.

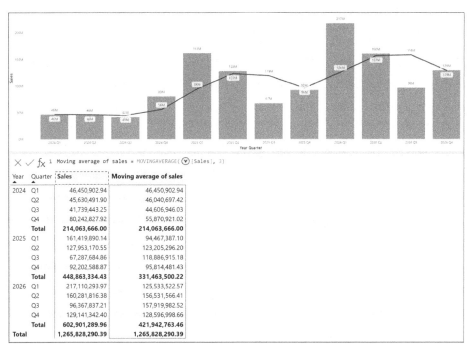

FIGURE 7-8 This is the visual and visual matrix for a simple moving average.

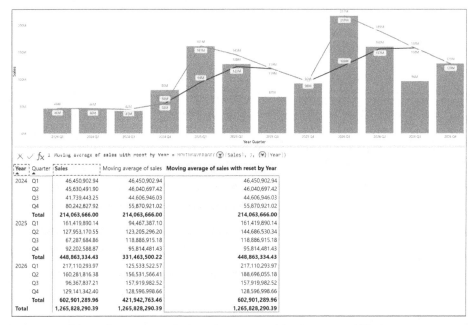

FIGURE 7-9 This moving average calculates the average of three quarters within the year.

> **Note** Relative *reset* references such as HIGHESTPARENT, LOWESTPARENT, and numerical values can also be used.

As before, you can implement a moving average in a visual calculation using the WINDOW foundational function or other foundational functions. For example, the following visual calculation is equivalent to the earlier *Moving average of Sales with Reset on Year* visual calculation:

```
Moving average of Sales Visual Calculation restart on Year WINDOW =
AVERAGEX ( WINDOW ( -2, REL, 0, REL, ROWS, HIGHESTPARENT ), [Sales] )
```

This visual calculation works as follows:

- The *axis* parameter for WINDOW is set to ROWS; therefore, we are operating over the rows in the visual matrix.

- The *from* and *from_type* parameters for WINDOW are set to -2 and REL (short for relative), respectively, which defines the start of the window as two elements earlier on the axis than the current position. Because *axis* is set to ROWS, the window will start two rows above the current row; because *from_type* is set to REL, the relative position will shift as the calculation traverses the axis.

- The *to* and *to_type* parameters to WINDOW are set to 0 and REL (short for relative), respectively. This ensures that the end of the window is always at the current element on the axis. Because *axis* is set to ROWS, the end of the window is always at the current row, including that row. If the calculation is calculated on the third row, the window spans from the first row up to and including the third row, and so on.

- The *reset* parameter is set to HIGHESTPARENT. This partitions the window into multiple slices—one for each distinct value of the column that is the HIGHESTPARENT on the ROWS axis, which is the Year column. Note that we could also have written [Year] or 1 here.

- WINDOW is passed as the table parameter to AVERAGEX, which then evaluates the *Sales* measure for every row in the window and returns the average of the results.

Measure equivalent

Of course, it's possible to write a moving average in a measure. In fact, as with RUNNINGSUM, there are multiple ways to achieve this. The first way shown here does not leverage foundational functions. The *Moving Average of Sales Measure* measure is equivalent to the previous *Moving average of Sales* visual calculation:

```
Moving Average of Sales Measure =
VAR QuartersInRange = 3
VAR LastQuarterRange =
    MAX ( 'Date'[YearQuarterNumber] )
```

```
VAR FirstQuarterRange = LastQuarterRange - QuartersInRange + 1
VAR PeriodQ =
    FILTER (
        ALL ( 'Date'[YearQuarterNumber] ),
        'Date'[YearQuarterNumber] >= FirstQuarterRange
            && 'Date'[YearQuarterNumber] <= LastQuarterRange
    )
VAR Result =
    CALCULATE (
        AVERAGEX ( PeriodQ, [Sales] ),
        REMOVEFILTERS ( 'Date' )
    )
RETURN
    Result
```

Another way to achieve the same result is to use foundational functions, in this case WINDOW:

```
Moving average of Sales Measure WINDOW =
AVERAGEX (
    WINDOW (
        -2,
        REL,
        0,
        REL,
        ALLSELECTED ( 'Date'[Year], 'Date'[Quarter] ),
    ),
    [Sales]
)
```

To implement the same calculation as the *Moving average of Sales with reset by Year* visual calculation in a measure using WINDOW, you'd use the following:

```
Moving average of Sales Measure restart on Year WINDOW =
AVERAGEX (
    WINDOW (
        -2,
        REL,
        0,
        REL,
        ALLSELECTED ( 'Date'[Year], 'Date'[Quarter] ),
        PARTITIONBY('Date'[Year] )
    ),
    [Sales]
)
```

Absolute movement functions

The functions in this category enable you to refer to the beginning or end of a visual matrix axis.

FIRST

FIRST retrieves a value from the first element on a specified axis. FIRST is often used to compare against a base period or entity—for example, against index years, baselines, or home markets. See Chapter 10, "Applied visual calculations," for an example of a benchmarking analysis using FIRST. Figure 7-10 provides a conceptual illustration of this function.

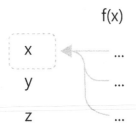

FIGURE 7-10 This is a conceptual illustration of FIRST.

FIRST retrieves the value of the column in the first element on the specified axis since the last time the calculation was reset and is an easier-to-use shortcut to the INDEX function with the *position* parameter set to 1, as follows: INDEX (1,…). For more details on INDEX see Chapter 6.

Parameters

FIRST takes the following parameters:

Parameter	Definition	Required	Skippable
column	Indicates the column to retrieve.	Yes	No
axis	Specifies an axis, which determines how the calculation traverses the visual matrix.	No	Yes
orderBy	Specifies how each partition on the axis is sorted; accepts the ORDERBY function.	No	Yes
blanks	Defines how blank values are handled.	No	Yes
reset	Dictates whether the calculation resets, and if so, how.	No	Yes

Examples

Let's start with a simple example of comparing sales by country and then comparing the sales for each store's country against the company's home market (Australia). First, create a visual that shows *Sales* by CountryName, sorted in ascending order by CountryName, as shown in Figure 7-11.

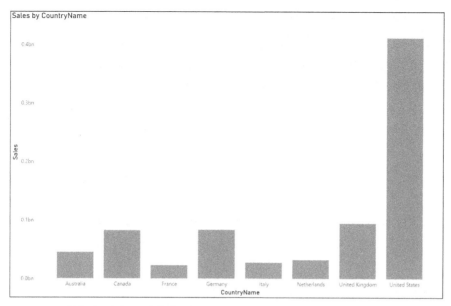

FIGURE 7-11 This visual shows *Sales* by CountryName.

Next, add a visual calculation that finds the sales for the first country on the rows (Australia):

```
Sales For First = FIRST ( [Sales] )
```

Now add a visual calculation that subtracts those sales for each country (*Sales For First*):

```
Vs First = [Sales] - [Sales For First]
```

Finally, hide the *Sales For First* visual calculation from the visual and show the *Sales* measure and the *Vs First* visual calculation, as shown in Figure 7-12.

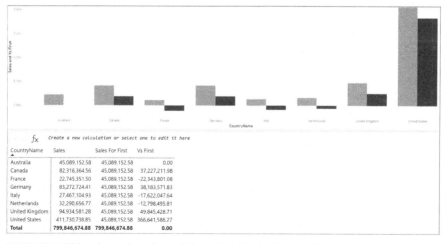

fx   Create a new calculation or select one to edit it here

CountryName	Sales	Sales For First	Vs First
Australia	45,089,152.58	45,089,152.58	0.00
Canada	82,316,364.56	45,089,152.58	37,227,211.98
France	22,745,351.50	45,089,152.58	-22,343,801.08
Germany	83,272,724.41	45,089,152.58	38,183,571.83
Italy	27,467,104.93	45,089,152.58	-17,622,047.64
Netherlands	32,290,656.77	45,089,152.58	-12,798,495.81
United Kingdom	94,934,581.28	45,089,152.58	49,845,428.71
United States	411,730,738.85	45,089,152.58	366,641,586.27
Total	**799,846,674.88**	**799,846,674.88**	**0.00**

FIGURE 7-12 This column chart shows *Sales* and *Vs First* by CountryName.

This shows the desired results, but you'd probably rather show a percentage comparison against the home country's sales. Let's add a final visual calculation to show that instead of the *Vs First* visual calculation:

```
% diff Sales of First = DIVIDE ( [Vs First], [Sales For First] )
```

After formatting the *% diff Sales of First* visual calculation and turning on data labels, the chart appears as shown in Figure 7-13.

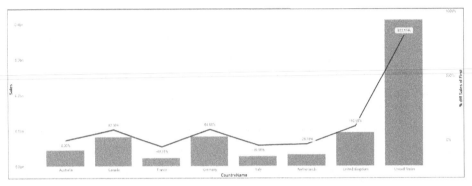

FIGURE 7-13 Now the chart shows *Sales* and *% diff Sales of First* by CountryName.

Because FIRST is a shortcut to INDEX, the following visual calculation returns the same result as *% diff Sales of First*:

```
% diff Sales of First INDEX =
VAR SalesForFirst =
    MAXX ( INDEX ( 1, ROWS ), [Sales] )
RETURN
    DIVIDE ( [Sales] - SalesForFirst, SalesForFirst )
```

Note We used MAXX here, but we could have used a different aggregation function like SUMX or MINX to get the same result.

This worked out well because we sorted the visual to match the visual matrix. So, the country we compared against happened to be first in the visual matrix and on the visual. If this is not the case, then you'll need to rely on other methods to achieve this.

Measure equivalent

Obtaining the exact same behavior as a visual calculation in a measure is difficult. The easiest way to get somewhat close to what the *% of Sales of First* visual calculation does is to create a measure that compares sales for a country against Australia, like this:

```
Sales Difference vs Australia =
VAR SalesInAustralia =
    CALCULATE ( [Sales], 'Store'[CountryName] = "Australia" )
RETURN
    DIVIDE ( [Sales] - SalesInAustralia, SalesInAustralia )
```

This approach works, but it's not quite as flexible as the visual calculation because Australia is part of the measure definition. To make this more flexible, you could take advantage of the fact that FIRST is a shortcut to INDEX(1, …) and write the following measure:

```
Sales Difference vs First Measure =
VAR SalesForFirst =
    CALCULATE (
        [Sales],
        INDEX (
            1,
            ALLSELECTED ( 'Store'[CountryName] ),
            ORDERBY ( 'Store'[CountryName] )
        )
    )
RETURN
    DIVIDE ( [Sales] - SalesForFirst, SalesForFirst )
```

LAST

LAST retrieves a value from the last element on a specified axis. It is the reverse of FIRST. LAST is often used to compare against the most recent entry—for example, against the previous month's sales to spot trends in sales. Figure 7-14 provides a conceptual illustration of this function.

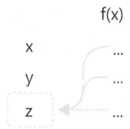

FIGURE 7-14 This conceptual illustration shows LAST.

LAST retrieves the value of the column in the last element on the specified axis since the last time the calculation was reset and is an easier-to-use shortcut to the INDEX function with the *position* parameter set to -1, as follows: INDEX (-1,…). For more details on INDEX see Chapter 6.

Parameters

LAST takes the following parameters:

Parameter	Definition	Required	Skippable
column	Indicates the column to retrieve.	Yes	No
axis	Specifies an axis, which determines how the calculation traverses the visual matrix.	No	Yes
orderBy	Specifies how each partition on the axis is sorted; accepts the ORDERBY function.	No	Yes
blanks	Defines how blank values are handled.	No	Yes
reset	Dictates whether the calculation resets, and if so, how.	No	Yes

Examples

Because LAST is the reverse of FIRST, we will not repeat the same examples. But we will show you what happens if you use *reset* while using LAST (or FIRST for that matter). We will also use the columns axis here, just to demonstrate that the same principles that apply to the rows axis apply to this one.

For this example, suppose you need to calculate the difference in sales per store country for each product subcategory against the last product subcategory in the same product category. You have decided to visualize this using a matrix and to put the product category and subcategory on the columns. You can use the LAST function in a visual calculation and set the *reset* parameter to CategoryName as follows:

```
Sales For Last in group = LAST ( [Sales], COLUMNS, [CategoryName] )
```

Figure 7-15 shows the result. Notice that *Sales For Last in group* indeed returns the *Sales* value for the last product subcategory in each category instead of the *Sales* value for the last subcategory across all categories.

FIGURE 7-15 This visual matrix is for *Sales For Last in group*.

> **Note** You could have written HIGHESTPARENT or 1 instead of the direct reference to CategoryName to make this visual calculation more resilient to changes.

Following the previous example, you can calculate the percentage difference in sales for each product subcategory against the last product in the same product category as follows using three visual calculations:

```
Sales For Last in group = LAST ( [Sales], COLUMNS, [CategoryName] )

Vs Last in group = [Sales] - [Sales For Last in group]

% diff Sales of Last in group = DIVIDE ( [Vs Last in group], [Sales For Last in group] )
```

Figure 7-16 shows the result.

Last							
CategoryName	Audio						
SubCategoryName	Bluetooth Headphones		MP4&MP3		Recording Pen		
CountryName	Sales	% diff Sales of Last in group	Sales	% diff Sales of Last in group	Sales	% diff Sales of Last in group	
Australia	535,292.86	13.67%	223,904.27	-52.45%	470,907.55	0.00%	
Canada	915,858.16	4.70%	406,932.53	-53.48%	874,781.47	0.00%	
France	257,757.06	10.59%	108,193.00	-53.58%	233,066.00	0.00%	
Germany	897,773.22	-3.44%	390,757.98	-57.97%	929,724.38	0.00%	
Italy	348,424.63	5.37%	130,639.47	-60.49%	330,666.72	0.00%	
Netherlands	361,205.63	6.97%	157,279.96	-53.42%	337,674.82	0.00%	
United Kingdom	1,109,686.66	-2.93%	437,201.40	-61.76%	1,143,168.20	0.00%	
United States	4,867,124.61	3.17%	1,860,762.32	-60.55%	4,717,357.25	0.00%	
Total	**9,293,122.83**	**2.83%**	**3,715,670.94**	**-58.89%**	**9,037,346.38**	**0.00%**	

FIGURE 7-16 This matrix shows *Sales* and *% diff Sales of Last in group* by CategoryName and SubCategoryName.

Of course, you could have done all of this in one visual calculation using the LAST function, or you could have used the fact that LAST is a shortcut to INDEX (-1, …) to your advantage. Just keep in mind that we used the columns axis in the visual calculation, so to get the same result, you need to specify that same axis here as well:

```
% diff Sales of Last in group INDEX =
VAR SalesForLastInGroup =
    SUMX ( INDEX ( -1, COLUMNS, PARTITIONBY ( [CategoryName] ) ), [Sales] )
RETURN
    DIVIDE ( [Sales] - SalesForLastInGroup, SalesForLastInGroup )
```

Measure equivalent

Again, because LAST is so much like FIRST, we will not repeat ourselves here. However, we will demonstrate how to write the *% diff Sales of Last in group* visual calculation in a measure, again keeping in mind that LAST is a shortcut to INDEX(-1, …):

```
Sales Difference vs Last in group Measure =
VAR SalesForLastInGroup =
    CALCULATE (
        [Sales],
        INDEX (
            -1,
            ALLSELECTED ( 'Product'[CategoryName], 'Product'[SubCategoryName] ),
            PARTITIONBY ( 'Product'[CategoryName] )
        )
```

```
    )
RETURN
    DIVIDE ( [Sales] - SalesForLastInGroup, SalesForLastInGroup )
```

 Note Because the *axis* and *reset* parameters are not available to measures, you must use the *relation*, *orderBy* and *partitionBy* parameters to achieve the same results.

LOOKUP

LOOKUP evaluates an expression with a value from a cell in the visual matrix that you identify using filters. Anything that is not specified is inferred from the context. LOOKUP is often used to compare against a specific value in the visual matrix—for example, against a company's home market's sales. Chapter 10 and Chapter 11 show more uses for LOOKUP, including creating a correlation matrix. Figure 7-17 provides a conceptual illustration of this function.

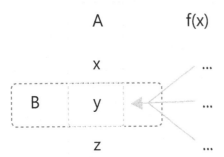

FIGURE 7-17 This is a conceptual illustration of LOOKUP.

LOOKUP returns the value of the expression provided at the "coordinates" you specify as filters for columns after filters and context have been applied. If no single value can be determined, an error is returned.

Parameters

LOOKUP takes the parameters shown in the following table. Notice that you can specify more than one column reference and expression pair for the filters.

Parameter	Definition	Required	Skippable
expression	Indicates the expression to evaluate.	Yes	No
colref	The column to be filtered. You can have multiple *colref / expression* pairs.	No	N/A
expression	The value to filter in the column. This is always paired to a *colref*.	No	N/A

Examples

Suppose you need to calculate the difference in sales for each store country versus a specific country. For our example, we picked the Netherlands as the country to compare against, but it could have been any country where there are stores. You can use the LOOKUP function in a visual calculation to retrieve the total sales for the Netherlands:

```
Sales NL = LOOKUP ( [Sales], [CountryName], "Netherlands" )
```

You can then use the result of *Sales NL* in more visual calculations to first determine the difference in sales between each country and the Netherlands and then determine the percentage difference between each country and the Netherlands:

```
Vs NL = [Sales] - [Sales NL]
```

```
% diff Sales NL = DIVIDE ( [Vs NL], [Sales NL] )
```

Figure 7-18 shows the results. Notice that *Sales NL* indeed returns the *Sales* value for the Netherlands per Brand.

| Brand | Adventure Works | | | | Contoso | | | |
CountryName	Sales	Sales NL	Vs NL	% diff Sales NL	Sales	Sales NL	Vs NL	% diff Sales NL
Australia	9,888,787.65	7,074,961.75	2,813,825.89	39.77%	7,907,575.54	5,485,446.46	2,422,129.08	44.16%
Canada	18,382,738.31	7,074,961.75	11,307,776.56	159.83%	13,870,521.94	5,485,446.46	8,385,075.47	152.86%
France	4,808,654.56	7,074,961.75	-2,266,307.20	-32.03%	3,906,521.10	5,485,446.46	-1,578,925.36	-28.78%
Germany	17,720,246.09	7,074,961.75	10,645,284.33	150.46%	14,315,225.60	5,485,446.46	8,829,779.14	160.97%
Italy	6,279,608.26	7,074,961.75	-795,353.49	-11.24%	4,354,268.65	5,485,446.46	-1,131,177.81	-20.62%
Netherlands	7,074,961.75	7,074,961.75	0.00	0.00%	5,485,446.46	5,485,446.46	0.00	0.00%
United Kingdom	21,305,634.75	7,074,961.75	14,230,673.00	201.14%	15,581,992.16	5,485,446.46	10,096,545.70	184.06%
United States	92,889,800.65	7,074,961.75	85,814,838.89	1212.94%	68,401,985.14	5,485,446.46	62,916,538.68	1146.97%
Total	**178,350,432.02**	**7,074,961.75**	**171,275,470.27**	**2420.87%**	**133,823,536.60**	**5,485,446.46**	**128,338,090.13**	**2339.61%**

FIGURE 7-18 This is the visual matrix for *Sales NL*, *Vs NL*, and *% diff Sales NL*.

The *Sales NL* visual calculation returns the sales for the Netherlands for each Brand because LOOKUP uses the current context to infer any filters you didn't specify. In this case, the *Sales NL* visual calculation did not specify any filter for Brand, so the current **Brand** in context is used, resulting in the results shown in Figure 7-18.

If, instead, you needed to compare the Sales for each Brand and Country against the Sales for the Contoso Brand in the Netherlands, you can simply add another filter to LOOKUP to retrieve the desired results:

```
Sales Contoso NL = LOOKUP ( [Sales], [CountryName], "Netherlands", [Brand],
"Contoso" )
```

```
Vs NL Contoso = [Sales] - [Sales Contoso NL]
```

```
% diff Sales Contoso NL = DIVIDE ( [Vs NL Contoso], [Sales Contoso NL] )
```

The results of these visual calculations are shown in Figure 7-19.

| Brand | Adventure Works | | | | Contoso | | | |
CountryName	Sales	Sales Contoso NL	Vs NL Contoso	% diff Sales NL	Sales	Sales Contoso NL	Vs NL Contoso	% diff Sales NL
Australia	9,888,787.65	548544646.33%	4,403,341.18	0.40	7,907,575.54	548544646.33%	2,422,129.08	0.44
Canada	18,382,738.31	548544646.33%	12,897,291.85	1.60	13,870,521.94	548544646.33%	8,385,075.47	1.53
France	4,808,654.56	548544646.33%	-676,791.91	-0.32	3,906,521.10	548544646.33%	-1,578,925.36	-0.29
Germany	17,720,246.09	548544646.33%	12,234,799.62	1.50	14,315,225.60	548544646.33%	8,829,779.14	1.61
Italy	6,279,608.26	548544646.33%	794,161.80	-0.11	4,354,268.65	548544646.33%	-1,131,177.81	-0.21
Netherlands	7,074,961.75	548544646.33%	1,589,515.29	0.00	5,485,446.46	548544646.33%	0.00	0.00
United Kingdom	21,305,634.75	548544646.33%	15,820,188.29	2.01	15,581,992.16	548544646.33%	10,096,545.70	1.84
United States	92,889,800.65	548544646.33%	87,404,354.18	12.13	68,401,985.14	548544646.33%	62,916,538.68	11.47
Total	178,350,432.02	548544646.33%	172,864,985.56	24.21	133,823,536.60	548544646.33%	128,338,090.13	23.40

FIGURE 7-19 This is a comparison of the sales per brand and per country against the sales for Contoso in the Netherlands.

Note Even though the preceding examples did not show it, it's perfectly legal to write an expression instead of just a measure or field reference in the first parameter of LOOKUP.

Measure equivalent

Readers with prior experience with DAX may have noticed that the structure of LOOKUP is a lot like CALCULATE. Therefore, it's no surprise that the measure equivalents of the previous visual calculations follow a very similar pattern. Here is the measure equivalent of the visual calculations that calculate the percentage difference in sales against the Netherlands:

```
Sales Difference vs the Netherlands Measure =
VAR SalesInTheNetherlands =
    CALCULATE ( [Sales], 'Store'[CountryName] = "Netherlands" )
RETURN
    DIVIDE ( [Sales] - SalesInTheNetherlands, SalesInTheNetherlands )
```

Finally, here's the measure equivalent of the visual calculations that calculate the percentage difference in sales against the total sales for Contoso in the Netherlands:

```
Sales Difference vs Contoso the Netherlands Measure =
VAR SalesContosoInTheNetherlands =
    CALCULATE (
        [Sales],
        'Store'[CountryName] = "Netherlands",
        'Product'[Brand] = "Contoso"
    )
RETURN
    DIVIDE ( [Sales] - SalesContosoInTheNetherlands, SalesContosoInTheNetherlands )
```

LOOKUPWITHTOTALS

LOOKUPWITHTOTALS is very similar to LOOKUP, with one important difference: instead of using the context to infer any filter that is not specified like LOOKUP does, LOOKUPWITHTOTALS will, as the name implies, use the total for any filter that is not specified. LOOKUPWITHTOTALS can be used to compare against a subtotal or total level—for example, to compare a value against the total value within a group. Often, the same result can be retrieved using COLLAPSE and COLLAPSEALL. The difference is that LOOKUPWITHTOTALS relies on absolute navigation in the visual matrix and COL-LAPSE and COLLAPSEALL rely on relative navigation on the lattice. Chapter 11 also shows how to use LOOKUPWITHTOTALS to create a correlation matrix. Figure 7-20 provides a conceptual illustration of this function.

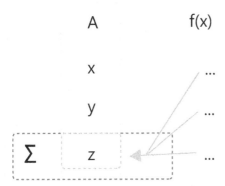

FIGURE 7-20 This conceptual illustration shows LOOKUPWITHTOTALS.

LOOKUPWITHTOTALS returns the value of the expression provided at the specified coordinates after filters have been applied. Any filter that is not specified is treated as referring to the total. If no single value can be determined, an error is returned.

Parameters

LOOKUPWITHTOTALS takes the same parameters as LOOKUP, shown in the following table. Notice that you can write more than one column reference and expression pair for the filters.

Parameter	Definition	Required	Skippable
expression	Indicates the expression to evaluate.	Yes	No
colref	The column to be filtered. You can have multiple *colref* / *expression* pairs.	No	N/A
expression	The value to filter in the column. This is always paired to a *colref*.	No	N/A

Examples

We will continue the examples of LOOKUP here to show the difference between LOOKUP and LOOKUPWITHTOTALS.

Instead of comparing against the current brand within context, as we did with the *% diff Sales NL* visual calculation, or a specific brand, as we did with the *% diff Sales Contoso NL* visual calculation, we will compare the sales per store country and brand against the sales for that store country for all brands. For that, we will add the following visual calculations:

```
Sales NL All Brands = LOOKUPWITHTOTALS ( [Sales], [CountryName], "Netherlands" )
```

Vs NL all Brands = [Sales] - [Sales NL All Brands]

% diff Sales NL all Brands = DIVIDE ([Vs NL for all Brands], [Sales NL All Brands])

Notice that the only real difference here, apart from the names of the visual calculations, is in the first visual calculation (*Sales NL All Brands*), which now uses LOOKUPWITHTOTALS instead of LOOKUP. The results of this are shown in Figure 7-21.

Brand	Adventure Works				Contoso			
CountryName	Sales	Sales NL All Brands	Vs NL all Brands	% diff Sales NL all Brands	Sales	Sales NL All Brands	Vs NL all Brands	% diff Sales NL all Brands
Australia	9,888,787.65	12,560,408.22	-2,671,620.57	-21.27%	7,907,575.54	12,560,408.22	-4,652,832.67	-37.04%
Canada	18,382,738.31	12,560,408.22	5,822,330.09	46.35%	13,870,521.94	12,560,408.22	1,310,113.72	10.43%
France	4,808,654.56	12,560,408.22	-7,751,753.66	-61.72%	3,906,521.10	12,560,408.22	-8,653,887.12	-68.90%
Germany	17,720,246.09	12,560,408.22	5,159,837.87	41.08%	14,315,225.60	12,560,408.22	1,754,817.38	13.97%
Italy	6,279,608.26	12,560,408.22	-6,280,799.96	-50.00%	4,354,268.65	12,560,408.22	-8,206,139.56	-65.33%
Netherlands	7,074,961.75	12,560,408.22	-5,485,446.46	-43.67%	5,485,446.46	12,560,408.22	-7,074,961.75	-56.33%
United Kingdom	21,305,634.75	12,560,408.22	8,745,226.54	69.63%	15,581,992.16	12,560,408.22	3,021,583.95	24.06%
United States	92,889,800.65	12,560,408.22	80,329,392.43	639.54%	68,401,985.14	12,560,408.22	55,841,576.92	444.58%
Total	**178,350,432.02**	**12,560,408.22**	**165,790,023.80**	**1319.94%**	**133,823,536.60**	**12,560,408.22**	**121,263,128.38**	**965.44%**

FIGURE 7-21 This is the visual matrix for *Sales NL All Brands*, *Vs NL All Brands*, and *% diff Sales NL all Brands*.

Notice that *Sales NL All Brands* is equivalent to a combined call to LOOKUP and COLLAPSE, as in this visual calculation:

Total Sales NL = COLLAPSE (LOOKUP ([Sales], [CountryName], "Netherlands"), COLUMNS)

We will discuss COLLAPSE later in this chapter.

For our final example of LOOKUPWITHTOTALS, we will compare the sales for each store country and brand to the total sales for all countries and brands. For this we create the following visual calculations:

Sales all Countries all Brands = LOOKUPWITHTOTALS ([Sales])

Vs total sales = [Sales] - [Sales all Countries all Brands]

% diff Sales of total = DIVIDE ([Vs total sales], [Sales all Countries all Brands])

Indeed, this does work, as Figure 7-22 shows.

Brand	Adventure Works				Contoso				Total
CountryName	Sales	Sales all Countries all Brands	Vs total sales	% diff Sales of total	Sales	Sales all Countries all Brands	Vs total sales	% diff Sales of total	Sales
Australia	9,888,787.65	312,173,968.62	-302,285,180.97	-0.97	7,907,575.54	312,173,968.62	-304,266,393.07	-0.97	17,796,363.19
Canada	18,382,738.31	312,173,968.62	-293,791,230.31	-0.94	13,870,521.94	312,173,968.62	-298,303,446.68	-0.96	32,253,260.25
France	4,808,654.56	312,173,968.62	-307,365,314.06	-0.98	3,906,521.10	312,173,968.62	-308,267,447.52	-0.99	8,715,175.66
Germany	17,720,246.09	312,173,968.62	-294,453,722.53	-0.94	14,315,225.60	312,173,968.62	-297,858,743.02	-0.95	32,035,471.69
Italy	6,279,608.26	312,173,968.62	-305,894,360.36	-0.98	4,354,268.65	312,173,968.62	-307,819,699.96	-0.99	10,633,876.92
Netherlands	7,074,961.75	312,173,968.62	-305,099,006.86	-0.98	5,485,446.46	312,173,968.62	-306,688,522.15	-0.98	12,560,408.22
United Kingdom	21,305,634.75	312,173,968.62	-290,868,333.86	-0.93	15,581,992.16	312,173,968.62	-296,591,976.45	-0.95	36,887,626.92
United States	92,889,800.65	312,173,968.62	-219,284,167.97	-0.70	68,401,985.14	312,173,968.62	-243,771,983.48	-0.78	161,291,785.79
Total	**178,350,432.02**	**312,173,968.62**	**-133,823,536.60**	**-0.43**	**133,823,536.60**	**312,173,968.62**	**-178,350,432.02**	**-0.57**	**312,173,968.62**

FIGURE 7-22 This compares sales by country and brand against the sales for all countries and brands.

Notice that the *Sales all Countries all Brands* visual calculation that uses LOOKUPWITHTOTALS is equivalent to a visual calculation that uses the COLLAPSEALL function, which we will discuss later in this chapter, where the *axis* parameter is set to COLUMNS ROWS:

Total Sales = COLLAPSEALL ([Sales], COLUMNS ROWS)

> **Note** Even though the preceding examples did not show it, it's perfectly legal to write an expression instead of just a measure or field reference in the first parameter to LOOKUPWITHTOTALS.

Measure equivalent

The measure equivalents for LOOKUPWITHTOTALS follow a similar pattern as the measure equivalents for LOOKUP. The main difference is that we omit any filters we do not want to specify and hence want to retrieve the total for all brands in the call to CALCULATE:

```
Sales Difference vs the Netherlands all Brands ALL Measure =
VAR SalesInTheNetherlandsAllBrands =
    CALCULATE (
        [Sales],
        'Store'[CountryName] = "Netherlands",
        ALL ( 'Product'[Brand] )
    )
RETURN
    DIVIDE (
        [Sales] - SalesInTheNetherlandsAllBrands,
        SalesInTheNetherlandsAllBrands
    )
```

Or, if you wanted to be explicit about it, you could also add ALLSELECTED in the call to CALCULATE:

```
Sales Difference vs the Netherlands all Brands ALLSELECTED Measure =
VAR SalesInTheNetherlandsAllBrands =
    CALCULATE (
        [Sales],
        'Store'[CountryName] = "Netherlands",
        ALLSELECTED ( 'Product'[Brand] )
    )
RETURN
    DIVIDE (
        [Sales] - SalesInTheNetherlandsAllBrands,
        SalesInTheNetherlandsAllBrands
    )
```

Notice that in the example pbix, a visual level filter has been set on the chart containing the LOOKUPWITHTOTALS example. Therefore, whether you specify ALLSELECTED or ALL does matter, as this measure will not return the exact same results in that visual:

```
Sales Difference vs the Netherlands all Brands ALL Measure =
VAR SalesInTheNetherlandsAllBrands =
    CALCULATE (
        [Sales],
        'Store'[CountryName] = "Netherlands",
        ALL ( 'Product'[Brand] )
    )
```

```
RETURN
    DIVIDE (
        [Sales] - SalesInTheNetherlandsAllBrands,
        SalesInTheNetherlandsAllBrands
    )
RETURN
    DIVIDE (
        [Sales] - SalesInTheNetherlandsAllBrands,
        SalesInTheNetherlandsAllBrands
    )
```

Relative movement functions

The functions in this category enable you to refer to positions on the axis of the visual matrix relative to the current position on that same axis.

PREVIOUS

PREVIOUS retrieves a value from a previous element on a specified axis. It's often used to compare periods, plants, products, or countries. Figure 7-23 provides a conceptual illustration of this function.

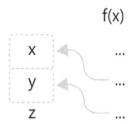

FIGURE 7-23 This is a conceptual illustration of PREVIOUS.

PREVIOUS retrieves the value of the column from an earlier element on the specified axis since the last time the calculation was reset. It is a shortcut to the OFFSET function with a negative value provided for the *delta* parameter. For example, PREVIOUS (..., 1, ...) is equivalent to OFFSET (-1, ...). PREVIOUS (..., 2, ...) is equivalent to OFFSET (-2, ...), and so on. For more details on OFFSET, see Chapter 6.

Parameters

PREVIOUS takes the following parameters:

Parameter	Definition	Required	Skippable
column	Indicates the column to retrieve.	Yes	No
steps	Specifies the number of steps back to take along the axis. Defaults to 1.	No	Yes
axis	Specifies an axis, which determines how the calculation traverses the visual matrix.	No	Yes
orderBy	Specifies how each partition on the axis is sorted; accepts the ORDERBY function.	No	Yes
blanks	Defines how blank values are handled.	No	Yes
reset	Dictates whether the calculation resets, and if so, how.	No	Yes

Examples

This example uses PREVIOUS to compare costs over quarters. Suppose you want to compare the costs for each quarter with the costs two quarters prior. First, create a table that shows costs by YearQuarter, as shown in Figure 7-24.

YearQuarter	Costs
Q1-2024	19,075,267.37
Q2-2024	18,825,129.28
Q3-2024	17,304,396.82
Q4-2024	33,331,701.81
Q1-2025	67,088,051.92
Q2-2025	53,178,817.88
Q3-2025	27,962,003.96
Q4-2025	38,280,784.63
Q1-2026	90,234,295.85
Q2-2026	66,436,947.38
Q3-2026	39,980,714.76
Q4-2026	53,437,053.82
Total	**525,135,165.47**

FIGURE 7-24 This table shows *Costs* by YearQuarter.

Next, create a visual calculation that calculates the difference between the costs for each quarter and the costs from two quarters ago as follows:

```
Versus previous = [Costs] - PREVIOUS ( [Costs], 2 )
```

Notice that the preceding expression specifies 2 as the value for the *steps* parameter to ensure that the comparison skips a quarter. Figure 7-25 shows the result.

Because PREVIOUS is a shortcut to OFFSET (-N, …), the following visual calculation is exactly the same as the *Versus previous* visual calculation:

```
Versus previous OFFSET = [Costs] - CALCULATE ( [Costs], OFFSET ( -2 ) )
```

> **Note**   Because the number of steps we provided to PREVIOUS was 2, and since PREVIOUS is a shortcut to OFFSET (-N, …), we provide -2 as the *delta* parameter for OFFSET.

YearQuarter	Costs	Versus previous
Q1-2024	19,075,267.37	19,075,267.37
Q2-2024	18,825,129.28	18,825,129.28
Q3-2024	17,304,396.82	-1,770,870.55
Q4-2024	33,331,701.81	14,506,572.52
Q1-2025	67,088,051.92	49,783,655.10
Q2-2025	53,178,817.88	19,847,116.07
Q3-2025	27,962,003.96	-39,126,047.96
Q4-2025	38,280,784.63	-14,898,033.24
Q1-2026	90,234,295.85	62,272,291.88
Q2-2026	66,436,947.38	28,156,162.75
Q3-2026	39,980,714.76	-50,253,581.09
Q4-2026	53,437,053.82	-12,999,893.56
Total	**525,135,165.47**	**525,135,165.47**

FIGURE 7-25 This result shows YearQuarter, *Costs*, and *Versus previous*.

Next, let's look at an example using the COLUMNS ROWS for the *axis* parameter. This axis enables you to write calculations that traverse over the visual matrix in a Z-like pattern, going over the columns first and then making its way down the rows. (Some people call this the typewriter movement, providing a more exact description of this pattern while also carbon-dating themselves at the same time.) The most common scenario we have seen for this is in a matrix visual with years on the rows and the quarter or month number on the columns, like the one in Figure 7-26, which shows costs.

Year	Q1	Q2	Q3	Q4	Total
2024	19,075,267.37	18,825,129.28	17,304,396.82	33,331,701.81	**88,536,495.27**
2025	67,088,051.92	53,178,817.88	27,962,003.96	38,280,784.63	**186,509,658.40**
2026	90,234,295.85	66,436,947.38	39,980,714.76	53,437,053.82	**250,089,011.81**
Total	**176,397,615.13**	**138,440,894.54**	**85,247,115.54**	**125,049,540.26**	**525,135,165.47**

FIGURE 7-26 This shows *Costs* by Quarter and Year.

In this scenario, if you want to calculate the difference between each quarter and the quarter before it, it's not enough to use the columns axis, like so, which returns the results shown in Figure 7-27.

(Notice that we're using an abbreviated name for the visual calculations in this section to improve readability of the figures.)

```
Vs prev cols = [Costs] - PREVIOUS ( [Costs], COLUMNS )
```

Quarter	Q1		Q2		Q3		Q4	
Year	Costs	Vs prev cols	Costs	Vs prev cols	Costs	Vs prev cols	Costs	Vs prev cols
2024	19,075,267.37	19,075,267.37	18,825,129.28	-250,138.08	17,304,396.82	-1,520,732.46	33,331,701.81	16,027,304.99
2025	67,088,051.92	67,088,051.92	53,178,817.88	-13,909,234.04	27,962,003.96	-25,216,813.91	38,280,784.63	10,318,780.67
2026	90,234,295.85	90,234,295.85	66,436,947.38	-23,797,348.46	39,980,714.76	-26,456,232.62	53,437,053.82	13,456,339.06

FIGURE 7-27 This matrix shows *Costs* and *Vs prev cols* by Quarter and Year.

This might look good at first glance. But notice that the result of the *Vs prev cols* calculation for Q1 2025 equals the value of *Costs* for that same quarter rather than showing the result of a comparison with the previous quarter. This is because there is no previous quarter in 2025 with which to compare the value for Q1 in that same year. To fix this, you need the calculation to reach across the year boundary, so that PREVIOUS returns the value for the previous quarter all the time, even for Q1. That way, the calculation for Q1 2025 would subtract the value from the previous quarter (Q4 2024) from the value of *Costs* in Q1 2025, and so on.

Specifying COLUMNS ROWS for the *axis* enables you to do exactly that. Here's our improved visual calculation, which returns the results shown in Figure 7-28:

```
Vs prev cols rows = [Costs] - PREVIOUS ( [Costs], COLUMNS ROWS )
```

Quarter	Q1		Q2		Q3		Q4	
Year	Costs	Vs prev cols rows	Costs	Vs prev cols rows	Costs	Vs prev cols rows	Costs	Vs prev cols rows
2024	19,075,267.37	19,075,267.37	18,825,129.28	-250,138.08	17,304,396.82	-1,520,732.46	33,331,701.81	16,027,304.99
2025	67,088,051.92	33,756,350.12	53,178,817.88	-13,909,234.04	27,962,003.96	-25,216,813.91	38,280,784.63	10,318,780.67
2026	90,234,295.85	51,953,511.21	66,436,947.38	-23,797,348.46	39,980,714.76	-26,456,232.62	53,437,053.82	13,456,339.06

FIGURE 7-28 This matrix shows *Costs* and *Vs prev cols rows* by Quarter and Year.

Measure equivalent

To perform the equivalent of the *Versus previous* visual calculation in a measure, you can leverage the fact that PREVIOUS is a shortcut to OFFSET (-N, …) as follows:

```
Costs Difference vs previous Measure =
VAR CostForPrevious =
    CALCULATE (
        [Costs],
        OFFSET (
            -2,
            ALLSELECTED ( 'Date'[YearQuarter], 'Date'[YearQuarterNumber] ),
            ORDERBY ( 'Date'[YearQuarterNumber] )
        )
    )
RETURN
    [Costs] - CostForPrevious
```

> **Note** We used ORDERBY here because the YearQuarter column is sorted by the YearQuarter-terNumber column. If you're doing time-based calculations, as we are doing here, you can also use the time intelligence functions built into DAX, such as DATEADD. However, this is beyond the scope of this book.

NEXT

NEXT retrieves a value from a next element on a specified axis. Similar to PREVIOUS, NEXT is often used to compare periods or other column values. Figure 7-29 provides a conceptual illustration of this function.

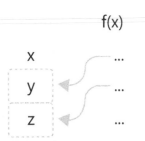

FIGURE 7-29 This is a conceptual illustration of NEXT.

NEXT retrieves the value of the column from a next element on the specified axis since the last time the calculation was reset. It's a shortcut to the OFFSET function with a positive value provided for the *delta* parameter. For example, NEXT (…, 1, …) is equivalent to OFFSET (1, …). NEXT (…, 2, …) is equivalent to OFFSET (2, …), and so on. For more details on OFFSET, see Chapter 6.

Parameters

NEXT takes the following parameters:

Parameter	Definition	Required	Skippable
column	Indicates the column to retrieve.	Yes	No
steps	Specifies the number of steps forward to take along the axis. Defaults to 1.	No	Yes
axis	Specifies an axis, which determines how the calculation traverses the visual matrix.	No	Yes
orderBy	Specifies how each partition on the axis is sorted; accepts the ORDERBY function.	No	Yes
blanks	Defines how blank values are handled.	No	Yes
reset	Dictates whether the calculation resets, and if so, how.	No	Yes

Examples

Because NEXT is so similar to PREVIOUS, we will skip the basic examples and show a more complex one: comparing manufacturers of our products. Specifically, we want to compare the average price for each manufacturer versus the next manufacturer on the list that manufactures products in the same category. To obtain the desired result, we will use NEXT with a reset, as follows:

```
Versus next in Category = [Average of Price] - NEXT ( [Average of Price],
HIGHESTPARENT )
```

The result of this visual calculation is indeed what we needed. Figure 7-30 shows the resulting visual matrix. This visual matrix also includes another visual calculation that does not reset:

```
Versus next = [Average of Price] - NEXT ( [Average of Price] )
```

CategoryName	Manufacturer	Average of Price	Versus next	Versus next in Category
Audio	Contoso, Ltd	146.06	75.72	75.72
	Northwind Traders	70.33	-96.05	-96.05
	Wide World Importers	166.38	-96.74	166.38
	Total	**135.88**	**-264.44**	**-264.44**
Cameras and camcorders	A. Datum Corporation	263.13	52.28	52.28
	Contoso, Ltd	210.85	-457.44	-457.44
	Fabrikam, Inc.	668.28	620.62	668.28
	Total	**400.32**	**225.45**	**225.45**
Cell phones	Contoso, Ltd	47.66	-238.51	-238.51
	The Phone Company	286.18	-223.77	286.18
	Total	**174.87**	**-156.83**	**-156.83**
Computers	Adventure Works	509.95	336.67	336.67
	Contoso, Ltd	173.27	-387.15	-387.15
	Fabrikam, Inc.	560.42	227.89	227.89
	Proseware, Inc.	332.54	267.51	267.51
	Southridge Video	65.02	-530.51	-530.51
	Wide World Importers	595.53	587.42	595.53
	Total	**331.70**	**289.17**	**289.17**
Games and Toys	Southridge Video	8.11	-39.68	-39.68
	Tailspin Toys	47.79	-298.44	47.79
	Total	**42.53**	**-495.27**	**495.27**

FIGURE 7-30 This visual matrix compares the average price by Manufacturer within the same category.

Like PREVIOUS, NEXT is a shortcut to OFFSET (N, …). This means you can create a visual calculation using OFFSET that does exactly the same thing as the *Versus next in Category* visual calculation:

```
Versus next in Category OFFSET =
[Average of Price]
    - CALCULATE ( [Average of Price], OFFSET ( 1, ROWS, HIGHESTPARENT ) )
```

Measure equivalent

As with PREVIOUS, to use NEXT to perform the equivalent of the *Versus next* visual calculation, you leverage the OFFSET function. Alternatively, you could avoid using OFFSET and write this monstrosity instead:

```
Average Product Price Difference versus next manufacturer Measure =
VAR _temp =
    ALLSELECTED ( 'Product'[Manufacturer] )
VAR _currentManufacturer =
    SELECTEDVALUE ( 'Product'[Manufacturer] )
VAR _nextManufacturer =
    TOPN (
        1,
        FILTER ( _temp, 'Product'[Manufacturer] > _currentManufacturer ),
        'Product'[Manufacturer], ASC
    )
RETURN
    CALCULATE (
        [Average Product Price],
        'Product'[Manufacturer] = _currentManufacturer
    )
        - CALCULATE (
            [Average Product Price],
            'Product'[Manufacturer] = _nextManufacturer
        )
```

This assumes you have already defined a simple measure to calculate the average product price:

```
Average Product Price = AVERAGE ( 'Product'[Price] )
```

In case this wasn't clear by now, we don't recommend you do this. Instead, we recommend using a visual calculation with NEXT, a visual calculation with OFFSET, or a measure with OFFSET, in that order of preference.

Lattice navigation functions

The lattice navigation functions get their name from their ability to navigate the fields on the axes on the visual matrix. Refer to Chapter 3 for an in-depth discussion of how the lattice is formed.

COLLAPSE and COLLAPSEALL

COLLAPSE and COLLAPSEALL navigate to a higher level in the lattice formed by the fields on the axes of the visual matrix. COLLAPSE takes extra parameters that specify how many levels to move or to which field to move; in contrast, COLLAPSEALL does not take extra parameters because it always moves to the highest level on the axis. Therefore, the *axis* parameter is required for COLLAPSEALL, but optional for COLLAPSE. COLLAPSE and COLLAPSEALL are most often used for percentage of parent, grandparent, and total calculations. Often, you can retrieve the same result using LOOKUPWITHTOTALS. The difference with LOOKUPWITHTOTALS is that COLLAPSE and COLLAPSEALL rely on relative navigation across the lattice, whereas LOOKUPWITHTOTALS uses absolute navigation on the visual matrix. Figure 7-31 provides a conceptual illustration of the COLLAPSE function.

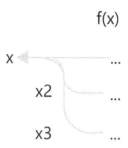

FIGURE 7-31 This is a conceptual illustration of COLLAPSE.

COLLAPSE and COLLAPSEALL either retrieve a value of the column from or return a context to a higher level in the lattice.

Parameters

COLLAPSE takes the parameters shown in the following table. Notice that even though none of these parameters are required, you need to specify the *expression* or *axis* or *column* parameter.

Parameter	Definition	Required	Skippable
expression	Specifies an expression to be evaluated after performing the navigation.	No*	Yes
axis	Specifies which axis of the visual matrix to navigate.	No*	Yes
columns	Identifies one or more columns to navigate to.	No*	Yes
n	The number of levels to navigate upward on the lattice.	No	Yes

* at least one of these parameters is required.

COLLAPSEALL takes these parameters:

Parameter	Definition	Required	Skippable
expression	Specifies an expression to be evaluated after performing the navigation.	No	Yes
axis	Specifies which axis of the visual matrix to navigate.	Yes	No

Examples

COLLAPSEALL takes fewer parameters, so we'll start there. In this example, we'll calculate a percentage of grand total sales by State. Each State is in a Country, which is in turn on a Continent (see Figure 7-32).

Continent	Sales
⊞ **Australia**	**74,986,599.07**
⊟ **Europe**	**408,952,943.30**
⊞ **DE**	**136,859,360.31**
⊞ **FR**	**37,472,316.91**
⊟ **GB**	**140,787,706.59**
⊞ **IT**	**40,149,175.04**
⊟ **NL**	**53,684,384.45**
DR	1,825,546.39
FL	1,350,663.71
FR	2,216,323.24
GE	6,987,467.68
GR	2,142,566.64
LI	3,493,731.19
NB	7,205,896.69
NH	8,412,893.46
OV	3,663,410.11
UT	3,932,669.73
ZE	1,941,521.56
ZH	10,511,694.05
⊞ **North America**	**781,888,748.03**
Total	**1,265,828,290.39**

FIGURE 7-32 This matrix shows *Sales* by State, Country, and Continent.

To calculate the percentage of grand total, you can write the following visual calculation:

```
Percent of grand total =
DIVIDE ( [Sales], COLLAPSEALL ( [Sales], ROWS ) )
```

Remember, COLLAPSEALL will navigate to the highest level of the lattice on the axis specified. So in this case, COLLAPSEALL ([Sales], ROWS) returns the grand total of *Sales* on the rows axis, which is 1,265,828,290.39. Now, it's easy to see that the result of the *Percent of grand total* visual calculation is simply dividing the value for *Sales* for each State, Country, and Continent by the grand total of *Sales*, as shown in Figure 7-33.

You could have achieved this exact same result with any of the following visual calculations:

```
Percent of parent 2 = DIVIDE ( [Sales], COLLAPSE ( [Sales], [Continent] ) )
```

```
Percent of parent 3 = DIVIDE ( [Sales], CALCULATE ( [Sales], COLLAPSE
( [Continent] ) ) )
```

```
Percent of parent 4 = DIVIDE ( [Sales], COLLAPSE ( [Sales], ROWS, 42 ) )
```

Continent	Sales	Percent of grand total
⊞ Australia	74,986,599.07	5.92%
⊟ Europe	408,952,943.30	32.31%
⊞ DE	136,859,360.31	10.81%
⊞ FR	37,472,316.91	2.96%
⊞ GB	140,787,706.59	11.12%
⊞ IT	40,149,175.04	3.17%
⊟ NL	53,684,384.45	4.24%
DR	1,825,546.39	0.14%
FL	1,350,663.71	0.11%
FR	2,216,323.24	0.18%
GE	6,987,467.68	0.55%
GR	2,142,566.64	0.17%
LI	3,493,731.19	0.28%
NB	7,205,896.69	0.57%
NH	8,412,893.46	0.66%
OV	3,663,410.11	0.29%
UT	3,932,669.73	0.31%
ZE	1,941,521.56	0.15%
ZH	10,511,694.05	0.83%
⊞ North America	781,888,748.03	61.77%
Total	1,265,828,290.39	100.00%

FIGURE 7-33 This matrix shows *Sales* and *Percent of grand total* by State, Country, and Continent.

All these visual calculations return the same result as the *Percent of grand total* visual calculation. Let's look at each one in more detail.

- **Percent of parent 2** This visual calculation specifies Continent as the column to collapse to. This enables you to collapse to a specific column, regardless of where it is on the lattice. DAX will automatically locate the Continent column on the axes of the visual matrix and collapse to the first table in the lattice that does not include Continent.

- **Percent of parent 3** This visual calculation uses a slightly different syntax, calling COLLAPSE without an expression. Because of this, COLLAPSE returns a context from the lattice that is collapsed to above the indicated column (Continent). This context is then used in a call to CALCULATE to evaluate *Sales* in that context, before finally dividing the current *Sales* by *Sales* calculated in the context COLLAPSE returns. Again, the results are the same. The only thing that's different is how we achieved the results.

- **Percent of parent 4** This visual calculation specifies both the axis on which to collapse and a number (in this case, 42). There is nothing special about the number 42 in DAX; DAX will automatically collapse to as many levels as there are on the axis or until it has performed the specified number of collapses, whichever comes first. Here, 42 is a high enough number that we can be confident there will be fewer levels on the axis, so effectively it's guaranteed to collapse all levels on the axis. In this situation, however, we could have replaced 42 with 3 and still have gotten the same result because 3 is the total number of levels on the specified axis.

If we replaced 42 with 2, though, we would have collapsed only two levels. Here's what that visual calculation would look like:

```
Percent of parent 5 = DIVIDE ( [Sales], COLLAPSE ( [Sales], ROWS, 2 ) )
```

In this example, on the state level, the calculation returns the percentage of sales on the continent level, and on the country and continent levels, the calculation still returns the same numbers as before (the sales as a percentage of the grand total sales). This is because there are no further levels on the axis to collapse (see Figure 7-34).

Continent	Sales	Percent of grand total	Percent of parent 5
⊞ **Australia**	**74,986,599.07**	**5.92%**	**5.92%**
⊟ **Europe**	**408,952,943.30**	**32.31%**	**32.31%**
⊞ **DE**	**136,859,360.31**	**10.81%**	**10.81%**
⊞ **FR**	**37,472,316.91**	**2.96%**	**2.96%**
⊞ **GB**	**140,787,706.59**	**11.12%**	**11.12%**
⊞ **IT**	**40,149,175.04**	**3.17%**	**3.17%**
⊟ **NL**	**53,684,384.45**	**4.24%**	**4.24%**
DR	1,825,546.39	0.14%	0.45%
FL	1,350,663.71	0.11%	0.33%
FR	2,216,323.24	0.18%	0.54%
GE	6,987,467.68	0.55%	1.71%
GR	2,142,566.64	0.17%	0.52%
LI	3,493,731.19	0.28%	0.85%
NB	7,205,896.69	0.57%	1.76%
NH	8,412,893.46	0.66%	2.06%
OV	3,663,410.11	0.29%	0.90%
UT	3,932,669.73	0.31%	0.96%
ZE	1,941,521.56	0.15%	0.47%
ZH	10,511,694.05	0.83%	2.57%
⊞ **North America**	**781,888,748.03**	**61.77%**	**61.77%**
Total	**1,265,828,290.39**	**100.00%**	**100.00%**

FIGURE 7-34 Collapsing two levels returns different results.

Finally, if you use COLLAPSEALL with the COLUMNS ROWS or ROWS COLUMNS for the *axis* parameter, you will get the grand total of the expression:

```
Grand total Sales = COLLAPSEALL ( [Sales], ROWS COLUMNS )
```

Indeed, the *Grand total Sales* visual calculation returns the grand total of *Sales*, as shown in Figure 7-35. In fact, because we're collapsing both axes, whether you specify ROWS COLUMNS or COLUMNS ROWS doesn't change the result; COLLAPSEALL will always return the grand total.

If you instead use COLLAPSE, you effectively collapse one level up on both axes:

```
Collapse both axes = COLLAPSE ( [Sales], ROWS COLUMNS )
```

Year	2024		2025		Total	
Continent	Sales	Grand total Sales	Sales	Grand total Sales	Sales	Grand total Sales
⊞ Australia	10,386,429.30	662,927,000.43	23,290,762.43	662,927,000.43	33,677,191.73	662,927,000.43
⊟ Europe	77,864,728.50	662,927,000.43	139,925,224.61	662,927,000.43	217,789,953.11	662,927,000.43
DE	19,715,064.98	662,927,000.43	42,676,870.00	662,927,000.43	62,391,934.99	662,927,000.43
FR	5,080,663.30	662,927,000.43	11,280,007.32	662,927,000.43	16,360,670.63	662,927,000.43
GB	35,466,497.54	662,927,000.43	53,228,633.46	662,927,000.43	88,695,130.99	662,927,000.43
IT	10,970,317.39	662,927,000.43	16,266,956.30	662,927,000.43	27,237,273.69	662,927,000.43
NL	6,632,185.28	662,927,000.43	16,472,757.53	662,927,000.43	23,104,942.81	662,927,000.43
⊞ North America	125,812,508.20	662,927,000.43	285,647,347.38	662,927,000.43	411,459,855.58	662,927,000.43
Total	214,063,666.00	662,927,000.43	448,863,334.43	662,927,000.43	662,927,000.43	662,927,000.43

FIGURE 7-35 Collapsing both axes completely returns the grand total.

Collapsing the columns axis up one level returns the sales for all years; collapsing the rows axis up one level returns the sales for each continent on the country level and the sales for all continents anywhere else. Therefore, the *Collapse both axes* visual calculation returns sales by continent and year, even when evaluated on the country level (see Figure 7-36.)

Year	2024		2025		Total	
Continent	Sales	Collapse both axes	Sales	Collapse both axes	Sales	Collapse both axes
⊞ Australia	10,386,429.30	662,927,000.43	23,290,762.43	662,927,000.43	33,677,191.73	662,927,000.43
⊟ Europe	77,864,728.50	662,927,000.43	139,925,224.61	662,927,000.43	217,789,953.11	662,927,000.43
DE	19,715,064.98	217,789,953.11	42,676,870.00	217,789,953.11	62,391,934.99	217,789,953.11
FR	5,080,663.30	217,789,953.11	11,280,007.32	217,789,953.11	16,360,670.63	217,789,953.11
GB	35,466,497.54	217,789,953.11	53,228,633.46	217,789,953.11	88,695,130.99	217,789,953.11
IT	10,970,317.39	217,789,953.11	16,266,956.30	217,789,953.11	27,237,273.69	217,789,953.11
NL	6,632,185.28	217,789,953.11	16,472,757.53	217,789,953.11	23,104,942.81	217,789,953.11
⊞ North America	125,812,508.20	662,927,000.43	285,647,347.38	662,927,000.43	411,459,855.58	662,927,000.43
Total	214,063,666.00	662,927,000.43	448,863,334.43	662,927,000.43	662,927,000.43	662,927,000.43

FIGURE 7-36 This matrix shows the result of collapsing on both axes.

Measure equivalent

The measure equivalent of the *Percent of grand total* visual calculation is as follows:

```
Percentage of Grand Total Sales Measure =
DIVIDE (
    [Sales],
    CALCULATE (
        [Sales], ALLSELECTED ( 'Customer' ), ALLSELECTED ( 'Date'[Year] )
    )
)
```

This measure is equivalent to the following one, which specifies the columns passed into ALLSELECTED. We slightly prefer this version because it's more explicit about what it's doing, but the results are the same in the visual:

```
Percentage of Grand Total Sales Measure 2 =
DIVIDE (
    [Sales],
    CALCULATE (
        [Sales],
```

```
        ALLSELECTED ( 'Customer'[Continent], 'Customer'[Country], 'Customer'[State] ),
        ALLSELECTED ( 'Date'[Year] )
    )
)
```

EXPAND and EXPANDALL

EXPAND and EXPANDALL navigate to a lower level in the lattice formed by the fields on the axes of the visual matrix. EXPAND takes extra parameters that specify how many levels to move or to which field to move. In contrast, EXPANDALL always moves down to the lowest level (leaf level) on the axis and doesn't take these parameters. Therefore, the *axis* parameter is required for EXPANDALL but is optional for EXPAND. EXPAND and EXPANDALL are most often used for aggregated descendant averages, such as average of direct descendants (children), or descendants of descendants (grandchildren), or other types of descendant calculations. Figure 7-37 provides a conceptual illustration of the EXPAND function.

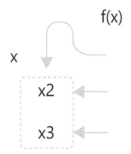

FIGURE 7-37 This is a conceptual illustration of EXPAND.

EXPAND and EXPANDALL either retrieve a value of the column from or return a context to a lower level in the lattice.

Parameters

EXPAND takes the parameters shown in the following table. Notice that even though none of these parameters are required, you need to either specify the *expression* or *axis* or *column* parameter.

Parameter	Definition	Required	Skippable
expression	Specifies an expression to be evaluated after performing the navigation.	No*	Yes
axis	Specifies which axis of the visual matrix to navigate.	No*	Yes
columns	Identifies one or more columns to navigate to.	No*	Yes
n	The number of levels to navigate downward on the lattice.	No	Yes

* at least one of these parameters is required.

EXPANDALL takes these parameters:

Parameter	Definition	Required	Skippable
expression	Specifies an expression to be evaluated after performing the navigation.	No	Yes
axis	Specifies which axis of the visual matrix to navigate.	Yes	No

Examples

Because EXPAND and EXPANDALL are effectively the reverse of COLLAPSE and COLLAPSEALL, we will not repeat the same basic examples here. Instead, we will focus on examples we have not shown previously, using EXPAND (or for that matter, COLLAPSE) with multiple columns and how different axis types influence the results.

The most common use of EXPAND is to calculate an average of children, so let's start there. The following visual calculation calculates the average sales for each level's children along the rows axis and returns the results shown in Figure 7-38:

```
Average of children = EXPAND ( AVERAGE ( [Sales] ), ROWS )
```

Continent	Sales	Average of children
⊞ **Australia**	**74,986,599.07**	**74,986,599.07**
⊟ **Europe**	**408,952,943.30**	**81,790,588.66**
⊞ **DE**	**136,859,360.31**	**8,553,710.02**
⊞ **FR**	**37,472,316.91**	**1,387,863.59**
⊟ **GB**	**140,787,706.59**	**368,554.21**
⊞ **IT**	**40,149,175.04**	**397,516.58**
⊟ **NL**	**53,684,384.45**	**4,473,698.70**
DR	1,825,546.39	1,825,546.39
FL	1,350,663.71	1,350,663.71
FR	2,216,323.24	2,216,323.24
GE	6,987,467.68	6,987,467.68
GR	2,142,566.64	2,142,566.64
LI	3,493,731.19	3,493,731.19
NB	7,205,896.69	7,205,896.69
NH	8,412,893.46	8,412,893.46
OV	3,663,410.11	3,663,410.11
UT	3,932,669.73	3,932,669.73
ZE	1,941,521.56	1,941,521.56
ZH	10,511,694.05	10,511,694.05
⊞ **North America**	**781,888,748.03**	**390,944,374.01**
Total	**1,265,828,290.39**	**421,942,763.46**

FIGURE 7-38 The matrix shows *Sales* and *Average of children*.

This *Average of children* visual calculation shows that you can pass any expression into the *expression* parameter to EXPAND, EXPANDALL, COLLAPSE, and COLLAPSEALL. This is something our examples for COLLAPSE and COLLAPSEALL did not show.

Let's see what happens if you provide columns to the *axis* parameter of EXPAND—in this case, the Country column. This returns the result shown in Figure 7-39.

```
Average of children Country = EXPAND ( AVERAGE ( [Sales] ), [Country] )
```

Continent	Sales	Average of children	Average of children Country
⊡ Australia	74,986,599.07	74,986,599.07	74,986,599.07
⊟ Europe	408,952,943.30	81,790,588.66	81,790,588.66
⊞ DE	136,859,360.31	8,553,710.02	136,859,360.31
⊞ FR	37,472,316.91	1,387,863.59	37,472,316.91
⊞ GB	140,787,706.59	368,554.21	140,787,706.59
⊞ IT	40,149,175.04	397,516.58	40,149,175.04
⊟ NL	53,684,384.45	4,473,698.70	53,684,384.45
DR	1,825,546.39	1,825,546.39	1,825,546.39
FL	1,350,663.71	1,350,663.71	1,350,663.71
FR	2,216,323.24	2,216,323.24	2,216,323.24
GE	6,987,467.68	6,987,467.68	6,987,467.68
GR	2,142,566.64	2,142,566.64	2,142,566.64
LI	3,493,731.19	3,493,731.19	3,493,731.19
NB	7,205,896.69	7,205,896.69	7,205,896.69
NH	8,412,893.46	8,412,893.46	8,412,893.46
OV	3,663,410.11	3,663,410.11	3,663,410.11
UT	3,932,669.73	3,932,669.73	3,932,669.73
ZE	1,941,521.56	1,941,521.56	1,941,521.56
ZH	10,511,694.05	10,511,694.05	10,511,694.05
⊞ North America	781,888,748.03	390,944,374.01	390,944,374.01
Total	1,265,828,290.39	421,942,763.46	158,228,536.30

FIGURE 7-39 This is the matrix for the *Average of children Country* visual calculation.

Notice that the results of *Average of children Country* and *Average of children* are the same when the calculation is performed on the Continent level. This is because countries are the direct descendants of continents. However, as shown in the following table, the value is different everywhere else.

Perhaps the most confusing result here is *Average of children Country* on the State level, which returns the same value as the *Average of children* visual calculation on the State level. After all, Country is not a child of State; in fact, the reverse is true. In this case, however, when evaluating *Average of children Country*, the EXPAND function will navigate down to the first level at which all the specified columns (Country and State) are present, which is the State level. So, that means that the contexts in which both calculations are performed are the same, and therefore the results are equal as well.

Level	Average of children context	Average of children Country context
Total	Continent	Country
Continent	Country	Country
Country	State	Country (itself)
State	State (itself)	Country and State

Similar things happen when you provide both Continent and Country, as in the following visual calculation:

```
Average of children Continent Country = EXPAND ( AVERAGE ( [Sales] ),
[Continent], [Country] )
```

Once again, the results are the same. And once again, the key to understanding this lies in the realization that if you provide multiple columns, EXPAND will navigate down to the level at which all the specified columns are present. Because Continent is the parent of Country, that level is at the Country level. Hence, the *Average of children Continent Country* and *Average of children Country* visual calculations return the same results, as shown in Figure 7-40.

Continent	Sales	Average of children	Average of children Country	Average of children Continent Country
⊞ Australia	74,986,599.07	74,986,599.07	74,986,599.07	74,986,599.07
⊟ Europe	408,952,943.30	81,790,588.66	81,790,588.66	81,790,588.66
⊞ DE	136,859,360.31	8,553,710.02	136,859,360.31	136,859,360.31
⊞ FR	37,472,316.91	1,387,863.59	37,472,316.91	37,472,316.91
⊞ GB	140,787,706.59	368,554.21	140,787,706.59	140,787,706.59
⊞ IT	40,149,175.04	397,516.58	40,149,175.04	40,149,175.04
⊟ NL	53,684,384.45	4,473,698.70	53,684,384.45	53,684,384.45
DR	1,825,546.39	1,825,546.39	1,825,546.39	1,825,546.39
FL	1,350,663.71	1,350,663.71	1,350,663.71	1,350,663.71
FR	2,216,323.24	2,216,323.24	2,216,323.24	2,216,323.24
GE	6,987,467.68	6,987,467.68	6,987,467.68	6,987,467.68
GR	2,142,566.64	2,142,566.64	2,142,566.64	2,142,566.64
LI	3,493,731.19	3,493,731.19	3,493,731.19	3,493,731.19
NB	7,205,896.69	7,205,896.69	7,205,896.69	7,205,896.69
NH	8,412,893.46	8,412,893.46	8,412,893.46	8,412,893.46
OV	3,663,410.11	3,663,410.11	3,663,410.11	3,663,410.11
UT	3,932,669.73	3,932,669.73	3,932,669.73	3,932,669.73
ZE	1,941,521.56	1,941,521.56	1,941,521.56	1,941,521.56
ZH	10,511,694.05	10,511,694.05	10,511,694.05	10,511,694.05
⊞ North America	781,888,748.03	390,944,374.01	390,944,374.01	390,944,374.01
Total	1,265,828,290.39	421,942,763.46	158,228,536.30	158,228,536.30

FIGURE 7-40 This matrix shows the *Average of children Continent Country* visual calculation.

To take this one step further, let's specify both Continent and State this time:

```
Average of children Continent State = EXPAND ( AVERAGE ( [Sales] ), [Continent],
[State] )
```

Again, because we specified multiple columns, EXPAND expands down the axis until all specified columns are present, which only happens at the State level. So, on any level, the average being calculated is on the State level. Hence, the *Average of children Continent State* visual calculation is equivalent to the following visual calculation, which uses EXPANDALL to expand down to the lowest (leaf) (State) level:

```
Average of leaf = EXPANDALL ( AVERAGE ( [Sales] ), ROWS )
```

Indeed, the *Average of leaf* and *Average of children Continent State* visual calculations do in fact return the same results, as shown in Figure 7-41.

Continent	Sales	Average of children Continent State	Average of leaf
⊞ **Australia**	**74,986,599.07**	**9,373,324.88**	**9,373,324.88**
⊖ **Europe**	**408,952,943.30**	**760,135.58**	**760,135.58**
⊞ **DE**	**136,859,360.31**	**8,553,710.02**	**8,553,710.02**
⊞ **FR**	**37,472,316.91**	**1,387,863.59**	**1,387,863.59**
⊞ **GB**	**140,787,706.59**	**368,554.21**	**368,554.21**
⊞ **IT**	**40,149,175.04**	**397,516.58**	**397,516.58**
⊖ **NL**	**53,684,384.45**	**4,473,698.70**	**4,473,698.70**
DR	1,825,546.39	1,825,546.39	1,825,546.39
FL	1,350,663.71	1,350,663.71	1,350,663.71
FR	2,216,323.24	2,216,323.24	2,216,323.24
GE	6,987,467.68	6,987,467.68	6,987,467.68
GR	2,142,566.64	2,142,566.64	2,142,566.64
LI	3,493,731.19	3,493,731.19	3,493,731.19
NB	7,205,896.69	7,205,896.69	7,205,896.69
NH	8,412,893.46	8,412,893.46	8,412,893.46
OV	3,663,410.11	3,663,410.11	3,663,410.11
UT	3,932,669.73	3,932,669.73	3,932,669.73
ZE	1,941,521.56	1,941,521.56	1,941,521.56
ZH	10,511,694.05	10,511,694.05	10,511,694.05
⊞ **North America**	**781,888,748.03**	**12,217,011.69**	**12,217,011.69**
Total	**1,265,828,290.39**	**2,075,128.34**	**2,075,128.34**

FIGURE 7-41 *Average of children Continent State* and *Average of leaf* return the same results.

Measure equivalent

The measure equivalent of the *Average of children* visual calculation is as follows:

```
Average Sales of Children Measure =
SWITCH (
    TRUE (),
```

```
      ISINSCOPE ( 'Customer'[State] ), [Sales], -- States don't have children
      ISINSCOPE ( 'Customer'[Country] ), AVERAGEX ( VALUES ( 'Customer'[State] ),
      [Sales] ),
      ISINSCOPE ( 'Customer'[Continent] ), AVERAGEX ( VALUES ( 'Customer'[Country]
      ), [Sales] ),
      AVERAGEX ( VALUES ( 'Customer'[Continent] ), [Sales] )
      )
)
```

Again, it's easy to see that visual calculations are much easier!

Other functions

ISATLEVEL

ISATLEVEL checks whether specified columns are on the current level of the axis. It functions much like ISINSCOPE, ISFILTERED, and others. However, unlike these other inspection functions, ISATLEVEL is guaranteed to work correctly in visual calculations with functions that navigate the levels of the lattice, such as EXPAND and COLLAPSE. The other functions might work or they might not, so it's recommended to use only ISATLEVEL in visual calculations. ISATLEVEL is most often used to return custom subtotals and totals as we show in the following example and in Chapter 10. Figure 7-42 provides a conceptual illustration of this function.

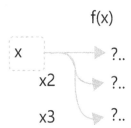

FIGURE 7-42 This is a conceptual illustration of ISATLEVEL.

ISATLEVEL returns a Boolean (True/False) value that reflects whether the specified column is at the current level of the axis.

Parameters

ISATLEVEL only takes one parameter:

Parameter	Definition	Required	Skippable
column	Specifies which column to test if it is at the current level of the visual matrix.	Yes	No

Examples

Recall that a lattice level can contain more than one column. For example, on an axis that contains Continent, Country, and State, the level that contains the Country column also contains the Continent column. Similarly, the level that contains the State column also contains both the Country and Continent columns (see Figure 7-43).

Continent	Continent At Level	Country At Level	State At Level
⊞ Australia	True	False	False
⊟ Europe	True	False	False
⊞ DE	True	True	False
⊞ FR	True	True	False
⊞ GB	True	True	False
⊞ IT	True	True	False
⊟ NL	True	True	False
DR	True	True	True
FL	True	True	True
FR	True	True	True
GE	True	True	True
GR	True	True	True
LI	True	True	True
NB	True	True	True
NH	True	True	True
OV	True	True	True
UT	True	True	True
ZE	True	True	True
ZH	True	True	True
⊞ North America	True	False	False
Total	False	False	False

FIGURE 7-43 A lower level contains higher levels as well.

The matrix visual in Figure 7-43 shows the results of the following visual calculations:

```
Continent At Level = ISATLEVEL ( [Continent] )

Country At Level = ISATLEVEL ( [Country] )

State At Level = ISATLEVEL ( [State] )
```

The *Continent At Level* visual calculation returns True for all levels except for the total row, where no continents are on the level. The *Country At Level* visual calculation returns True for all levels except the total row and the total rows for each continent. The *State At Level* visual calculation returns True only on the State level and returns False everywhere else.

Using this, one can influence the value returned on each level. For example, the following visual calculation leverages a SWITCH (TRUE(), …) pattern to influence what is returned on each level:

```
Custom Totals =
SWITCH (
    TRUE (),
    ISATLEVEL ( [State] ), [Sales],
    ISATLEVEL ( [Country] ), EXPAND ( MAX ( [Sales] ), ROWS ),
    ISATLEVEL ( [Continent] ), EXPAND ( MIN ( [Sales] ), ROWS ),
    EXPAND ( AVERAGE ( [Sales] ), ROWS )
)
```

This visual calculation returns the following:

- On the lowest level, the State level, it returns the sales for that state.

- On the next level up, the Country level, it expands the rows axis one level down and returns the maximum sales value for the states in that country.

- On the next level up, the Continent level, it expands the rows axis one level down and returns the minimum sales value for the countries in that continent.

- On the highest level, the Total level, this visual calculation again expands the rows axis one level down and calculates the average sales value for all continents.

Figure 7-44 shows the results.

Continent	Sales	Continent At Level	Country At Level	State At Level	Custom Totals
⊞ Australia	74,986,599.07	True	False	False	74,986,599.07
⊟ Europe	408,952,943.30	True	False	False	37,472,316.91
⊞ DE	136,859,360.31	True	True	False	39,135,084.12
⊞ FR	37,472,316.91	True	True	False	11,997,530.85
⊞ GB	140,787,706.59	True	True	False	7,080,513.52
⊞ IT	40,149,175.04	True	True	False	1,241,209.05
⊟ NL	53,684,384.45	True	True	False	10,511,694.05
DR	1,825,546.39	True	True	True	1,825,546.39
FL	1,350,663.71	True	True	True	1,350,663.71
FR	2,216,323.24	True	True	True	2,216,323.24
GE	6,987,467.68	True	True	True	6,987,467.68
GR	2,142,566.64	True	True	True	2,142,566.64
LI	3,493,731.19	True	True	True	3,493,731.19
NB	7,205,896.69	True	True	True	7,205,896.69
NH	8,412,893.46	True	True	True	8,412,893.46
OV	3,663,410.11	True	True	True	3,663,410.11
UT	3,932,669.73	True	True	True	3,932,669.73
ZE	1,941,521.56	True	True	True	1,941,521.56
ZH	10,511,694.05	True	True	True	10,511,694.05
⊞ North America	781,888,748.03	True	False	False	133,587,098.93
Total	1,265,828,290.39	False	False	False	421,942,763.46

FIGURE 7-44 Custom totals can be implemented with ISATLEVEL.

Measure equivalent

As mentioned, DAX provides multiple inspection functions. These include ISINSCOPE, ISFILTERED, and HASONEVALUE. The following measure is an equivalent of the *Custom Totals* visual calculation, which uses ISINSCOPE:

```
Custom totals Measure =
SWITCH (
    TRUE (),
    ISINSCOPE ( 'Customer'[State] ), [Sales], -- States don't have children
    ISINSCOPE ( 'Customer'[Country] ), MAXX ( VALUES ( 'Customer'[State] ),
    [Sales] ),
    ISINSCOPE ( 'Customer'[Continent] ), MINX ( VALUES ( 'Customer'[Country] ),
    [Sales] ),
    AVERAGEX ( VALUES ( 'Customer'[Continent] ), [Sales] )
)
```

This time the visual calculation and the equivalent measure are almost the same.

RANGE

RANGE is a shortcut to WINDOW that provides a range of rows relative from the current position on the axis. Because RANGE simply returns a context, it must be used with other functions, such as CALCU-LATE, to actually perform a calculation. This makes it slightly more complicated to work with than many other visual calculation functions. RANGE can be used for many things but is often employed to calcu-late a moving sum. A moving sum is almost the same thing as a running sum (which is easily calculated using RUNNINGSUM), except that the start of the window is not fixed to the first element on the axis. Instead, it slides across the axis in a position relative to the current position. You can also use RANGE to calculate a moving maximum or to perform any other calculation that involves a sliding window. Figure 7-45 provides a conceptual illustration of this function.

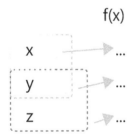

FIGURE 7-45 This is a conceptual illustration of RANGE.

RANGE returns an interval of data rows on the axis and is an easier-to-use shortcut to `WINDOW ( N, REL, M, REL, … )`, with N and M being the relative position where the window starts and ends, respectively.

Parameters

RANGE takes the following parameters:

Parameter	Definition	Required	Skippable
step	Specifies the number of elements on the axis before or after the current position to include.	Yes	No
includeCurrent	A true/false parameter that specifies whether to include the current row in the range.	No	Yes
axis	Specifies an axis, which determines how the calculation traverses the visual matrix.	No	Yes
orderBy	Specifies how each partition on the axis is sorted; accepts the ORDERBY function.	No	Yes
blanks	Defines how blank values are handled.	No	Yes
reset	Dictates whether the calculation resets, and if so, how.	No	Yes

Examples

Let's create a visual calculation that returns the sales in the previous six months, including the current month, per product category. In a visual that contains the months on the rows axis, we can create the following visual calculation to do just that:

```
Sales Last 6 Months = CALCULATE ( SUM ( [Sales] ), RANGE ( -5 ) )
```

As shown in Figure 7-46, this visual calculation returns the desired result.

CategoryName	Audio		Cameras and camcorders	
Year	Sales	Sales Last 6 Months	Sales	Sales Last 6 Months
⊟ **2024**	**6,816,313.48**	**6,816,313.48**	**32,944,784.71**	**32,944,784.71**
January	296,010.71	296,010.71	4,389,449.01	4,389,449.01
February	420,357.58	716,368.29	5,107,224.83	9,496,673.84
March	322,558.21	1,038,926.50	3,606,807.54	13,103,481.38
April	387,911.30	1,426,837.80	2,758,638.96	15,862,120.34
May	470,263.52	1,897,101.32	2,860,719.89	18,722,840.22
June	494,796.18	2,391,897.50	2,449,571.23	21,172,411.46
July	490,872.22	2,586,759.01	2,096,084.05	18,879,046.50
August	332,160.03	2,498,561.46	879,802.69	14,651,624.35
September	521,764.48	2,697,767.73	1,625,627.73	12,670,444.54
October	803,224.42	3,113,080.84	1,879,218.59	11,791,024.17
November	908,135.52	3,550,952.84	2,073,515.00	11,003,819.29
December	1,368,259.32	4,424,415.98	3,218,125.20	11,772,373.25
⊞ **2025**	**13,765,422.62**	**20,581,736.10**	**47,767,301.24**	**80,712,085.95**
⊞ **2026**	**12,713,044.19**	**33,294,780.29**	**37,194,710.10**	**117,906,796.05**
Total	**33,294,780.29**	**33,294,780.29**	**117,906,796.05**	**117,906,796.05**

FIGURE 7-46 This matrix shows *Sales Last 6 Months*.

If you look across the years, however, you will soon notice that the *Sales Last 6 Months* visual calculation crosses the year boundary. A small tweak that uses the *reset* parameter enables us to ensure that we calculate only the total sales over the last six months in the same year:

```
Sales Last 6 Months within the Year = CALCULATE ( SUM ( [Sales] ), RANGE ( -5,
[Year] ) )
```

Figure 7-47 shows that the *Sales Last 6 Months within the Year* visual calculation returns the correct results.

CategoryName Year	Audio Sales	Sales Last 6 Months	Sales Last 6 Months within the Year
⊟ **2024**	**6,816,313.48**	**6,816,313.48**	**6,816,313.48**
January	296,010.71	296,010.71	296,010.71
February	420,357.58	716,368.29	716,368.29
March	322,558.21	1,038,926.50	1,038,926.50
April	387,911.30	1,426,837.80	1,426,837.80
May	470,263.52	1,897,101.32	1,897,101.32
June	494,796.18	2,391,897.50	2,391,897.50
July	490,872.22	2,586,759.01	2,586,759.01
August	332,160.03	2,498,561.46	2,498,561.46
September	521,764.48	2,697,767.73	2,697,767.73
October	803,224.42	3,113,080.84	3,113,080.84
November	908,135.52	3,550,952.84	3,550,952.84
December	1,368,259.32	4,424,415.98	4,424,415.98
⊟ **2025**	**13,765,422.62**	**20,581,736.10**	**13,765,422.62**
January	1,906,604.34	5,840,148.11	1,906,604.34
February	2,325,698.42	7,833,686.49	4,232,302.76
March	1,545,047.94	8,856,969.95	5,777,350.70
April	1,429,036.73	9,482,782.27	7,206,387.43
May	1,357,654.57	9,932,301.32	8,564,042.00
June	1,085,456.24	9,649,498.24	9,649,498.24
July	1,042,803.35	8,785,697.24	8,785,697.24
August	460,318.26	6,920,317.09	6,920,317.09
September	626,503.09	6,001,772.24	6,001,772.24
October	622,373.15	5,195,108.65	5,195,108.65
November	585,072.05	4,422,526.13	4,422,526.13
December	778,854.48	4,115,924.38	4,115,924.38
⊞ **2026**	**12,713,044.19**	**33,294,780.29**	**12,713,044.19**
Total	**33,294,780.29**	**33,294,780.29**	**33,294,780.29**

FIGURE 7-47 This matrix shows *Sales Last 6 Months within the Year*.

You could also do a forward-looking range or even skip the current value. For example, the following visual calculation calculates the difference between the sales for the current month and the average of the next three months, not including the current month:

```
Sales vs average next 3 Months within Year =
[Sales] - CALCULATE ( AVERAGE ( [Sales] ), RANGE ( 3, FALSE, [Year] ) )
```

This visual calculation uses the AVERAGE function instead of the SUM function and averages *Sales* over the next three elements on the axis, while still making sure to never cross the year boundary. So, for every December, the *Sales vs average next 3 months within Year* visual calculation returns the sales for that month because there are no further months to average. For each November, however, the sales for the following December are subtracted from the sales for November, and so on. Figure 7-48 shows the results.

CategoryName	Audio		Cameras and camcorders	
Year	Sales	Sales vs avg next 3 Mon in Year	Sales	Sales vs avg next 3 Mon in Year
⊟ 2024	**6,816,313.48**	**6,816,313.48**	**32,944,784.71**	**32,944,784.71**
January	296,010.71	-80,931.65	4,389,449.01	565,225.23
February	420,357.58	26,779.90	5,107,224.83	2,031,836.04
March	322,558.21	-128,432.13	3,606,807.54	917,164.18
April	387,911.30	-97,399.34	2,758,638.96	289,847.24
May	470,263.52	30,987.38	2,860,719.89	1,052,233.90
June	494,796.18	46,530.60	2,449,571.23	915,733.08
July	490,872.22	-61,510.76	2,096,084.05	634,534.38
August	332,160.03	-412,214.77	879,802.69	-979,651.08
September	521,764.48	-504,775.27	1,625,627.73	-764,658.53
October	803,224.42	-334,973.01	1,879,218.59	-766,601.51
November	908,135.52	-460,123.80	2,073,515.00	-1,144,610.19
December	1,368,259.32	1,368,259.32	3,218,125.20	3,218,125.20
⊟ 2025	**13,765,422.62**	**13,765,422.62**	**47,767,301.24**	**47,767,301.24**
January	1,906,604.34	140,009.98	5,355,471.81	-316,002.54
February	2,325,698.42	881,785.34	6,764,001.45	1,533,818.77
March	1,545,047.94	254,332.09	5,178,120.95	89,851.32
April	1,429,036.73	267,065.34	5,072,300.65	499,260.52
May	1,357,654.57	494,795.29	5,440,126.46	2,102,706.27
June	1,085,456.24	375,581.34	4,752,381.76	2,238,590.41
July	1,042,803.35	473,071.85	3,526,612.17	1,366,448.89
August	460,318.26	-150,997.84	1,733,266.62	-589,734.39
September	626,503.09	-35,596.81	2,281,495.28	-273,012.75
October	622,373.15	-59,590.12	2,465,727.92	-133,170.16

FIGURE 7-48 This matrix shows *Sales vs average next 3 Months within the Year.*

Measure equivalent

It should be no surprise that the easiest measure equivalent of the *Sales vs average next 3 months within the Year* visual calculation relies on WINDOW:

```
Sales vs average next 3 Months within Year Measure =
[Sales] - AVERAGEX (
    WINDOW (
        1,
        REL,
```

```
            3,
            REL,
            ALLSELECTED ( 'Date'[Year], 'Date'[Month], 'Date'[MonthNumber] ),
            ORDERBY('Date'[Year], ASC, 'Date'[MonthNumber], ASC),
            PARTITIONBY ( 'Date'[Year] )
        ),
        [Sales]
    )
)
```

Notice that because Month is sorted by MonthNumber, it needs to be included in the *relation* and the *orderBy* parameter to WINDOW to produce the same results.

In summary

Congratulations! You made it through the most detailed chapter in this book. Together, we went deep into all visual calculations exclusive functions. These functions are unique to visual calculations and provide capabilities that make many calculations in DAX much easier than before. We identify the following visual calculations exclusive function groups:

- **Business functions**   These perform a running sum or running total calculation (RUNNING-SUM) or a moving average (MOVINGAVERAGE). Both functions are easier-to-use versions of the WINDOW foundational function.

- **Absolute movement functions**   These enable you to jump to a fixed position on the axis. FIRST retrieves a value from the first element on the axis, while LAST retrieves a value from the last element on the axis. These functions are an easier-to-use version of the INDEX foundational function. The other functions in this group, LOOKUP and LOOKUPWITHTOTALS, allow you to retrieve values in the visual matrix by specifying filters, similar to how XLOOKUP works in Excel.

- **Relative movement functions**   These enable you to perform movements from the current position on the axis. PREVIOUS retrieves a value from a previous element on the axis, while NEXT retrieves a value from a next element on the axis. For both these functions, you can determine how many steps to take along the axis.

- **Lattice navigation functions**   These enable you to navigate upward (COLLAPSE) or downward (EXPAND) within the hierarchy levels on the axes. Whereas COLLAPSE and EXPAND enable you to determine how many levels to move up or down on the axis, the special variants COLLAPSEALL and EXPANDALL enable you to jump to the highest and lowest level on the axis, respectively.

- **Other functions**   These enable you to check whether a column is at the current level (ISAT-LEVEL) so you can return a different result as the subtotal and total. The RANGE function returns an interval of rows on the axis. RANGE is an easier-to-use version of the WINDOW foundational function.

We started the discussion of the visual calculations exclusive functions by identifying their shared signature and parameters as well as introducing the concept of skippable parameters.

Many of the visual calculations exclusive functions are easier-to-use versions of foundational or other functions that are available anywhere DAX can be used. When we discussed each function, we indicated which shortcut it provides. Also, for each function, we discussed the parameters and use cases and provided examples of visual calculations using these functions and their measure equivalents.

Armed with this knowledge, you are ready to take on any challenge using visual calculations! Rest assured, we will use these functions again in Part IV, where we discuss practical applications of visual calculations.

## PART III

Mastering visual calculations

Visual calculations are a new tool in your toolbox, but Power BI already offers a variety of ways to perform approximately the same job. To master visual calculations, it's important to know the options available to you. It's also important to understand how visual calculations work so you can get the most out of them. This part discusses and compares the tools available before diving deep into the inner workings of visual calculations and the queries they generate so you can troubleshoot their results and tweak their performance.

## CHAPTER 8

Comparing calculation options

Power BI offers a variety of options to add calculations—some based on Power Query, and others on DAX. This chapter discusses the different calculation options and each one's purpose, offers examples, and compares them.

Available calculation options

Simply having data in a semantic model in Power BI doesn't do you much good. The value of your data lies in the calculations you create on it, such as business logic related to company-defined performance indicators. These calculations—which are not part of your data—enable you to compare values, such as actual values versus target values.

Roche's Maxim of Data Transformation, expressed by Matthew Roche of Microsoft, states that "Data should be transformed as far upstream as possible, and as far *downstream* as necessary." Upstream data is source data (for example, data in a database), whereas downstream data is data that has been transformed in some way (for example, data in a report). We mention this maxim because you can apply calculations to data that is upstream, downstream, or anywhere in between. Figure 8-1 illustrates this concept in the form of a waterfall. The further upstream you go, the closer to the origin of the data you are. The further downstream you go, the closer to the visualization on the report you are, like the lake at the bottom of the waterfall. Full details on Roche's Maxim of Data Transformation can be found at *https://ssbipolar.com/2021/05/31/roches-maxim/*.

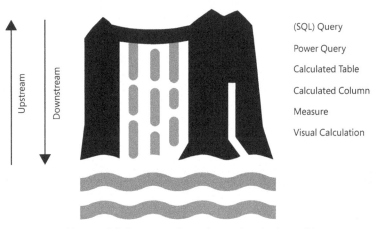

FIGURE 8-1 This waterfall shows transformation options in Power BI.

Power BI provides multiple ways of adding calculations. To start with, the query editor allows you to add calculations by adding custom columns. The query editor uses Power Query (also known as M) for these calculations. Further downstream in the calculation options in Power BI, you use DAX to add additional logic to your solution. In the Introduction to this book, we introduced the DAX language. DAX in Power BI is used for many different tasks, but you will use it primarily to add a measure, a calculated column, or a calculated table to your semantic model. DAX is also used to create a field parameter or numeric range (what-if) parameters (which are themselves related to measures, calculated columns, and calculated tables, and which both result in the addition of a calculated table to the semantic model) and to define row-level security by defining a filter condition based on an expression.

Note   This chapter focuses on measures, calculated columns, and calculated tables, and contrasts them with visual calculations. It doesn't discuss custom columns because these are defined using M, nor does it discuss the use of DAX for field parameters or row-level security rules.

Understanding calculated columns

Calculated columns are one way to add calculations to your semantic model. They enable you to add new data to your model. Like measures, calculated columns are defined using DAX. Adding calculated columns in DAX is similar to adding columns with the query editor using Power Query. The calculations used for calculated columns have many answers. It's important to understand that the calculations are executed in row context; therefore, each row will have its own individual answer. For more information about row context, refer to Chapter 1, "Introduction to visual calculations."

As an example, you can use a calculated column to calculate the total sales in the following table by way of the following DAX expression:

```
Total Sales = [Quantity] * [UnitPrice]
```

As shown, this expression generates an answer for each row individually.

OrderKey	ProductKey	Quantity	UnitPrice	Total Sales
10960865	1683	1	$ 4.99	$ 4.99
10961015	419	2	$ 369.00	$ 738.00
10961062	1635	6	$ 22.89	$ 137.44

The result of a calculated column is not dynamic. Rather, it's calculated only when the semantic model is refreshed. You can schedule this refresh in the Power BI Service or run it ad hoc using the refresh button in Power BI Desktop.

> **Note** Although this is a working example of a calculated column, ideally this scenario would be solved through a measure using an iterator. One reason for this is that calculated columns persist the result in memory, and adding many columns can lead to extreme increases in model size. Also, measures add more flexibility based on cross-filtering and highlighting by the user.

Example: calculating customer age

One typical example of calculated columns is to calculate the age of your customers. For example, suppose you have a table that contains the birth date of each customer. You could add a calculated column to refer to that data to calculate each customer's age in years. The following DAX expression achieves this:

```
Age in Years =
        DATEDIFF ( Customer[BirthDate], TODAY (), YEAR )
```

The following table shows the result.

CustomerKey	FirstName	BirthDate	Age in Years
1200337	Mark	09/06/1982	42
1219923	Christian	03/20/1983	41
934045	Amila	06/23/1979	45

As you saw, this calculation uses the DATEDIFF function, which enables you to easily calculate the difference between two points in time. As a parameter of this function, you can choose the interval that should be applied: SECOND, MINUTE, HOUR, DAY, WEEK, MONTH, QUARTER, or YEAR. Because we wanted to calculate the age in years, we added YEAR as the interval.

The second function is TODAY. This function returns a datetime value for which only the date is updated upon refresh. Time is not included in this function. If you're using this with the DATEDIFF function, and you require an interval smaller than DAY, consider using the NOW function, which includes the time as well. In all scenarios, TODAY returns the date at 12:00:00 AM on that day.

Calculating the customer age in a calculated column is a good use case. Compared to the total sales described earlier, the customer age is not a dynamic value that can change due to filters or report interactions. Therefore, calculating the age for each customer once and persisting the result in the model is fine. Also, the value only has to be recalculated at most once per day, where sales could be a dynamically changing value.

Evaluating calculated columns

Calculated columns update results only upon model or table refresh. Alternatively, you can use the recalculate command in the Tabular Model Scripting Language to recalculate the result of calculated columns. Therefore, calculating age is a valid example in which calculated columns can be used.

Use cases in which an age is given in seconds, minutes, or hours are rare. Another typical use case for calculated columns is the creation of concatenated fields, like combining City and State in a single field. However, in the case of the concatenation of fields, you could argue that this calculation should be applied further upstream using the query editor, or even in a data platform.

Use cases of calculated columns

Although most calculated columns can be pushed further upstream using the query editor, calculated columns still have a relevant place in your semantic model. The following sections explain some of them.

Calculated columns as filters

A calculated column can be created to use in a slicer or any other type of visual. For example, suppose your data contains a datetime column that you want to filter by year. By adding a calculated column, you can easily extract the year, which you can then use as a slicer on the report page to show data only for the selected year. Here's how:

```
Order Year = YEAR ( 'Order'[OrderDate] )
```

Following this example, you could work with a dimension to provide this filter option where you can precalculate the years for all values in your fact table. However, adding a dedicated dimension with a datetime column and a year column will have a significant impact on performance due to the high granularity of the datetime column. Therefore, think about the required granularity of the dimensions. Perhaps rather than requiring the datetime, you really only need the date, which reduces the granularity of the dimension.

Alternatively, you could add the year column to the original table to limit performance impact. For example, you might be able to use Power Query in the query editor to add the year column rather than using a DAX calculated column. However, you might not have access to the query editor in all cases to push transformations or enrichments like these further upstream, like in the following example.

Calculated columns in composite models

Another use case in which you may be forced to use calculated columns is when you are dealing with a composite model in which two different source groups are connected. In general, a composite model is created when you combine two different data source groups or you combine imported data with DirectQuery.

Let's have a closer look at a practical example. Your semantic model can connect to another semantic model that has been shared with you, which you combine with your local imported data. The model that results from combining an existing remote semantic model with a local imported table is called a composite model. By combining with another data source, the connection to the remote semantic model will change from live connection to DirectQuery. For your local table, you can easily add logic and push transformations upstream using Power Query. However, for the remote semantic model, you're only allowed to consume data. As a reader, you're not allowed to add or change the logic of the model. This means that adding columns further upstream isn't possible. In this scenario, your only option is to employ calculated columns using DAX to, for example, extract the year from a datetime column. Alternatively, you could write more complex DAX in a calculated table, depending on your use case.

Calculated columns to look up values across relationships

A third scenario for calculated columns is calculating a result across two different tables, using functions like RELATED and RELATEDTABLE to combine columns from one table with columns from another table in the same semantic model. This could be done in Power Query using a join or merge statement, both of which are heavy operations that are executed when the semantic model is refreshed. In DAX, you can leverage the RELATED function to look up a specific row on the other end of a relationship between two tables.

Be aware that the RELATED function works only when both tables are part of a regular relationship. A regular relationship is a relationship between two tables in the same source group. Both tables are either imported to the semantic model or reside in the same DirectQuery data source. In contrast to these are limited relationships, which are relationships that do not have a guaranteed one side. This can happen with many-to-many relationships or cross-source group relationships. As with the previous scenario, you can consider using RELATED in a calculated column if you don't have access to the query editor like in composite models.

Understanding calculated tables

DAX does not have any data connectors or ways to reach out to anything outside of Power BI to collect data. Therefore, all data must be connected to the semantic model first. After this has been done, you can use calculated tables to enrich your semantic model and apply calculations. Calculated tables let you add new tables based on data you loaded into the model. Instead of querying and loading values into your new table's columns from a data source, you create a DAX formula to define the table's values. For example, you could use calculated tables to generate an aggregated table. Using calculated tables for this purpose is not recommended because it's always based on data that already exists in the model, and therefore, calculated tables duplicate data in the model and bloat the model. Following Roche's Maxim of Data Transformation, data transformations should be done as far upstream as possible. So, in the example use case of aggregating data, it would be better to do this in the query editor using Power Query.

Another use case for calculated tables—or better said, a table-valued expression—is precalculating in-memory tables that are used within measures. In this scenario, not all data has to be persisted in a table in the model first, but the table can be calculated and generated in memory as part of a larger calculation. In this scenario, you are not duplicating data because the table is not saved to the model, but only exists in the context of the measure. Also, this step cannot be pushed further upstream and is therefore a perfect example of doing it as far downstream as necessary, following Roche's Maxim.

Functions for calculated tables

Various DAX functions are commonly used for calculated tables, including SUMMARIZE, CALCULATETABLE, and ADDCOLUMNS. These can be used individually or in combination with each other.

As its name implies, the SUMMARIZE function helps to aggregate data, like a group by expression in SQL. SUMMARIZE is often used within a measure to precalculate a result in a variable. Using the SUMMARIZE function also enables you to directly add new calculations to the table that might not exist in the semantic model.

The CALCULATETABLE function is similar to the CALCULATE function, and enables you to change the filter context of a table definition. This function takes a table as a whole and allows filters on top. These are often simple filter expressions to eliminate a set of rows from the table but can be made more complex by way of functions like USERELATIONSHIP and TREATAS.

With ADDCOLUMNS, you can add a new column to an in-memory table. This can be used to add a describing column or calculation.

Example: percentage sales of top three countries

Suppose you want to show the percentage of total sales from the top three countries in which your company operates for marketing purposes or to decide where to locate new stores. The higher the number returned, the more dependent the business is on these countries. The following DAX statement returns this:

```
% Sales top 3 countries =
VAR SalesAllCountries =
        CALCULATE ( [Sales], ALL ( Customer[CountryFull] ) )
VAR SalesTop3Countries =
    SUMX (
        TOPN (
            3,
            SUMMARIZE ( Customer, Customer[CountryFull], "CountrySales", [Sales] ),
            [CountrySales], DESC
        ),
        [CountrySales]
    )
RETURN
    DIVIDE ( SalesTop3Countries, SalesAllCountries )
```

Note This example is imperfect because total sales should not be the only metric in the calculation. To derive more valuable insights, you should also take into account the population of each country.

The preceding calculation uses variables defined with the VAR function to precalculate certain numbers in a specific context. The first variable (SalesAllCountries) calculates the total sales for all countries. The ALL function resets the filter context based on countries and returns the total value for all countries, even if you're evaluating in a context in which you are looking at one specific country.

The second variable (SalesTop3Countries) uses the SUMMARIZE function to create an in-memory table of countries and the total sales for those countries. Out of the generated table, a top three is derived based on the TOPN function, which enables you to take the top or bottom of the table, depending on whether values are sorted in an ascending or descending order. In this example, the sales are sorted in descending order from high to low. The result is a small table in which only the sales of the top three countries are left. At this point, the result of this second variable is a table, but it's not possible to compare a table object with multiple rows to a scalar value, which you calculated in the first variable. To get the total sales for the top three countries, the SUMX iterator function is wrapped around to convert the table to a scalar value.

To end the section in which you defined the variables, you use the RETURN function. There you divide both scalar values by each other because they were calculated in the variables. This will return a value between 0 and 1 that can be formatted as a percentage in the measure tools. The result is shown in the card visual in Figure 8-2.

73.15%
% Sales top 3 countries

FIGURE 8-2 The result of a calculation to show sales for the top three countries.

This example used a temporary table calculated by way of the SUMMARIZE function within a measure. The resulting table expression of the SUMMARIZE function was not persisted to the model. Calculated tables are usually saved in the model, like calculated columns—meaning they refresh only when the semantic model is refreshed. This is not the case when the temporary table is created in the context of a measure as in this example. In that case, the benefits of measures being calculated on demand at evaluation time will apply, and it's referred to as a table-valued expression or simply a table expression instead of a calculated table.

Understanding measures

A measure is the most commonly used method to add calculations to your Power BI semantic model. Measure definitions are saved in the model and are indicated by a calculator icon (see Figure 8-3).

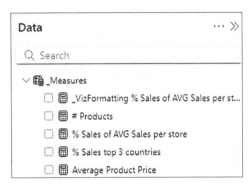

FIGURE 8-3 Measures are shown with a calculator icon in the Data pane of Power BI Desktop.

The result of a measure is not saved within the model itself. Instead, measures are evaluated at run-time and in context. Measures aggregate a column based on the defined expression such as SUM, MIN, MAX, or AVERAGE. The following example takes the sum of a column to calculate the total sales:

```
Sales = SUMX ( Sales, Sales[Quantity] * Sales[UnitPrice] )
```

Applying this measure in the following sample table will result in the total over three rows being $657.

OrderKey	ProductKey	Quantity	UnitPrice	Total Sales
8230434	1577	1	$ 219.00	$ 219.00
8230739	1622	1	$ 219.00	$ 219.00
8240338	1626	1	$ 219.00	$ 219.00

Creating measures

To create a measure in a semantic model, you click the New measure button in the Modeling tab of the Power BI Desktop ribbon (see Figure 8-4). This opens the formula bar (see Figure 8-5), where you can use DAX to define the measure.

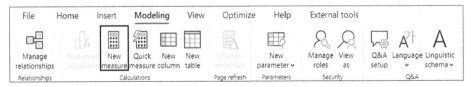

FIGURE 8-4 Use the top ribbon in Power BI Desktop to add measures to the model.

FIGURE 8-5 Measure tools in the top ribbon of Power BI Desktop include the New measure button.

Within Power BI, you can also create measures from DAX Query View. This view enables you to bulk create and edit measures, along with advanced debugging capabilities and Copilot integration.

You can also create and debug measures using third-party tools like Tabular Editor. With this tool, more advanced users can run scripts in bulk to generate measures, format measures, and perform transformations on measures. For even more advanced users, the Tabular Model Scripting Language (TMSL) and the Tabular Model Definition Language (TMDL) offer options for bulk editing and scripting from code editors rather than through a user interface.

Note The location of the newly created measure in the model is defined by the selected table at creation time. You can move a measure to other tables at any time using the measure tools in the ribbon or in bulk in the model view.

Nested measures

Nested measures are a common practice. For example, you might calculate the sales amount in one measure and, in a separate measure, refer to the *Sales Amount* measure to calculate the sales amount year to date. Here's an example:

```
Sales Amount = SUM ( 'Order Detail'[Total Sales] )
Sales Amount YTD = TOTALYTD ( [Sales Amount], 'Date'[Date] )
```

Notice that in this example, the *Sales Amount YTD* measure refers to the *Sales Amount* measure and uses it as a parameter for the TOTALYTD function. You could also write TOTALYTD differently by using the CALCULATE function. CALCULATE is used often in measures to apply filters to an expression—what we call filter context (refer to Chapter 1). Filter context is frequently used to apply time intelligence like year to date or month to date, as in the preceding example.

Note Frequently used filters in measures relate to excluding certain data from a calculation, like filtering the measure result by a dimension value.

Iterators

With measures, the simplest calculations are based on aggregations. Another option, however, is to use iterators. As its name implies, an iterator iterates over all rows in a table to calculate the result. Typically, iterators have an X in the function name. For example, AVERAGEX is the iterator version of AVERAGE and so on.

Suppose that for the following table, you wanted to calculate the total sales over all orders. One solution could be first to create a calculated column to calculate the sales per row and determine the sales amount per order as described earlier in this chapter. This would add a column to the table that you could reuse to take the sum over all orders. Alternatively, you could write a DAX measure with an iterator. Using an iterator in this scenario would make the calculated column obsolete.

OrderKey	ProductKey	Quantity	UnitPrice
8230434	1577	1	$ 219.00
8230739	1622	1	$ 219.00
8240338	1626	1	$ 219.00

SUMX is a commonly used iterator that allows a row-by-row calculation to calculate the sum over the in-row calculations. When you use a measure with an iterator like SUMX, the multiplication of the quantity and the price for each row is done in-memory. Afterward, the iterator applies an aggregation to these in-memory generated results to obtain the requested result. In the case of SUMX, the aggregation is a sum, so it returns the total. The following DAX measure could be used to achieve this:

```
Sales Amount = SUMX ( 'Order Detail', [Quantity] * [UnitPrice] )
```

Iterators are typically a better alternative to creating calculated columns because they're dynamic and calculated on demand. Compared to calculated columns, using measures saves memory and adds extra flexibility to respond to any filters that may be applicable.

Evaluation of measures

Measures typically aggregate a column by performing a SUM, AVERAGE, or any other function. They evaluate a total, not a row-by-row calculation.

Measures evaluate at runtime in the CPU. The results are not precalculated and stored in memory, as with calculated columns and tables. Therefore, they are dynamic and work well with user interactions like cross-filtering and cross-highlighting on report visuals.

It's not possible to return a table as a result of a measure. Instead, measures always have one answer in the defined context. For example, when you apply the SUM measure over a column, the engine returns only one answer. Similarly, if you build a visual in which you use a product category column and a measure to show the total sales by product category, the measure returns one answer for each record (see Figure 8-6)—to be precise, one answer for each product category as presented on the y-axis.

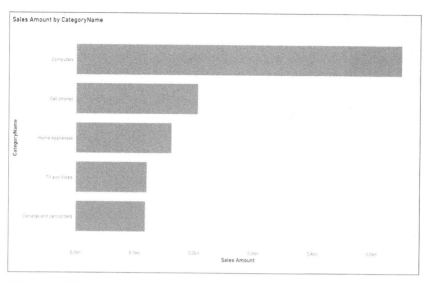

FIGURE 8-6 This bar chart shows total *Sales Amount* by product category.

Use cases of measures

There are many use cases of measures in Power BI. The most obvious one is to define calculations in the semantic model.

By creating a measure, you make the calculation explicit, and the definition of the measure is saved in the semantic model. This is called an explicit measure. This is in contrast to an implicit measure. An implicit measure is created when columns are directly put in visuals by using auto summarization features of Power BI, and numeric columns will automatically be summed. With implicit measures, you're relying on the auto summarization feature of the model or another configuration of the auto summarization set by the person who built the visualization. Auto summarization of columns can be set as part of column tools (see Figure 8-7).

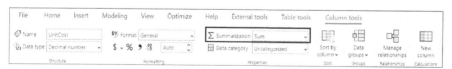

FIGURE 8-7 Auto summarization settings of a column are in the column tools section in the top ribbon of Power BI Desktop.

Explicit measures are often created to ensure a single source of truth and for reusability of a calculation. Implicit measures, on the other hand, are generated by the drag-and-drop experience of users who pick a column from the Fields pane and put it on the Power BI reporting canvas.

Measures reside in a home table. Within this table, you can put measures in display folders to group them together by category. You can also nest these display folders to set up a structure. After a measure is created, anyone who uses the semantic model can take advantage of it, whether they use the semantic model from within Power BI or perhaps Excel.

Measures for dynamic visual titles

Measures need not always result in an integer or number. The result of a measure could also be a text value. This brings us to another use case for measures: creating a dynamic visual title.

By default, Power BI visual titles change only when you drill through a hierarchy—for example, from product category to subcategory to product. These visual titles always use the object names as they appear in the semantic model, which are not always as intuitive and might not match user expectations. Using a measure, you can easily change the title of a visual dynamically. One scenario might be to present the applied filters in a visual title. In that way, users can easily see which selection made in a slicer is applicable as a filter on the visual.

> **Note** When creating a measure for a dynamic title, keep in mind that measures must always return a single value.

Figure 8-8 shows a visual title that includes the years selected in the slicer shown next to the visual. You can achieve this result by using the following measure:

```
_TotalSales VisualTitle =
VAR Sel_SingleYear =
    CONCATENATE ( "$ Total Sales for year ", SELECTEDVALUE ( 'Date'[Year] ) )
VAR Sel_MultipleYears =
    CONCATENATEX ( VALUES ( 'Date'[Year] ), 'Date'[Year], ", " )
VAR Dyn_Title =
    CONCATENATE ( "$ Total Sales for years ", Sel_MultipleYears )
RETURN
    IF(
        AND ( ISFILTERED ( 'Date'[Year] ), NOT ( HASONEVALUE ( 'Date'[Year] ) ) ),
        Dyn_Title,
        Sel_SingleYear
    )
```

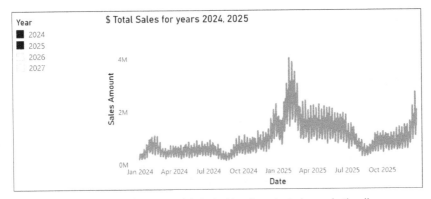

FIGURE 8-8 This line chart shows total *Sales* by Year for selected years in the slicer.

A measure like the one shown here checks multiple conditions, such as whether there is a filter applied using the ISFILTERED function. If so, it determines whether one Year is selected or multiple years are in scope by using the HASONEVALUE function. If only one Year is selected, it changes the visual title dynamically to display the selected year in the visual title. In the case of multiple selected years, the title will list all selected years with commas between them. These possible titles are defined in the variables before the IF expression.

You can select a measure to use as a dynamic visual title in the visual's Format pane. To do so, expand the Title section of the pane, click the fx button, and select the measure that returns the dynamic title (see Figure 8-9).

FIGURE 8-9 Use the Format pane to change the visual title to conditional formatting based on a DAX expression.

In addition to the title, you can use measures to control other visual elements. For example, you can fully control the x-axis and y-axis by applying measures that define the minimum and maximum value for each axis. You can also use measures to set the line color for horizontal and vertical gridlines.

Note Visual calculations can also support visual elements such as titles. To achieve this, add a visual calculation to the visual and then select it when configuring the title using the fx button in the Format pane.

Measures for conditional formatting

On the topic of visual formatting, there is another area in which measures can be useful: to check and validate certain conditions and apply conditional formatting. Taking a matrix visual as an example, you can apply conditional formatting to cell elements to dynamically change the background color and font color, to generate data bars in the matrix cells, and to present icons or even clickable URLs. This helps make the matrix visual more intuitive and highlights relevant data. Any place where measures can be used for conditional formatting can be recognized by the fx button (see Figure 8-10).

FIGURE 8-10 The fx button indicates that conditional formatting is supported.

Suppose you have a matrix visual that contains the total sales amount for each Store split by product categories. As shown in Figure 8-11, by default, the way this information is presented is not terribly intuitive; conditional formatting could highlight the data points that need attention.

Description	Cell phones	Computers	Games and Toys	Home Appliances	Music, Movies and Audio Books	TV and Video	Total
Contoso Store Alaska	2,845,140.79	8,395,596.55	151,092.82	2,007,756.39	908,414.97	1,608,675.83	15,916,677.36
Contoso Store Arkansas	3,480,214.80	9,308,113.33	183,448.73	2,678,140.35	1,034,221.33	1,752,655.31	18,436,793.85
Contoso Store Armagh	2,231,471.28	7,392,694.40	136,329.82	1,872,916.84	637,941.41	1,607,216.09	13,878,569.84
Contoso Store Australian Capital Territory	884,356.36	2,087,576.98	48,986.56	632,004.41	289,353.55	536,260.00	4,478,546.94
Contoso Store Ayrshire	2,231,652.92	6,787,109.05	115,632.69	2,035,296.49	706,015.51	1,473,805.05	13,349,521.71
Contoso Store Basse-Normandie	535,935.86	1,556,301.34	24,305.21	421,038.79	167,962.90	329,476.11	3,035,020.20
Contoso Store Belfast	2,246,244.46	7,234,010.34	122,160.05	2,018,679.81	726,032.18	1,314,004.19	13,661,131.03
Contoso Store Berlin	1,647,620.19	4,353,359.97	81,922.93	1,341,797.10	545,627.92	976,030.94	8,946,359.05
Contoso Store Blaenau Gwent	2,222,355.30	7,350,617.24	118,749.37	1,976,245.39	714,187.71	1,285,646.45	13,667,801.46
Contoso Store Connecticut	3,215,365.56	9,490,898.81	188,264.74	2,528,805.04	1,040,117.27	1,747,059.09	18,210,510.51
Contoso Store Corse	532,517.71	1,344,581.02	27,780.56	363,831.28	168,893.88	239,560.45	2,677,164.90
Contoso Store Drenthe	1,270,291.55	3,917,092.93	74,438.83	938,465.47	454,271.42	772,504.72	7,427,064.91
Contoso Store Dungannon and South Tyrone	2,156,067.49	6,976,503.42	127,514.45	1,978,273.04	714,928.37	1,366,657.14	13,319,943.91
Contoso Store Enna	1,835,870.48	6,097,215.76	104,358.79	1,755,420.94	573,103.57	1,311,638.18	11,677,607.70
Contoso Store Flevoland	1,238,190.52	3,371,142.94	68,189.91	900,373.02	402,790.34	734,736.86	6,715,423.60
Contoso Store Franche-Comté	551,742.34	1,365,970.85	26,564.62	430,333.02	171,757.19	243,752.50	2,790,120.53
Contoso Store Freie Hansestadt Bremen	1,475,360.54	4,067,323.24	89,230.89	1,252,642.98	532,127.79	774,925.74	8,191,611.19
Contoso Store Freistaat Thüringen	1,888,826.51	5,360,402.93	110,832.18	1,410,674.28	634,205.93	1,155,053.27	10,559,995.10
Contoso Store Friesland	1,395,219.34	3,450,392.06	70,489.75	1,098,607.01	432,315.09	649,879.79	7,096,903.03
Contoso Store Groningen	1,296,635.05	3,557,664.34	64,244.27	1,077,836.15	434,169.82	670,087.06	7,100,636.69
Contoso Store Hamburg	1,714,682.96	4,554,078.72	98,917.19	1,434,832.56	552,257.41	918,402.44	9,273,171.28
Contoso Store Hawaii	2,880,545.28	8,628,201.00	154,923.94	2,208,572.24	919,370.44	1,692,642.07	16,484,254.96
Contoso Store Hessen	1,686,827.83	4,790,092.52	87,546.37	1,326,932.18	524,151.96	957,694.04	9,373,244.90
Contoso Store Idaho	2,819,021.08	8,388,321.13	142,254.53	2,359,356.53	894,300.28	1,562,259.55	16,165,513.11
Contoso Store Iowa	3,267,605.93	9,653,420.05	180,770.36	2,724,840.29	1,060,191.44	1,828,136.06	18,714,964.12
Contoso Store Kansas	3,402,414.33	10,117,513.92	179,370.36	2,745,657.63	995,693.59	2,007,904.91	19,448,554.74
Contoso Store La Réunion	489,680.34	1,234,315.73	32,262.87	366,472.21	143,055.53	300,104.21	2,565,890.90
Contoso Store Limousin	550,922.68	1,497,356.48	32,796.00	495,716.83	167,866.33	309,155.17	3,053,813.49
Contoso Store Maine	2,868,220.91	8,181,319.66	161,707.41	2,176,870.12	872,942.63	1,651,962.45	15,913,023.20
Contoso Store Martinique	504,692.66	1,587,453.03	33,394.68	366,021.86	178,655.15	334,532.34	3,004,749.72
Contoso Store Mayotte	520,087.62	1,530,347.78	27,557.35	330,164.58	158,355.39	238,950.76	2,805,463.48
Contoso Store Mecklenburg-Vorpommern	1,594,122.51	4,623,230.83	86,210.08	1,294,118.67	549,575.78	987,997.22	9,135,255.10
Contoso Store Montana	2,841,801.36	8,245,876.67	152,228.94	2,074,665.05	956,270.68	1,557,072.86	15,827,915.56
Total	**205,114,321.30**	**549,446,768.74**	**10,617,789.15**	**161,683,450.31**	**67,641,532.13**	**120,122,852.43**	**1,114,626,714.05**

FIGURE 8-11 This matrix visual shows the sales amount per store and per product category.

A measure can help you identify which cells you want to highlight by checking each cell's value against another value. For example, suppose you want to see which stores have fewer sales in a certain product category—in other words, stores whose sales in the product category are lower than the average over all stores (not counting online sales). You could use the following expression to apply conditional formatting to stores that meet this criterion:

```
% Sales of AVG Sales per store =
VAR TotalSalesAllPhysicalStores =
    CALCULATE (
        [Sales Amount],
        ALL ( Store ),
        Store[Description] <> "Online store"
    )
VAR StoresWithsales =
    CALCULATE (
        DISTINCTCOUNT ( Sales[StoreKey] ),
        Store[Description] <> "Online store"
    )
VAR AverageSalesPerStore =
    DIVIDE ( TotalSalesAllPhysicalStores, StoresWithsales )
RETURN
    DIVIDE ( [Sales Amount], AverageSalesPerStore )
```

This expression calculates the total sales for all physical stores and the number of total stores. It then divides these numbers to obtain to the average sales per Store. Finally, it divides the sales of the Store in the current row by the average sales of all stores to obtain a percentage. This percentage shows a contribution to the average sales for the Store in the current row.

As expected, for some stores, this number is far higher than 100 percent because these stores make many more sales than the average sales per store (see Figure 8-12).

CategoryName / Description	Cell phones Sales Amount	% Sales of AVG Sales per store	Computers Sales Amount	% Sales of AVG Sales per store	Games and Toys Sales Amount	% Sales of AVG Sales per store	Home Appliances Sales Amount
Contoso Store Alaska	2,845,140.79	131.87%	8,395,596.55	133.78%	151,092.82	129.47%	2,007,756.39
Contoso Store Arkansas	3,480,214.80	161.31%	9,308,113.33	148.32%	183,448.73	157.19%	2,678,140.35
Contoso Store Armagh	2,231,471.28	103.43%	7,392,694.40	117.80%	136,329.82	116.82%	1,872,916.84
Contoso Store Australian Capital Territory	884,356.36	40.99%	2,087,576.98	33.26%	48,986.56	41.97%	632,004.41
Contoso Store Ayrshire	2,231,662.92	103.44%	6,787,109.05	108.15%	115,632.69	99.08%	2,035,296.49
Contoso Store Basse-Normandie	535,935.86	24.84%	1,556,301.34	24.80%	24,305.21	20.83%	421,038.79
Contoso Store Belfast	2,246,244.46	104.11%	7,234,010.34	115.27%	122,160.05	104.67%	2,018,619.81
Contoso Store Berlin	1,647,620.19	76.37%	4,353,359.97	69.37%	81,922.93	70.20%	1,341,797.10
Contoso Store Blaenau Gwent	2,222,355.30	103.01%	7,350,617.24	117.13%	118,749.37	101.75%	1,976,245.39
Contoso Store Connecticut	3,215,365.56	149.03%	9,490,898.81	151.23%	188,264.74	161.32%	2,528,805.04
Contoso Store Corse	532,517.71	24.68%	1,344,581.02	21.43%	27,780.56	23.80%	363,831.28
Contoso Store Drenthe	1,270,291.55	58.88%	3,917,092.93	62.42%	74,438.83	63.78%	938,465.47
Contoso Store Dungannon and South Tyrone	2,156,067.49	99.93%	6,976,503.42	111.17%	127,514.45	109.26%	1,978,273.04
Contoso Store Enna	1,835,870.48	85.09%	6,097,215.76	97.16%	104,358.79	89.42%	1,755,420.94
Contoso Store Flevoland	1,238,190.52	57.39%	3,371,142.94	53.72%	68,189.91	58.43%	900,373.02
Contoso Store Franche-Comté	551,742.34	25.57%	1,365,970.85	21.77%	26,564.62	22.76%	430,333.02
Contoso Store Freie Hansestadt Bremen	1,475,360.54	68.38%	4,067,323.24	64.81%	89,230.89	76.46%	1,252,642.98
Contoso Store Freistaat Thüringen	1,888,826.51	87.55%	5,360,402.93	85.42%	110,832.18	94.97%	1,410,674.28
Contoso Store Friesland	1,395,219.34	64.67%	3,450,392.06	54.98%	70,489.75	60.40%	1,098,607.01
Contoso Store Groningen	1,296,635.05	60.10%	3,557,664.34	56.69%	64,244.27	55.05%	1,077,836.15
Contoso Store Hamburg	1,714,682.96	79.47%	4,554,078.72	72.57%	96,917.19	84.76%	1,434,832.56
Contoso Store Hawaii	2,880,545.28	133.51%	8,628,201.00	137.49%	154,923.94	132.75%	2,208,572.24
Contoso Store Hessen	1,686,827.83	78.18%	4,790,092.52	76.33%	87,546.37	75.02%	1,326,932.18
Contoso Store Idaho	2,819,021.08	130.66%	8,388,321.13	133.67%	142,254.53	121.89%	2,359,356.53
Contoso Store Iowa	3,267,605.93	151.45%	9,653,420.05	153.82%	180,770.36	154.90%	2,724,840.29
Contoso Store Kansas	3,402,414.33	157.70%	10,117,513.92	161.22%	179,370.36	153.70%	2,745,657.63
Contoso Store La Réunion	489,680.34	22.70%	1,234,315.73	19.67%	32,262.87	27.64%	366,472.21
Contoso Store Limousin	550,922.68	25.53%	1,497,356.48	23.86%	32,796.00	28.10%	495,716.83
Contoso Store Maine	2,868,220.91	132.94%	8,181,319.68	130.37%	161,707.41	138.56%	2,176,870.12
Contoso Store Martinique	504,692.66	23.39%	1,587,453.03	25.30%	33,394.68	28.61%	366,021.86
Contoso Store Mayotte	520,087.62	24.11%	1,530,347.78	24.39%	27,557.35	23.61%	330,164.58
Contoso Store Mecklenburg-Vorpommern	1,504,127.51	72.80%	4,633,530.93	73.67%	94,310.09		1,304,119.67
Total	205,114,321.30	9506.95%	549,446,768.74	8755.28%	10,617,789.15	9098.00%	161,683,450.31

FIGURE 8-12 This matrix visual shows the *Sales Amount* per Store and the *% of AVG Sales per store* measure.

So far, only the percentage is shown. To configure conditional formatting, you must open the Format pane, expand the Cell elements section, choose the Sales Amount as the Series to apply the settings to, and click the fx button under Background color. This opens the dialog shown in Figure 8-13. Then choose Rules from the Format style dropdown, choose Values only from the Apply to menu, and choose *% Sales of AVG Sales per store* from the dropdown: What field should we base this on? Finally, under Rules, specify the parameters of the if-then-else statement as shown in Figure 8-13. This will apply a red background color to cells for stores whose sales are between 0 percent and 80 percent of the average sales per Store (see Figure 8-14).

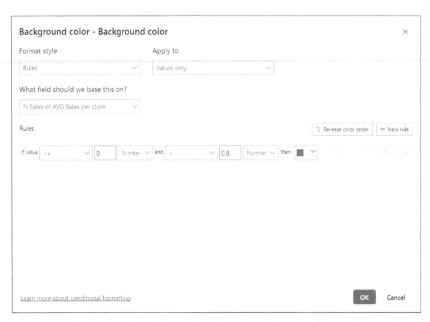

FIGURE 8-13 Use the conditional formatting window to color the cells based on another measure.

CategoryName	Audio		Cameras and camcorders		Cell phones		Computers
Description	Sales Amount	% Sales of AVG Sales per store	Sales Amount	% Sales of AVG Sales per store	Sales Amount	% Sales of AVG Sales per store	Sales Amount
Contoso Store Alaska	513,761.98	132.83%	1,802,075.57	125.44%	2,845,140.79	131.87%	8,395,596.
Contoso Store Arkansas	558,010.75	144.27%	2,145,220.78	149.32%	3,480,214.80	161.31%	9,308,113.
Contoso Store Armagh	449,533.84	116.23%	1,703,763.51	118.60%	2,231,471.28	103.43%	7,392,694.
Contoso Store Australian Capital Territory	133,638.14	34.55%	527,772.93	36.74%	884,356.36	40.99%	2,087,576
Contoso Store Ayrshire	451,300.92	116.68%	1,686,011.60	117.36%	2,231,662.92	103.44%	6,787,109.
Contoso Store Basse-Normandie	91,569.24	23.68%	369,553.87	25.72%	535,935.86	24.84%	1,556,301
Contoso Store Belfast	451,294.65	116.66%	1,818,960.64	126.61%	2,246,244.46	104.11%	7,234,010.
Contoso Store Berlin	267,320.21	69.12%	977,048.85	68.01%	1,647,620.19	76.37%	4,353,359
Contoso Store Blaenau Gwent	491,720.52	127.13%	1,781,095.40	123.98%	2,222,355.30	103.01%	7,350,617.
Contoso Store Connecticut	546,082.59	141.19%	2,252,421.50	156.79%	3,215,365.56	149.03%	9,490,898.
Contoso Store Corse	87,320.23	22.58%	269,615.25	18.77%	532,517.71	24.68%	1,344,581
Contoso Store Drenthe	221,296.86	57.22%	862,186.52	60.01%	1,270,291.35	58.88%	3,917,092
Contoso Store Dungannon and South Tyrone	419,459.31	108.45%	1,828,397.08	127.27%	2,156,067.49	99.93%	6,976,503.
Contoso Store Enna	400,248.99	103.48%	1,482,894.67	103.22%	1,835,870.48	85.09%	6,097,215.
Contoso Store Flevoland	189,213.79	48.92%	786,757.53	54.76%	1,238,190.52	57.39%	2,371,142
Contoso Store Franche-Comté	86,330.28	22.32%	328,264.25	22.85%	551,742.34	25.57%	1,365,970
Contoso Store Freie Hansestadt Bremen	255,677.69	66.11%	894,298.45	62.25%	1,475,360.54	68.38%	4,067,323
Contoso Store Freistaat Thüringen	313,689.32	81.10%	1,124,434.79	78.27%	1,888,826.51	87.55%	5,360,402.
Contoso Store Friesland	203,701.69	52.67%	720,038.63	50.12%	1,395,219.34	64.67%	3,450,392
Contoso Store Groningen	241,948.05	62.56%	725,485.45	50.50%	1,296,635.05	60.10%	3,557,664
Contoso Store Hamburg	283,844.48	73.39%	988,274.21	68.79%	1,714,682.96	79.47%	4,554,078
Contoso Store Hawaii	509,798.95	131.81%	1,872,201.66	130.32%	2,880,545.28	133.51%	8,628,201.
Contoso Store Hessen	288,279.74	74.53%	1,022,326.28	71.16%	1,686,827.83	78.18%	4,790,092
Contoso Store Idaho	551,052.33	142.47%	2,052,101.60	142.84%	2,819,021.08	130.66%	8,388,321.
Contoso Store Iowa	598,320.21	154.69%	2,176,943.75	151.53%	3,267,605.93	151.45%	9,653,420.
Contoso Store Kansas	598,772.16	154.81%	2,034,770.51	141.64%	3,402,414.33	157.70%	10,117,513.
Contoso Store La Réunion	92,546.51	23.93%	280,468.49	19.52%	489,680.34	22.70%	1,234,315
Contoso Store Limousin	93,100.66	24.07%	374,494.15	26.07%	550,922.68	25.53%	1,497,356
Contoso Store Maine	546,507.39	141.30%	1,963,108.09	136.65%	2,868,220.91	132.94%	8,181,319.
Contoso Store Martinique	80,059.73	20.70%	253,943.29	17.68%	504,692.66	23.39%	1,567,453
Contoso Store Mayotte	68,099.40	17.60%	337,772.92	23.51%	520,087.62	24.11%	1,530,347
Contoso Store Mecklenburg-Vorpommern	[illegible]	73.36%	[illegible]	66.32%	[illegible]	73.89%	[illegible]
Total	**33,294,780.29**	**8608.32%**	**117,906,796.05**	**8207.23%**	**205,114,321.30**	**9506.95%**	**549,446,768.**

FIGURE 8-14 The conditional formatting is applied in the matrix visual based on 80 percent or lower compared to average sales.

Alternatively, you can define this logic in a DAX statement. However, the statement must be slightly adjusted to contain an IF statement to set up the logic as part of the conditional formatting.

In the dialog box for conditional formatting, you must select the option for Field value as the Format style, which follows the DAX expression logic. Finally, you must select a DAX measure as the field to base the conditional formatting on. No other configuration is needed in the dialog box. You could then use the following DAX measure to highlight all stores that contribute less than 100 percent:

```
_VizFormatting % Sales of AVG Sales per store =
VAR TotalSalesAllPhysicalStores =
    CALCULATE (
        [Sales Amount],
        ALL ( Store ),
        Store[Description] <> "Online store"
    )
VAR StoresWithsales =
    CALCULATE (
        DISTINCTCOUNT ( Sales[StoreKey] ),
        Store[Description] <> "Online store"
    )
VAR AverageSalesPerStore =
    DIVIDE ( TotalSalesAllPhysicalStores, StoresWithsales )
VAR StoreContribution =
    DIVIDE ( [Sales Amount], AverageSalesPerStore )
RETURN
    IF (
        StoreContribution < 0.8,
        "#D64550" //hex color coding when true, result for false is left out as
we don't want to color this
    )
```

Notice that the logic in the IF function compares the calculated value to 0.8. This is because percentages are calculated as a decimal number between 0 and 1. If the condition is true, we return the hex color code, which will be picked up by Power BI to color the matrix cell. If the evaluated condition is false, nothing will be returned, and the cell will not be colored.

> **Note** This section discusses just two examples of how conditional formatting can be set using a measure. Many alternative setups are possible, also using visual calculations. The main difference is that the visual calculation is part of the visual itself, whereas the measure for formatting can be reused across multiple visuals or even multiple reports as long as the measure definitions are stored in the semantic model.

Measures as visual level filters

In principle, measures cannot be used as filters. This is because measure results are dynamically evaluated on demand. Contrast this with a calculated column, which persists the result in the model and therefore can easily be put on the reporting canvas as a filter or slicer. Measures can, however, be used as visual level filters.

You apply a measure as a filter in the Filter pane in Power BI. You'll notice when you open this pane that filters can be applied to the selected visual, to the current report page, or to the entire report. However, measures can only be used as filters on visuals.

Suppose you have a visual in your report that shows total sales by Manufacturer (see Figure 8-15), and you want to identify which Manufacturers' products you sell the most to ensure there are enough of their products in your company warehouse.

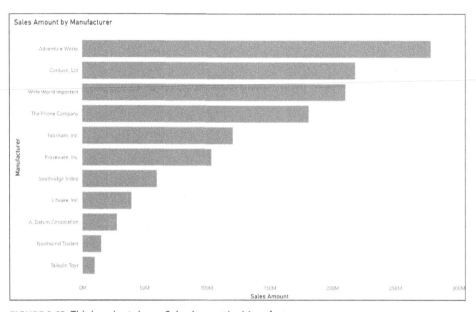

FIGURE 8-15 This bar chart shows *Sales Amount* by Manufacturer.

Now suppose you also want to find out which of these manufacturers supply you with more than 200 products because these will likely be among your most important manufacturers. To achieve this, you could apply a measure like this one:

```
Total Sales for Manufacturers more than 200 products =
IF ( COUNT ( 'Product'[ProductKey] ) >= 200, [Sales Amount] )
```

The resulting visual shows total sales and sales for manufacturers that supply you with more than 200 products (see Figure 8-16). From this visual, you can conclude that Adventure Works has significant total sales but a relatively small portfolio of products.

Creating a dedicated measure for this purpose bloats the model with numerous measures because new measures for each visual may be required. Also, from a maintenance perspective, developers will have a hard time finding out where the logic is hidden in the event a business definition changes.

An alternative approach is to create reusable measures. In this case, you can simply split the preceding measure into two reusable components, making it a lot more flexible to change the threshold value. The first measure, shown here, calculates the total sales, which is already saved in the model:

```
Sales Amount = SUM ( 'Order Detail'[Total Sales] )
```

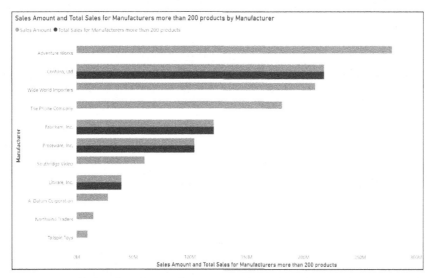

FIGURE 8-16 This bar chart shows *Sales Amount* and *Total Sales for Manufacturers more than 200 products*.

This results in the original visual. Now you can create another measure to obtain a simple count of unique products, like so:

```
# Products = DISTINCTCOUNT ( 'Product'[ProductKey] )
```

At this point, the base visual simply visualizes the total sales by Manufacturer. However, you can use the Filter pane to add the *# Products* measure as a visual-level filter and configure it to return values greater than or equal to 200 (see Figure 8-17).

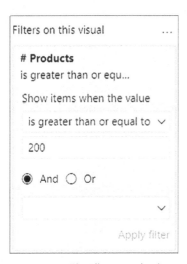

FIGURE 8-17 The Filter pane is where a visual-level filter is applied based on the *# Products* measure.

The resulting visual could be achieved by putting all the logic in the same measure expression, but now, the result is generated using two reusable measures (see Figure 8-18). As you can see, this visual illustrates that you have four manufacturers that supply you with more than 200 products.

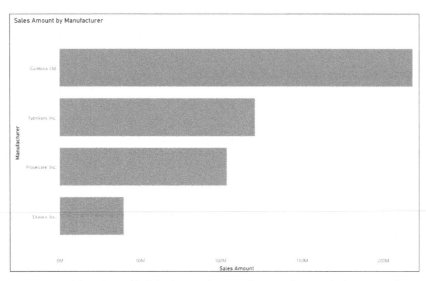

FIGURE 8-18 A bar chart with *Sales Amount* by Manufacturer shows only those manufacturers with more than 200 products.

Calculation groups

You may end up with many measures in your semantic model that repeat the same logic. This is often the case with time intelligence measures and measures for format string changes.

Suppose you have a semantic model that uses several measures, such as one that calculates the sales amount, one that calculates the total order count, and one that calculates the quantity of products sold. Granted, three measures is not many. However, for each of these calculations, you will likely also need to generate year-to-date calculations, quarter-to-date calculations, and month-to-date calculations, which means the number of measures will grow significantly.

In addition to the growing number of measures, the same filter expression is saved multiple times in various measures. This can be a problem when it comes to maintaining measures. For example, if the definition of the filter context changes, the developer will need to find all measures that use the same exact logic to update them.

Calculation groups can help reduce the number of redundant measures using the same filter expression. Calculation groups provide a way to change the type of calculation without adding another measure to the model. In this way, you can avoid adding more measures and duplicating logic in multiple measures.

Note Calculation groups only work with explicit measures. They do not work with other types of calculations in the semantic model, such as calculated columns or calculated tables. Find more about calculation groups in the documentation at *https://learn.microsoft.com/power-bi/transform-model/calculation-groups*.

You can create calculation groups in the semantic model to define the calculation items. DAX contains multiple expressions that are used explicitly for calculation groups, which can be dynamically filled with your measures of choice.

 Note Because calculation groups are not a primary focus of this book, we won't cover them further.

How do all other calculation options compare to visual calculations?

Visual calculations are different from all other calculation options discussed so far. This section describes and compares the various calculation options.

The following table shows the differences between calculated tables, calculated columns, measures, and visual calculations.

Aspect	Calculated Tables	Calculated Columns	Measures	Visual Calculations
Expression Language	DAX, M	DAX, M	DAX	DAX
Editor	Query editor, DAX formula bar	Query editor, DAX formula bar	DAX formula bar	DAX formula bar in visual editing mode
Calculation Context	Model	Model	Model	Visual Matrix
Evaluation	Model refresh	Model refresh	Runtime	Runtime
Persistence of data	Saved in model	Saved in model	Dynamic	Dynamic
Result change based on user interaction	Not influenced	Not influenced	Dynamic	Dynamic

Expression language

Like all the previously discussed calculation options, visual calculations use DAX as an expression language. As noted in Chapter 1, most regular DAX functions that can be used in measures, calculated columns, and calculated tables can be used in visual calculations as well. That being said, there are a few DAX functions that can only be used with visual calculations, such as RUNNINGSUM and MOVINGAVERAGE. In addition, functions like PREVIOUS, NEXT, EXPAND, and COLLAPSE, as well as variations of these functions, are not available in regular DAX.

Editor

Measures, calculated columns, and calculated tables use the DAX formula bar (see Figure 8-19). This is where the semantic model developer types and edits DAX expressions. You can open the DAX formula bar from the model view, the table view, and the report view in Power BI Desktop.

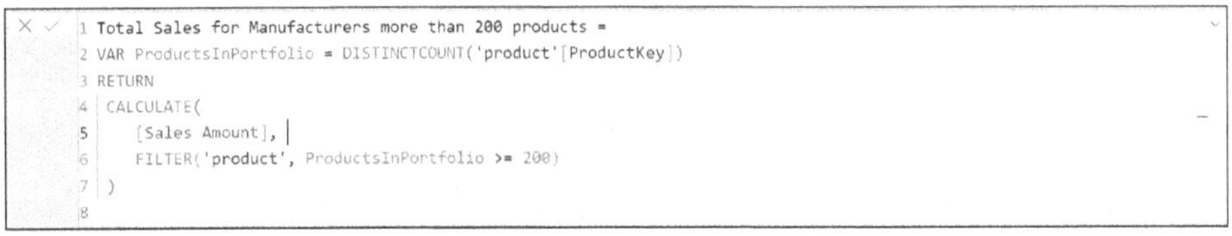

```
1 Total Sales for Manufacturers more than 200 products =
2 VAR ProductsInPortfolio = DISTINCTCOUNT('product'[ProductKey])
3 RETURN
4 CALCULATE(
5     [Sales Amount],
6     FILTER('product', ProductsInPortfolio >= 200)
7 )
8
```

FIGURE 8-19 DAX formula bar in Power BI Desktop is where you edit DAX.

Visual calculations also use the DAX formula bar but only in the visual calculations edit mode window, which also presents the visual matrix. Visual calculations follow a What You See Is What You Get (WYSIWYG) pattern. Results of visual calculation expressions are easy to validate using the rows and columns in the visual matrix. Any column that is part of the visual matrix can be referenced and used in the visual calculation. For a step-by-step tutorial on creating and editing visual calculations, refer to Chapter 2, "My first visual calculation."

Calculation context

To build more complex calculations, you must think in the context of the semantic model, taking into account aspects like the relationships between tables, the direction of these relationships, and storage modes when you write the expression. Functions like USERELATIONSHIP and CROSSFILTERDIRECTION help users influence these model aspects in measures, calculated columns, and calculated tables.

Visual calculations are calculated in the context of the visual matrix. All model objects that are in the visual matrix can be used in a visual calculation. These can consist of columns from various tables, but also explicit measures saved in the model or implicit measures that are part of the visual. Calculation context and related topics are discussed in more detail in Chapter 1.

Evaluation

Similar to measures, visual calculations are evaluated at runtime and consume CPU instead of memory. Other calculation options, such as calculated tables and calculated columns, are evaluated at model refresh and consume memory as part of the total semantic model size. Because measures and visual calculations are calculated at runtime, they're dynamic and can change depending on context and user interaction.

Persistence of data

Calculated columns, calculated tables, and measures are saved in the semantic model as definitions. Calculated columns and calculated tables persist the data in the model, where measures are dynamic and calculate the results in CPU at evaluation time. In contrast, with visual calculations, no definition is saved in the model. Also, visual calculations do not persist data in the semantic model. Visual calculations are saved on a visual level as part of a visual object in a Power BI report.

> **Note** Measures can also be saved in a thin-report as report-level measures. In this scenario, they're not saved to the model but as part of the report definition.

Changes with user interactions

Because visual calculations evaluate at runtime, like measures do, they can be fully dynamic in the context of the visual. Filters applied using the Filter pane or cross-filtering and highlighting from other visual objects will influence the result of the visual calculation. In contrast, calculated columns and calculated tables are not updated based on user interactions but instead are recalculated only when the data is refreshed.

Conditional formatting

Conditional formatting can be applied to any object in your report. Typical use cases could be dynamic visual titles but also data bars, font colors, or background colors in a matrix visual. All this can be achieved by using measures as described in the section "Understanding measures" in this chapter. However, visual calculations are perfectly capable of achieving the same goal as described in Chapter 4, "Organization and use of visual calculations."

There are pros and cons to each setup. One pro of using measures for conditional formatting is that you can reuse them across many visuals and even in different reports because the measure definition is saved to the model. At the same time, though, this is a con of using measures because creating too many measures can clutter the semantic model and make it harder to manage and maintain. In contrast, visual calculations only live on the visual, which will avoid cluttering of the semantic model, but cannot be reused across visuals without duplicating logic.

In summary

This chapter discussed the different calculation options in Power BI and how they compare. Calculations in Power BI are built within the context of the semantic model. This involves considering relationships between tables, the direction of these relationships, and storage modes when writing expressions.

Visual calculations, on the other hand, are computed within the context of the visual matrix. They can use everything that is part of the visual itself but can't reach back out to the model. These calculations are evaluated at runtime, consuming CPU resources rather than memory, making them dynamic and capable of changing based on the context and user interaction.

Calculated tables and calculated columns are evaluated at model refresh, consuming memory as part of the total semantic model size. In contrast, measures and visual calculations are runtime-evaluated and do not consume memory. Visual calculations do not persist in the semantic model but on a visual level within Power BI reports.

## CHAPTER 9

Breaking down visual calculations execution

This chapter looks under the hood of visual calculations, revealing how they work. Grasping the mechanics of visual calculations will make it easier for you to apply complex patterns. This chapter begins with a section on the characteristics of visual calculations, offering a general overview of what makes visual calculations so special. After that, it dives into the DAX queries that are executed to populate the visuals—first showing you how to obtain these DAX queries and then breaking them down to really explain what's happening.

> **Note** This chapter goes far beyond the beginner level of understanding visual calculations. If you're not interested in how visual calculations work under the hood, don't worry about skipping it. You will still be able to enjoy all the benefits of visual calculations without this knowledge. But if you do want to know exactly how things work so you can get the most out of visual calculations, this chapter is written for you!

Characteristics of visual calculations

Before we dive deep into visual calculations, let's take one step back to examine regular visuals in Power BI reports without visual calculations. These visuals are populated with data values, which the Power BI engine obtains from the semantic model by executing DAX queries. A DAX query is a question that is written in the DAX language and can be executed in a Power BI semantic model to obtain results in the form of a flat table. So, every visual has a DAX query behind it. When visual calculations come into play, the underlying DAX query is enhanced such that a visual calculations table with specific metadata is defined.

This chapter compares the DAX query behind a regular visual and the DAX query behind a visual that contains visual calculations. Although there's a lot of overlap, there are also some important differences. Because the output of any DAX query is always a flat table, you might need some additional tricks to generate the information needed for a hierarchy and data sorting order. This helps to display the output of the flat table in a visual that has a hierarchy and sorting order, like a matrix visual. This is done in the DAX query by creating additional columns to indicate whether the value of a row is a raw data field value or a subtotal or a grand total of some kind. By adding these columns, you can display all the calculated results in a flat table and have all the values available to view the results within a visual in a hierarchy that contain subtotals and grand totals as well.

To provide a specific sorting order, you might also need to add additional columns to the flat table. For example, the sorting order of a month column might depend on a different column, like a month number column. This is usually set in the metadata of the month column in the definition of the semantic model itself. To use this metadata, you must include the column for the month number in the output of the DAX query to be able to sort the visual according to this specified sorting order.

The hierarchy and sorting order are two vital pieces of information that are missing in a regular flat table but are of vital importance for creating visual calculations. These are used in the DAX query behind a visual with visual calculations through the introduction of two new concepts inside the DAX language:

- **Visual shape**   This enables you to enrich tables in DAX with metadata to provide a hierarchy and a sorting order by defining axes in the table. These axes can in turn be referenced by visual calculations. This makes the creation of visual calculations intuitive and easy to understand. The complex DAX code is well hidden from the regular business user when visual calculations are created.

- **Densification**   This ensures that you do not lose any values when you create a visual calculation in a visual. Although densification is an important technical concept to ensure you obtain correct and complete output, the regular user does not need to wrap their head around it to be able to create visual calculations. Therefore, visual calculations make DAX easier.

Another very important visual calculation operation that occurs in the DAX query is the renaming of columns. This renaming process takes place in the SELECTCOLUMNS DAX function when the input variable for the visual calculations table is defined. In the visual calculations table, the visual calculations are defined as new columns. This section represents the core of the DAX query executed by the Power BI engine. It generates the calculated values used to populate the visual, which contains the visual calculations shown in the report. The renaming process is necessary to map the column names of the original query to the names used in the visual with visual calculations—and thus, the underlying visual matrix. This ensures that business users can directly reference the columns as they are named in the visual when they create visual calculations, making this creation process simple and intuitive.

 Note   We discuss visual shape and densification, as well as the renaming of columns, later in this chapter, in the section "Understanding how visuals work".

Finally, visual calculations are defined and evaluated only on the filtered and aggregated data that is visible in the visual and thus in the visual matrix in which you create the visual calculation. This is the visual calculations table that's defined in the DAX query. The DAX query contains all the filtered and aggregated data needed to populate the original visual without the visual calculations and by extension, the visual matrix that is visible when you start creating visual calculations. The visual calculations are basically new columns added to this virtual table of filtered and aggregated data, which is not directly connected to the rest of the semantic model.

This has the added benefit of providing performance optimization. When evaluating regular measures, DAX queries run through the tables in your semantic model, and these tables can become quite large. Of course, considerable optimization is performed to ensure that these queries are as efficient and fast as possible, but how easily this optimization occurs depends on how the user set up the measure. A regular user cannot be expected to have all deep insights in contexts and create only DAX formulas that perform optimally. We have already seen that DAX is too hard for most business users to grasp all that. However, because visual calculations are not evaluated over the tables defined in the semantic model, but instead are evaluated over the visual calculations table, they do not have this problem. Because visual calculations run through the filtered and aggregated data, there is a much smaller chance that a user will create calculations that perform suboptimally.

In an excellent blog post found at *https://pbidax.wordpress.com/2024/04/17/visual-calculations-introducing-a-two-layer-approach-in-dax-calculations/*, Jeffrey Wang shows that this optimization can be explained on a deeper level in the number of queries used by the storage engine to obtain the results. There is a lot of optimization done here when you use visual calculations compared to regular DAX measures. In his example of a year-to-date calculation, the number of queries used to obtain the result is reduced from four to one when you use a visual calculation instead of a DAX measure. Because of this, visual calculations often perform better than their measure equivalent.

Obtaining and running DAX queries

In the next section, we explain the DAX query behind every visual and what kind of output table it generates to populate the visual with values. But how do you obtain this DAX query, and where can you see the resulting flat table? The answer is the performance analyzer. The performance analyzer is a Power BI Desktop tool that analyzes the performance of your reports. You access it from a pane available on the right side of Power BI Desktop. To display this pane, click the View tab in the ribbon at the top of the screen and, in the Show Panes section, click Performance analyzer (see Figure 9-1).

FIGURE 9-1 The Show panes option for the performance analyzer is on the View ribbon.

When you open the performance analyzer, you have the option to start recording. If you select this option, Power BI will analyze every action you perform and report the time it took to load each visual that is changed by this action. You can also choose to refresh the visuals on the current report page to obtain data about the performance of those visuals. Figure 9-2 shows the performance analyzer pane after a matrix visual for the current page has been refreshed.

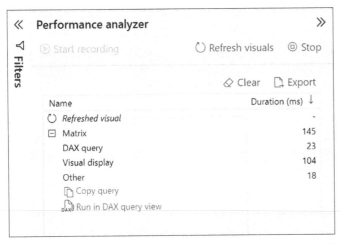

FIGURE 9-2 The performance analyzer pane shows the performance of a matrix visual.

The performance of a visual is always split into categories. All categories have a duration in milliseconds; this reflects how much time is spent in that category.

The three categories shown in Figure 9-2—DAX query, Visual display, and Other—are always present. The DAX query category reports the time it takes for the visual to send the query and the engine to return the results. The Visual display category reports the time needed for the visual to draw on the screen. Finally, the Other category is for all other operations on which time was spent. This could include preparing queries, background processing, or waiting for other visuals to complete. Depending on the storage mode of your semantic model, Additional categories may be available, like DirectQuery or Direct Lake.

At the moment, we're more interested in the other two options shown in Figure 9-2:

- **Copy query** This copies the DAX query used to populate the visual to your clipboard. You can use any text editor to paste the code in, and then you have access to the DAX query that is behind the visual.

- **Run in DAX Query View** DAX Query View is one of the views available in Power BI. It can be used to write, edit, and view the results of DAX queries that you run in your semantic model. If you click this option, Power BI will navigate to the DAX Query View, open a new query, paste in the DAX query, and run it, all in one go (see Figure 9-3).

The DAX query appears at the top of the screen, where it can be adapted, while the query result appears in the bottom of the screen in the form of a flat table. This enables you to easily modify the query and immediately evaluate the result.

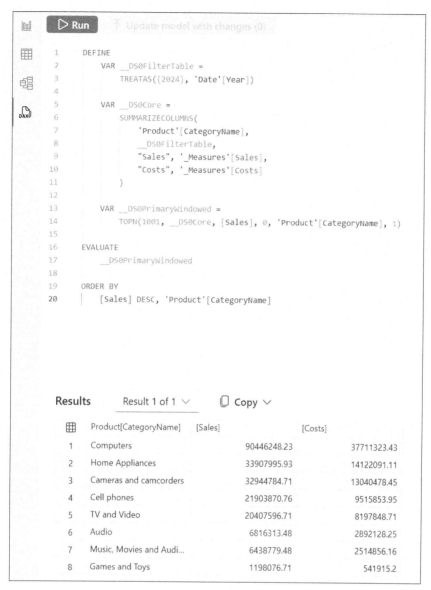

```
   ▷ Run      ⊤ Update model with changes (0)

1    DEFINE
2        VAR __DS0FilterTable =
3            TREATAS({2024}, 'Date'[Year])
4
5        VAR __DS0Core =
6            SUMMARIZECOLUMNS(
7                'Product'[CategoryName],
8                __DS0FilterTable,
9                "Sales", '_Measures'[Sales],
10               "Costs", '_Measures'[Costs]
11           )
12
13       VAR __DS0PrimaryWindowed =
14           TOPN(1001, __DS0Core, [Sales], 0, 'Product'[CategoryName], 1)
15
16   EVALUATE
17       __DS0PrimaryWindowed
18
19   ORDER BY
20       [Sales] DESC, 'Product'[CategoryName]
```

Results   Result 1 of 1 ∨   ☐ Copy ∨

Product[CategoryName]	[Sales]	[Costs]
1	Computers	90446248.23	37711323.43
2	Home Appliances	33907995.93	14122091.11
3	Cameras and camcorders	32944784.71	13040478.45
4	Cell phones	21903870.76	9515853.95
5	TV and Video	20407596.71	8197848.71
6	Audio	6816313.48	2892128.25
7	Music, Movies and Audi...	6438779.48	2514856.16
8	Games and Toys	1198076.71	541915.2

FIGURE 9-3 The output of running a DAX query from a visual in the DAX Query View shows the results in a table.

If you want to obtain the DAX query that contains the visual shape, be aware that this DAX query is created only when visual calculations have been added to a visual, not before. When you want to obtain the DAX query with the visual shape, you will have to add a visual calculation to a visual first, close the visual calculations edit mode, and refresh the visual while using the performance analyzer to obtain the DAX query in the performance analyzer. You can then use the Run in DAX Query View option to directly run the DAX query and see the results. This shows you the end results immediately, but you can always modify the DAX query to evaluate an intermediate table or variable instead of the end result. This will be further explained in the remainder of this chapter.

> **Note** We could write another book about all the available options and operations in the DAX Query View, but in this book, we'll focus on just showing the output.

Understanding how visuals work

To grasp how visual calculations work, you must understand how visuals work in Power BI. In this section, we'll take a closer look at a Power BI visual to help you gain this understanding—specifically, a clustered bar chart, which is a basic visual used in many reports.

What we describe in this section holds true for every visual you create in a report in Power BI. Some visuals, like a card visual, will be much simpler than what we describe; others will be more and more complex depending on the type of visual.

Understanding a regular visual

Recall that in Chapter 2, "My first visual calculation," we started with a clustered bar chart with *Sales* and *Costs* per product category. This visual looked like the one in Figure 9-4, with two bars per product category. We then extended this visual with our first visual calculation by calculating the *Profit*. This created a new bar to display *Profit* for each product category.

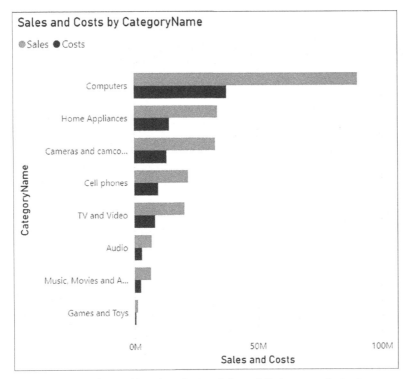

FIGURE 9-4 This clustered bar chart displays *Sales* and *Costs* per product category.

When we created the visual calculation, we also viewed the visual matrix of this visual. As explained in Chapter 3, "Visual calculations concepts," in the section "Visual matrix," the visual matrix represents the data used to create the visual. Figure 9-5 shows the visual matrix for a new visual calculation for our example.

CategoryName	Sales	Costs	Calculation
Audio	6,816,313.48	2,892,128.25	
Cameras and camcorders	32,944,784.71	13,040,478.45	
Cell phones	21,903,870.76	9,515,853.95	
Computers	90,446,248.23	37,711,323.43	
Games and Toys	1,198,076.71	541,915.20	
Home Appliances	33,907,995.93	14,122,091.11	
Music, Movies and Audio Books	6,438,779.48	2,514,856.16	
TV and Video	20,407,596.71	8,197,848.71	
Total	**214,063,666.00**	**88,536,495.27**	

FIGURE 9-5 This visual matrix of a clustered bar chart displays *Sales* and *Costs* per product category and has an empty column called Calculation, where the visual calculation can be added.

Every visual can be represented in this way: by a matrix with data. This is an important thing to realize. By creating visual calculations, we add new columns to this visual matrix and thereby extend the data that's used to populate the visual itself.

To create the data for the visual matrix of a visual, Power BI executes a query to obtain all the data. To be exact, the query is not executed with the purpose of creating the visual matrix; it's created by the Power BI engine to obtain all the necessary data that could be needed to populate the visual shown in the report, as shown in Figure 9-4.

To show this visual to a user, the data to populate that visual must be retrieved. The semantic model definition states which measures and columns from which tables are used, and this information is used to create a query that's executed to populate the visual with data values. This query is written in the DAX language, and this is called a DAX query. The DAX query that's executed returns only the data that's necessary to populate the visual. The output of a DAX query is always a set of data that can be represented in a flat table, as mentioned earlier in this chapter.

The visual matrix that can be accessed in the visual calculations edit mode also contains this information needed to populate the visual, but it's created only after the visual has been created. It's the data used to generate the visual, represented in a table format. One difference with the output table of the DAX query described previously is that the visual matrix has some formatting available. It doesn't consist of just flat data. The total row is an example of a formatted row that has a different role than the other rows. A visual matrix can also have total columns, depending on the visual and the data that's in it, and even rows or columns with subtotals.

A DAX query output table can't have formatted rows or columns; it just consists of a flat table with data. But every visual has a DAX query behind it to retrieve the data that's necessary to populate the visual. As described in the previous section, "Obtaining and running DAX queries," you can view the DAX query behind a visual, and you can also view the output of this DAX query.

Let's go back to the clustered bar chart that contains the *Sales* and *Costs* per product category, shown in Figure 9-4. Before we dive into the DAX query statement, let's review the output of the DAX query, which is shown in Figure 9-6.

⊞	Product[CategoryName]	[Sales]	[Costs]
1	Computers	90446248.23	37711323.43
2	Home Appliances	33907995.93	14122091.11
3	Cameras and camcorders	32944784.71	13040478.45
4	Cell phones	21903870.76	9515853.95
5	TV and Video	20407596.71	8197848.71
6	Audio	6816313.48	2892128.25
7	Music, Movies and Audi...	6438779.48	2514856.16
8	Games and Toys	1198076.71	541915.2

FIGURE 9-6 This DAX query output of a clustered bar chart displays *Sales* and *Costs* per product category.

Consider the differences between the two tables displayed in Figures 9-5 and 9-6. Figure 9-5 shows the visual matrix of the visual, where we add a visual calculation to the clustered bar chart. Figure 9-6 shows the output of the DAX query underneath the clustered bar chart containing *Sales* and *Costs*, which is needed to populate the visual with values. This is the query that is sent to the Power BI engine to calculate the values that we need to show in the visual.

We want to point out two differences here. The first difference is the total row. In the visual matrix (Figure 9-5), there is a total row, even though there is no total displayed in the visual. The data in this row is not even shown in the bar chart. But in the DAX query output table (Figure 9-6), this total row isn't present. Showing it would be a waste of calculation power because we aren't displaying it in the bar chart. When we're gathering the values to populate the visual, there's no need to query the result of the total either. Moreover, the DAX query output table consists of all the data that's retrieved to populate the visual in the first place. The total row isn't displayed in the clustered bar chart; therefore, it isn't included in the DAX query. But if we take the clustered bar chart and ask for the visual matrix of it, suddenly a total row is shown. Where is this calculated? Because it isn't present in the DAX query output table of the visual without any visual calculations, it must be calculated on the spot when you go into the visual calculations edit mode. Once you add a visual calculation to a visual, the DAX query that's executed to obtain the values for the visual is changed. We'll look at these changes in depth in this chapter.

The second difference is the sorting of the product categories. In the visual matrix, the product categories are sorted in an alphabetical order, whereas the DAX query output table is sorted in descending order on the value of *Sales*.

Now let's look at the actual DAX query code that's executed to produce the output table shown in Figure 9-6:

```
DEFINE
    VAR __DS0FilterTable =
        TREATAS({2024}, 'Date'[Year])
```

```
    VAR __DS0Core =
        SUMMARIZECOLUMNS(
            'Product'[CategoryName],
            __DS0FilterTable,
            "Sales", '_Measures'[Sales],
            "Costs", '_Measures'[Costs]
        )

    VAR __DS0PrimaryWindowed =
        TOPN(1001, __DS0Core, [Sales], 0, 'Product'[CategoryName], 1)

EVALUATE
    __DS0PrimaryWindowed

ORDER BY
    [Sales] DESC, 'Product'[CategoryName]
```

A DAX query can have three parts:

- **Definition**   The definition, which is always preceded by the keyword DEFINE, in this case defines three variables. The first one (__DS0FilterTable) creates a table that is used to propagate filters that were present on the visual report page to the calculation we want to do here. Apparently, there was a slicer for the year present on the report page, which was set to the year 2024, and that filter is defined in __DS0FilterTable to pass on in an argument later. The second variable (__DS0Core) is the core results table, where the actual output table is created. In this case, it's a fairly simple statement. The DAX function SUMMARIZECOLUMNS is used, which summarizes one or more tables with respect to the given groupings. In this case, the column CategoryName from the Product table is retrieved. The second parameter provides the filter table defined in __DS0FilterTable to ensure we look only at the year 2024. Finally, the summarized table for the category names is extended with two new columns called Sales and Costs, whose values are calculated by evaluating the *Sales* and *Costs* measures, respectively. The third variable (__DS0PrimaryWindowed) is the windowed results variable. Power BI never returns all the necessary values for the output of a DAX query. Rather, it wants to limit the results to optimize performance. In a visual, there are never 1 million data values visible at the same time. Even if you were to create a table visual with a million rows, you would just see a subset in the first view, and you would need to scroll down to view more rows. In addition, to optimize performance, the Power BI engine does not return all the results in the first go, but only a subset instead. This is what is called the windowed results in the variable definition. In this example, it will only return the first 1001 values.

- **Evaluation**   This is the only mandatory section in a DAX query and is always preceded by the keyword EVALUATE. This is where you define what you want to execute and show in the output of the DAX query. In this case, we want to evaluate the windowed results, so that's the only output.

- **Modifier**   This is where you can specify how you would like to view the results. This is an optional section in a DAX query; only the evaluation part is mandatory. You can use the modifier part in a DAX query to influence the order in which output data is sorted by adding an ORDER BY expression, as is done in this example. This is why the rows in Figure 9-6 are sorted by *Sales* and not in alphabetical order of the product categories.

The preceding DAX query is fairly simple. But what happens if we add a visual calculation and then look at the underlying DAX query and the output table? We'll explore this in the next section.

The DAX query behind a visual with visual calculations

Let's go back to our clustered bar chart visual and add a visual calculation to see what happens in the DAX query and the output. We'll use the same example as in Chapter 2, adding *Profit* as a visual calculation using the following DAX statement:

```
Profit = [Sales] - [Costs]
```

If you look at the DAX query output, shown in Figure 9-7, it's as expected. Indeed, it looks very similar to the output in Figure 9-6, except there's an additional column to display the values of the profit per product category, and the names of the columns are somewhat more complex. The column with the product category is suddenly called __SQDS0VisualCalcs[CategoryName], and the three columns with data for the sales, costs, and profit also have the prefix __SQDS0VisualCalcs.

⊞	__SQDS0VisualCalcs[CategoryName]	__SQDS0VisualCalcs[Sales]	__SQDS0VisualCalcs[Costs]	__SQDS0VisualCalcs[Profit]
1	Computers	90446248.23	37711323.43	52734924.8
2	Home Appliances	33907995.93	14122091.11	19785904.82
3	Cameras and camcorders	32944784.71	13040478.45	19904306.25
4	Cell phones	21903870.76	9515853.95	12388016.81
5	TV and Video	20407596.71	8197848.71	12209748
6	Audio	6816313.48	2892128.25	3924185.23
7	Music. Movies and Audio Books	6438779.48	2514856.16	3923923.32
8	Games and Toys	1198076.71	541915.2	656161.5

FIGURE 9-7 This DAX query output of a clustered bar chart displays *Sales* and *Costs* per product category and is extended with a visual calculation to calculate *Profit* per product category.

The prefix hints that the DAX query is more complex than before. To start, it indicates that the column for the product category is not taken from the Product table but rather from a virtual table called __SQDS0VisualCalcs. This virtual table is created inside the DAX query and generates the output.

Let's have a look at the DAX query itself. Whereas the previous DAX query was only 20 lines long, this one has 74 lines of code. Therefore, we'll examine it in pieces to ensure you understand what happens. You can find the whole DAX query in the sample model, as explained in the introduction for this book. You can also view it in Appendix A. The first 30-odd lines of code are as follows:

```
DEFINE
COLUMN '__SQDS0VisualCalcs'[Profit] =
    (/* USER DAX BEGIN */
    [Sales] - [Costs]
    /* USER DAX END */)

    VAR __SQDS0FilterTable =
        TREATAS({2024}, 'Date'[Year])
```

```
VAR __SQDS0Core =
    SUMMARIZECOLUMNS(
        ROLLUPADDISSUBTOTAL('Product'[CategoryName],
        "IsSQDS0GrandTotalRowTotal"),
        __SQDS0FilterTable,
        "Sales", '_Measures'[Sales],
        "Costs", '_Measures'[Costs]
    )

VAR __SQDS0VisualCalcsInput =
    SELECTCOLUMNS(
        KEEPFILTERS(
            SELECTCOLUMNS(
                __SQDS0Core,
                "CategoryName", 'Product'[CategoryName],
                "IsSQDS0GrandTotalRowTotal", [IsSQDS0GrandTotalRowTotal],
                "Sales", [Sales],
                "Costs", [Costs]
            )
        ),
        "CategoryName", [CategoryName],
        "IsSQDS0GrandTotalRowTotal", [IsSQDS0GrandTotalRowTotal],
        "Sales", [Sales],
        "Costs", [Costs]
    )
```

You might recognize a lot of this code from the previous DAX query, which had the *Sales* and *Costs* per product category. It defines the same filter table and a similar core table. However, the core variable, __SQDS0Core, contains a new column and a new row that were not present in the earlier DAX query. Figure 9-8 shows the output table for the __SQDS0Core variable.

	Product[CategoryName]	[IsSQDS0GrandTotalRowTotal]	[Sales]	[Costs]
1	Audio	False	6816313.48	2892128.25
2	TV and Video	False	20407596.71	8197848.71
3	Computers	False	90446248.23	37711323.43
4	Cameras and camcorders	False	32944784.71	13040478.45
5	Cell phones	False	21903870.76	9515853.95
6	Music, Movies and Audi...	False	6438779.48	2514856.16
7	Games and Toys	False	1198076.71	541915.2
8	Home Appliances	False	33907995.93	14122091.11
9		True	214063666	88536495.27

FIGURE 9-8 The DAX query output of the __SQDS0Core variable contains a new column.

The output table in Figure 9-8 has four columns. Three of these—Product[CategoryName], [Sales], and [Costs] are familiar. The new column is called [IsSQDS0GrandTotalRowTotal]; it contains only the Boolean values True or False. This column imposes a hierarchy on the table by marking whether a row contains raw data (False) or is in fact a total row (True). For all the rows shown in the output table in Figure 9-6, the value is False; these are the rows that also contain a specific product category. However, the new row, the last one in Figure 9-8, has no product category, and the value for this total column is

True, indicating that it is in fact a total row. This is where the total row is added in the DAX query, which suddenly appeared in the visual matrix.

Note however that the total row is also not present in the output table shown in Figure 9-7, which is the DAX query executed to obtain all the data values needed to populate the visual itself. Because there's no total displayed in the final visual, there's no need to execute this total value there. In the intermediate steps, however, it's necessary; therefore, it's included in the __SQDS0Core variable.

Often, a visual calculation needs to know the total value to calculate the results. An example could be when a visual calculation is added to calculate a percentage of the grand total. Instead of inspecting the visual calculations that are present and figuring out whether they need the total, the total row is always added regardless of whether it's needed. From this, we can deduce that the visual matrix is set up using some intermediate result of the DAX query rather than the final result of the DAX query.

If you look at the next variable defined in the DAX query, __SQDS0VisualCalcsInput, this is also pretty familiar. Figure 9-9 shows the output of this variable.

	[CategoryName]	[IsSQDS0GrandTotalRowTotal]	[Sales]	[Costs]
1	Audio	False	6816313.48	2892128.25
2	TV and Video	False	20407596.71	8197848.71
3	Computers	False	90446248.23	37711323.43
4	Cameras and camcorders	False	32944784.71	13040478.45
5	Cell phones	False	21903870.76	9515853.95
6	Music, Movies and Audi...	False	6438779.48	2514856.16
7	Games and Toys	False	1198076.71	541915.2
8	Home Appliances	False	33907995.93	14122091.11
9		True	214063666	88536495.27

FIGURE 9-9 The DAX query output of the __SQDS0VisualCalcsInput variable is similar to before.

This is almost identical to the output of the __SQDS0Core variable, except for the name of the first column. Specifically, the Product[CategoryName] column is now named simply [CategoryName]. This is due to the use of the SELECTCOLUMNS function, in which all the columns from the core variable are renamed to match the names as they appear in the final visual, and thus the visual matrix (refer to Figure 9-5).

In this case, apart from the removal of the word Product from the first column name, the columns wind up with the exact same name they already had. So why bother renaming them? Actually, what happens here is slightly more elegant: the column names in the original query are in fact mapped to the column names of the visual column names, so the names used in the visual are also displayed in the visual matrix. If you were to change the name of a field that should be displayed in the visual, you would see a different mapping here. For example, if you had renamed the CategoryName to Category, Sales to Sales Amount, and Costs to Cost Amount in the clustered bar chart, these names would be visible in this mapping in the SELECTCOLUMNS function.

Note The Boolean total column is not present in the visual matrix, so that column is not renamed to any other name than it already had.

So far, a lot of the DAX query is familiar and relates to the DAX query for the visual that did not yet contain the visual calculation for the profit. However, we skipped the first few lines in the DAX query, which were as follows:

```
DEFINE
    COLUMN '__SQDS0VisualCalcs'[Profit] =
        (/* USER DAX BEGIN */
        [Sales] - [Costs]
        /* USER DAX END */)
```

In this code, a column called Profit is defined inside a table called __SQDS0VisualCalcs, as some object Sales minus an object Costs. We recognize this as the calculation we defined for the visual calculation inside the visual, but we haven't defined any table called SQDS0VisualCalcs. So, where is this table, and what is in this table? And what objects does it call in this calculation? Are they measures or columns? We will answer these questions below, when we look at the rest of the DAX query code.

The next piece of DAX query, which is still in the DEFINE section, is as follows:

```
    TABLE '__SQDS0VisualCalcs' =
        __SQDS0VisualCalcsInput
    WITH VISUAL SHAPE
        AXIS rows
            GROUP [CategoryName] TOTAL [IsSQDS0GrandTotalRowTotal]
            ORDER BY
                [CategoryName] ASC
        DENSIFY "IsDensifiedRow"
```

This is where the __SQDS0VisualCalcs table is defined, which is used in the first few lines of the DAX query. The very first lines of the DAX query defined a column inside this table, which contains the visual calculation definition created in the visual. In the preceding part of the DAX query, the table itself is defined as the variable __SQDS0VisualCalcsInput (which was also defined earlier) but with another new piece of DAX code for the visual shape.

In the preceding piece of DAX, the __SQDS0VisualCalcs table is defined with a WITH VISUAL SHAPE statement. This is some new DAX that has been created specifically for visual calculations. It enables you to enrich tables with metadata to provide a hierarchical structure and a sorting order, which are precisely the two pieces of information missing in a flat output table of a visual, but which are both essential to create visual calculations. This is the visual shape.

The preceding WITH VISUAL SHAPE DAX statement defines only one axis—namely rows—because this is a DAX query for a simple visual with only one field on the rows. For this axis, the column CategoryName is grouped and marked as the column that should define the rows, and with the keyword TOTAL, the column that contains the totals for this group is defined. An axis can have multiple groups (more on this later), and each axis can have a sort order. In the preceding DAX, the rows axis is sorted by the CategoryName column ascending. Because the column contains text values, an alphabetical sorting order is applied.

Axes in the visual shape are always provided in order, with ROWS first and COLUMNS second. Since the default value of the *axis* parameter is the first axis in the visual shape, the default value is ROWS for most visuals, unless the visual does not have a ROWS axis; then the default value is COLUMNS. For example, a matrix visual that does not include a field on rows but does include a field on columns only has a columns axis; in that situation, the default value for *axis* is COLUMNS.

These axes are used extensively in visual calculations. The concept of the axis is explained in detail in Chapter 3. In this part of the DAX query, axes are defined to be used directly in visual calculation functions, making it easy and intuitive for any user to create visual calculations.

Note We will explain the DENSIFY "IsDensifiedRow" line at the end of the preceding DAX query later in this chapter.

Let's see what the __SQDS0VisualCalcs table looks like if you evaluate it. Figure 9-10 shows the result.

	__SQDS0VisualCalcs[Profit]	__SQDS0VisualCalcs[CategoryName]	_SQDS...	__SQDS0VisualCalcs[Sales]	__SQDS0VisualCalcs[Costs]	__SQDS0VisualCalcs[IsDensifiedRow]
1	125527170.73		True	214063666	88536495.27	False
2	3924185.23	Audio	False	6816313.48	2892128.25	False
3	12209748	TV and Video	False	20407596.71	8197848.71	False
4	52734924.8	Computers	False	90446248.23	37711323.43	False
5	19904306.25	Cameras and camcorders	False	32944784.71	13040478.45	False
6	12388016.81	Cell phones	False	21903870.76	9515853.95	False
7	3923923.32	Music, Movies and Audio Books	False	6438779.48	2514856.16	False
8	656161.5	Games and Toys	False	1198076.71	541915.2	False
9	19785904.82	Home Appliances	False	33907995.93	14122091.11	False

FIGURE 9-10 The DAX query output of the __SQDS0VisualCalcs variable contains extra columns.

Compare this table with the output for the __SQDS0VisualCalcsInput variable shown in Figure 9-9. Because this new table has been defined from the variable as a starting point, but with additional metadata, you would expect to find the same values here.

This output table does contain the same nine rows as the output table for the __SQDS0VisualCalcsInput variable. It also contains the same four columns: the CategoryName, the column that indicates whether the row is a total, the Sales, and the Costs.

There is a slight difference in the column headers, however; they now contain the name of the table (__SQDS0VisualCalcs). This indicates that they are part of the __SQDS0VisualCalcs virtual table defined in the DAX query. Also, the rows have a different sorting order; this is explained by the ORDER BY statement in the DAX query, which enforces an alphabetical sorting order based on the category name. This is also the sorting order shown in Figure 9-10.

This table also contains two new columns on either end. The right-most one, IsDensifiedRow, contains only False values and derives from the DENSIFY statement (explained later in this section).

The left-most one, Profit—which you might also recognize—is defined in the first few lines of the DAX query, where you recognize the visual calculation definition created in the visual. Because the DAX query begins with the definition of this new column in this table, it is placed at the left-most position and is the starting point of the output table.

Now we can also answer the question of which objects Sales and Costs are in this column definition: they're the Sales and Costs columns from the __SQDS0VisualCalcs table in which we're creating the new column. Because we're creating a column in a table using other columns from this same table, it isn't necessary to append the table name as a prefix. This is also not necessary when you create a calculated column in a table in Power BI; you can directly reference the columns from the table in which you're creating the new calculated column. This definition of a new column is like that process, even if it happens in a virtual table instead of a physical one.

We now seem to have all the information we need to populate the clustered bar chart, including the visual calculation for the profit. The remainder of the DAX query also supports this. The next definition that takes place in the DAX query is the definition of another variable, __SQDS0RemoveEmptyDensified, where we filter out any empty or densified rows in the table we just defined. Because densification plays no role yet in this example, we will not discuss it in detail here. However, to be thorough, we do provide the DAX code of this part of the DAX query:

```
VAR __SQDS0RemoveEmptyDensified =
    FILTER(
        KEEPFILTERS('__SQDS0VisualCalcs'),
        OR(
            NOT('__SQDS0VisualCalcs'[IsDensifiedRow]),
            NOT(ISBLANK('__SQDS0VisualCalcs'[Profit]))
        )
    )
```

Figure 9-11 shows the output of this variable, also for the sake of completeness. As you can see, it is no different from the output of the __SQDS0VisualCalcs table shown in Figure 9-10.

⊞	__SQDS0VisualCalcs[Profit]	__SQDS0VisualCalcs[CategoryName]	__SQDS0Vi...	__SQDS0VisualCalcs[Sales]	__SQDS0VisualCalcs[Costs]	__SQDS0VisualCalcs[IsD...
1	125527170.73		True	214063666	88536495.27	False
2	3924185.23	Audio	False	6816313.48	2892128.25	False
3	12209748	TV and Video	False	20407596.71	8197848.71	False
4	52734924.8	Computers	False	90446248.23	37711323.43	False
5	19904306.25	Cameras and camcorders	False	32944784.71	13040478.45	False
6	12388016.81	Cell phones	False	21903870.76	9515853.95	False
7	3923923.32	Music, Movies and Audio Books	False	6438779.48	2514856.16	False
8	656161.5	Games and Toys	False	1198076.71	541915.2	False
9	19785904.82	Home Appliances	False	33907995.93	14122091.11	False

FIGURE 9-11 The DAX query output of the variable __SQDS0RemoveEmptyDensified contains the same columns as before.

We're nearing the end of the DAX query, but there are two more variables defined. The next piece of the DAX query defines a variable with a name that should be familiar: __DS0Core. You saw this name in the simple DAX query behind the clustered bar chart before we added the visual calculation.

Even though the name is familiar, the code itself is a bit more complex than what you saw earlier:

```
VAR __DS0Core =
    SELECTCOLUMNS(
        KEEPFILTERS(
            FILTER(
                KEEPFILTERS(__SQDS0RemoveEmptyDensified),
                '__SQDS0VisualCalcs'[IsSQDS0GrandTotalRowTotal] = FALSE
            )
        ),
        "'__SQDS0VisualCalcs'[CategoryName]",
        '__SQDS0VisualCalcs'[CategoryName],
        "'__SQDS0VisualCalcs'[Sales]", '__SQDS0VisualCalcs'[Sales],
        "'__SQDS0VisualCalcs'[Costs]", '__SQDS0VisualCalcs'[Costs],
        "'__SQDS0VisualCalcs'[Profit]", '__SQDS0VisualCalcs'[Profit]
    )
```

To define the variable, you take the previous variable, __SQDS0RemoveEmptyDensified, filter out the total row, and select only the columns we need for the next steps by using the SELECTCOLUMNS DAX function.

The output of the __DS0Core variable, shown in Figure 9-12, is likely also familiar; it's starting to look much like the final output, shown in Figure 9-7 (and repeated in Figure 9-13). The number of rows and columns match, and the naming of the columns is as you would expect in the final output. The only difference is in the sorting order of the rows. Because this table is the output of an intermediate step, no sorting order is applied, unlike in the final output table.

	_SQDS0VisualCalcs[CategoryName]	_SQDS0VisualCalcs[Sales]	_SQDS0VisualCalcs[Costs]	_SQDS0VisualCalcs[Profit]
1	Audio	6816313.48	2892128.25	3924185.23
2	TV and Video	20407596.71	8197848.71	12209748
3	Computers	90446248.23	37711323.43	52734924.8
4	Cameras and camcorders	32944784.71	13040478.45	19904306.25
5	Cell phones	21903870.76	9515853.95	12388016.81
6	Music, Movies and Audio Books	6438779.48	2514856.16	3923923.32
7	Games and Toys	1198076.71	541915.2	656161.5
8	Home Appliances	33907995.93	14122091.11	19785904.82

FIGURE 9-12 The DAX query output of the __DS0Core variable is not yet sorted.

	_SQDS0VisualCalcs[CategoryName]	_SQDS0VisualCalcs[Sales]	_SQDS0VisualCalcs[Costs]	_SQDS0VisualCalcs[Profit]
1	Computers	90446248.23	37711323.43	52734924.8
2	Home Appliances	33907995.93	14122091.11	19785904.82
3	Cameras and camcorders	32944784.71	13040478.45	19904306.25
4	Cell phones	21903870.76	9515853.95	12388016.81
5	TV and Video	20407596.71	8197848.71	12209748
6	Audio	6816313.48	2892128.25	3924185.23
7	Music, Movies and Audio Books	6438779.48	2514856.16	3923923.32
8	Games and Toys	1198076.71	541915.2	656161.5

FIGURE 9-13 This DAX query output of a clustered bar chart displays *Sales* and *Costs* per product category and is extended with a visual calculation to calculate *Profit* per product category.

There's not much to the final piece of the DAX query, shown here:

```
VAR __DSOPrimaryWindowed =
    TOPN(1001, __DSOCore, '__SQDSOVisualCalcs'[Sales], 0,
    '__SQDSOVisualCalcs'[CategoryName], 1)

EVALUATE
    __DSOPrimaryWindowed

ORDER BY
    '__SQDSOVisualCalcs'[Sales] DESC, '__SQDSOVisualCalcs'[CategoryName]
```

The only variable left is __DSPrimaryWindowed. This represents the windowed result of the previous variable. You already saw this in the DAX query behind the visual of the simple clustered bar chart, where only measures were used, and no visual calculation was added. Then the query reaches the evaluation stage, where it evaluates this last windowed variable and adds a modifier to apply the sorting order based on the Sales column.

 Note The entire DAX query can be found in Appendix A.

From visual to DAX query and output table

Take a moment to review what you've learned so far. We started with a simple visual—a clustered bar chart with two measures—and looked at the DAX query behind it to retrieve all the necessary data values to populate it. We also looked at the output table of this DAX query where the data values are visible in a flat table format. We then extended the clustered bar chart with a visual calculation and checked the DAX query and the output table again, comparing them to the DAX query and output table of the simple clustered bar chart. In this process, we explained the following:

- Every visual has a DAX query behind it.

- Every visual is populated with values because the Power BI engine executes this DAX query.

- The output of a DAX query can always be displayed in a flat table output.

- The DAX query of a visual with visual calculations is a lot more complex than the DAX query for a visual without visual calculations.

- There are some new concepts introduced in a DAX query where visual calculations are involved: visual shape and densification. (More on these in a moment.)

- In a DAX query where visual calculations are involved, there's a mapping between the column names in the original query and the visual's column names. This makes it possible to reference the visual's column names directly when creating visual calculations.

Note We have not yet seen much of the new concepts of visual shape and densification introduced with visual calculations because we started with a simple example visual. We will explain that in more detail in the remainder of this chapter.

Extending the visual shape with a hierarchy

The visual shape is a table modifier that can be used in DAX queries. It enriches a flat table with metadata that's needed to define the axes for visual calculations. It also defines the hierarchy and the sorting order within these axes—which is vital information we're missing in a flat table but that's needed to create visual calculations. So far, you've only seen a definition of the rows axis, and no hierarchy or complex sorting order yet, but this can also be defined with the help of the visual shape. We'll explore these options in the next sections.

To illustrate the capabilities of the visual shape modifier in a DAX query, we'll reuse an example from Chapter 2, in the section "Reset your calculation." This example starts with a simple matrix visual with Year and Month on the rows and the *Sales* measure as values (see Figure 9-14).

Year	Sales
⊟ **2024**	**214,063,666.00**
January	14,091,130.12
February	18,652,745.19
March	13,707,027.63
April	13,617,953.40
May	16,025,489.67
June	15,987,048.83
July	15,846,857.82
August	9,561,371.47
September	16,331,213.97
October	20,374,371.26
November	23,371,076.56
December	36,497,380.10
⊟ **2025**	**448,863,334.43**
January	51,886,482.12
February	64,923,153.55
March	44,610,254.48
April	43,794,064.91
May	44,782,137.77
June	39,376,967.87
July	29,708,944.66
Total	**1,265,828,290.39**

FIGURE 9-14 This matrix visual shows *Sales* per Month and Year.

If you look at the DAX query behind this visual, you'll see the same structure as the one for the simple clustered bar chart. The query itself, however, is a bit more complicated. We'll use a slightly simplified version of the DAX query to explain a few new concepts; you can find the original DAX query in Appendix B. The simplified version is as follows:

```
DEFINE
    VAR __DSOCore =
        SUMMARIZECOLUMNS(
            ROLLUPADDISSUBTOTAL(
                'Date'[Year], "IsGrandTotalRowTotal",
                ROLLUPGROUP('Date'[Month], 'Date'[MonthNumber]),
                "IsDM1Total"
            ),
            "Sales", '_Measures'[Sales]
        )
EVALUATE
    __DSOCore
ORDER BY
    [IsGrandTotalRowTotal] DESC,
    'Date'[Year],
    [IsDM1Total] DESC,
    'Date'[MonthNumber],
    'Date'[Month]
```

Note The difference between this simplified version of the DAX query and the full version is that we removed the windowed results variable (which ensures that only the top 502 values are calculated when populating the visual) and we removed a filter table that was defined to calculate the values that appear in the matrix when the user clicks the expand icons for the years.

The DAX query defines a __DSCore variable that uses the SUMMARIZECOLUMNS DAX function to create a summary table over the Year and Month column from the Date table. The MonthNumber column is also used here, even though we did not put it in the visual. This is because in the Date table in the semantic model, we used the Sort by column option for the Month column to ensure that this column is sorted based on the MonthNumber column rather than alphabetically. The DAX query includes this metadata to populate a visual containing the Month column to ensure that the sorting in the visual is done correctly. The query also applies a hierarchy by adding two columns—IsGrandTotalRowTotal and IsDM1Total—to distinguish between rows that contain the raw data for one single month from rows that contain data for the subtotals per year or even the grand total for all years. Finally, this table is extended with a Sales column that uses the *Sales* measure to calculate the sales for each row.

This __DSCore variable is evaluated in the DAX query with an extensive ORDER BY expression. This statement ensures that the grand total is on top of the output table, and the subtotal for each year is above the monthly values. You also see the MonthNumber column here again to ensure that the months are sorted in a logical order and not alphabetically.

The output of this DAX query is still a flat table, but now it contains additional columns to create a hierarchy and sorting orders. Figure 9-15 shows the first few rows of the output table of the DAX query.

	Date[Year]	Date[Month]	Date[MonthNumber]	[IsGrandTotalRowTotal]	[IsDM1Total]	[Sales]
1				True	True	1265828290.39
2	2024			False	True	214063666
3	2024	January	1	False	False	14091130.12
4	2024	February	2	False	False	16652745.19
5	2024	March	3	False	False	13707027.63
6	2024	April	4	False	False	13617953.4
7	2024	May	5	False	False	16025489.67
8	2024	June	6	False	False	15987048.83
9	2024	July	7	False	False	15846857.82

FIGURE 9-15 The output table of the DAX query that is executed to populate the matrix visual with *Sales* per Month and Year contains additional columns to create a hierarchy and sorting orders.

What would happen if we were to define a visual calculation in this visual? We would expect the visual shape to be more complex, because now we have some hierarchy and sorting in our visual. So, let's add the YTD Sales as a visual calculation that resets for each year, like we did in Chapter 2, in the section "Reset your calculation," and look at the resulting DAX query and the output table.

The DAX query itself is a lot longer and more complex than before, but that was expected. We'll only highlight the relevant differences with the DAX query for the simple visual and not analyze the complete DAX query part for part. The DAX query as a whole can be found in the sample model and in Appendix C.

The DAX query starts again with the definition of a column called YTD Sales, which is the visual calculation we added to the visual. You will likely recognize the DAX that we used to create the visual calculation, which is as follows, from Chapter 2:

```
DEFINE
    COLUMN '__DS0VisualCalcs'[YTD Sales] =
    (/* USER DAX BEGIN */
    RUNNINGSUM([Sales], [Year])
    /* USER DAX END */)
```

Next, the __DS0Core variable is defined in the same way as in the preceding simplified DAX query to populate the matrix visual that shows *Sales* per Month and Year. From this, a variable called __DS0VisualCalcsInput is defined to create a table as input for the visual calculations table. In this variable, all the columns from the core variable are renamed to match the names as they are displayed in the visual itself, and thus in the visual matrix.

After that, the __DS0VisualCalcs table is defined, where the visual shape is used again. The DAX query code for this table is as follows:

```
TABLE '__DS0VisualCalcs' =
        __DS0VisualCalcsInput
        WITH VISUAL SHAPE
```

```
AXIS rows
    GROUP [Year] TOTAL      [IsGrandTotalRowTotal]
    GROUP
        [Month],
        [MonthNumber]
         TOTAL [IsDM1Total]
    ORDER BY
        [Year] ASC,
        [MonthNumber] ASC,
        [Month] ASC
    DENSIFY "IsDensifiedRow"
```

In the visual shape, there is still only one axis defined, namely rows. However, it's more extensive than the previous example, which only defined one group. The preceding statement has one group for the year column, where the total values are defined by the IsGrandTotalRowTotal column, and then another group that contains both the Month and the MonthNumber columns, where the total is defined by the IsDM1Total column. As before, the MonthNumber column is included so it can be used for the sorting order, which is done in the next few lines of code. The ORDER BY statement calls for this axis to be sorted ascending on the Year column first, then ascending on the MonthNumber column, and finally ascending on the Month column. This ensures a logical sort order in the axis that matches the metadata that was already defined in the Date table of the semantic model itself. The table definition ends with the DENSIFY statement, which we'll explain later in this chapter.

This shows how the visual shape can be extended to more complex situations: the visual shape defines one or more axes that contain a hierarchy and a sorting order, two important concepts relating to visual calculations. Once defined, these axes can be used in visual calculations to refer to the visual structure of a visual. In this case, we defined a visual calculation that uses a running sum over the rows axis, and we can directly refer to this rows axis because it's defined in the visual structure that lies behind the visual.

For completeness, Figure 9-16 shows the output table of the DAX query. This output table matches the output table of the visual without the visual calculation displayed in Figure 9-15, but with two additional columns for the YTD sales and the IsDensifiedRow, and the table name __DS0VisualCalcs before each column name.

	__DS0VisualCalcs[YTD Sal...	_DS...	_DS0Vi...	_DS...	__DS0Visual...	__DS0Visual...	__DS0VisualCalcs[Sales]	__DS0VisualCalcs[IsDens...
1	1265828290.39				True	True	1265828290.39	False
2	214063666	2024			False	True	214063666	False
3	14091130.12	2024	January	1	False	False	14091130.12	False
4	32743875.31	2024	February	2	False	False	18652745.19	False
5	46450902.94	2024	March	3	False	False	13707027.63	False
6	60068856.34	2024	April	4	False	False	13617953.4	False
7	76094346	2024	May	5	False	False	16025489.67	False
8	92081394.84	2024	June	6	False	False	15987048.83	False
9	107928252.65	2024	July	7	False	False	15846857.82	False

FIGURE 9-16 The output table of the DAX query that is executed to populate the matrix visual with *Sales* and *YTD Sales* per Month and Year contains columns with added table names.

Extending the visual shape with a columns axis

Let's look at one more example to see how the visual shape can also define the columns axis. We'll use the example from Chapter 2, in the section "Create calculations that navigate over the columns," where we created a matrix visual with the CategoryName on the rows, the quarters of the year on the columns, the *Sales* measure, and a visual calculation to calculate the moving average. Figure 9-17 displays the matrix visual.

| YearQuarter | Q1-2024 | | Q2-2024 | | Q3-2024 | | Q4-2024 | | Q1-2025 | |
CategoryName	Sales	MA	Sales	MA	Sales	MA	Sales	MA	Sales	MA
Audio	1,038,926.50	1,038,926.50	1,352,971.01	1,195,948.75	1,344,796.73	1,245,564.74	3,079,619.26	1,704,078.37	5,777,350.70	2,888.6
Cameras and camcorders	13,103,481.38	13,103,481.38	8,068,930.08	10,586,205.73	4,601,514.46	8,591,308.64	7,170,858.79	8,236,196.18	17,297,594.21	9,284.7
Cell phones	3,457,961.86	3,457,961.86	4,192,581.24	3,825,271.55	4,415,694.79	4,022,079.29	9,837,632.88	5,475,967.69	21,766,278.14	10,053.0
Computers	12,486,032.00	12,486,032.00	17,535,223.77	15,010,627.89	20,574,798.78	16,865,351.52	39,850,193.68	22,611,562.06	84,033,897.88	40,498.5
Games and Toys	309,864.12	309,864.12	217,915.36	263,889.74	153,667.18	227,148.88	516,630.05	299,519.18	1,476,095.23	591.0
Home Appliances	7,959,507.47	7,959,507.47	7,835,943.35	7,897,725.41	6,484,927.45	7,426,792.76	11,627,617.65	8,476,998.98	16,542,900.10	10,622.8
Music, Movies and Audio Books	1,530,020.19	1,530,020.19	1,220,315.86	1,375,172.52	937,936.91	1,229,427.32	2,750,497.52	1,609,694.87	5,613,217.98	2,630.4
TV and Video	6,565,100.43	6,565,100.43	5,206,611.23	5,885,855.83	3,226,106.96	4,999,272.87	5,409,778.09	5,101,899.18	8,912,555.80	5,698.7
Total			46,450,902.94 46,450,902.94	45,630,491.90	46,040,697.42	41,739,443.25	44,606,946.03	80,242,827.92	53,515,916.50	161,419,890.14	82,258,1(

FIGURE 9-17 This matrix visual displays *Sales* and a moving average per category and quarter of each year.

If you look at the DAX query behind this visual—in particular, the part where the table __DS0VisualCalcs is defined—it includes the following DAX code. The whole DAX query can be found in the example model and in Appendix D.

```
TABLE '__DS0VisualCalcs' =
        __DS0VisualCalcsInput
    WITH VISUAL SHAPE
        AXIS rows
            GROUP [CategoryName] TOTAL [IsGrandTotalRowTotal]
            ORDER BY
                [CategoryName] ASC
        AXIS columns
            GROUP
                [YearQuarter],
                [YearQuarterNumber]
                TOTAL [IsGrandTotalColumnTotal]
            ORDER BY
                [YearQuarterNumber] ASC,
                [YearQuarter] ASC
        DENSIFY "IsDensifiedRow"
```

Here, two axes are defined in the WITH VISUAL SHAPE statement. The first is the rows axis, which consists only of the CategoryName column and which is sorted alphabetically on that same column. After that, an axis for the columns is defined by grouping the values of the YearQuarter column and the YearQuarterNumber column. Here, the YearQuarterNumber column is again used to ensure that the sorting order of the YearQuarter column is maintained as it was defined in the metadata of the Date table in the semantic model. This column's axis is sorted primarily by the YearQuarterNumber column. Again, the visual shape statement adds the axis to the __DS0VisualCalcs table that includes the hierarchy and sorting order needed to create the visual calculations.

The densification concept explained

You have seen that all the __DS0VisualCalcs table definitions end with a DENSIFY "IsDensifiedRow" statement, but we have skipped over it in all the previous examples so far.

In short, densification ensures that any visual calculation is calculated for every combination of the axes in your visual, even if the original value for the measure used in the visual is returning a blank value for those combinations. With densification, you don't lose any values when creating visual calculations, and the results shown are complete. This is done for you in the background. You don't have to switch on any process or option, so you don't have to worry about it. Indeed, densification is quite a technical concept, and you don't really need to know much about it at all to understand and work with visual calculations. But for the sake of completeness, we will explain how it works in this section, with the help of an example.

> **Note** By default, Power BI filters out rows that return only blank values in a visual. In a regular visual without visual calculations, it's possible to show items with no data, which would also show the combinations that return a blank result. However, this option is disabled when your visual includes visual calculations. Conversely, if you have a visual and turn on the option to show items with no data, it's no longer possible to add visual calculations to that visual. In the current setup, visual calculations do not work together with this option because it would result in performance issues.

To illustrate the concept of densification and demonstrate what happens in the visual and the DAX query, we created a matrix visual with the Color of the Product on the rows, the Brand on the columns, and the *Sales* measures as the values. Furthermore, we selected three products in the table to create empty spots in our matrix visual. We'll need these to show the densification. Figure 9-18 shows the resulting matrix visual.

Color	Adventure Works	Northwind Traders	Southridge Video	Total
Brown	4,135,383.00			4,135,383.00
Green		418,379.11		418,379.11
Yellow			21,658.10	21,658.10
Total	**4,135,383.00**	**418,379.11**	**21,658.10**	**4,575,420.20**

FIGURE 9-18 This matrix visual displays *Sales* per Color and Brand, for three specific products.

For each row of data, only one combination of Color and Brand is populated with a value (if you don't include the totals). For the combinations of Brown and Northwind Traders and Yellow and Adventure Works, there have been no sales.

Recall that the matrix visual is populated with values because the Power BI engine executes a DAX query to calculate these values, and that the output of such a DAX query is always a flat table. If you look at the underlying DAX query, you can obtain something like the table shown in Figure 9-19.

Note This is not the exact result you get if you just run the DAX query. The DAX query for a matrix visual is always split into two parts and evaluates two results: one for the header names that are enriched with a header index, and one for the values, where the header indices can be used to identify the corresponding columns. The reason for this is technical, so we will not take a deep dive into it, but it has to do with the fact that the DAX engine returns only nonblank values and with simplifying and optimizing the queries that are used.

In Figure 9-19, the output from the intermediate variable __DS0Core is displayed, which shows the view that we're looking for.

	Product[Color]	Product[Brand]	[IsGrandTotalRowTotal]	[IsGrandTotalColumnTotal]	[Sales]
1			True	True	4575420.2
2		Adventure Works	True	False	4135383
3		Northwind Traders	True	False	418379.11
4		Southridge Video	True	False	21658.1
5	Brown		False	True	4135383
6	Brown	Adventure Works	False	False	4135383
7	Green		False	True	418379.11
8	Green	Northwind Traders	False	False	418379.11
9	Yellow		False	True	21658.1
10	Yellow	Southridge Video	False	False	21658.1

FIGURE 9-19 The output table of the variable __DS0Core contains rows for each of the values in the matrix visual.

There are 10 rows in the output table—one for each of the values that is populated in the matrix visual. Only three rows are actual data values from the lowest level; the other seven are subtotals and the grand total.

In the output table, only the three rows are displayed where the *Sales* measure returns a nonblank value for the combination of Color and Brand. So, for the combination of the Adventure Works Brand and the Color Green, there are no sales, so the *Sales* measure returns a blank value. The same holds for the combinations of Southridge Video and Brown, and so on. Therefore, these rows are not present in the output table needed to populate the matrix visual.

What if you want to add visual calculations to this visual? There are visual calculations functions that would return a nonblank value for the combination of Adventure Works and the Color Green, like the RANK function. But because there are no sales for this combination, there's no row in the table that would serve as the input table for the visual calculations to be created as an additional column. If the row does not exist, the newly added column for the visual calculation would not calculate for that combination either, so you would miss values in your visual when the visual calculation is added. This is where densification comes into play.

Densification occurs in the WITH VISUAL SHAPE statement in the DAX query. It ensures that combinations that are not populated in the visual are present in the visual calculations table to which the visual calculations are added as new columns. So, in this example, the densification statement adds rows to the __DS0VisualCalcs table that is defined when you add a visual calculation to the matrix visual and execute the underlying DAX query. The added rows are for the following combinations of Color and Brand:

- Brown with Northwind Traders

- Brown with Southridge Video

- Green with Adventure Works

- Green with Southridge Video

- Yellow with Adventure Works

- Yellow with Northwind Traders

The corresponding *Sales* values for all these combinations are empty. The column added to the table, IsDensifiedRow, has a True value for all these combinations, making it clear that these rows are added by the densification process.

If you add a visual calculation to the matrix visual, you can see this process in action. Here, we have added a visual calculation to calculate the rank of the rows because we want to see some output for our visual calculation for the combinations for which the output of the *Sales* measure is empty. The RANK function was explained in Chapter 6, "The foundation: foundational functions," so we won't explain it here again. We just added the following visual calculation to our visual:

```
Rank = RANK ( ROWS )
```

Figure 9-20 shows the resulting matrix visual. You can see that the densification process has done its work, and there are values calculated for the combinations of Color and Brand that do not have any *Sales* value.

Brand	Adventure Works		Northwind Traders		Southridge Video		Total	
Color	Sales	Rank	Sales	Rank	Sales	Rank	**Sales**	**Rank**
Brown	4,135,383.00	1.00		1.00		1.00	**4,135,383.00**	**1.00**
Green		2.00	418,379.11	2.00		2.00	**418,379.11**	**2.00**
Yellow		3.00		3.00	21,658.10	3.00	**21,658.10**	**3.00**
Total	**4,135,383.00**	**1.00**	**418,379.11**	**1.00**	**21,658.10**	**1.00**	**4,575,420.20**	**1.00**

FIGURE 9-20 This matrix visual has a visual calculation for the rank added.

If you look at the DAX query behind this visual, you can again see where the table for the visual calculation is defined, with the DENSIFY statement in the WITH VISUAL SHAPE statement:

```
TABLE '__DS0VisualCalcs' =
       __DS0VisualCalcsInput
       WITH VISUAL SHAPE
```

```
AXIS rows
    GROUP [Color] TOTAL [IsGrandTotalRowTotal]
    ORDER BY
        [Color] ASC
AXIS columns
    GROUP [Brand] TOTAL [IsGrandTotalColumnTotal]
    ORDER BY
        [Brand] ASC
DENSIFY "IsDensifiedRow"
```

The entire DAX query can again be found in the sample model and in Appendix E. If you look at the output of this table, __DS0VisualCalcs, you get a table that indeed has more rows than the one in Figure 9-19. There are now six rows added for the combinations of Color and Brand that do not have any *Sales* value, and they are recognizable by the True value in the IsDensifiedRow column. Figure 9-21 shows the output of the __DS0VisualCalcs table, with the added rows highlighted.

	__DS0VisualCalcs[Rank]	__DS0VisualCalcs[Color]	__DS0VisualCalcs[Brand]	_DS0...	_DS0...	__DS0VisualCalcs[Sales]	__DS0VisualCalcs[IsDensifiedRow]
1	1			True	True	4575420.2	False
2	1		Adventure Works	True	False	4135383	False
3	1		Northwind Traders	True	False	418379.11	False
4	1		Southridge Video	True	False	21658.1	False
5	1	Brown		False	True	4135383	False
6	1	Brown	Adventure Works	False	False	4135383	False
7	1	Brown	Northwind Traders	False	False		True
8	1	Brown	Southridge Video	False	False		True
9	2	Green		False	True	418379.11	False
10	2	Green	Adventure Works	False	False		True
11	2	Green	Northwind Traders	False	False	418379.11	False
12	2	Green	Southridge Video	False	False		True
13	3	Yellow		False	True	21658.1	False
14	3	Yellow	Adventure Works	False	False		True
15	3	Yellow	Northwind Traders	False	False		True
16	3	Yellow	Southridge Video	False	False	21658.1	False

FIGURE 9-21 The output table of the __DS0VisualCalcs variable contains extra rows.

The first column in this table is the added column for the visual calculation for the rank that we added. The DAX query starts with defining this new column, which is why it's also present if you evaluate the results of the newly defined table.

Another thing to observe is that the densification added only the combinations for colors and brands that are actually in the visual that we started with. There are more colors—like Silver, Blue, and Pink—present in the data (as well as brands), but these colors do not appear in the output table for the visual calculations table. This is because the visual calculations operate only on the data that's in the visual itself. Only the combinations that could be made from the data that's in the visual are considered—not any combinations that could come from the model as a whole.

Note This is one of the reasons visual calculations have such a good performance.

Finally, densification adds rows to the table used for the visual calculations. In the preceding example, the visual calculation we defined has an output value for all these new rows, but that's not necessarily the case. If we were to create a visual calculation that has an output value only for the combination of the Color Green and the Brand Adventure Works, we would be left with five newly added rows that wouldn't give us any more information for populating the visual. Therefore, in the DAX query, after defining the table for the visual calculation, this table is also filtered again to remove any obsolete rows with the following piece of DAX code:

```
VAR __DSORemoveEmptyDensified =
    FILTER(
        KEEPFILTERS('__DSOVisualCalcs'),
        OR(
            NOT('__DSOVisualCalcs'[IsDensifiedRow]),
            NOT(ISBLANK('__DSOVisualCalcs'[Rank]))
        )
    )
```

Here, all rows that are added by the densification process (all rows that have a value True in the column IsDensifiedRow) and have a blank value for the visual calculation column (Rank) that we added are removed, leaving a clean output table to populate the visual itself. This ensures that the visual performs optimally as well.

In summary

This chapter looks under the hood of visual calculations by exploring the DAX query that's executed to populate a visual with values. It started by breaking down the DAX query for a simple visual without visual calculations and then extended the visual with a visual calculation. It also broke down the DAX query that's behind a visual with visual calculations, revealing two new concepts in the process: the visual shape and densification.

The visual shape ensures that we can extend a flat table output with a hierarchy and (sub)totals, and a sorting order, by defining axes in the table. These axes can be referenced by visual calculations, making the creation of a visual calculation very intuitive.

The densification concept ensures that you don't lose any values when you create visual calculations and is quite a technical concept about which a regular user does not need to know in order to be able to use visual calculations.

The art of practical visual calculations

Something we love about visual calculations is the creativity they enable; in this final part of the book, we show you some of our favorite uses of visual calculations. This is hardly an exhaustive list, so we encourage you to explore the Power BI community for more examples.

> **Note**   Many of the examples in this part are inspired by the Power BI community. In particular, we want to mention Fowmy Abdulmuttalib (*https://www.linkedin. com/in/fowmy/*), Injae Park (*https://www.linkedin.com/ in/injae-park/*), and Erik Svensen (*https://www.linkedin. com/in/eriksvensen/*) for sharing their ideas. Many of the examples in this part are either inspired by them or gracefully provided by them.

The first chapter in this part (Chapter 10, "Applied visual calculations") shows you how to make real-world calculations that you can apply to many visuals, while Chapter 11, "Charting with visual calculations," explains how to create specific visuals using visual calculations.

This part of the book is meant as an inspirational guide for your work with visual calculations, showcasing what visual calculations can do from the straightforward-yet-useful to the complicated-and-awesome and everything in between. We won't be overly exhaustive here in the instructions; we assume you have read the book to this point. After working through all details in the previous chapters, it's time to put what you've learned into practice, have some fun, and go a little crazy!

## CHAPTER 10

Applied visual calculations

We've collected some of our favorite uses of visual calculations that do not involve creating specific visual types (those we saved for Chapter 11, "Charting with visual calculations").

The examples in this chapter range from straightforward to hard to a bit "out there":

- **Benchmarking analysis** This compares current values with an index, or a reference value.

- **Highest and lowest point indicators** These make it easy to spot the outliers, particularly in line charts or tabular visuals.

- **Best-in-class analysis** This is a neat trick that allows you to highlight the best (or worst) performers.

- **Custom totals** These show how easy it is to influence what a matrix returns on the subtotal and total level using visual calculations.

- **Dynamic titles and subtitles** The sky is the limit when you combine visual calculations and conditional formatting, as we show you in this example that highlights important information in the subtitle of the visual.

- **Dynamic ranked contribution analysis** By far the most involved and complicated example in this chapter, this is an implementation of a very popular pattern using visual calculations exclusively.

- **Focus highlighting** With this simple trick, you can help users focus on particular parts of the data shown in busy visuals.

Feel free to pick and choose and refer to this chapter any time you need a refresher. And don't worry. We won't tell anyone that you can't create the dynamic ranked contribution analysis example in this chapter with your eyes closed! Neither can we.

Benchmarking analysis

These calculations compare against a fixed reference value or benchmark, such as a specific period. Alternative names for this type of analysis are indexing, variance analysis, trend analysis, and fixed-point comparison.

Many industries rely on some kind of comparative calculations against fixed reference values, such as a specific period or benchmark. A common use is in finance to value assets against an index period, most often a year. Other examples are in manufacturing, where performance or quality is often compared to industry benchmarks, and utilities, which often need to compare against regulatory standards.

Benchmarking analysis makes it easy to track growth, compare performance, and spot deviations. Whatever industry you work in, or whatever you call this type of analysis, visual calculations make it easy to add these calculations to your visuals.

Figure 10-1 shows the result of our benchmarking analysis in an area chart. This benchmarking analysis compares the sales for each month against the first month's sales (January 2024). It's immediately clear that August 2024 is the only period in which sales were remarkably lower than the benchmark. Also, this area chart shows regular and predictable patterns (seasonality) and growth in the business year over year.

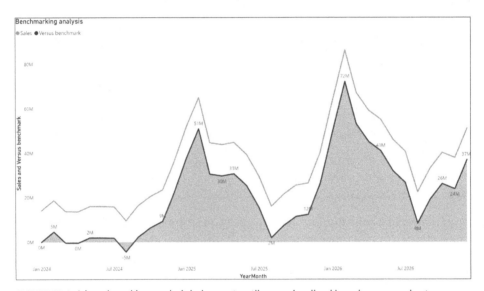

FIGURE 10-1 A benchmarking analysis helps spot outliers as visualized here in an area chart.

Our benchmarking analysis is based on a simple visual calculation that uses the provided Versus First expression template:

```
Versus benchmark = [Sales]  - FIRST ( [Sales] )
```

To create the visual shown in Figure 10-1, begin by creating an area chart that shows *Sales* by Year-Month. Then open visual calculations edit mode and use the Versus First expression template or type the *Versus benchmark* visual calculation that precedes this paragraph. Be sure that both the *Sales* measure and the *Versus benchmark* visual calculation are on the Y-axis of your visual, as shown in Figure 10-2.

The calculation is now done! We recommend that you remove the area color for the *Sales* to help users focus on the *Versus benchmark* visual calculation. Also, enable data labels for *Versus benchmark*. Both settings are shown in Figure 10-3.

FIGURE 10-2 This is the visual configuration for the benchmarking analysis.

FIGURE 10-3 The Shade area and Data labels are turned on.

Although we don't think this visual needs more updates to help the user focus, you could, of course, use conditional formatting rules to indicate the low point, as you will see later in this chapter.

A variant of benchmarking analysis that is also easy to create is a comparison against a previous element, such as three months back. Instead of the FIRST function, you'd instead use the PREVIOUS function. Both FIRST and PREVIOUS are discussed in much more detail in Chapter 7, "The floors and rooms: visual calculations exclusive functions."

Highest and lowest point indicators

Indicating the highest and lowest point in a visual is often very useful to grab users' attention. Visual calculations make it extremely easy to do this. This technique can be used in many visuals, including matrices and line charts. Here we will limit ourselves to one example using line charts, and two more for matrices.

In a line chart

Create a line chart showing *Sales* by Year Month. Then open visual calculations edit mode and add the *MinAndMaxVal* visual calculation:

```
MinAndMaxVal =
VAR Min_var =
    MINX ( ROWS, [Sales] )
VAR Max_var =
    MAXX ( ROWS, [Sales] )
RETURN
    SWITCH ( [Sales], Min_var, Min_var, Max_var, Max_var, BLANK () )
```

This visual calculation first defines two variables (Min_var and Max_var) to return the minimum and maximum values of *Sales* across the rows. Then, a simple SWITCH statement is used to compare the actual *Sales* value for each row with the minimum and maximum values. If the values match, then the *MinAndMaxVal* visual calculation returns that value; otherwise, it returns a blank value. Make sure both *Sales* and *MinAndMaxVal* are on the Y-axis of your visual. At this point, the minimum and maximum values in the chart are connected with a line. In the Format pane of the line visual, change the X-axis settings to type Categorical to only show a dot on the chart for the min and max values. By default, the X-axis is set to continuous. That's it; your visual should look like Figure 10-4. As you can see, visual calculations make this extremely easy.

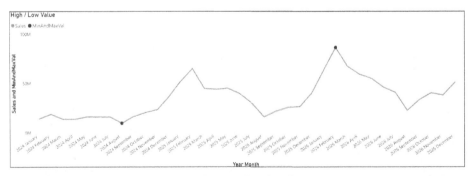

FIGURE 10-4 Highlighting high and low points on a line chart is made easy using visual calculations.

In a matrix

Using conditional formatting rules, the possibilities are truly endless. With a small adaptation, you can show any icon in a matrix visual to highlight the months with the lowest and highest *Sales* per Year, as shown in Figure 10-5.

High / Low Sales per year

Month	2024		2025		2026		Total
January	14,091,130.12		51,886,482.12		63,672,376.76		129,649,988.99
February	18,652,745.19	✓	64,923,153.55	✓	86,214,246.78		169,790,145.52
March	13,707,027.63		44,610,254.48		67,223,670.43		125,540,952.54
April	13,617,953.40		43,794,064.91		59,185,328.15		116,597,346.46
May	16,025,489.67		44,782,137.77		55,118,198.36		115,925,825.79
June	15,987,048.83		39,376,967.87		45,978,289.87		101,342,306.57
July	15,846,857.82		29,708,944.66		40,754,203.12		86,310,005.60
August	✗ 9,561,371.47	✗	16,054,829.64	✗	22,415,217.90		48,031,419.01
September	16,331,213.97		21,523,910.57		33,198,416.18		71,053,540.72
October	20,374,371.26		25,471,590.22		40,210,297.84		86,056,259.31
November	23,371,076.56		26,442,100.96		37,896,676.95		87,709,854.47
December	✓ 36,497,380.10		40,288,897.70		51,034,367.61		127,820,645.41
Total	**214,063,666.00**		**448,863,334.43**		**602,901,289.96**		**1,265,828,290.39**

FIGURE 10-5 The high and low points for each Year are highlighted on the matrix.

To do this, first create a matrix visual that shows *Sales* as values, Month on rows, and Year on columns. Then add the *MinAndMaxVal* visual calculation, but this time, change the output to two numbers (1 and 2 in this example, but you could use any values). We use these values later to define rules for conditional formatting:

```
MinAndMaxVal =
VAR Min_var = MINX ( COLUMNS ROWS, [Sales] )
VAR Max_var = MAXX ( COLUMNS ROWS, [Sales] )
RETURN
    IF ( [Sales] = Min_var, 1, IF ( [Sales] = Max_var, 2, BLANK () ) )
```

Then, hide the *MinAndMaxVal* visual calculation and set an icon conditional formatting rule for *Sales* by right-clicking *Sales*, selecting Conditional formatting, and choosing Icons. In the dialog that opens, select Rules as the Format style and select *MinAndMaxVal* for What field should we base this on? Finally, set up two rules. One rule should check if the value equals 1. This is the lowest value, so pick a corresponding icon. We selected a red X. The other rule should check if the value equals 2. Because this is the highest value, we picked a green check mark. Figure 10-6 shows the full setup.

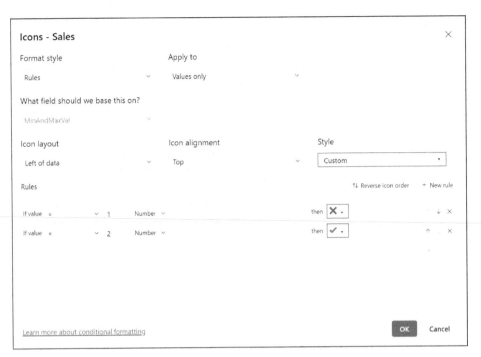

FIGURE 10-6 Setting up rules to show icons for the lowest and highest values.

Now your matrix should show icons for the lowest and highest selling Month for each Year and resemble Figure 10-5.

If you want to show icons for the lowest and highest selling Month across all years, a quick change of how the Min_var and Max_var variables in *MinAndMaxVal* are determined is all that is needed. Simply change the ROWS axis to COLUMNS ROWS or ROWS COLUMNS, and the icons will be shown for the lowest and highest value across all years:

```
MinAndMaxVal =
VAR Min_var = MINX ( COLUMNS ROWS, [Sales] )
VAR Max_var = MAXX ( COLUMNS ROWS, [Sales] )
RETURN
    IF ( [Sales] = Min_var, 1, IF ( [Sales] = Max_var, 2, BLANK () ) )
```

The matrix should now look like the one shown in Figure 10-7.

High / Low Sales across all years				
Month	2024	2025	2026	**Total**
January	14,091,130.12	51,886,482.12	63,672,376.76	**129,649,988.99**
February	18,652,745.19	64,923,153.55 ✓	86,214,246.78	**169,790,145.52**
March	13,707,027.63	44,610,254.48	67,223,670.43	**125,540,952.54**
April	13,617,953.40	43,794,064.91	59,185,328.15	**116,597,346.46**
May	16,025,489.67	44,782,137.77	55,118,198.36	**115,925,825.79**
June	15,987,048.83	39,376,967.87	45,978,289.87	**101,342,306.57**
July	15,846,857.82	29,708,944.66	40,754,203.12	**86,310,005.60**
August	✗ 9,561,371.47	16,054,829.64	22,415,217.90	**48,031,419.01**
September	16,331,213.97	21,523,910.57	33,198,416.18	**71,053,540.72**
October	20,374,371.26	25,471,590.22	40,210,297.84	**86,056,259.31**
November	23,371,076.56	26,442,100.96	37,896,676.95	**87,709,854.47**
December	36,497,380.10	40,288,897.70	51,034,367.61	**127,820,645.41**
Total	**214,063,666.00**	**448,863,334.43**	**602,901,289.96**	**1,265,828,290.39**

FIGURE 10-7 On the matrix, the high and low points across all years are highlighted.

Best-in-class analysis

A best-in-class analysis identifies the highest performers in a group, such as a group of students or sales representatives. Alternative names for this analysis are leader analysis, ranking analysis, or champion analysis. We often see these types of analysis being done in hospitality and travel to identify popular destinations or travel packages, but this is also commonly used in manufacturing, healthcare, and retail.

This analysis not only shows a numerical value for, for example, the total sales or the amount of sales of the highest performer but also who the highest performer was. Regardless of whether you're talking about students, sales representatives, medications, machinery, or sensors, the benefits are the same; it allows you to focus on the top performer so you can see what sets them apart from all competitors. Of course, you could also use this technique to identify the lowest performer, but we'll leave that as an exercise for you. (Hint: It's not hard; it just involves replacing MAX with MIN.)

In our example, we will create a best-in-class analysis to show the highest performing Product for each product category and subcategory. We will show *Sales* for the (sub)category as well as the *Sales* for the highest performing product within each product (sub)category. Figure 10-8 shows the finished best-in-class analysis.

To create this, let's start with a simple matrix with CategoryName, SubCategoryName, and Product Name on rows and *Sales* as values, as shown in Figure 10-9.

Best-in-class analysis		
CategoryName	Sales	Best Performer
⊟ **Computers**	**$549,446,769**	**$11,299,025 (Adventure Works Desktop PC2.33 XD233 Black)**
Desktops	$242,616,719	$11,299,025 (Adventure Works Desktop PC2.33 XD233 Black)
Projectors & Screens	$120,400,114	$4,312,025 (Contoso Projector 1080p X981 Silver)
Laptops	$102,694,213	$2,934,441 (Adventure Works Laptop19W X1980 White)
Monitors	$51,256,496	$1,927,008 (WWI LCD24W X300 Black)
Printers, Scanners & Fax	$25,136,761	$418,004 (Proseware High-Performance Business-Class Laser Fax X200 White)
Computers Accessories	$7,342,467	$195,803 (Contoso Laptop Keyboard X105 Brown)
⊞ **Cell phones**	**$205,114,321**	**$3,043,599 (The Phone Company Touch Screen Phone 1600 TFT-1.4" L250 Black)**
⊞ **Home Appliances**	**$161,683,450**	**$3,480,130 (Contoso Water Heater 7.2GPM X1800 Silver)**
⊞ **TV and Video**	**$120,122,852**	**$6,936,486 (Adventure Works 52" LCD HDTV X590 Silver)**
⊞ **Cameras and camcorders**	**$117,906,796**	**$1,402,080 (Fabrikam Independent filmmaker 1'' 25mm X400 White)**
⊞ **Music, Movies and Audio Books**	**$67,641,532**	**$2,076,444 (SV DVD 15-Inch Player Portable L200 White)**
⊞ **Audio**	**$33,294,780**	**$1,017,595 (WWI 4GB Video Recording Pen X200 Yellow)**
⊞ **Games and Toys**	**$10,617,789**	**$832,452 (MGS Age of Empires Expansion: The Rise of Rome X900)**
Total	**$1,265,828,290**	**$11,299,025 (Adventure Works Desktop PC2.33 XD233 Black)**

FIGURE 10-8 A best-in-class analysis helps identify high performers.

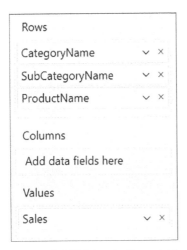

FIGURE 10-9 This is a starting point for a best-in-class analysis matrix.

Now add these three visual calculations:

```
HighestSellingProductSales = EXPANDALL ( MAX ( [Sales] ), ROWS )

HighestSellingProduct =
VAR MaxSalesPerCategory = [HighestSellingProductSales]
RETURN
    EXPANDALL (
        LOOKUP ( [ProductName], [Sales], MaxSalesPerCategory ),
        ROWS
    )

Best Performer = FORMAT ( [HighestSellingProductSales], "$#,##0" ) &
" (" & [HighestSellingProduct] & ")"
```

HighestSellingProductSales returns the highest sales per (sub)category. *HighestSellingProduct* uses EXPANDALL to find the highest sales and returns the corresponding ProductName. We used EXPANDALL here because we had three levels on the rows axis, but if you have only two or you want more control, you can also use EXPAND. Also, note that *HighestSellingProduct* uses LOOKUP to find the ProductName for the *HighestSellingProductSales* value. Finally, *Best Performer* concatenates the other two visual calculations and applies a bit of formatting.

After you've added these, hide *HighestSellingProduct* and *HighestSellingProductSales* so the visual shows only the *Sales* and *Best Performer* values. After some quick model-level formatting (see Chapter 4, "Organization and use of visual calculations") of the *Sales* measure to make it display as a currency, you're done! Notice that *Best Performer* not only works not only for product categories and subcategories, but also for the total level (see Figure 10-8). Visual calculations enable you to add a very flexible best-in-class analysis.

Custom totals

One common challenge for users has to do with influencing what is shown on the subtotal or total lines of a matrix. Totals in Power BI work by reevaluating the calculation in the context that is available on the subtotal or total level. This holds true for any type of calculation, including, of course, visual calculations. This is often mistaken for a bug because it can lead to totals seemingly not adding up. But in fact, this is a deliberate and correct design choice.

Luckily, visual calculations make it easy to influence what is returned on the subtotal and total levels using the ISATLEVEL function, as explained in Chapter 7. Collectively, we call these custom totals. In some cases, using EXPAND or COLLAPSE to navigate across the lattice also works to change what will be calculated and shown for the total row. ISATLEVEL allows for more customization and complex requirements.

As an illustrative (although admittedly kind of "out there") example, let's say you are using a running sum to see the cumulated product cost for each year and quarter. You've added a basic visual calculation to calculate the running sum:

```
Cost Running Sum = RUNNINGSUM ( [Costs] )
```

The total row now shows the last value of the *Cost Running Sum* visual calculation, as shown in Figure 10-10.

However, you actually need to show the sum of the quarterly running sum cost values that you just calculated in the total row. For example, you can add the following visual calculation and hide *Cost Running Sum*:

```
Cost Running Sum with total = EXPAND ( SUM ( [Cost Running Sum] ), ROWS )
```

Now the total row shown for *Cost Running Sum with total* shows the value of all the running sum values together (see Figure 10-11).

Custom total

YearQuarter	Costs	Cost Running Sum
Q1-2024	19,075,267.37	19,075,267.37
Q2-2024	18,825,129.28	37,900,396.65
Q3-2024	17,304,396.82	55,204,793.46
Q4-2024	33,331,701.81	88,536,495.27
Q1-2025	67,088,051.92	155,624,547.19
Q2-2025	53,178,817.88	208,803,365.07
Q3-2025	27,962,003.96	236,765,369.03
Q4-2025	38,280,784.63	275,046,153.67
Q1-2026	90,234,295.85	365,280,449.51
Q2-2026	66,436,947.38	431,717,396.89
Q3-2026	39,980,714.76	471,698,111.65
Q4-2026	53,437,053.82	525,135,165.47
Total	**525,135,165.47**	**525,135,165.47**

FIGURE 10-10 Total values in Power BI are determined by evaluating the calculation in context.

Custom total

YearQuarter	Costs	Cost Running Sum with total
Q1-2024	19,075,267.37	19,075,267.37
Q2-2024	18,825,129.28	37,900,396.65
Q3-2024	17,304,396.82	55,204,793.46
Q4-2024	33,331,701.81	88,536,495.27
Q1-2025	67,088,051.92	155,624,547.19
Q2-2025	53,178,817.88	208,803,365.07
Q3-2025	27,962,003.96	236,765,369.03
Q4-2025	38,280,784.63	275,046,153.67
Q1-2026	90,234,295.85	365,280,449.51
Q2-2026	66,436,947.38	431,717,396.89
Q3-2026	39,980,714.76	471,698,111.65
Q4-2026	53,437,053.82	525,135,165.47
Total	**525,135,165.47**	**2,870,787,511.24**

FIGURE 10-11 It's easy to influence the total row value in visual calculations.

Dynamic titles and subtitles

The combination of conditional formatting and visual calculations is a match made in heaven. Most, if not all, conditional formatting calculations are inherently tied to the visual. This is a trait they share with visual calculations.

One example we particularly like is using visual calculations to dynamically determine the value for a title or subtitle of a visual. Instead of entering a static value, you can use a dynamic title or dynamic subtitle to convey important information about the data in your visual. Figure 10-12 shows an example of a dynamic subtitle created with visual calculations.

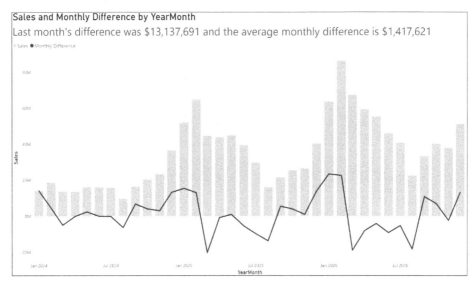

FIGURE 10-12 This dynamic subtitle was created with visual calculations.

To create this, start with a line and stacked column chart that shows *Sales* on the columns and Year-Month on the X-axis. Next, add the *Monthly Difference* visual calculation using the provided expression template or by typing it yourself:

```
Monthly Difference = [Sales] - PREVIOUS ( [Sales] )
```

Move the *Monthly Difference* visual calculation to the Line Y-axis. Now, add three more visual calculations:

```
AvgMonthDiff = AVERAGEX ( ROWS, [Monthly Difference] )

LastMonthsDiff = LAST ( [Monthly Difference] )

Subtitle =
"Last month's difference was " & FORMAT ( [LastMonthsDiff], "$#,##0" ) & " and
the average monthly difference is " & FORMAT ( [AvgMonthDiff], "$#,##0" )
```

The *AvgMonthDiff* visual calculation calculates the average of *Monthly Difference* over all the rows using AVERAGEX. *LastMonthsDiff* returns the last YearMonth's value of *Monthly Difference*. Finally, the *Subtitle* visual calculation concatenates the results, performs some formatting, and adds some text. Because you don't want to show the results of these visual calculations as part of the chart, but only as subtitle, mark each of them as hidden.

You're almost finished. But because the data type of visual calculations at the time of this writing is always set to decimal number (described in more detail in Chapter 4), you need to change it for the *Subtitle* visual calculation so you can use it as the subtitle value, as shown in Figure 10-13. The order for doing this is relevant here; you first need to change the *Subtitle* visual calculation's data type to Text in the Data Format section before you can assign it as dynamic subtitle.

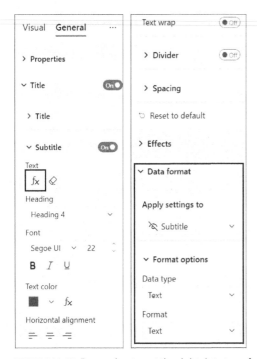

FIGURE 10-13 Remember to set the right data type for your visual calculation.

After the *Subtitle* visual calculation's data type is set to text, you can use the fx button for Subtitle in the Visualizations pane, as highlighted in Figure 10-13, to open the conditional formatting window for it. Here, select Field value for Format style and choose *Subtitle* as the field on which to base the formatting, as shown in Figure 10-14. After you apply these changes, your dynamic subtitle will show. If not, double-check that you set the *Subtitle* visual calculation's data type to text. After you change the color of the columns that show *Sales*, your visual should look like Figure 10-12!

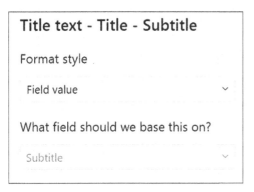

FIGURE 10-14 Set the Subtitle text to the *Subtitle* visual calculation.

Dynamic ranked contribution analysis

Many reports include some kind of top-N calculation. Often, users want to see data represented in a ranked contribution format, where, for example, the top three brands by *Sales* are shown and all the other brands that are not part of the top three are combined as a new entry (often labeled Others). Alternative names for this type of analysis are top-N with others, segmented performance analysis, and leaderboard analysis.

We're tackling two challenges at once here. The first one is grouping all the items that fall outside of the rank into Others. The second one is doing all this dynamically. While technically not necessary to show you a ranked contribution analysis done using visual calculations, we labeled this section "dynamic" for a reason. Figure 10-15 shows the result we're after.

To start, create a numeric range parameter that ranges between 1 and the maximum number of brands you want to show to the user. To do that, select New parameter on the Modeling tab in the ribbon and select Numeric range, as shown on Figure 10-16.

We called our new numeric range parameter Number of Rows for Rank, but feel free to pick something that makes more sense to you for your situation. Select Whole number as Data type and enter a minimum value of 1 and a maximum value of brands you want to show to your user. We picked 11 because that is the number of brands in the sample data. Finally, make sure the increment is set to 1, pick a default value (we picked 3), and select the Add slicer to this page option. Figure 10-17 shows the settings we used.

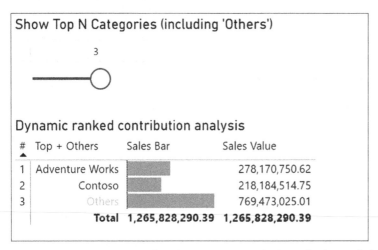

FIGURE 10-15 This matrix and slicer show a dynamic ranked contribution analysis.

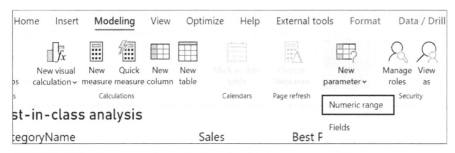

FIGURE 10-16 Use New parameter on the Modeling tab to create a numeric range parameter.

Now that you have the numeric range parameter and slicer, format the slicer as you see fit, but make sure to set the slicer style to Less than or equal to using the Visualizations pane as shown in Figure 10-18 so the visual shows the range from 1 to the selected value.

Now, you can finally create your matrix! Create a matrix that shows the numeric range parameter's column (not the measure) and Brand on rows. Using the column here ensures that the visual shows the range from 1 to the selected value. Also put *Sales* on values. Change the name of the column with the numeric range parameter to # and sort it in ascending order. Your matrix should now look like Figure 10-19.

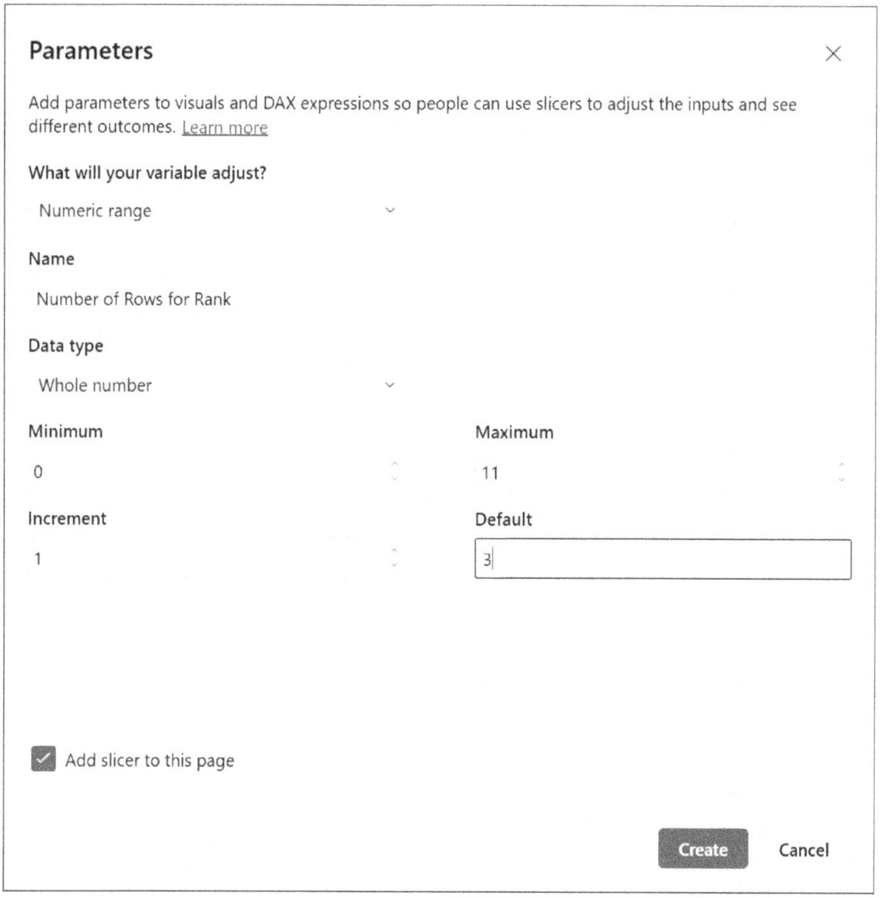

Parameters   ✕

Add parameters to visuals and DAX expressions so people can use slicers to adjust the inputs and see
different outcomes. Learn more

What will your variable adjust?

Numeric range   ⌄

Name

Number of Rows for Rank

Data type

Whole number   ⌄

Minimum   **Maximum**

0   11

Increment   **Default**

1   3

☑ Add slicer to this page

                                              [Create]   Cancel

FIGURE 10-17 Set up a numeric range parameter.

FIGURE 10-18 Set the slicer style to Less than or equal to.

# ▲	Sales
⊞ 1	1,265,828,290.39
⊞ 2	1,265,828,290.39
⊞ 3	1,265,828,290.39
Total	**1,265,828,290.39**

FIGURE 10-19 This is the starting point for our dynamic ranked contribution analysis.

You're still a long way off from the matrix we showed you in Figure 10-15, but don't worry, you'll get there! Now enter visual calculations edit mode. Here, add a new visual calculation that uses RANK to rank each Brand in descending order within each value for our numeric parameter (#):

```
Rank Rows = RANK ( DENSE, ROWS, ORDERBY ( [Sales], DESC ) )
```

Refer to Chapter 6 for more information on RANK.

Now, compare the value of *Rank Rows* with the value of the numeric parameter (#) and return the value of *Sales* if they are equal; otherwise, return nothing:

```
In Rank = IF ( [Rank Rows] = [#], [Sales] )
```

In Rank returns the value of *Sales* if *Rank Rows* equals the value of the numeric parameter. For the first group, where the numeric parameter equals 1, *In Rank* returns the value of *Sales* for the Brand ranked first in that group; in the second group, *In Rank* returns the value of *Sales* for the Brand ranked second in that group; and so on.

The next step is to add a visual calculation that returns the Brand name if *In Rank* is not blank or equal to 0:

```
Group = IF ( [In Rank] <> 0, [Brand] )
```

Group returns the value of Brand if *In Rank* is not blank or 0, so like *In Rank*, it only returns a Brand name if the position of the Brand within the group matches the value of the numeric parameter.

You want to calculate the average of the *In Rank* value but expand it so you return a value on the total row as well:

```
Sales in Rank = EXPAND ( AVERAGE ( [In Rank] ), ROWS )
```

As a final helper visual calculation, return the maximum of your numeric parameter (#):

```
Other Group = MAXX ( ROWS, [#] )
```

Other Group is a static value that is set to the maximum of the value of the numeric parameter—that is, the number of groups, which also equals the index of the group that will be the Others group.

By now, you should have the following fields on your matrix:

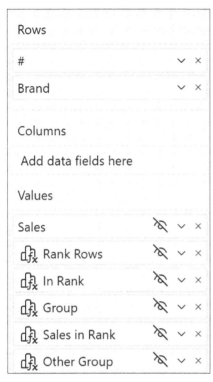

FIGURE 10-20 This is the halfway point for the dynamic ranked contribution analysis.

You should hide all these fields, as shown in Figure 10-20. Don't worry, we're going to show something on the matrix (eventually). Confirm that your visual matrix looks like the one in Figure 10-21 before continuing.

#	Brand	Sales	Rank Rows	In Rank	Group	Sales in Rank	Other Group
1	A. Datum	27,865,953.89	9.00				3.00
	Adventure Works	278,170,750.62	1.00	278,170,750.62	Adventure Works	278,170,750.62	3.00
	Contoso	218,184,514.75	2.00				3.00
	Fabrikam	121,197,856.89	5.00				3.00
	Litware	39,840,230.04	8.00				3.00
	Northwind Traders	15,017,709.70	10.00				3.00
	Proseware	104,050,853.59	6.00				3.00
	Southridge Video	60,086,249.68	7.00				3.00
	Tailspin Toys	9,833,060.31	11.00				3.00
	The Phone Company	181,172,587.20	4.00				3.00
	Wide World Importers	210,408,523.71	3.00				3.00
	Total	**1,265,828,290.39**	**1.00**	**1,265,828,290.39**		**278,170,750.62**	**3.00**
2	A. Datum	27,865,953.89	9.00				3.00
	Adventure Works	278,170,750.62	1.00				3.00
	Contoso	218,184,514.75	2.00	218,184,514.75	Contoso	218,184,514.75	3.00
	Fabrikam	121,197,856.89	5.00				3.00

FIGURE 10-21 This visual matrix is for the halfway point for the dynamic ranked contribution analysis.

Now, add the *Other Group Sales* visual calculation, which takes a difference between the total value of *Sales* for each value in the range selected by the numeric parameter and the running sum of *Sales in Rank* up to that point:

```
Other Group Sales = COLLAPSE ( [Sales], ROWS ) - RUNNINGSUM ( [Sales in Rank],
ROWS )
```

This is the final helper visual calculation you will need for your basic version, so hide the *Other Group Sales* visual calculation.

Now, add the actual value you will show for the groups:

```
Sales Value =
SWITCH (
    TRUE (),
    NOT ( ISATLEVEL ( [#] ) ), [Sales],
    [#] = [Other Group], [Other Group Sales] + [Sales in Rank],
    [Sales in Rank]
)
```

The *Sales Value* visual calculation checks if the value for the numeric parameter is not on the current level, which happens only on the total row. Therefore, it returns only the value of *Sales* on the total row. For all other rows, it then checks if the current value belongs to the Others group; if so, it returns the total of *Other Group Sales* and *Sales in Rank*. If the value does not belong to the Others group, then *Sales Value* will return the value of *Sales in Rank*, without adding the value of *Other Group Sales*. As a result, it returns the same value for all brands in the Others group and returns one value for each group that equals that Brand's sales.

Now, you're finally going to work on showing the brands themselves. Add another visual calculation:

```
Top + Others =
SWITCH (
    TRUE (),
    NOT ( ISATLEVEL ( [#] ) ), "Total",
    [Other Group] = [#], "Others",
    EXPAND ( CONCATENATEX ( VALUES ( [Group] ), [Group] ), ROWS )
)
```

This visual calculation is very similar to the *Sales Value* visual calculation you created earlier. It checks if the current row is the total row or belongs to the Others group, and if so, returns the text "Total" or "Others", respectively. If not, then it returns the value of *Group*, which is the Brand.

Move the visual calculations around so *Top + Others* is shown on the left and *Sales Value* is shown next to it. Your matrix should now look like Figure 10-22. You're almost done!

Disable the expand and collapse icons on the row headers using the Visualizations pane and turning off +/- icons in the Row headers submenu, as shown in Figure 10-23.

While you're here, make your matrix a bit cleaner by turning off the row subtotals for the # column. Do this by opening the Row subtotals submenu and enabling the Per row level setting. Then, select # as the Row level and enter a space as the Subtotal label as shown in Figure 10-24.

# ▲	Top + Others	Sales Value
⊟ 1	Adventure Works	278,170,750.62
⊞ 2	Contoso	218,184,514.75
⊟ 3	Others	769,473,025.01
Total	**Total**	**1,265,828,290.39**

FIGURE 10-22 Almost completed dynamic ranking contribution analysis.

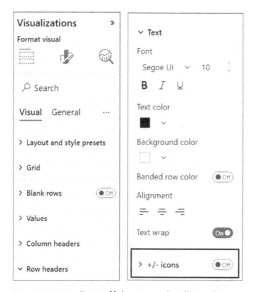

FIGURE 10-23 Turn off the expand/collapse icons.

FIGURE 10-24 Replace the Subtotal label for the # column.

And that's it. You're done! Your matrix should now look like Figure 10-25 and be fully responsive to the selections you make using the slicer for the numeric parameter.

#	Top + Others	Sales Value
1	Adventure Works	278,170,750.62
2	Contoso	218,184,514.75
3	Others	769,473,025.01
	Total	**1,265,828,290.39**

FIGURE 10-25 Here's the completed dynamic ranking contribution analysis.

If you want to take this a couple steps further, you can add conditional formatting to the Others group to clarify that it's not a Brand. Also, you can add a Sales bar. We did both by adding these two visual calculations:

```
Others Color = IF ( [Top + Others] = "Others", "darkgray" )

Sales Bar =
SWITCH (
    TRUE (),
    NOT ( ISATLEVEL ( [#] ) ), [Sales],
    [#] = [Other Group], [Other Group Sales],
    [Sales in Rank]
)
```

Sales Bar returns the *Sales* on the total row, the *Other Group Sales* for the row for Others, and the *Sales in Rank* value otherwise. Because we will be using *Others Color* exclusively for a conditional formatting rule, let's hide it. Also set the data type of *Others Color* to text by selecting the General tab in the Visualizations pane, opening the Data format submenu, and setting Data type for *Others Color* to Text. Move the *Sales Bar* visual calculation to between *Top + Others* and *Sales Value*.

Now, set up a font color conditional formatting rule for *Top + Others* and base it on *Others Color* as shown in Figure 10-26.

Finally, set the data bar conditional formatting for *Sales Bar* as shown in Figure 10-27. Make sure to select the Show bar only option.

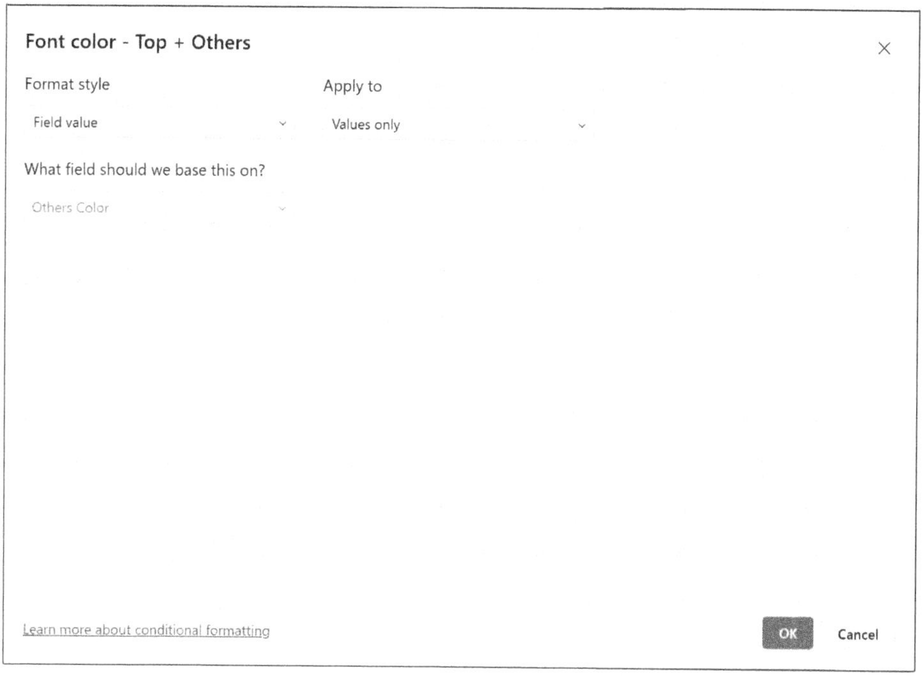

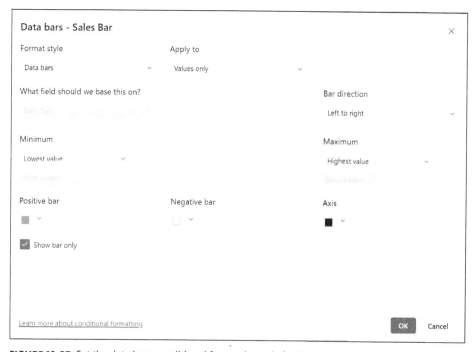

FIGURE 10-26 Set the font color conditional formatting rule for the *Top + Others* visual calculation.

FIGURE 10-27 Set the data bars conditional formatting rule for the *Sales Bar* visual calculation.

And that's it! Your dynamic rank contribution analysis is finished and should look like Figure 10-28. Pat yourself on the back. You deserve it!

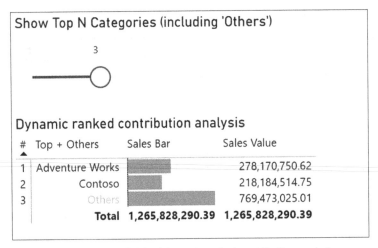

FIGURE 10-28 This is the finished dynamic ranked contribution analysis.

Focus highlighting

In a visual containing a lot of information, it can be very helpful to add a visual guide for your users to help them focus on what is important. In this example, we will show you how to highlight a specific Month on a line chart, but you can also use this to highlight other time periods or parts of the chart that are above or below a threshold. Figure 10-29 shows the visual we will be making. Notice how a slicer is provided to allow the user to set the highlight on the chart, in this case by selecting a month number to highlight.

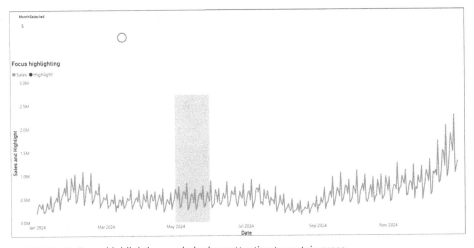

FIGURE 10-29 Focus highlighting can help draw attention to certain areas

To do this, first add a filter on Year to ensure that the visual only shows one Year. We used 2024. Then, add a numeric parameter for the month number, ranging from 1 to 12. If you're not familiar with adding a numeric parameter, we recommend checking the previous example. In our example, we called the numeric range parameter MonthSelected. (Note that there are other ways of doing this as well.) Once you have a way to select the range to highlight, create a line chart that shows Date on the X-axis and the selected value of the month number and *Sales* on the Y-axis. Then add the following visual calculation:

```
Highlight =
VAR __h =
    MAXX ( ROWS, [Sales] )
RETURN
    IF ( MONTH ( [Date] ) = [MonthSelected Value], __h * 1.2, BLANK () )
```

The *Highlight* visual calculation checks if the current month is the selected month and, if so, shows the highlight as a line that equals the highest amount + 20%, so it always shows just a little above the line (hence the multiplication of __h by 1.2). Be sure to put the *Highlight* visual calculation on the Y-axis as well. Hide the selected value of the month number so your visualization configuration looks like Figure 10-30.

FIGURE 10-30 This is the end configuration for the focus highlight visualization.

Finally, turn on the Shade area for the *Highlight* visual calculation. Also turn off the line for the *Highlight* visual calculation. By now, your visual should start to look like Figure 10-29. You can adjust the percentage of shade in the settings to make the highlight more obvious.

In the preceding example, a single year was selected (2024). If the line chart contains multiple years, however, the highlight will span from the first selected month in the first year all the way to the end of that month in the last year. Connecting the data points with a line is an effect of the continuous X-axis. If you set the axis to categorical, the highlight will appear for each year individually. However, that may defeat the purpose of the highlight because highlights will appear in each year instead of in one specific year.

## CHAPTER 11

Charting with visual calculations

If you felt like some of the examples in Chapter 10, "Applied visual calculations," were not "out there" enough, this is the chapter for you. This chapter takes you on a tour of the laboratories of the most creative masters of visual calculations. It shows some of the most spectacular charts created using visual calculations. That's right, you can create complete charts using visual calculations! You can also use charts that are already built into Power BI but take them to the next level. You can even create charts that don't exist in Power BI unless you use a custom visual, **Deneb**, or some other way of using or creating custom visuals. Some are useful and some are outright insane. In this chapter you will find:

- Pareto analysis

- Correlation matrix

- Waterfall chart in a matrix

- Bullet chart

- Tornado chart

- Gantt chart

- Box-and-whisker plot

- Bump chart

Don't say we didn't warn you!

> **Note** To optimize space, we arranged sections of the Format pane side by side in the screenshots for this chapter rather than stacking them vertically as they appear in Power BI.

Pareto analysis

A Pareto analysis is a decision-making tool based on the 80/20 rule, which suggests that 80 percent of outcomes comes from 20 percent of causes. This rule was originally observed by economist Vilfredo Pareto (hence the name Pareto analysis). He was a Paris-born Italian economist, sociologist, and philosopher. Pareto first observed that 80 percent of Italy's wealth was owned by 20 percent of the population, which led him to the broader 80/20 rule we still use today in many business analyses.

> **Note** A Pareto analysis helps you focus on what matters most by highlighting the biggest issues, but you might miss rare but unpredictable events that have a major impact (Black Swans).

Pareto analyses are most commonly used in manufacturing, healthcare, retail, and finance, although they are present in almost any industry. Alternative names for the Pareto analysis are the law of the vital few and the principle of factor sparsity, although people typically just call the chart a Pareto chart or an 80/20 chart. The Pareto chart consists of multiple parts:

- **Column chart** This is sorted by a numerical value in descending order, so the biggest contributor is listed first.

- **Line chart** This shows the cumulative percentage of the total. Because the biggest factors are sorted first, the line starts off steep and then gradually arcs toward 100 percent in the top right.

Figure 11-1 shows an example of a Pareto chart made in Power BI. With this Pareto chart, it's clear that Computers, Cell phones, and Home Appliances are the big contributors to *Sales*, as together they comprise more than 70 percent of the total sales.

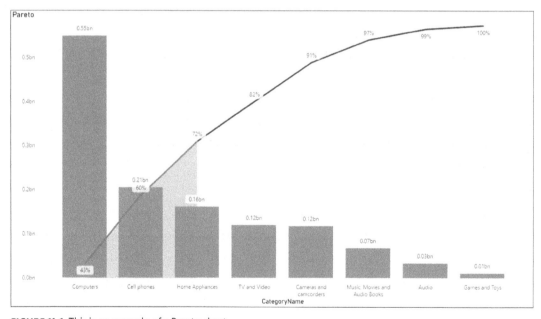

FIGURE 11-1 This is an example of a Pareto chart.

To make the Pareto chart shown in Figure 11-1, first create a combo chart (either a line and stacked column or line and clustered column chart). Put Product CategoryName on the X-axis and *Sales* on the column Y-axis, ensuring that the chart is sorted by *Sales* in descending order (see Figure 11-2).

Sales by CategoryName
0.5bn
0.4bn
0.3bn
0.2bn
0.1bn
0.0bn
Sales
Computers
Cell phones
Home Appliances
TV and Video
Cameras and camcorders
Music, Movies and Audio Books
Audio
Games and Toys
CategoryName

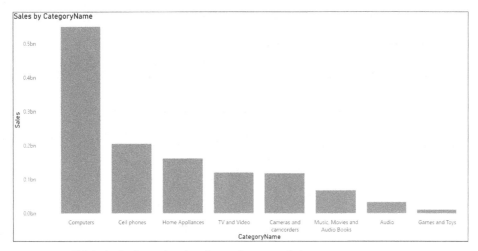

FIGURE 11-2 This is the basic combo chart for our Pareto analysis.

Next, enter visual calculations edit mode and add a percent of grand total visual calculation by selecting it from the expression templates menu (as shown in Figure 11-3). Of course, you can also enter this manually.

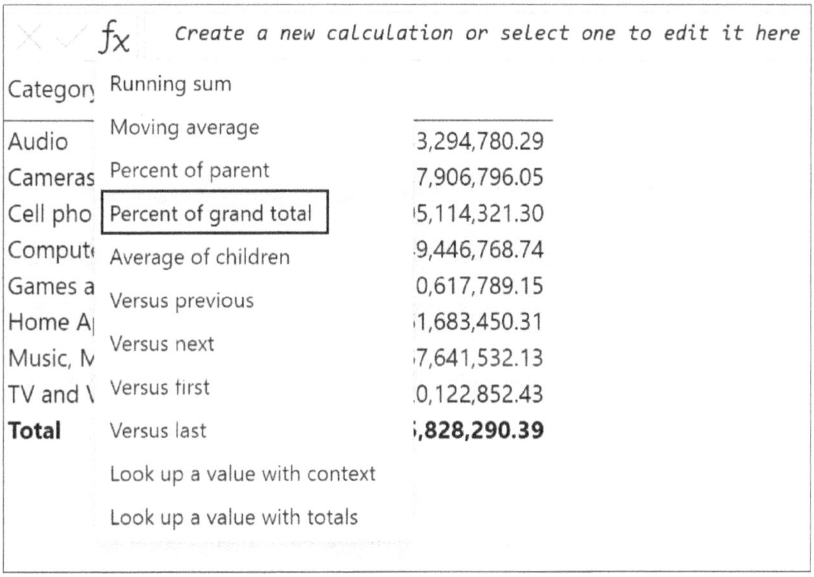

fx
Create a new calculation or select one to edit it here
Categor
Audio
Cameras
Cell pho
Comput
Games a
Home A
Music, M
TV and \
Total
Running sum
Moving average
Percent of parent
Percent of grand total
Average of children
Versus previous
Versus next
Versus first
Versus last
Look up a value with context
Look up a value with totals
3,294,780.29
7,906,796.05
5,114,321.30
9,446,768.74
0,617,789.15
1,683,450.31
7,641,532.13
0,122,852.43
,828,290.39

FIGURE 11-3 Percent of grand total is one of the expression templates provided for visual calculations.

Now fill out the template using the provided parameter pickers. As shown in Figure 11-4, your *Percent of grand total* visual calculation should look as follows:

```
Percent of grand total = DIVIDE ( [Sales], COLLAPSEALL ( [Sales], ROWS ) )
```

	f_x 1 Percent of grand total = DIVIDE(⊙ [Sales], COLLAPSEALL(⊙ [Sales], ⊙ ROWS))	
CategoryName	Sales	Percent of grand total
Audio	33,294,780.29	0.03
Cameras and camcorders	117,906,796.05	0.09
Cell phones	205,114,321.30	0.16
Computers	549,446,768.74	0.43
Games and Toys	10,617,789.15	0.01
Home Appliances	161,683,450.31	0.13
Music, Movies and Audio Books	67,641,532.13	0.05
TV and Video	120,122,852.43	0.09
Total	**1,265,828,290.39**	**1.00**

FIGURE 11-4 Use the parameter pickers to fill out the parameters for the expression template.

Hide the *Percent of grand total* visual calculation. After that, add the Pareto line with the following visual calculation:

```
Pareto = RUNNINGSUM ( [Percent of grand total], ORDERBY ( [Sales], DESC ) )
```

Move the *Pareto* visual calculation you have just created to the line Y-axis and format the *Pareto* visual calculation as a percentage by following the next steps:

1. Click the General tab, open Data Format, and choose *Pareto* from the Apply setting to menu.

2. Open the Format menu and set the Data type to Decimal number and select Percentage as the format. Set the decimal places to 0.

You should have the settings displayed in Figure 11-5.

Add data labels to both the line showing the *Pareto* visual calculation and the column showing the *Sales* measure. To finish up, hide the legend and the secondary Y-axis title. We also set the color of the secondary Y-axis labels to the background color to avoid displaying them, as shown in Figure 11-6.

Optionally, you can emphasize the biggest contributors using another visual calculation. For example, the following *Big contributor* visual calculation will return a blank value for any CategoryName that is higher than or equal to 80 percent, resulting in a highlight for only the first three categories:

```
Big contributor = IF ( [Pareto] < 0.80, [Pareto], BLANK () )
```

FIGURE 11-5 You can set data formats for visual calculations in the General section of the Format pane, under the Data Format header.

Note Because adding the *Sales* value for the fourth category brings the *Pareto* value to 82 percent, it isn't highlighted.

FIGURE 11-6 You can hide the legend, title, and values for the secondary Y-axis.

Move the *Big contributor* visual calculation to the line Y-axis next to the *Pareto* visual calculation. Format it as a percentage, as before. Finally, turn on shading for the *Big contributor* visual calculation; click the Visual tab, and turn on Shade area. Be sure to turn it off for the *Pareto* visual calculation and leave it on for *Big contributor*. The final visual configuration should look like Figure 11-7; Figure 11-8 shows the resulting Pareto chart.

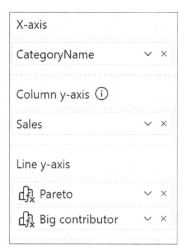

X-axis		
CategoryName	∨	×

Column y-axis ⓘ

| Sales | ∨ | × |

Line y-axis

| 📊 Pareto | ∨ | × |
| 📊 Big contributor | ∨ | × |

FIGURE 11-7 This is the final configuration for the Pareto chart.

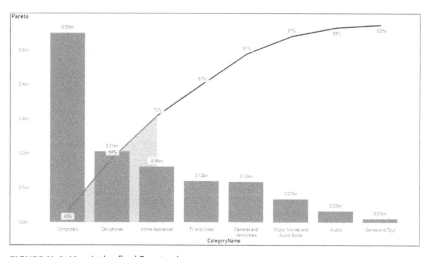

FIGURE 11-8 Here's the final Pareto chart.

Correlation matrix

A correlation matrix is a table that displays the correlation coefficients between multiple variables or attributes, where each value in the matrix represents the strength and direction of the relationship between two variables. This type of analysis helps users understand relationships between data points and what-if scenarios because it visualizes what effects a change in one variable will have on the other tracked variables. For example, it's often used in finance to understand how value swings in one asset impact others and in healthcare to relate lifestyle and medical conditions. The key features of this type of analysis are as follows:

- The values shown are correlation coefficients that range from -1 to 1, where 1 indicates a perfect positive correlation (as one variable increases, the other also increases), -1 indicates a perfect negative correlation (as one increases, the other decreases), and 0 means no correlation: there is no measured effect between changes in one variable on the value of the other.

- The matrix is always symmetrical on the diagonal because the correlation between A and B is the same as between B and A.

- The diagonal values are always 1 because each variable is perfectly correlated with itself.

Note Perfect correlations (positive or negative) are rare. A nonperfect positive correlation still means that an increase in one variable often results in an increase in the other variable, just not that it happens always.

Other names for the correlation matrix are correlation plot, diagonal correlation matrix, covariance matrix, dependency matrix, association matrix, similarity matrix, and relationship matrix. In finance, variance-covariance matrices are also popular, although technically, these are not correlation matrices because the diagonal values are not 1. Instead, they show the variance within the variable. Popular statistical languages such as R and Python have their own tools for calculating correlations. The R language even provides a dedicated package for creating a correlation matrix, aptly called corrplot. In Python, most often you use matplotlib to create these types of matrices. A close cousin of this type of analysis is a correlogram, which shows small charts (mostly scatter plots or column charts) instead of correlation coefficients.

Figure 11-9 shows the correlation matrix we will make.

Correlation matrix

Attribute	Age in Years	NetPrice	Quantity	Square meters	Total Orders	Weight
Age in Years	1.00	0.42	0.66	0.68	0.64	0.43
NetPrice	0.42	1.00	0.41	0.42	0.41	0.34
Quantity	0.66	0.41	1.00	0.64	0.61	0.40
Square meters	0.68	0.42	0.64	1.00	0.65	0.41
Total Orders	0.64	0.41	0.61	0.65	1.00	0.40
Weight	0.43	0.34	0.40	0.41	0.40	1.00

FIGURE 11-9 This is the final correlation matrix.

Note that as the Store's area (as measured by the Square meters attribute) increases, the quantity of orders does not increase linearly, leading to the conclusion that bigger stores do not lead to more orders. Whether customers do indeed prefer smaller stores cannot be concluded from this analysis, but it's interesting, nonetheless. Also note that the correlation coefficient between the Square meters and

NetPrice is 0.42, which implies that as Stores grow in size, the price of products sold does not grow linearly. This is another potential indicator that smaller stores might perform better. Also, the correlation coefficient of Quantity and Weight is 0.40, which implies that as the quantity of products in an order increases, the order's total weight does not increase linearly. This potentially leads to the conclusion that the upsell and cross-sell strategies used at the cash register and by store clerks pay off, as customers seem to buy a limited number of main (heavy) products in combination with smaller products. (Let's face it, we have all been victims of this same technique, causing us to buy that extra maintenance spray, spare battery, or set of tools!)

To create this matrix, you first need to create an unpivoted table. Most if not all data used for Power BI is stored in a dimensional model with facts and dimensions. A fact from our sample model is NetPrice. For the correlation matrix, you need to create a new column that contains the names of the facts and a column that contains the values of the facts. You also need to add some kind of identifier to separate the individual fact values. In this case, we picked OrderKey as our index column, and we added NetPrice and Quantity from the Sales table as attributes, as well as the Age in Years of the Customer who placed the order and the area of the Store in which the order was placed in square meters. Additionally, we calculated the total orders placed by that customer as well as the total weight of the products ordered. Note that this results in multiple rows being created for each order that contains more than one product. To create this unpivoted table, we used a calculated table called SalesUnpivot:

```
SalesUnpivot =
VAR LimitedSales =
    FILTER (
        TOPN ( 50000, Sales, Sales[OrderKey], ASC ),
        Sales[StoreKey] <> 999999
            && NOT ISBLANK ( RELATED ( Product[Weight] ) )
    )
VAR ExpandedSales =
    ADDCOLUMNS (
        UNION (
            SELECTCOLUMNS (
                LimitedSales,
                "Index", Sales[OrderKey],
                "Attribute", "NetPrice",
                "Value", Sales[NetPrice]
            ),
            SELECTCOLUMNS (
                LimitedSales,
                "Index", Sales[OrderKey],
                "Attribute", "Quantity",
                "Value", Sales[Quantity]
            ),
            SELECTCOLUMNS (
                LimitedSales,
                "Index", Sales[OrderKey],
                "Attribute", "Age in Years",
                "Value", RELATED ( Customer[Age in Years] )
            ),
            SELECTCOLUMNS (
                LimitedSales,
```

```
            "Index", Sales[OrderKey],
            "Attribute", "Total Orders",
            "Value", CALCULATE ( COUNTROWS ( Sales ), ALLEXCEPT ( Sales,
            Sales[CustomerKey] ) )
        ),
        SELECTCOLUMNS (
            LimitedSales,
            "Index", Sales[OrderKey],
            "Attribute", "Weight",
            "Value", RELATED ( Product[Weight] )
        ),              SELECTCOLUMNS (
            LimitedSales,
            "Index", Sales[OrderKey],
            "Attribute", "Square meters",
            "Value", RELATED ( Store[SquareMeters] )
        )
    ),
    "Attribute 2", [Attribute]
    )
)
RETURN
    ExpandedSales
```

Notice that we limited the number of orders in SalesUnpivot to 50,000. We also removed any products that have a blank weight, as well as a specific store (999999), which represents stores with missing information, including square-meter information for each store. As shown in Figure 11-10, SalesUnpivot has four columns:

- **Index**   This is the order number.

- **Attribute and Attribute 2**   These contain the name of the attribute.

- **Value**   This contains the value of the attribute for that order.

Index	Attribute	Value	Attribute 2
1180093	Total Orders	1	Total Orders
1160174	Total Orders	1	Total Orders
1170041	Total Orders	1	Total Orders
1160125	Total Orders	1	Total Orders
1170025	Total Orders	1	Total Orders
1020152	Total Orders	1	Total Orders
1130090	Total Orders	1	Total Orders

FIGURE 11-10 This is part of the SalesUnpivot calculated table.

With this, it's relatively easy to create the correlation matrix. To get started, create a matrix that shows Attribute and Index on rows, Attribute 2 on columns, and Value as the values.

As mentioned, the correlation matrix displays correlation coefficients that indicate the direction and strength of the correlation between the attributes. The correlation coefficient shown is the Pearson correlation coefficient and is calculated with this formula:

$$r = \frac{n(\Sigma xy) - (\Sigma x)\,(\Sigma y)}{\sqrt{(n\Sigma x^2 - (\Sigma x)^2)\,(n\Sigma y^2 - (\Sigma y)^2)}}$$

To calculate the coefficient, you need to add the following three visual calculations:

```
X^2 = EXPAND ( SUMX ( ROWS, [Value] * [Value] ) , ROWS )
Y^2 = LOOKUP ( [X^2], [Attribute 2], [Attribute] )
Corr =
    VAR __n = EXPANDALL ( DISTINCTCOUNT ( [Index] ), ROWS )
    VAR __x = LOOKUPWITHTOTALS ( [Value], [Attribute 2], [Attribute 2] )
    VAR __y = LOOKUPWITHTOTALS ( [Value], [Attribute], [Attribute] )
    VAR __xy =
    EXPAND (
        SUMX (
            VALUES ( ROWS ),
            LOOKUP ( [Value], [Attribute], [Attribute 2] )
                * LOOKUP ( [Value], [Attribute 2], [Attribute] )
        ),
        ROWS
    )
    VAR __toSQRT =
        (
            __n * [X^2]
                - POWER ( __x, 2 )
        )
            * (
                __n * [Y^2]
                    - POWER ( __y, 2 )
            )
    VAR result =
        DIVIDE (
            __n * __xy - __x * __y,
            SQRT ( IF ( ISNUMBER ( __toSQRT ), __toSQRT, 0 ) )
        )
    RETURN
        IF (
            OR ( ISBLANK ( [Attribute] ), ISBLANK ( [Attribute 2] ) ),
            BLANK (),
            result
        )
```

Note The *Corr* visual calculation does not have particularly good performance. This is largely due to the IF statement that checks whether Attribute and/or Attribute 2 are blank. A measure-based approach would offer faster performance but has far higher complexity. But because visual calculations allow you to create these kinds of calculations, we still wanted to share it.

Hide the *X^2* and *Y^2* visual calculations, as well as the Value column, keeping only *Corr* visible. You should now have your correlation matrix; adding a conditional formatting rule for the background will finish it up. Create a background conditional formatting rule for *Corr* as a gradient. Set -1 or lowest value to red and 1 or highest value to green and add a middle color for 0 (middle value). It's OK to leave this white or whatever makes sense for your scenario (see Figure 11-11).

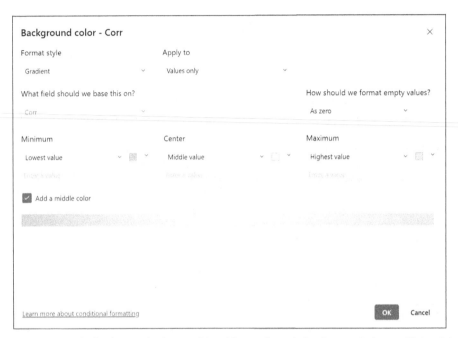

FIGURE 11-11 The background color conditional formatting rule for the correlation coefficient is based on the *Corr* visual calculation.

Congratulations! Your correlation matrix should now look like Figure 11-9.

Waterfall chart in a matrix

Power BI offers a waterfall chart, just as it offers a matrix. Combining the two, however, is useful to give more context for income statements. A waterfall chart built into the matrix adds color to the endless rows of numbers and allows the user to spot positive and negative outliers with ease.

Even though our sample dataset does not include data to create a proper income statement, we wanted to show you this technique using the data available. Figure 11-12 shows part of the waterfall chart in a matrix we will create next.

Start with a matrix with CategoryName and SubCategoryName on rows and *Sales* on values. Next, change the Style to Minimal and set the Layout to Outline. To do this, open the Format pane, select Layout and style presets, and select the correct style and layout. While you're here, turn off the Column subtotals and move the Row subtotals to the bottom. Figure 11-13 shows these layout changes.

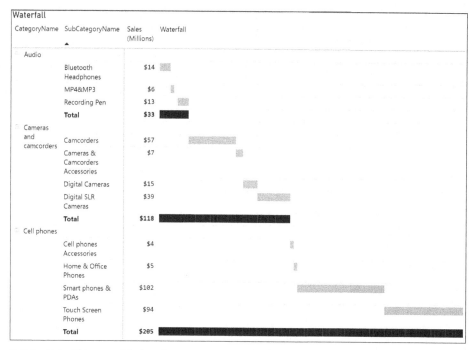

CategoryName	SubCategoryName	Sales (Millions)	Waterfall
Audio			
	Bluetooth Headphones	$14	
	MP4&MP3	$6	
	Recording Pen	$13	
	Total	**$33**	
Cameras and camcorders			
	Camcorders	$57	
	Cameras & Camcorders Accessories	$7	
	Digital Cameras	$15	
	Digital SLR Cameras	$39	
	Total	**$118**	
Cell phones			
	Cell phones Accessories	$4	
	Home & Office Phones	$5	
	Smart phones & PDAs	$102	
	Touch Screen Phones	$94	
	Total	**$205**	

FIGURE 11-12 This waterfall chart in a matrix was created solely with visual calculations.

Now, enter visual calculations edit mode and add the following visual calculation:

```
Sales (Millions) = DIVIDE ( [Sales], 1000000 )
```

You're going to show *Sales (Millions)* instead of *Sales* to reduce the clutter on the chart and make it look more like an aggregated income statement. Hide the *Sales* measure so the *Sales (Millions)* visual calculation is the only thing shown in the values of your matrix and set the format of *Sales (Millions)* to Currency with 0 decimal places.

Now, add a couple of helper visual calculations that you'll hide:

```
Denominator = DIVIDE ( COLLAPSEALL ( [Sales (Millions)], ROWS ), 300 )
RS = DIVIDE ( RUNNINGSUM ( [Sales (Millions)], ROWS ), [Denominator] )
```

Denominator calculates the maximum of *Sales (Millions)* and divides this by 300. This is done to scale down the length of the bars. We selected 300 based on our data and the space available. You will have to play around with this value to find an optimal value for your data and the space available on your visual report page. Your goal is to make the waterfall bars fit in the space so you avoid the need for a horizontal scrollbar. *RS* calculates the running sum of *Sales (Millions)* and divides this by the *Denominator*. Of course, you use RUNNINGSUM for this.

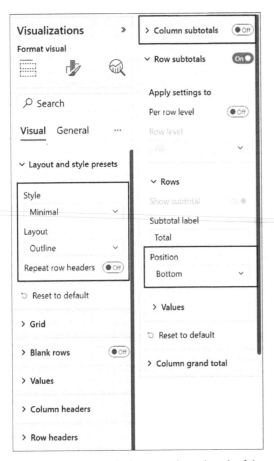

FIGURE 11-13 Change the layout, style, and totals of the matrix.

Finally, let's add the waterfall itself by adding yet another visual calculation:

```
Waterfall =
VAR __sales =
    DIVIDE ( [Sales (Millions)], [Denominator] )
VAR __sales_RS =
    DIVIDE ( RUNNINGSUM ( [Sales (Millions)] ), [Denominator] )
VAR __sales_RS_diff =
    __sales_RS - DIVIDE ( [Sales (Millions)], [Denominator] )
VAR __sales_RS_min =
    MINX ( ROWS, EXPANDALL ( MIN ( [RS] ), ROWS ) )
VAR __negative_min =
    ABS ( MIN ( 0, __sales_RS_min ) )
VAR __waterfall_bar =
    IF ( __sales > 0, __sales_RS_diff, __sales_RS ) + __negative_min
RETURN
    SWITCH (
        TRUE,
        ISATLEVEL ( [SubCategoryName] ),
```

```
           REPT ( UNICHAR ( 8202 ), ABS ( __waterfall_bar ) )
               & REPT ( UNICHAR ( 9608 ), ABS ( __sales ) ),
       NOT ( ISATLEVEL ( [SubCategoryName] ) ),
           IF (
               __sales_RS > 0,
               REPT ( UNICHAR ( 8202 ), __negative_min )
                   & REPT ( UNICHAR ( 9608 ), ABS ( __sales - __negative_min +
                   __waterfall_bar ) ),
               REPT ( UNICHAR ( 9608 ), ABS ( __sales ) )
           )
   )
)
```

A lot of things are happening here, so let's unpack this.

First, you define a __sales variable that simply returns the current value of *Sales (Millions)* and divides this by the *Denominator*. This is immediately followed by another variable definition (__sales_RS), which calculates the running sum of *Sales (Millions)* and divides it by the *Denominator*. Of course, you again use RUNNINGSUM for this. Then, you define __sales_RS_diff, which takes the difference of the running sum of the *Sales (Millions)* as stored in __sales_RS and subtracts the current value (again divided by *Denominator*). This enables you to position the bars nicely one after each other.

To consider negative values of *Sales (Millions)*—for example, when a loss is reported—we need to determine the minimum value, which is stored in __sales_RS_min. This is followed by __negative_min, which determines the absolute value of __sales_RS_min or 0, whichever is lower.

Then your final variable (__waterfall_bar) calculates the length of the waterfall bars by checking if the value of __sales is larger than 0. If so, the value of __sales_RS_diff is returned; otherwise, the value of __sales_RS is returned. In all cases, the value of __negative_min is also added to the value of __waterfall_bar, which is going to be 0 if there are no negative values in the data.

Finally, you get to the heart of the calculation. This is where the magic happens. First, you use ISATLEVEL to check if you are on the detail row by confirming SubCategoryName is present. If so, you will return the Unicode character 8202 __waterfall_bar times using REPT. This Unicode character gives you the empty space before the bars so the bars align. You can't use a regular space (Unicode character 32) here because of the next call to REPT, which repeats the Unicode character for a vertical bar (9608) __sales times. Notice we used the absolute value of __sales in case of negative values. Effectively, the bars shown in the waterfall chart in Figure 11-12 are just long text strings of carefully chosen Unicode characters. Conditional formatting will make them look good in a second.

To finish up the code in the *Waterfall* visual calculation, the final clause to the SWITCH statement confirms that SubCategoryName is not present. This means that the calculation is being calculated on the subtotal or total level, and therefore you need to return the total bar, which consists of repeating Unicode char 9806 __sales times if __sales_RS value is smaller than or equal to 0. If it is larger than 0, we put whitespaces (Unicode char 8202) in front to adjust the bar while also making sure the bar itself (Unicode char 9806) is of the correct length. Again, notice we used absolute values here. Your waterfall chart should now look like Figure 11-14 after scrolling to the right.

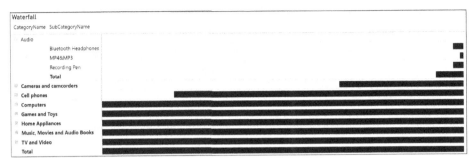

FIGURE 11-14 This is a very dark almost-waterfall chart in a matrix.

To make this look like an actual waterfall chart, you need to align the *Waterfall* visual calculation to the left, change the font, and add conditional formatting. To align the *Waterfall* visual calculation to the left, open the Format pane and left-align the Waterfall series in the Specific column submenu as shown in Figure 11-15. Make sure to also turn on the Apply to total toggle.

FIGURE 11-15 Use the Format pane to left-align the waterfall.

While you're here, you can also set the font to a monospaced font. This is important to make sure the bars line up perfectly. After all, they are composed of long strings of characters. We picked Consolas as our font by selecting it in the Values submenu.

Now, add one more visual calculation, this time to color the waterfall chart bars:

```
Waterfall color =
VAR __colorRed = "#ff0000"
VAR __colorGreen = "#8CB400"
VAR __colorBlack = "#000000"
RETURN
    IF (
        [Sales (Millions)] > 0,
        IF ( NOT ( ISATLEVEL ( [SubCategoryName] ) ), __colorBlack, __colorGreen
        ),
        __colorRed
    )
```

Hide the *Waterfall color* visual calculation and set up a conditional formatting rule for font color for the values and totals of the *Waterfall* visual calculation using the *Waterfall color* as the field value. Remember to set the data type of the *Waterfall color* visual calculation to text before setting up this conditional formatting rule. You're setting up the conditional formatting rule for font color and not the background color because you're using text strings to create the waterfall bars.

That's it! You should now have a waterfall chart in a matrix, and it should look like Figure 11-16.

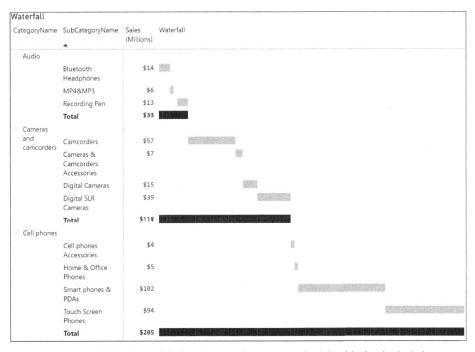

FIGURE 11-16 This finished waterfall chart in a matrix was created solely with visual calculations.

In case you do have negative values in your data, the *Waterfall* calculation will continue to work as shown in Figure 11-17.

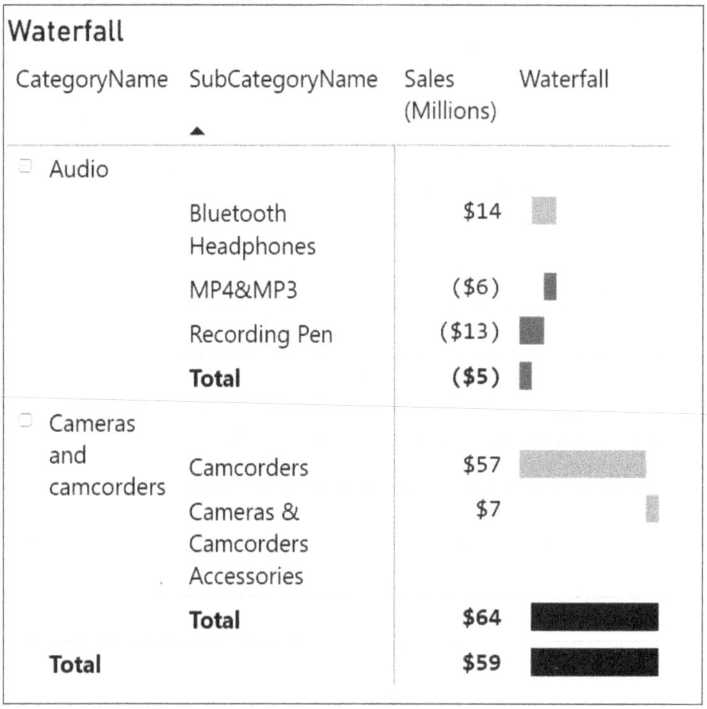

Waterfall			
CategoryName	SubCategoryName ▲	Sales (Millions)	Waterfall
Audio			
	Bluetooth Headphones	$14	
	MP4&MP3	($6)	
	Recording Pen	($13)	
	Total	($5)	
Cameras and camcorders	Camcorders	$57	
	Cameras & Camcorders Accessories	$7	
	Total	$64	
Total		$59	

FIGURE 11-17 The finished waterfall chart in a matrix also works with negative values.

Bullet chart

A bullet chart is a variation of a bar chart that shows performance against a target or benchmark. It was developed by Stephen Few and offers high information density per pixel. It allows easy comparison against the benchmark and is great at giving a lot of insight in a short time and minimal space. Because the target is often shown as a vertical line, it's easy to see the bars that are below the target and ones that are above; the below-target bars do not form a + sign shape with the target line and the ones that are above target do. The gray areas around the bars are used to give visual context to the value to indicate a poor, satisfactory, good, or excellent performance.

Power BI does not offer a built-in bullet chart, but thanks to visual calculations, you can make a similar chart using two overlaid bar charts. After all, a bullet chart is just a variation of a bar chart. The technique we will demonstrate here, however, includes putting two bar charts on top of each other, which is not ideal for many reasons, including duplication of code, needing to maintain two visuals, and performance. Figure 11-18 shows the bullet chart we will be making.

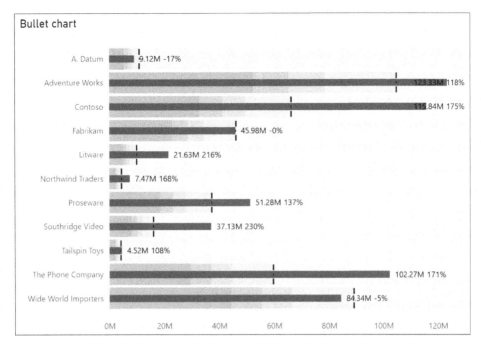

FIGURE 11-18 A bullet chart is great at showing a lot of information in a small space and is way less lethal than an actual bullet.

The chart in Figure 11-18 compares the *Sales* for 2026 with the *Sales* of the year before for each Brand. It makes it easy to see that most brands are either performing the same or better in 2026 as they did in 2025, but the A. Datum and Wide World Importers brands are underperforming, with 17 percent and 5 percent below target, respectively. The biggest percentage increase is with the Contoso brand, which grew 175 percent.

To create this bullet chart, you need two extra measures:

```
Sales Previous Year =
CALCULATE (
    [Sales],
    SAMEPERIODLASTYEAR ( 'Date'[Date] )
)

Sales vs. Previous Year (%) =
VAR _Actual = [Sales]
VAR _Target = [Sales Previous Year]
VAR _Delta = _Actual - _Target

AR _Perc =
    DIVIDE ( _Delta, _Target )
RETURN
    IF ( _Perc >= 0, 1 + _Perc, _Perc )
```

Sales Previous Year calculates *Sales* for the same period last year. This will help you to create the comparison and benchmark values in your bar chart. The *Sales vs. Previous Year (%)* measure then compares *Sales* with the results of *Sales Previous Year* and calculates the percentage difference against the benchmark. If it's larger than or equal to 0, this will return 1+ the percentage difference. You will use this for the data label in the finished bullet chart. If the difference is negative, it will just return the negative percentage difference.

With this in place, let's start the construction of the bullet chart with the first bar chart. You will start with the background first and later put another bar chart on top.

First, create a stacked bar chart and put Brand on the Y-axis and *Sales* and *Sales Previous Year* on the X-axis. Sort the chart by Brand in ascending order so that A. Datum is at the top. To re-create the example, make sure that only the Year 2026 is selected by adding a filter to the visual or using a slicer.

Open visual calculations edit mode and hide *Sales* and *Sales Previous Year*. Then add the following four visual calculations:

```
Sales Previous Year 50 % = [Sales Previous Year] * 0.50
Sales Previous Year 62.5 % = [Sales Previous Year] * 0.125
Sales Previous Year 75 % = [Sales Previous Year] * 0.125
Sales Previous Year 100 % = [Sales Previous Year] * 0.25
```

The preceding calculations are not typos because you'll be showing them stacked. Adding 12.5 percent of *Sales Previous Year* to the 50 percent already displayed will indeed make it look like it is 62.5 percent. In the same way, adding another 12.5 percent will create a bar that ends at 75 percent, and finally, adding another 25 percent creates a bar that ends at exactly 100 percent. These measures are necessary to create gray backgrounds for the bars with the *Sales* value in the bar chart. Your bullet chart should now look like Figure 11-19.

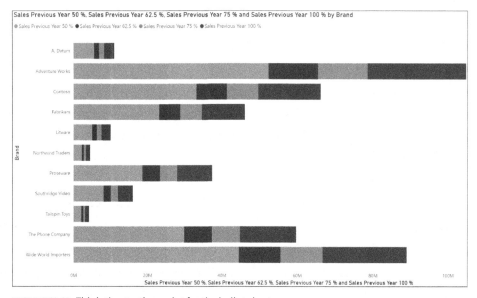

FIGURE 11-19 This is the starting point for the bullet chart.

Now, you need to add a visual calculation to determine the maximum value the chart will show:

```
Max Value to display =
EXPAND (
    ROUNDUP ( MAXX ( ROWS, MAX ( [Sales Previous Year], [Sales] ) ), -7 ),
    ROWS
)
```

Go ahead and hide *Max Value to display*. Because you don't know if that is going to be a value of *Sales* or *Sales Previous Year*, *Max Value to display* calculates the maximum value of all the rows for both *Sales and Sales Previous Year* and compares the two values. Notice we use EXPAND here to calculate the maximum of just the individual rows, ensuring that the total row will also return just the maximum value of the individual rows. If you just used MAXX without the EXPAND, then the total row would be equal to the total value of *Sales* or *Sales Previous Year*. Finally, you will round them up with a negative value for the NumberOfDigits parameter, so you end up with a value that's a bit higher than the maximum value. We used -7 in *Max Value to display*, but you might have to experiment with a good value for your own data. This brings us to the next visual calculation you need to add:

```
Diff to max = [Max Value to display] - [Sales Previous Year]
```

This straightforward visual calculation subtracts the value of the previous year's sales from the result of *Max Value to display*, so you can fill out the chart, effectively turning it into a 100 percent stacked bar chart but using numbers instead of percentages to determine the length of the bars (see Figure 11-20).

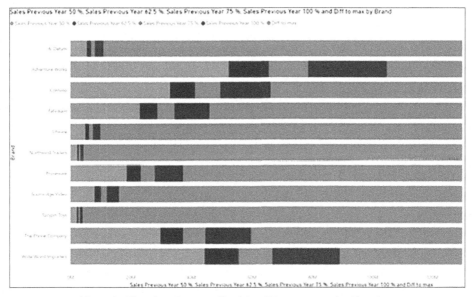

FIGURE 11-20 This stacked bar chart is pretending it's a 100 percent stacked bar chart.

You're almost finished with the bottom of the two bar charts to create your bullet chart. Wrap up the first one by doing some formatting using the Format pane, as shown in Figure 11-21:

1. Set the values color for the Y-axis to white or your background color.

2. Turn off the Y-axis title.

3. Use the fx button to set the Maximum value for the X-axis range to the value of *Max Value to display*.

4. Set the Values color for the X-axis to white or to your background color.

5. Turn off the X-axis title.

6. Turn off the legend.

7. Turn off the vertical gridlines.

8. Set the color for the bars to these increasingly lighter tints of gray using the following values:

   - #B3B3B3 for *Sales Previous Year 50%*
   - #C3C3C3 for *Sales Previous Year 62.5%*
   - #D3D3D3 for *Sales Previous Year 75%*
   - #E3E3E3 for *Sales Previous Year 100%*
   - #F3F3F3 for *Diff to max*

Finally, set the title text of this visual to an empty text (space), but don't turn it off. You can find the title text in the Visualizations pane in the General section under the Title submenu. The bottom layer of your bullet chart is now finished and should look like Figure 11-22.

Now, let's create the top layer. To do this, create a new clustered bar chart. Be careful not to create another stacked bar chart this time. The first setup is the same as before: Put Brand on the Y-axis and *Sales* and *Sales Previous Year* on the X-axis. Sort the chart by Brand in ascending order so that A. Datum is at the top. Again, to follow along, make sure Year is set to 2026 as before.

Now, open visual calculations edit mode and add the following three visual calculations:

```
Sales 1 = [Sales]
Sales 2 = [Sales]
Max Value to display =
    EXPAND (
        ROUNDUP ( MAXX ( ROWS, MAX ( [Sales Previous Year], [Sales] ) ), -7 ),
        ROWS
    )
```

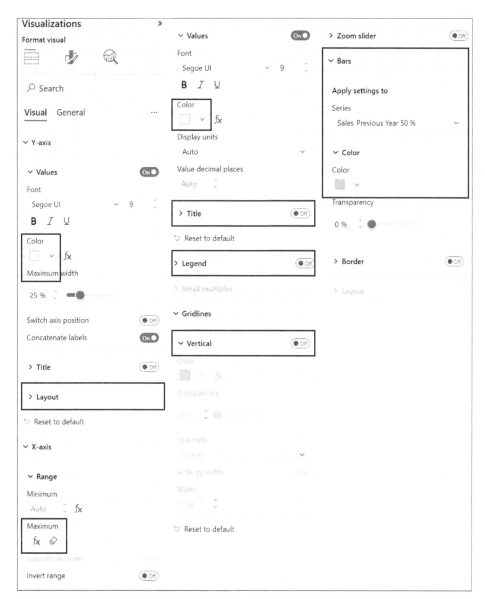

FIGURE 11-21 Use the Visualizations pane to make formatting changes to the first layer of your bullet chart.

The *Max Value to display* visual calculation is the same as before and will serve the same purpose. The *Sales 1* and *Sales 2* visual calculations are trivial; they just repeat the same value as *Sales* but are critical to turn this into a bullet chart.

Move *Sales* between *Sales 1* and *Sales 2*. Then hide *Max Value to display* and hide *Sales Previous Year*, as shown in Figure 11-23.

FIGURE 11-22 This is the finished bottom layer of the bullet chart.

X-axis		
Sales 1	⊙ ∨ ×
Sales	⊙ ∨ ×
Sales 2	⊙ ∨ ×
Sales Previous Year	⊘ ∨ ×
Max Value to display	⊘ ∨ ×

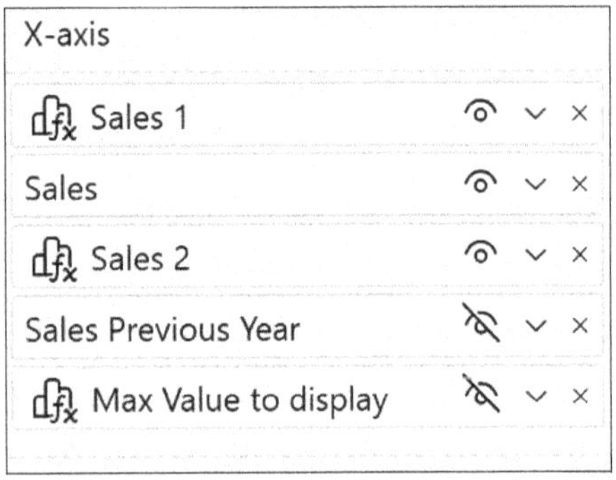

FIGURE 11-23 This is the X-axis configuration for the top layer of the bullet chart.

Now, you are ready for a lot of formatting changes to finish up the bullet chart using the Format pane as shown in Figure 11-24:

1. Turn off the Y-axis title.

2. Use the fx button to set the Maximum value for the X-axis range to the value of *Max Value to display*.

3. Turn off the X-axis title.

4. Turn off the legend.

5. Turn off the vertical gridlines.

6. Make the *Sales 1* and *Sales 2* bars 100 percent transparent.

7. Set the color of the *Sales* bar to #666666.

8. Turn data labels on for *Sales* (turn them off for *Sales 1* and *Sales 2*). Then set the position of the data labels to Outside end and set the value color to black.

9. Turn on detail for the data labels for *Sales* and add *Sales vs. Previous Year (%)* as data to display. Set the color to black, set the display units to None, and set the value decimal places to 0.

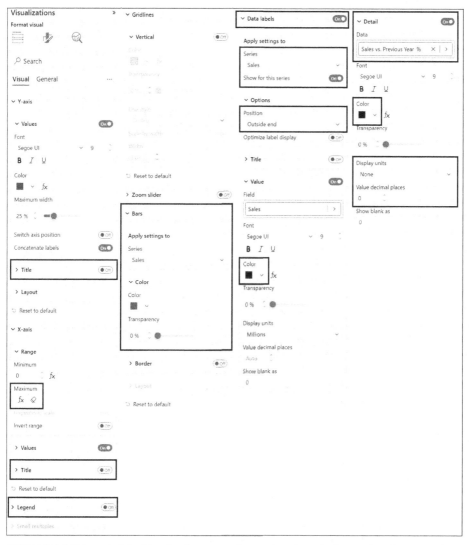

FIGURE 11-24 This part of the Visualizations pane shows where to make formatting changes to the top layer of your bullet chart.

Open the General tab in the Format pane, set the title text to Bullet chart, and turn off the background color, which you can find in the Effect submenu, as shown in Figure 11-25.

FIGURE 11-25 Change the title and turn off the background for the top layer of the bullet chart.

Finally, add errors bars using the Analytics pane, as shown in Figure 11-26. Apply the same settings to all three series (*Sales 1*, *Sales*, and *Sales 2*):

1. Turn the error bars on.

2. Select *Sales Previous Year* as the upper bound.

3. Select *Sales Previous Year* as the lower bound.

4. Set the bar and border color to black.

5. Turn the markers off.

6. Turn the tooltip off.

FIGURE 11-26 Set the error bars on the bullet chart.

Now, carefully resize and position the two charts on top of each other. Your finished bullet chart should look like Figure 11-27. You have just created a bullet chart using built-in visualizations, measures, and visual calculations!

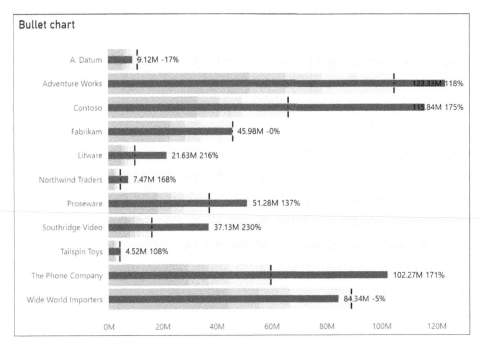

FIGURE 11-27 This is the finished bullet chart.

Tornado chart

A tornado chart is a type of bar chart used for comparative analysis, with bars arranged in descending order to create a tornadolike shape. A slightly less scary name for this chart is a butterfly chart; depending on the industry, the same chart is sometimes called a risk analysis chart or a sensitivity analysis chart.

> **Note** To create this kind of chart, you need at least two values to compare, as in our example. You can easily extend a tornado chart to show more than two values, but it would technically no longer be called a tornado chart.

Power BI does not offer this chart type built in, but thanks to visual calculations, it's straightforward to make. Figure 11-28 shows the tornado chart we will make. It compares the sales for 2026 with the sales for 2025 for each of the different brands.

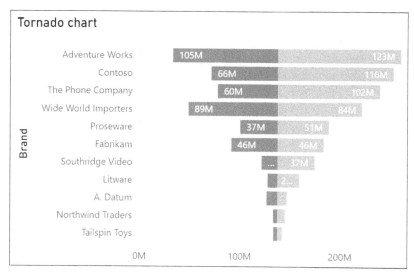

FIGURE 11-28 This is a scary tornado chart.

To create this chart, you will reuse the *Sales Previous Year* measure you created for the bullet chart:

```
Sales Previous Year =
CALCULATE (
    [Sales],
    SAMEPERIODLASTYEAR ( 'Date'[Date] )
)
```

As with the bullet chart, you will use a stacked bar chart, but make it look like a 100 percent bar chart using similar techniques to determine the maximum value to plot. You will also use the same technique of limiting the X-axis range to that maximum value.

To start, create a stacked bar chart and put Brand on the Y-axis and the *Sales* and *Sales Previous Year* measures on the X-axis. Filter the Year to 2026. Sort the chart by *Sales* in descending order.

Now, enter visual calculations edit mode and add the following three visual calculations:

```
Total = [Sales] + [Sales Previous Year]
MaxToShow = EXPAND ( ROUNDUP ( MAXX ( ROWS, [Total] ), -7 ) * 1.2, ROWS )
MidPoint = DIVIDE ( [MaxToShow], 2 )
```

As its name implies, the *Total* visual calculation calculates the sum of *Sales* and *Sales Previous Year*. If you wanted to compare more than two values, you'd need to add those to the sum here. The *MaxToShow* visual calculation determines the maximum value to show by calculating the maximum value of *Total* and returning it for all the rows including the total, using EXPAND. We have added an extra buffer by rounding the resulting value up to a higher value (hence the -7 parameter) and multiplying it by 1.2. The third visual calculation you just added is *MidPoint*, which simply divides the *MaxToShow* value by 2.

Before going any further, set the X-axis maximum range to the *MaxToShow* visual calculation, as shown in Figure 11-29.

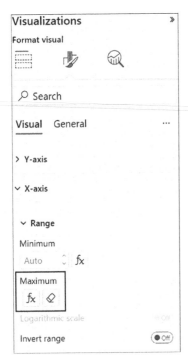

FIGURE 11-29 Setting the maximum range of the X-axis.

Now, hide all visual calculations you've added so far so that only *Sales Previous Year* and *Sales* are visible. It's time to add two more visual calculations to calculate the space to the left of the *Sales Previous Year* and the space to the right of the *Sales*:

```
LeftBuffer = [MidPoint] - [Sales Previous Year]
RightBuffer = [MaxToShow] - [Total]
```

LeftBuffer calculates the difference between *MidPoint* and *Sales Previous Year*, while *RightBuffer* calculates the difference between the end of the chart as indicated by *MaxToShow* and *Total*.

Now, reorder the fields on the X-axis so that *LeftBuffer* is shown first, followed by *Sales Previous Year*, *Sales*, and finally *RightBuffer*, as shown in Figure 11-30.

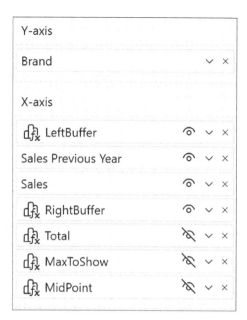

FIGURE 11-30 This is the order of fields on the X-axis of the tornado chart.

Now, it's time for a couple of formatting changes, as shown in Figure 11-31:

1. Turn off the X-axis title.

2. Turn off the legend.

3. Set the transparency of the bars (in the bars settings) for *LeftBuffer* and *RightBuffer* to 100 percent (or set the colors to your background color).

4. Set the colors for the *Sales Previous Year* and *Sales* bars. We used #808080 and #B3B3B3.

5. Turn on data labels for *Sales Previous Year* and set the position to inside base.

6. Turn on data labels for *Sales* and set the position to inside end.

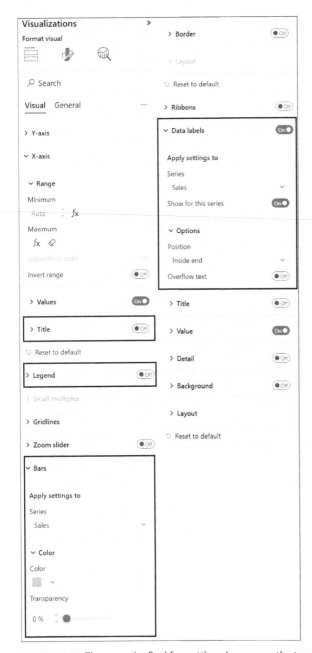

FIGURE 11-31 These are the final formatting changes on the tornado chart.

Finally, set the title text. Your final tornado chart should look like Figure 11-32.

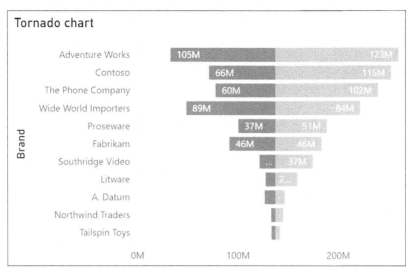

FIGURE 11-32 This is the final tornado chart.

Gantt chart

A Gantt chart mimics a Kanban board and is often used to visualize the progress of a project or process. It is also often called a project progress chart because it shows the steps in the project in an easy-to-understand timeline.

The chart is named after Henry Gantt, an American mechanical engineer and management consultant who developed this type of project-scheduling tool between 1910 and 1915. His goal was to create a visual method for tracking tasks, timelines, and progress in industrial settings. It became popular during World War I, when it was used by the U.S. military for managing production schedules. A similar concept, however, was developed even earlier, in 1896, by a Polish engineer called Karol Adamiecki. He gave the chart the much more beautiful and less megalomaniacal name, harmonogram, but it didn't gain the widespread adoption that the Gantt chart did.

A Gantt chart often includes a task or step breakdown; a timeline, including start and (estimated) end dates; the number of days to complete the task; and a completion percentage. While you can show all this information in a simple table, a timeline is often added to show progression. The timeline also makes it easier to see if tasks run sequentially or simultaneously. This helps in spotting potential areas for optimization.

Using a technique similar to the one we used to show a waterfall chart in a matrix (described earlier in this chapter), you can create such a Gantt chart in Power BI. Figure 11-33 shows the Gantt chart you'll be creating.

Gantt Chart

ID	TaskName	StartDate	EndDate	Days	Timeline + Completion %	Progress (%)
1	Project Kickoff	1/1/2024	1/1/2024	1.00		100%
2	Requirements Gathering	1/1/2024	1/10/2024	10.00		80%
3	Functional Specification	1/10/2024	1/22/2024	13.00		60%
4	Technical Specification	1/18/2024	1/31/2024	14.00		50%
5	Development	1/31/2024	2/12/2024	13.00		10%
6	Test	2/12/2024	2/23/2024	12.00		0%
7	Go-Live	2/23/2024	2/28/2024	6.00		0%

FIGURE 11-33 It's easy to show a project's progress and timeline with a Gantt chart.

Our sample dataset does not really include project information, so we created a calculated table to mimic a project plan by picking a couple of orders from the Order table like so:

```
ProjectStages =
VAR OrderKeys = { 10000, 10001, 100010, 180127, 310013, 430002, 540001, 590008 }
RETURN
    ADDCOLUMNS (
        SELECTCOLUMNS (
            FILTER ( 'Order', 'Order'[OrderKey] IN OrderKeys ),
            "ID", RANK ( ORDERBY ( 'Order'[OrderKey] ) ),
            "StartDate", 'Order'[OrderDate],
            "EndDate", 'Order'[DeliveryDate]
        ),
        "TaskName",
            SWITCH (
                [ID],
                1, "Project Kickoff",
                2, "Requirements Gathering",
                3, "Functional Specification",
                4, "Technical Specification",
                5, "Development",
                6, "Test",
                7, "Go-Live"
            ),
        "Progress (%)", SWITCH ( [ID], 1, 1, 2, .8, 3, .6, 4, .5, 5, .1, 6, 0, 7, 0 )
    )
```

Note Of course, the dates, task names, and progress should not be hardcoded, as they are in this example. Rather, they should be loaded from an actual source system. We just did this for illustration purposes.

To begin creating the Gantt chart shown in Figure 11-33, start with a table visual that shows the ID, TaskName, StartDate, EndDate, and Progress (%) columns from the ProjectStages calculated table. Then enter visual calculations edit mode and add this visual calculation, which calculates the difference in the EndDate and StartDate for each task:

```
Days =
VAR duration =
  INT ( [EndDate] - [StartDate] )
```

```
RETURN
  IF ( duration = 0, 1, duration )
```

For tasks that start and end on the same day (duration is 0), you return 1; otherwise, you just return the duration.

Now, add another visual calculation that's similar to what you did for the waterfall chart, where you used UNICHAR characters to create blocks:

```
Timeline + Completion % =
REPT ( UNICHAR ( 8202 ), INT ( [StartDate] - FIRST ( [StartDate] ) ) )
    & REPT ( UNICHAR ( 9608 ), [Days] )
    & FORMAT ( [Progress (%)], " 0%" )
```

The *Timeline + Completion %* visual calculation uses the FIRST function to calculate the number of days between the start date of each task and the first start date to ensure that each bar is aligned properly. It repeats an empty space (Unicode character 8202) for that number of days. Then it repeats the block character (Unicode character 9608) to show the bar, and finally, it shows the Progress % value.

Move the Progress (%) column to the end of the table. Then add a conditional formatting rule for the font color for the *Timeline + Completion %* visual calculation and base it on Progress (%). We created a gradient from gray to green, as shown in Figure 11-34.

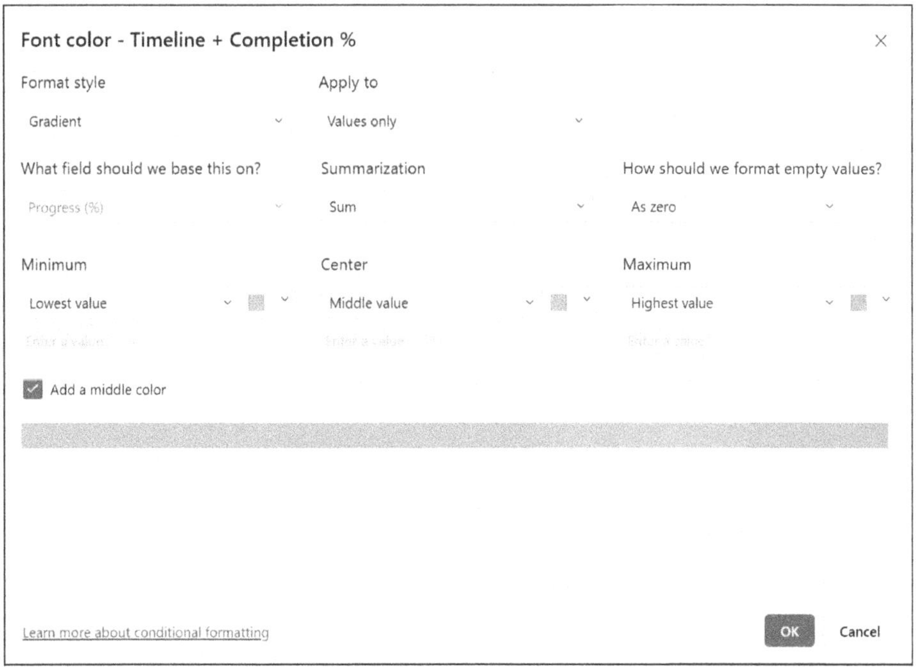

FIGURE 11-34 These are the font color conditional formatting settings for *Timeline + Completion %*.

Now, you need to make a couple of quick formatting changes, as shown in Figure 11-35:

1. Set the values font to a monospaced font to make sure the bars line up correctly. We picked Consolas as our font by selecting it in the Values submenu.

2. Turn off the total values.

3. Left-align *Timeline + Completion %* in the specific column section.

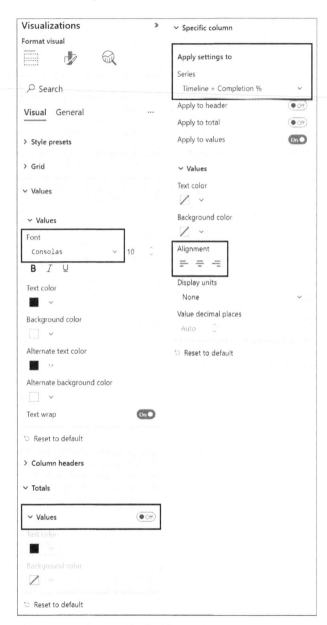

FIGURE 11-35 These are the final formatting changes on the Gantt chart.

That's it! Your Gantt chart is complete, and it should look like Figure 11-36.

Gantt Chart

ID	TaskName	StartDate	EndDate	Days	Timeline + Completion %	Progress (%)
1	Project Kickoff	1/1/2024	1/1/2024	1.00		100%
2	Requirements Gathering	1/1/2024	1/10/2024	10.00		80%
3	Functional Specification	1/10/2024	1/22/2024	13.00		60%
4	Technical Specification	1/18/2024	1/31/2024	14.00		50%
5	Development	1/31/2024	2/12/2024	13.00		10%
6	Test	2/12/2024	2/23/2024	12.00		0%
7	Go-Live	2/23/2024	2/28/2024	6.00		0%

FIGURE 11-36 This is the final Gantt chart.

Box-and-whisker plot

Introduced in 1970 by American John Tukey and based partly on the work of Mary Eleanor Spear in 1952, a box-and-whisker plot, or box plot for short, conveys a lot of information at a glance. The box plot enables the user to analyze distribution and variability of values, and it often shows:

- **The median value**   This represents the middle of the data; that is, 50 percent of the data is below that point and 50 percent is above it.

- **The first quartile (or 25th percentile)**   This is the median of the lower half of the data.

- **The third quartile (or 75th percentile)**   This is the median of the upper half of the data.

- **The range between the first and third quartile**   This represents the middle 50 percent of the data.

- **The maximum and minimum values**   These are represented by whiskers.

These information-packed plots have quickly become a standard tool in statistics but are applied to business information as well. They excel at contrasting multiple members of a population and are popular in finance and medical research.

Power BI does not offer a built-in box plot, but thanks to visual calculations, they're not hard to make. Figure 11-37 shows the box plot you'll create. It contains information about size of stores per country and includes the 25th to 75th percentile, maximum, minimum, median, average, and even the number of stores per country. It's easy to see that France is the outlier, with the biggest store in that country being only 400 square meters in size (which is only marginally higher than the smallest store in Germany, which is 350 square meters), and all other countries have significantly bigger stores. Not everything is bigger in America, though, as Canada has the U.S. beat for the average, median, and minimum store size (1884 versus 1543, 1500 versus 1313, and 1105 versus 840, respectively). If you look at the difference between the 75th and 25th percentile, Canada also has a far wider distribution of store sizes than the U.S., although Australia has the biggest distribution of all countries in the middle 50 percent of the data.

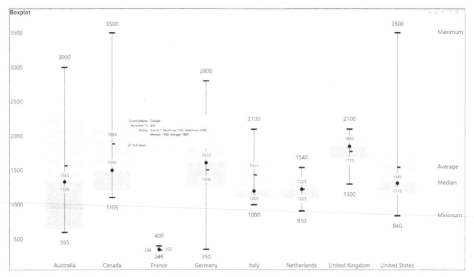

FIGURE 11-37 A box plot can pack a lot of information.

To get started, create a line and stacked column chart that shows CountryName, SquareMeters, and StoreCode on the X-axis. Drill it up so that only CountryName is shown, sort the chart by CountryName in ascending order, and set a filter on CountryName to exclude the Online country, as it has no stores. The chart will be empty, but that's exactly what you need because you will create visual calculations to show the information in the chart. Because visual calculations can only access what is on the visual, you need the fields on the chart, although you do not show them.

Enter visual calculations edit mode and create the following four visual calculations to calculate median value, the 25th and 75th percentile, and show the range to and from the median value:

```
Median = EXPAND ( MEDIAN ( [SquareMeters] ), ROWS )

Percentile 25 Start =
EXPAND (
    PERCENTILEX.INC ( VALUES ( [SquareMeters] ), [SquareMeters], .25 ),
    ROWS
)

25 to median = [Median] - [Percentile 25 Start]

Percentile 75 =
EXPAND (
    PERCENTILEX.INC ( VALUES ( [SquareMeters] ), [SquareMeters], .75 ),
    ROWS
) - [25 to median] - [Percentile 25 Start]
```

Move the *Median* visual calculation to the Line Y-axis and place the rest of these visual calculations on the Column Y-axis. Order them so that *Percentile 25 Start* is at the top, *25 to median* is shown next, and *Percentile 75* is shown last.

Now, add the following three visual calculations to determine the minimum, average, and maximum values:

```
Minimum = EXPAND ( MIN ( [SquareMeters] ), ROWS )
Maximum = EXPAND ( MAX ( [SquareMeters] ), ROWS )
Average = EXPAND ( AVERAGE ( [SquareMeters] ), ROWS )
```

Place the *Minimum*, *Maximum*, and *Average* on the Line Y-axis. Next, add the *Count* visual calculation:

```
Count = EXPANDALL ( COUNT ( [StoreCode] ), ROWS )
```

Place the *Count* on the Column Y-axis and hide it. You will use it in the tooltips later. The X-axis, Column Y-axis, and Line Y-axis should now contain the fields shown in Figure 11-38.

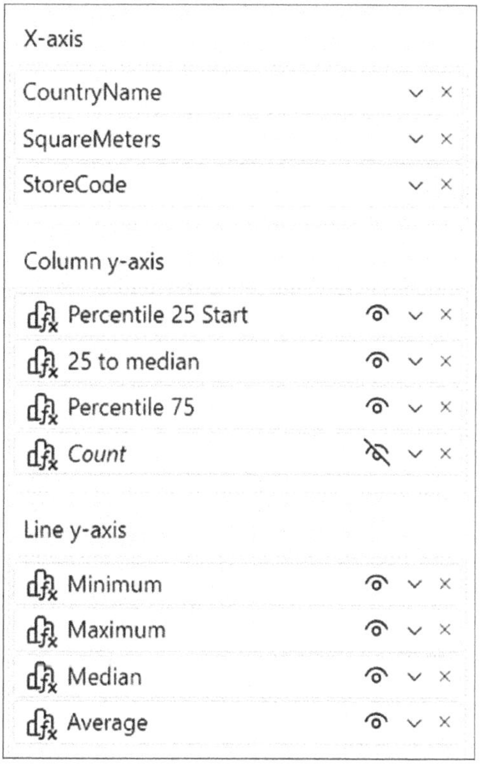

FIGURE 11-38 The configuration of the X-axis, Column Y-axis, and Line Y-axis for the box plot includes a lot of visual calculations.

Now, add a visual calculation for the tooltip to the Tooltips bucket:

```
Tooltip =
"Count: " & [Count] & ", Minimum: " & FORMAT ( [Minimum], "#" ) & ",
Maximum: " & FORMAT ( [Maximum], "#" ) & ", Median: " &
FORMAT ( [Median], "#" ) & ", Average: " & FORMAT ( [Average], "#" )
```

Finally, add two more helper visual calculations to the Tooltips bucket and hide them:

```
Min on Axis = EXPAND ( MINX ( ROWS, [SquareMeters] ), ROWS, 2 ) * .8
Max on Axis = EXPAND ( MAXX ( ROWS, [SquareMeters] ), ROWS, 2 ) * 1.05
```

You will use these helper visual calculations to set the minimum and maximum values of the Y-axis. We multiplied these by 0.8 and 1.05 to provide a bit more room at the bottom and top of the Y-axis. The final visual configuration should look like Figure 11-39.

FIGURE 11-39 This is the final configuration of the box plot.

Your visual should look like Figure 11-40. As you can see, this does not look like a box plot at all! Don't worry, you'll make it look like one soon enough.

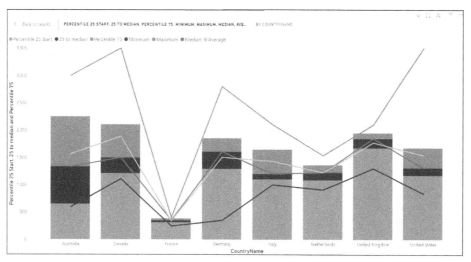

FIGURE 11-40 This doesn't look like a box plot at all.

OK, it's time for a lot of formatting changes. The first set is shown in Figure 11-41. Make these changes:

1. Turn off the X-axis title.

2. Turn off the Y-axis title.

3. Use the fx buttons to set the Y-axis range minimum value to the *Min on Axis* visual calculation and set the maximum value to the *Max on Axis* visual calculation.

4. Turn off the legend.

5. Turn off the horizontal gridlines.

6. Make the *Percentile 25 Start* column 100 percent transparent in the settings for columns.

7. Make the *25 to median* column 75 percent transparent and give it a contrasting color. We picked an orange hue (#E66C37).

8. Make the *Percentile 75* column 75 percent transparent and give it another contrasting color. We picked a light gray (#B3B3B3).

9. In the Lines settings, toggle off Show for all series.

10. Turn on the markers for all series. Set the following markers using a dark color. We used black for all markers:

    • For the *Minimum* and *Maximum* series, use an em dash (—) and set the size to 10 px.

    • For the *Median* series, use a filled circle (•) and set the size to 5 px.

    • For the *Average* series, use a hyphen (-) and set the size to 10 px.

11. Turn on the data labels.

12. Turn on the series labels.

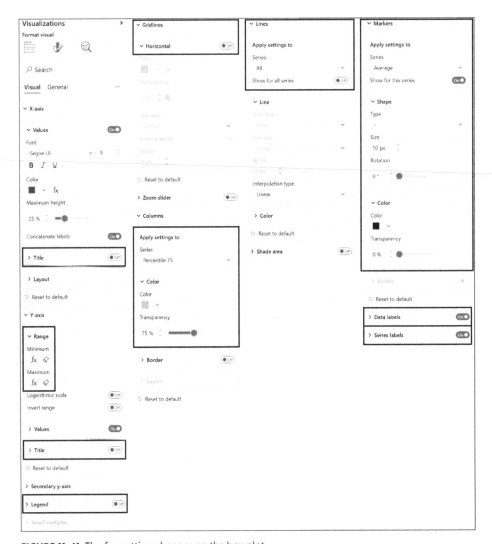

FIGURE 11-41 The formatting changes on the box plot.

Finally, you need an error bar. Use the Analytics pane to set an error bar for the *Minimum* series and set the upper bound to the max of SquareMeters, as shown in Figure 11-42. And that's it! Your box plot should now look like Figure 11-43.

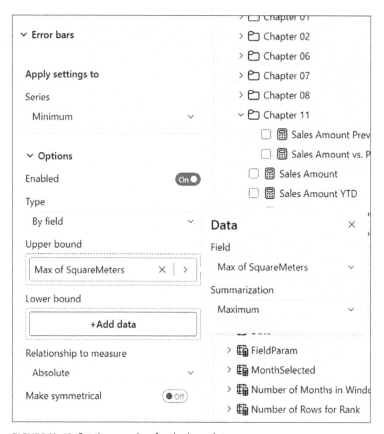

FIGURE 11-42 Set the error bar for the box plot.

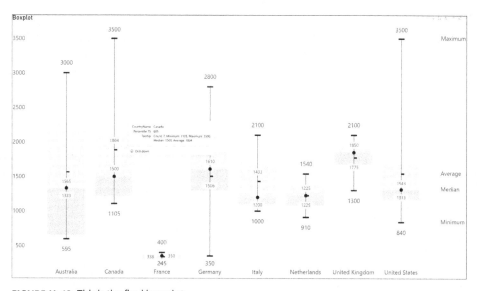

FIGURE 11-43 This is the final box plot.

Bump chart

A bump chart or ranking chart compares values as they progress, most commonly over time. Each line presents a category, and each category is ranked based on the value for that category for that specific moment. It helps highlight trends, rankings, or shifts in data over time—for example, company revenue streams (which we will use for our example) or performance before and after an event. This is also commonly used to show shifts in public opinion or to visualize survey results across time. The name is believed to have originated from boat races, where competitors "bump" each other to move up in the ranking. When comparing just two values, this chart is instead called a slope chart or slope graph. The slope chart was popularized by Edward Tufte in his classic book The Visual Display of Quantitative Information (1983) as a cleaner, more insightful way to visualize changes over time, compared to more traditional charts.

Figure 11-44 shows the bump chart you'll make. It also shows why some people call this chart type a subway chart; it looks a lot like a subway map.

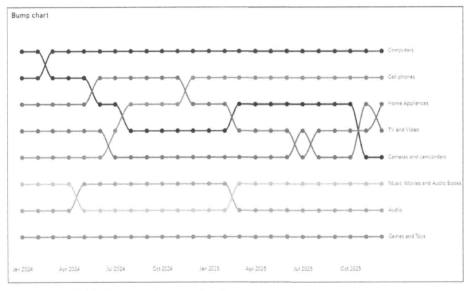

FIGURE 11-44 This is the bump chart we will make.

Reading a bump chart is pretty straightforward. Looking at the bump chart in Figure 11-44, you can see that the Cameras and camcorders product category massively lost popularity in the first half year of 2024. Despite the little spike in the beginning of 2025, the leading position was taken over by Computers. Similarly, between January 2025 and April 2025, Audio decreased in popularity, whereas Music, Movies, and Audio Books increased.

To create this bump chart, start with a basic line chart with YearMonth on the X-axis, CategoryName on the Legend, and *Sales* on the Tooltips. At this point, the chart is still blank. Set a filter on Year so that only 2024 and 2025 are showing. Then add the following visual calculation:

```
Rank = RANK ( DENSE, COLUMNS, ORDERBY ( [Sales], DESC ) )
```

The *Rank* visual calculation uses the RANK function to order each CategoryName by *Sales* descending, so the highest selling category gets the highest rank. We also specified DENSE to make sure there are no gaps in the ranking.

Next, add another visual calculation that determines the maximum value for the Y-axis:

```
MaxAxisValue = COLLAPSE ( EXPAND ( MAX ( [Rank] ), COLUMNS ROWS ), COLUMNS ROWS ) + 1
```

MaxAxisValue calculates the maximum value of *Rank* across the whole visual matrix and adds 1 to give a bit more room on the Y-axis. Hide this new visual calculation and confirm *Rank* is still visible.

Now, do some formatting to make the chart look like the one in Figure 11-44:

1. Hide the X-axis title.

2. Set the maximum value for the Y-axis to the *MaxAxisValue* visual calculation and the minimum value to 0.

3. Invert the range on the Y-axis so the lowest performer (lowest rank) is shown at the bottom and hide the values and title.

4. Turn off the legend.

5. In the Lines settings, set the interpolation type for the line to smooth.

6. Turn on the markers using the Show for all series toggle.

7. Turn on the series labels.

8. Set the title.

Figure 11-45 shows where to make these changes.

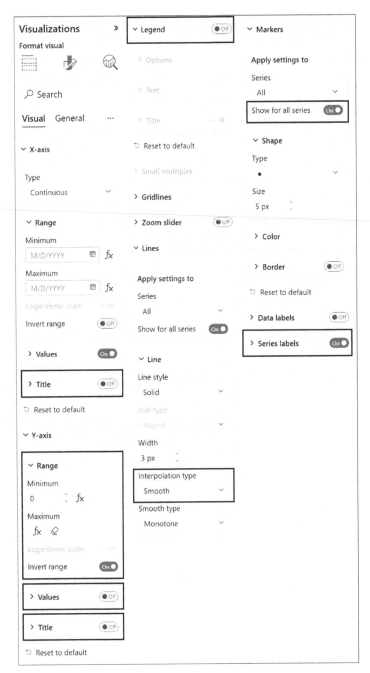

FIGURE 11-45 These are the formatting changes for the bump chart.

And that's it! Your bump chart is complete. It should look like Figure 11-44.

## CHAPTER 42

Beyond the page

Congratulations! You've made it to the end of this book on visual calculations. Now, it's time to put what you learned into practice.

As we said all the way back on the first pages of this book, we had two goals in mind when writing:

- We wanted to enable you to use visual calculations to perform calculations in Power BI.

- We hoped to inspire you to explore new, innovative ways to use visual calculations while also looking beyond them toward the wide world of DAX.

This book was not meant to be just a technical guide. It's a launchpad. Now that you've arrived at the end, it's time to launch visual calculations into your workflow! You've explored the universe of visual calculations. You've charted new territories. And now? It's time to apply it all. If Douglas Adams is correct in *The Hitchhiker's Guide to the Galaxy*, and 42 is the answer to the Ultimate Question of Life, the Universe, and Everything, the right visual calculation at the right moment might just be a close second. Better strap in and put your helmet on. Don't Panic. Lift-off begins with your next report.

Thanks for joining us on this journey. So long and thanks for all the fish. Good luck!

Appendices

Appendix A

This appendix contains the complete DAX query executed to obtain the output shown in Figure 9-7 in Chapter 9, which is the visual matrix for a clustered bar chart displaying *Sales* and *Costs* per product category and extended with a visual calculation to calculate the *Profit* per product category.

```
DEFINE
    COLUMN '__SQDS0VisualCalcs'[Profit] =
        (/* USER DAX BEGIN */
[Sales] - [Costs]
/* USER DAX END */)

    VAR __SQDS0FilterTable =
        TREATAS({2024}, 'Date'[Year])

    VAR __SQDS0Core =
        SUMMARIZECOLUMNS(
            ROLLUPADDISSUBTOTAL('Product'[CategoryName],
"IsSQDS0GrandTotalRowTotal"),
            __SQDS0FilterTable,
            "Sales", '_Measures'[Sales],
            "Costs", '_Measures'[Costs]
        )

    VAR __SQDS0VisualCalcsInput =
        SELECTCOLUMNS(
            KEEPFILTERS(
                SELECTCOLUMNS(
                    __SQDS0Core,
                    "CategoryName", 'Product'[CategoryName],
                    "IsSQDS0GrandTotalRowTotal", [IsSQDS0GrandTotalRowTotal],
                    "Sales", [Sales],
                )
            ),
            "CategoryName", [CategoryName],
            "IsSQDS0GrandTotalRowTotal", [IsSQDS0GrandTotalRowTotal],
            "Sales", [Sales],
            "Costs", [Costs]
        )
```

```
TABLE '__SQDS0VisualCalcs' =
    __SQDS0VisualCalcsInput
    WITH VISUAL SHAPE
        AXIS rows
            GROUP [CategoryName] TOTAL [IsSQDS0GrandTotalRowTotal]
            ORDER BY
                [CategoryName] ASC

VAR __SQDS0RemoveEmptyDensified =
    FILTER(
        KEEPFILTERS('__SQDS0VisualCalcs'),
        OR(
            NOT('__SQDS0VisualCalcs'[IsDensifiedRow]),
            NOT(ISBLANK('__SQDS0VisualCalcs'[Profit]))
        )
    )

VAR __DS0Core =
    SELECTCOLUMNS(
        KEEPFILTERS(
            FILTER(
                KEEPFILTERS( __SQDS0RemoveEmptyDensified),
                '__SQDS0VisualCalcs'[IsSQDS0GrandTotalRowTotal] = FALSE
            )
        ),
        "'__SQDS0VisualCalcs'[Sales]", '__SQDS0VisualCalcs'[Sales],
        "'__SQDS0VisualCalcs'[Costs]", '__SQDS0VisualCalcs'[Costs],
        "'__SQDS0VisualCalcs'[Profit]", '__SQDS0VisualCalcs'[Profit]
    )

VAR __DS0PrimaryWindowed =
    TOPN(1001, __DS0Core, '__SQDS0VisualCalcs'[Sales], 0, '__SQDS0VisualCalcs
'[CategoryName], 1)

EVALUATE
    __DS0PrimaryWindowed

ORDER BY
    '__SQDS0VisualCalcs'[Sales] DESC, '__SQDS0VisualCalcs'[CategoryName]
```

Appendix B

This appendix contains the complete DAX query executed to populate the matrix visual showing *Sales* per Month and Year in Figure 9-14. In Chapter 9, a simplified version of the DAX query is described and explained.

```
DEFINE
    VAR __DM3FilterTable =
        TREATAS({2024,
            2025,
            2026}, 'Date'[Year])

    VAR __DS0Core =
        SUMMARIZECOLUMNS(
            ROLLUPADDISSUBTOTAL(
                'Date'[Year], "IsGrandTotalRowTotal",
                ROLLUPGROUP('Date'[Month], 'Date'[MonthNumber]),
                "IsDM1Total",
                NONVISUAL(__DM3FilterTable)
            ),
            "Sales", '_Measures'[Sales]
        )

    VAR __DS0PrimaryWindowed =
        TOPN(
            502,
            __DS0Core,
            [IsGrandTotalRowTotal],
            0,
            'Date'[Year],
            1,
            [IsDM1Total],
            0,
            'Date'[MonthNumber],
            1,
            'Date'[Month],
            1
        )

EVALUATE
    __DS0PrimaryWindowed

ORDER BY
    [IsGrandTotalRowTotal] DESC,
    'Date'[Year],
    [IsDM1Total] DESC,
    'Date'[MonthNumber],
    'Date'[Month]
```

Appendix C

This appendix contains the complete DAX query executed to populate a matrix visual that shows *Sales* per Month and Year, which was extended with a visual calculation *YTD Sales* that resets for each Year. The resulting output table can be found in Figure 9-16, in Chapter 9.

```
DEFINE
    COLUMN '__DS0VisualCalcs'[YTD Sales] =
        (/* USER DAX BEGIN */
RUNNINGSUM([Sales], [Year])
/* USER DAX END */)

    VAR __DS0Core =
        SUMMARIZECOLUMNS(
            ROLLUPADDISSUBTOTAL(
                'Date'[Year], "IsGrandTotalRowTotal",
                ROLLUPGROUP('Date'[Month], 'Date'[MonthNumber]), "IsDM1Total"
            ),
            "Sales", '_Measures'[Sales]
        )

    VAR __DS0VisualCalcsInput =
        SELECTCOLUMNS(
            KEEPFILTERS(
                SELECTCOLUMNS(
                    __DS0Core,
                    "Year", 'Date'[Year],
                    "IsGrandTotalRowTotal", [IsGrandTotalRowTotal],
                    "Month", 'Date'[Month],
                    "MonthNumber", 'Date'[MonthNumber],
                    "IsDM1Total", [IsDM1Total],
                    "Sales", [Sales]
                )
            ),
            "Year", [Year],
            "Month", [Month],
            "MonthNumber", [MonthNumber],
            "IsGrandTotalRowTotal", [IsGrandTotalRowTotal],
            "IsDM1Total", [IsDM1Total],
            "Sales", [Sales]
        )

    TABLE '__DS0VisualCalcs' =
        __DS0VisualCalcsInput
        WITH VISUAL SHAPE
            AXIS rows
                GROUP [Year] TOTAL [IsGrandTotalRowTotal]
                GROUP
                    [Month],
                    [MonthNumber]
                    TOTAL [IsDM1Total]
                ORDER BY
                    [Year] ASC,
```

```
                        [MonthNumber] ASC,
                        [Month] ASC
                DENSIFY "IsDensifiedRow"
    VAR __DS0RemoveEmptyDensified =
        FILTER(
            KEEPFILTERS('__DS0VisualCalcs'),
            OR(
                NOT('__DS0VisualCalcs'[IsDensifiedRow]),
                NOT(ISBLANK('__DS0VisualCalcs'[YTD Sales]))
            )
        )

    VAR __DS0CoreWithInstanceFilters =
        FILTER(
            KEEPFILTERS(__DS0RemoveEmptyDensified),
            OR(
                OR(
                    '__DS0VisualCalcs'[IsGrandTotalRowTotal],
                    AND(NOT('__DS0VisualCalcs'[IsGrandTotalRowTotal]),
'__DS0VisualCalcs'[IsDM1Total])
                ),
                AND(
                    NOT('__DS0VisualCalcs'[IsDM1Total]),
                    '__DS0VisualCalcs'[Year] IN {2024,
                        2025,
                        2026}
                )
            )
        )

    VAR __DS0PrimaryWindowed =
        TOPN(
            502,
            __DS0CoreWithInstanceFilters,
            '__DS0VisualCalcs'[IsGrandTotalRowTotal],
            0,
            '__DS0VisualCalcs'[Year],
            1,
            '__DS0VisualCalcs'[IsDM1Total],
            0,
            '__DS0VisualCalcs'[MonthNumber],
            1,
            '__DS0VisualCalcs'[Month],
            1
        )
EVALUATE
    __DS0PrimaryWindowed

ORDER BY
    '__DS0VisualCalcs'[IsGrandTotalRowTotal] DESC,
    '__DS0VisualCalcs'[Year],
    '__DS0VisualCalcs'[IsDM1Total] DESC,
    '__DS0VisualCalcs'[MonthNumber],
    '__DS0VisualCalcs'[Month]
```

Appendix D

This appendix contains the complete DAX query executed to populate a matrix visual that displays *Sales* and a moving average per Category and Quarter of each Year, which can be found in Figure 9-17 in Chapter 9.

```
DEFINE
    COLUMN '__DS0VisualCalcs'[MA] =
        (/* USER DAX BEGIN */
MOVINGAVERAGE([Sales], 4, TRUE, COLUMNS)
/* USER DAX END */)
    VAR __DS0Core =
        SUMMARIZECOLUMNS(
            ROLLUPADDISSUBTOTAL('Product'[CategoryName], "IsGrandTotalRowTotal"),
            ROLLUPADDISSUBTOTAL(
                ROLLUPGROUP('Date'[YearQuarter], 'Date'[YearQuarterNumber]),
"IsGrandTotalColumnTotal"
            ),
            "Sales", '_Measures'[Sales]
        )

    VAR __DS0VisualCalcsInput =
        SELECTCOLUMNS(
            KEEPFILTERS(
                SELECTCOLUMNS(
                    __DS0Core,
                    "CategoryName", 'Product'[CategoryName],
                    "IsGrandTotalRowTotal", [IsGrandTotalRowTotal],
                    "YearQuarter", 'Date'[YearQuarter],
                    "YearQuarterNumber", 'Date'[YearQuarterNumber],
                    "IsGrandTotalColumnTotal", [IsGrandTotalColumnTotal],
                    "Sales", [Sales]
                )
            ),
            "CategoryName", [CategoryName],
            "YearQuarter", [YearQuarter],
            "YearQuarterNumber", [YearQuarterNumber],
            "IsGrandTotalRowTotal", [IsGrandTotalRowTotal],
            "IsGrandTotalColumnTotal", [IsGrandTotalColumnTotal],
            "Sales", [Sales]
        )

    TABLE '__DS0VisualCalcs' =
        __DS0VisualCalcsInput
        WITH VISUAL SHAPE
            AXIS rows
                GROUP [CategoryName] TOTAL [IsGrandTotalRowTotal]
                ORDER BY
                    [CategoryName] ASC
            AXIS columns
                GROUP
                    [YearQuarter],
                    [YearQuarterNumber]
```

```
                            TOTAL [IsGrandTotalColumnTotal]
                    ORDER BY
                        [YearQuarterNumber] ASC,
                        [YearQuarter] ASC
                DENSIFY "IsDensifiedRow"

VAR __DS0RemoveEmptyDensified =
    FILTER(
        KEEPFILTERS('__DS0VisualCalcs'),
        OR(
            NOT('__DS0VisualCalcs'[IsDensifiedRow]),

        )
    )

VAR __DS0PrimaryWindowed =
    TOPN(
        102,
        SUMMARIZE(
            __DS0RemoveEmptyDensified,
            '__DS0VisualCalcs'[CategoryName],
            '__DS0VisualCalcs'[IsGrandTotalRowTotal]
        ),
        '__DS0VisualCalcs'[IsGrandTotalRowTotal],
        0,
        '__DS0VisualCalcs'[CategoryName],
        1
    )

VAR __DS0SecondaryBase =
    SUMMARIZE(
        __DS0RemoveEmptyDensified,
        '__DS0VisualCalcs'[YearQuarter],
        '__DS0VisualCalcs'[YearQuarterNumber],
        '__DS0VisualCalcs'[IsGrandTotalColumnTotal]
    )
VAR __DS0Secondary =
    TOPN(
        102,
        __DS0SecondaryBase,
        '__DS0VisualCalcs'[IsGrandTotalColumnTotal],
        1,
        '__DS0VisualCalcs'[YearQuarterNumber],
        1,
        '__DS0VisualCalcs'[YearQuarter],
        1
    )

VAR __DS0BodyLimited =
    NATURALLEFTOUTERJOIN(
        __DS0PrimaryWindowed,
        SUBSTITUTEWITHINDEX(
            __DS0RemoveEmptyDensified,
            "ColumnIndex",
            __DS0Secondary,
```

```
                        '__DSOVisualCalcs'[IsGrandTotalColumnTotal],
                        ASC,
                        '__DSOVisualCalcs'[YearQuarterNumber],
                        ASC,
                        '__DSOVisualCalcs'[YearQuarter],
                        ASC
                )
        )

EVALUATE
    __DSOSecondary

ORDER BY
    '__DSOVisualCalcs'[IsGrandTotalColumnTotal],
    '__DSOVisualCalcs'[YearQuarterNumber],
    '__DSOVisualCalcs'[YearQuarter]

EVALUATE
    __DSOBodyLimited

ORDER BY
    '__DSOVisualCalcs'[IsGrandTotalRowTotal] DESC,
    '__DSOVisualCalcs'[CategoryName],
    [ColumnIndex]
```

Appendix E

This appendix contains the complete DAX query executed to populate a matrix visual that displays *Sales* and *Rank* for some combinations of Color and Brand, which can be found in Figure 9-20 in Chapter 9.

```
DEFINE
    COLUMN '__DS0VisualCalcs'[Rank] =
        (/* USER DAX BEGIN */
RANK(ROWS)
/* USER DAX END */)

    VAR __DS0FilterTable =
        TREATAS({106026,
            303016,
            701025}, 'Product'[ProductCode])

    VAR __DS0Core =
        SUMMARIZECOLUMNS(
            ROLLUPADDISSUBTOTAL('Product'[Color], "IsGrandTotalRowTotal"),
            ROLLUPADDISSUBTOTAL('Product'[Brand], "IsGrandTotalColumnTotal"),
            __DS0FilterTable,
            "Sales", '_Measures'[Sales]
        )

    VAR __DS0VisualCalcsInput =
        SELECTCOLUMNS(
            KEEPFILTERS(
                SELECTCOLUMNS(
                    __DS0Core,
                    "Color", 'Product'[Color],
                    "IsGrandTotalRowTotal", [IsGrandTotalRowTotal],
                    "Brand", 'Product'[Brand],
                    "IsGrandTotalColumnTotal", [IsGrandTotalColumnTotal],
                    "Sales", [Sales]
                )
            ),
            "Color", [Color],
            "Brand", [Brand],
            "IsGrandTotalRowTotal", [IsGrandTotalRowTotal],
            "IsGrandTotalColumnTotal", [IsGrandTotalColumnTotal],
            "Sales", [Sales]
        )

    TABLE '__DS0VisualCalcs' =
        __DS0VisualCalcsInput
        WITH VISUAL SHAPE
            AXIS rows
                GROUP [Color] TOTAL [IsGrandTotalRowTotal]
                ORDER BY
                    [Color] ASC
```

```
            AXIS columns
                GROUP [Brand] TOTAL [IsGrandTotalColumnTotal]
                ORDER BY
                    [Brand] ASC
            DENSIFY "IsDensifiedRow"

    VAR __DSORemoveEmptyDensified =
        FILTER(
            KEEPFILTERS('__DSOVisualCalcs'),
            OR(
                NOT('__DSOVisualCalcs'[IsDensifiedRow]),
                NOT(ISBLANK('__DSOVisualCalcs'[Rank]))
            )
        )

    VAR __DSOPrimaryWindowed =
        TOPN(
            102,
            SUMMARIZE(
                __DSORemoveEmptyDensified,
                '__DSOVisualCalcs'[Color],
                '__DSOVisualCalcs'[IsGrandTotalRowTotal]
            ),
            '__DSOVisualCalcs'[IsGrandTotalRowTotal],
            0,
            '__DSOVisualCalcs'[Color],
            1
        )

    VAR __DSOSecondaryBase =
        SUMMARIZE(
            __DSORemoveEmptyDensified,
            '__DSOVisualCalcs'[Brand],
            '__DSOVisualCalcs'[IsGrandTotalColumnTotal]
        )

    VAR __DSOSecondary =
        TOPN(
            102,
            __DSOSecondaryBase,
            '__DSOVisualCalcs'[IsGrandTotalColumnTotal],
            1,
            '__DSOVisualCalcs'[Brand],
            1
        )

    VAR __DSOBodyLimited =
        NATURALLEFTOUTERJOIN(
            __DSOPrimaryWindowed,
            SUBSTITUTEWITHINDEX(
                __DSORemoveEmptyDensified,
```

```
                    "ColumnIndex",
                    __DS0Secondary,
                    '__DS0VisualCalcs'[IsGrandTotalColumnTotal],
                    ASC,
                    '__DS0VisualCalcs'[Brand],
                    ASC
                )
            )

EVALUATE
    __DS0Secondary

ORDER BY
    '__DS0VisualCalcs'[IsGrandTotalColumnTotal], '__DS0VisualCalcs'[Brand]

EVALUATE
    __DS0BodyLimited

ORDER BY
    '__DS0VisualCalcs'[IsGrandTotalRowTotal] DESC,
    '__DS0VisualCalcs'[Color],
    [ColumnIndex]
```

Appendix F

This appendix contains sample code that can be used in a Fabric Notebook to detect visual calculations in reports. This code uses semantic link labs as an open-source package to report metadata. More details are described in Chapter 4.

 Disclaimer   The code provided in this appendix is intended for illustrative purposes only. It's not meant to represent best practices or production-ready Python code. Because Python isn't our primary area of expertise, and some portions have been generated with the assistance of AI tools, please treat this code as a conceptual guide rather than a definitive implementation.

This notebook extracts visual calculations from an existing report. The following steps are applied:

1. Obtain the report definition (base64).

2. Convert base64 to json.

3. Identify visuals containing visual calculations.

4. Extract visual calculation definition(s) from each visual.

5. Print the visual calculation name, language, and expression to the dataframe.

Code cell 1

```
# Importing semantic link labs packages
%pip install semantic-link-labs
import sempy_labs as labs
import sempy_labs.report as rep
from sempy_labs.report import ReportWrapper
import json
import base64
import pandas as pd
```

Code cell 2

```
# Define variables
report_name = "Contoso Sales" # Enter the report name
report_workspace = "Visual Calculations book" # Enter the workspace in which the
report exists
```

```
rpt = ReportWrapper(report=report_name, workspace=report_workspace) # Setting up
the report wrapper to be used later
```

Code cell 3

```
# This step extracts the base64 payload for the different report elements
# if you want to reuse report elements, this can be useful,
# though we cannot directly extract the visual calculations
reportdef = labs.report.get_report_definition(
    report=report_name,
    workspace=report_workspace , # defaults to the current workspace,
    return_dataframe= True # if True, returns a dataframe. If False, returns a
json dictionary.
    )
```

Code cell 4

```
# Extract and decode the JSON payload from Base64
row = reportdef[reportdef["path"] == "report.json"].iloc[0]
base64_payload = row["payload"]
json_bytes = base64.b64decode(base64_payload)
json_str = json_bytes.decode("utf-8")
json_obj = json.loads(json_str)
```

Code cell 5

```
# Recursive function to find all NativeVisualCalculation objects anywhere in a
nested JSON
def find_native_visual_calculations(obj):
    results = []
    if isinstance(obj, dict):
        for k, v in obj.items():
            if k == "NativeVisualCalculation" and isinstance(v, dict):
                results.append(v)
            else:
                results.extend(find_native_visual_calculations(v))
    elif isinstance(obj, list):
        for item in obj:
            results.extend(find_native_visual_calculations(item))
    return results
```

Code cell 6

```python
# trying to find the rows in the json which contain a definition like visual
calculations
def find_strings_with_substring(obj, substring="NativeVisualCalculation"):
    found_strings = []
    if isinstance(obj, dict):
        for v in obj.values():
            found_strings.extend(find_strings_with_substring(v, substring))
    elif isinstance(obj, list):
        for item in obj:
            found_strings.extend(find_strings_with_substring(item, substring))
    elif isinstance(obj, str):
        if substring in obj:
            found_strings.append(obj)
    return found_strings
# Search all strings in json_obj that contain the key substring
strings_with_nvc = find_strings_with_substring(json_obj,
"NativeVisualCalculation")
print(f"Found {len(strings_with_nvc)} visuals containing Visual Calculation in
{report_name}")
```

Code cell 7

```python
# as a line may contain multiple visual calculations, extracting the number of
visual calculations from the strings

all_nvc_objects = []
for s in strings_with_nvc:
    try:
        # Sometimes the string might be JSON escaped (like config fields)
        parsed = json.loads(s)
    except Exception:
        # Not JSON, skip or continue
        continue
    # Now find native visual calculations inside this parsed JSON snippet
    nvc_objs = find_native_visual_calculations(parsed)
    all_nvc_objects.extend(nvc_objs)
print(f"Extracted {len(all_nvc_objects)} NativeVisualCalculation objects from
embedded JSON strings")
```

Code cell 8

```python
# Build list of dictionaries to extract the Language, Expression and Name of the
visual calculations
records = []
for nvc in all_nvc_objects:
    language = nvc.get("Language", "").strip()
    expression = nvc.get("Expression", "").replace('\n', ' ').strip()
```

```
        name = nvc.get("Name", "").strip()
        records.append({"Name": name, "Language": language, "Expression":
expression})
# Create DataFrame
df = pd.DataFrame(records)
# Remove duplicates and reset index
df = df.drop_duplicates().reset_index(drop=True)
# Display with better formatting: no index, wrap text for expressions
from IPython.display import display
pd.set_option('display.max_colwidth', None)  # show full Expression text without
truncation
display(df.style.set_properties(**{
    'text-align': 'left',
    'white-space': 'pre-wrap',
    'word-wrap': 'break-word',
}))
```

Index

A

absolute movement functions, 72, 94, **95**, 129–141, 166

absolute mode, **62**–63

APIs, 85

association matrix, 256

audit logs, 86

axes

    collapsing both, 152

    definition of, **53**

    lattices of fields on all, 54

    navigation of, 53

    visibility of fields on, 68

    in visual shape, 207–208, 212, 215, 216, 221

axis parameter

    COLUMNS ROWS value, 57, 60, 61, 144, 145

    COLUMNS value, 57, 58–59, 61, 208

    default value of, 46, 53–54, 208

    definition of, **53**

    overview of, 118

    ROWS COLUMNS value, 57, 59–60

    ROWS value, 40, 43, 46, 57–58, 208

    values for, 57–60

B

benchmarking analysis, **225**–228

best-In-class analysis, 225, **231**–233

blanks parameter, 102, **103**, 116, **118**

blocked functions, 72

box-and-whisker plot (box plot), 285–291

bullet chart, 266–276

bump chart, 292–294

business functions, 72, 94, **95**, 119–129, 166

butterfly chart, 276

C

calculated column

    adding calculations via, 172

    in composite models, 174–175

    context transition in, 10

    definition of, **172**

    filter context for, 8

    as filters, 174

    measures vs., 180

    use cases for, 173, 174–175

    visual calculations and, 22, 191

calculated table

    definition of, **175**

    evaluation of, 193

    filter context for, 8

    functions for, 176

    use cases for, 175, 176

    visual calculations and, 191

CALCULATE function

    context transition performed by, 10, 14–15

CALCULATETABLE function, 10, 176

calculation groups, 190–191

calculation options

    calculated columns, 172–175

    calculated tables, 175–177

    compared, **171**

    measures, 177–191

    visual calculations, 191–193

champion analysis, 231

COLLAPSEALL function

    axis parameter for, 53, 54

    lattice navigation via, 54–56

    overview of, **148**–154

    as visual calculation exclusive, 72, 95

    in visual calculation structure, 94

COLLAPSE function

    axis parameter for, 53, 54

    custom totals via, 233

    ISATLEVEL and, 159

    lattice navigation via, 54–56

    overview of, **148**–154

    as visual calculation exclusive, 72, 95, 192

    in visual calculation structure, 94

W

Plug into learning at

MicrosoftPressStore.com

The Microsoft Press Store by Pearson offers:

- Free U.S. shipping

- Buy an eBook, get multiple formats – PDF and EPUB – to use on your computer, tablet, and mobile devices

- Print & eBook Best Value Packs

- eBook Deal of the Week – Save up to 60% on featured title

- Newsletter – Be the first to hear about new releases, announcements, special offers, and more

- Register your book – Find companion files, errata, and product updates, plus receive a special coupon* to save on your next purchase

 Pearson